CCNP Self-Study
CCNP BCMSN
Exam Certification Guide
Third Edition

David Hucaby, CCIE No. 4594

Cisco Press

800 East 96th Street
Indianapolis, IN 46240 USA

CCNP BCMSN Exam Certification Guide, Third Edition

David Hucaby

Copyright © 2006 Cisco Systems, Inc.

Published by:
Cisco Press
800 East 96th Street
Indianapolis, IN 46240 USA

Printed in the United States of America 1 2 3 4 5 6 7 8 9 0

First Printing October 2005

Library of Congress Cataloging-in-Publication Number: 2004113165

ISBN: 1-58720-142-9

Warning and Disclaimer

This book is designed to provide information about selected topics for the Building Cisco Multilayer Switched Networks (BCMSN) exam for the CCNP certification. Every effort has been made to make this book as complete and as accurate as possible, but no warranty or fitness is implied.

The information is provided on an "as is" basis. The authors, Cisco Press, and Cisco Systems, Inc., shall have neither liability nor responsibility to any person or entity with respect to any loss or damages arising from the information contained in this book or from the use of the discs or programs that may accompany it.

The opinions expressed in this book belong to the author and are not necessarily those of Cisco Systems, Inc.

Feedback Information

At Cisco Press, our goal is to create in-depth technical books of the highest quality and value. Each book is crafted with care and precision, undergoing rigorous development that involves the unique expertise of members from the professional technical community. Readers' feedback is a natural continuation of this process. If you have any comments regarding how we could improve the quality of this book or otherwise alter it to better suit your needs, you can contact us through e-mail at feedback@ciscopress.com. Please make sure to include the book title and ISBN in your message.

We greatly appreciate your assistance.

Trademark Acknowledgments

All terms mentioned in this book that are known to be trademarks or service marks have been appropriately capitalized. Cisco Press or Cisco Systems, Inc., cannot attest to the accuracy of this information. Use of a term in this book should not be regarded as affecting the validity of any trademark or service mark.

Corporate and Government Sales

Cisco Press offers excellent discounts on this book when ordered in quantity for bulk purchases or special sales.

For more information, please contact: **U.S. Corporate and Government Sales,** 1-800-382-3419 or corpsales@pearsontechgroup.com.

For sales outside the U.S., please contact: **International Sales,** international@pearsoned.com.

Publisher: John Wait

Editor-In-Chief: John Kane

Executive Editor: Brett Bartow

Senior Development Editor: Christopher Cleveland

Copy Editor: Krista Hansing

Editorial Assistant: Tammi Ross

Indexer: Tim Wright

Cisco Representative: Anthony Wolfenden

Cisco Press Program Manager: Jeff Brady

Production Manager: Patrick Kanouse

Senior Project Editor: San Dee Phillips

Technical Editors: Stephen Daleo, Steve McQuerry, Geoff Tagg

Book and Cover Designer: Louisa Adair

Composition: Mark Shirar

CISCO SYSTEMS

Corporate Headquarters
Cisco Systems, Inc.
170 West Tasman Drive
San Jose, CA 95134-1706
USA
www.cisco.com
Tel: 408 526-4000
800 553-NETS (6387)
Fax: 408 526-4100

European Headquarters
Cisco Systems International BV
Haarlerbergpark
Haarlerbergweg 13-19
1101 CH Amsterdam
The Netherlands
www-europe.cisco.com
Tel: 31 0 20 357 1000
Fax: 31 0 20 357 1100

Americas Headquarters
Cisco Systems, Inc.
170 West Tasman Drive
San Jose, CA 95134-1706
USA
www.cisco.com
Tel: 408 526-7660
Fax: 408 527-0883

Asia Pacific Headquarters
Cisco Systems, Inc.
Capital Tower
168 Robinson Road
#22-01 to #29-01
Singapore 068912
www.cisco.com
Tel: +65 6317 7777
Fax: +65 6317 7799

Cisco Systems has more than 200 offices in the following countries and regions. Addresses, phone numbers, and fax numbers are listed on the **Cisco.com Web site at www.cisco.com/go/offices.**

Argentina • Australia • Austria • Belgium • Brazil • Bulgaria • Canada • Chile • China PRC • Colombia • Costa Rica • Croatia • Czech Republic Denmark • Dubai, UAE • Finland • France • Germany • Greece • Hong Kong SAR • Hungary • India • Indonesia • Ireland • Israel • Italy Japan • Korea • Luxembourg • Malaysia • Mexico • The Netherlands • New Zealand • Norway • Peru • Philippines • Poland • Portugal Puerto Rico • Romania • Russia • Saudi Arabia • Scotland • Singapore • Slovakia • Slovenia • South Africa • Spain • Sweden Switzerland • Taiwan • Thailand • Turkey • Ukraine • United Kingdom • United States • Venezuela • Vietnam • Zimbabwe

About the Author

David Hucaby, CCIE No. 4594, is a lead network engineer for the University of Kentucky, where he works with healthcare networks based on the Cisco Catalyst, IP telephony, PIX, and VPN product lines. David has a bachelor of science degree and master of science degree in electrical engineering from the University of Kentucky. He is the author of three previous books for Cisco Press, including *Cisco ASA and PIX Firewall Handbook*, *Cisco Field Manual: Router Configuration*, and *Cisco Field Manual: Catalyst Switch Configuration*.

David lives in Kentucky with his wife, Marci, and two daughters.

About the Technical Reviewers

Steve McQuerry, CCIE No. 6108, is a systems engineer with the Enterprise group at Cisco Systems, specializing in data center technologies. He has 15 years of networking industry experience in routed and switched environments. Steve has written several networking titles for Cisco Press and was formerly a certified Cisco instructor, teaching routing and switching concepts throughout the world.

Geoff Tagg runs a networking consultancy in the United Kingdom, where he has more than 20 years of experience in working with companies ranging from small local businesses to large multinationals. Before that, he was a systems programmer for a number of years. Geoff's main specialty is IP network design and implementation. He lives in Oxford, England, with his wife, Christine, and family, and is a visiting professor at nearby Oxford Brookes University.

John Tiso, CCIE No. 5162, MCSE, CCDP, holds a bachelor of science degree from Adelphi University in New York. He currently serves as a customer support engineer in the Cisco Heartland TAC. Before joining the team at Cisco, John was the lead AVVID consultant and installer for a Cisco Gold Partner. John has written and edited for Cisco Press for many years. He has also published papers in several industry publications and coauthored a book for Cisco Learning Systems.

Dedications

As always, this book is dedicated to the most important people in my life: my wife, Marci, and my two little daughters, Lauren and Kara. Their love, encouragement, and support carry me along. I'm so grateful to God, who gives endurance and encouragement (Romans 15:5), and has allowed me to work on projects like this.

Acknowledgments

It has been my great pleasure to work on another Cisco Press project. I enjoy the networking field very much, and technical writing even more. And more than that, I'm thankful for the joy and inner peace that Jesus Christ gives, making everything more abundant.

Technical writing may be hard work, but I'm finding that it's also quite fun because I'm working with very good friends. I can't say enough good things about Chris Cleveland. Somehow Chris is able to handle many book projects all at once, while giving each one an incredible amount of attention and improvement. Brett Bartow is a constant source of organization, project management, and encouragement. I'm glad he agreed to have me back for another project! Dayna Isley and San Dee Phillips were both very helpful during the review process.

I am very grateful for the insight, suggestions, and helpful comments that Steve McQuerry, Geoff Tagg, and John Tiso contributed. Each one offered a different perspective, which helped make this a more well-rounded book and me a more educated author.

This Book Is Safari Enabled

The Safari® Enabled icon on the cover of your favorite technology book means the book is available through Safari Bookshelf. When you buy this book, you get free access to the online edition for 45 days.

Safari Bookshelf is an electronic reference library that lets you easily search thousands of technical books, find code samples, download chapters, and access technical information whenever and wherever you need it.

To gain 45-day Safari Enabled access to this book:

- Go to http://www.ciscopress.com/safarienabled
- Enter the ISBN of this book (shown on the back cover, above the bar code)
- Log in or Sign up (site membership is required to register your book)
- Enter the coupon code UJR5-DRBP-CI23-KDPR-X72H

If you have difficulty registering on Safari Bookshelf or accessing the online edition, please e-mail customer-service@safaribooksonline.com.

Contents at a Glance

x

Table of Contents

Icons Used in This Book

Router

Bridge

Hub

DSU/CSU

Catalyst
Switch

Multilayer
Switch

Modem

ATM
Switch

ISDN/Frame Relay
Switch

Communication
Server

Gateway

Access
Server

PC

PC with
Software

Sun
Workstation

Macintosh

Terminal

Cisco Works
Workstation

Web
Server

File
Server

Laptop

Printer

IBM
Mainframe

Front End
Processor

Cluster
Controller

Line: Ethernet

Line: Serial

Line: Switched Serial

Token Ring

FDDI

Network Cloud

Command Syntax Conventions

The conventions used to present command syntax in this book are the same conventions used in the Cisco IOS Command Reference. The Command Reference describes these conventions as follows:

- Vertical bars (|) separate alternative, mutually exclusive elements.

- Square brackets ([ ]) indicate optional elements.

- Braces ({ }) indicate a required choice.

- Braces within brackets ([{ }]) indicate a required choice within an optional element.

- **Boldface** indicates commands and keywords that are entered literally as shown. In actual configuration examples and output (not general command syntax), boldface indicates commands that are manually input by the user (such as a **show** command).

- *Italics* indicate arguments for which you supply actual values.

segment page number header

Foreword

CCNP BCMSN Exam Certification Guide, Third Edition, is an excellent self-study resource for the CCNP BCMSN exam. Passing the exam validates the knowledge, skills, and understanding needed to build scalable multilayer switched networks, create and deploy a global intranet, and implement basic troubleshooting techniques in environments that use Cisco multilayer switches for client hosts and services. It is one of several exams required to attain the CCNP certification.

Cisco Press Exam Certification Guide titles are designed to help educate, develop, and grow the community of Cisco networking professionals. The guides are filled with helpful features that allow you to master key concepts and assess your readiness for the certification exam. Developed in conjunction with the Cisco certifications team, Cisco Press books are the only self-study books authorized by Cisco Systems.

Most networking professionals use a variety of learning methods to gain necessary skills. Cisco Press self-study titles are a prime source of content for some individuals, and can also serve as an excellent supplement to other forms of learning. Training classes, whether delivered in a classroom or on the Internet, are a great way to quickly acquire new understanding. Hands-on practice is essential for anyone seeking to build, or hone, new skills. Authorized Cisco training classes, labs, and simulations are available exclusively from Cisco Learning Solutions Partners worldwide. Please visit www.cisco.com/go/training to learn more about Cisco Learning Solutions Partners.

I hope and expect that you'll find this guide to be an essential part of your exam preparation and a valuable addition to your personal library.

Don Field
Director, Certifications
Cisco System, Inc.
September, 2005

Introduction: Overview of Certification and How to Succeed

Professional certifications have been an important part of the computing industry for many years and will continue to become more important. Many reasons exist for these certifications, but the most popularly cited reason is that of credibility. All other considerations held equal, the certified employee/consultant/job candidate is considered more valuable than one who is not.

Objectives and Methods

The most important and somewhat obvious objective of this book is to help you pass the Cisco BCMSN exam (642-811). In fact, if the primary objective of this book were different, the book's title would be misleading; however, the methods used in this book to help you pass the BCMSN exam are designed to also make you much more knowledgeable about how to do your job. Although this book and the accompanying CD-ROM have many example test questions, the method in which they are used is not to simply make you memorize as many questions and answers as you possibly can.

One key methodology used in this book helps you discover the exam topics about which you need more review, to help you fully understand and remember those details, and to help you prove to yourself that you have retained your knowledge of those topics. So this book helps you pass not by memorization, but by helping you truly learn and understand the topics. The BCMSN exam is just one of the foundation topics in the CCNP and CCDP certifications, and the knowledge contained within is vitally important to consider yourself a truly skilled routing and switching engineer or specialist. This book would do you a disservice if it did not attempt to help you learn the material. To that end, the book can help you pass the BCMSN exam by using the following methods:

- Helping you discover which test topics you have not mastered
- Providing explanations and information to fill in your knowledge gaps
- Supplying exercises and scenarios that enhance your ability to recall and deduce the answers to test questions
- Providing practice exercises on the topics and the testing process through test questions on the CD-ROM

Who Should Read This Book?

This book is not designed to be a general networking topics book, although it can be used for that purpose. This book is intended to tremendously increase your chances of passing the Cisco BCMSN exam. Although other objectives can be achieved from using this book, the book is written with one goal in mind: to help you pass the exam.

The BCMSN exam is primarily based on the content of the Building Cisco Multilayer Switched Networks (BCMSN) 2.2 CCNP course. You should have either taken the course, read through the BCMSN coursebook or this book, or have a couple of years of LAN switching experience.

Exam Overview

Cisco offers three levels of certification, each with an increasing level of proficiency: Associate, Professional, and Expert. These are commonly known by their acronyms CCNA/CCDA (Cisco Certified Network/Design Associate), CCNP/CCDP (Cisco Certified Network/Design Professional), and CCIE (Cisco Certified Internetworking Expert). There are others as well, but this book focuses on the certifications for enterprise networks.

For the CCNP certification, you must pass a series of four core exams or pass a longer foundations exam plus one support exam. The BCMSN exam or its content is included and required for either path. For most exams, Cisco does not publish the scores needed for passing. You need to take the exam to find that out for yourself.

To see the most current requirements for the CCNP or CCDP certifications, go to cisco.com; then click Learning and Events, followed by Career Certifications and Paths.

The BCMSN exam itself is composed of 60 to 70 questions, presented in a variety of formats. You can expect to find multiple-choice, single-answer; multiple-choice, multiple-answer; drag-and-drop; fill-in-the-blank; and simulation questions. To find more specific information about the topics that can be covered on the BCMSN exam, go to cisco.com; then click Learning and Events, followed by Exam Information and then Certification Exams. The exam lasts 90 minutes and is offered through either Pearson VUE or Prometric testing centers only. See http://www.cisco.com/en/US/learning/le3/le11/learning_about_registering_for_exams.html for the most current information about registering for the exam.

Strategies for Exam Preparation

The strategy you use to prepare for the BCMSN exam might be slightly different than strategies used by other readers, mainly based on the skills, knowledge, and experience you already have obtained. For instance, if you have attended the BCMSN course, you might take a different approach than someone who learned switching through on-the-job training.

Regardless of the strategy you use or the background you have, this book is designed to help you get to the point that you can pass the exam with the least amount of time required. For instance, there is no need for you to practice or read about IP addressing and subnetting if you fully understand it already. However, many people like to make sure that they truly know a topic and read over material that they already know. Several book features help you gain the confidence that you know some material already and also help you know what topics you need to study more.

How This Book Is Organized

Although this book can be read cover to cover, it is designed to be flexible and allow you to easily move between chapters and sections of chapters to cover only the material that you need more work with. Chapters 1 through 18 are the core chapters and can be covered in any order, though some chapters are related and build upon each other. If you do intend to read them all, the order in the book is an excellent sequence to use.

When you finish with the core chapters, you have several options on how to finish your exam preparation. Chapter 19, "Scenarios for Final Preparation," provides many scenarios to help you review and refine your knowledge, without giving you a false sense of preparedness that you would get with simply reviewing a set of multiple-choice questions. You can review the questions at the end of each chapter, and you can use the CD-ROM testing software to practice the exam.

Each core chapter covers a subset of the topics on the BCMSN exam. The core chapters are organized into parts. The core chapters cover the following topics:

PART I: Overview and Design of a Campus Network

- **Chapter 1, "Campus Network Overview"**—This chapter covers the use of switches in the OSI model's various layers, the different campus network models, hierarchical network design, and how Cisco's switching products fit into a hierarchical network design.

- **Chapter 2, "Modular Network Design"**—This chapter covers how to design, size, and scale a campus network using a modular approach

PART II: Building a Campus Network

- **Chapter 3, "Switch Operation"**—This chapter covers Layer 2 and multilayer switch operation, how various CAM and TCAM tables are used to make switching decisions, and how to monitor these tables to aid in troubleshooting.

- **Chapter 4, "Switch Configuration"**—This chapter covers the operating system software available on Cisco Catalyst switches, basic switch configuration and administration, switch file management, and how to verify that a switch is functioning properly to aid in troubleshooting.

- **Chapter 5, "Switch Port Configuration"**—This chapter covers basic Ethernet concepts, how to use scalable Ethernet, how to connect switch block devices, and how to verify switch port operation to aid in troubleshooting.

- **Chapter 6, "VLANs and Trunks"**—This chapter covers basic VLAN concepts, how to transport multiple VLANs over single links, how to configure VLAN trunks, and how to verify VLAN and trunk operation.

- **Chapter 7, "VLAN Trunking Protocol (VTP)"**—This chapter covers VLAN management using VTP, VTP configuration, traffic management through VTP pruning, and how to verify VTP operation.

- **Chapter 8, "Aggregating Switch Links"**—This chapter covers switch port aggregation with EtherChannel, EtherChannel negotiation protocols, EtherChannel configuration, and how to verify EtherChannel operation.

- **Chapter 9, "Traditional Spanning Tree Protocol"**—This chapter covers IEEE 802.1D Spanning Tree Protocol (STP) and gives an overview of the other STP types that might be running on a switch.

- **Chapter 10, "Spanning Tree Configuration"**—This chapter covers the STP root bridge, how to customize the STP topology, how to tune STP convergence, redundant link convergence, and how to verify STP operation.

- **Chapter 11, "Protecting the Spanning Tree Protocol Topology"**—This chapter covers protecting the STP topology using Root Guard, BPDU Guard, and Loop Guard, and also how to use BPDU filtering and how to verify that these STP protection mechanisms are functioning properly.

- **Chapter 12, "Advanced Spanning Tree Protocol"**—This chapter covers Rapid Spanning Tree Protocol (RSTP) for Rapid PVST+ and Multiple Spanning Tree (MST) Protocol.

PART III: Layer 3 Switching

- **Chapter 13, "Multilayer Switching"**—This chapter covers interVLAN routing, multilayer switching with CEF, and how to verify that multilayer switching is functioning properly.

- **Chapter 14, "Router, Supervisor, and Power Redundancy"**—This chapter covers providing redundant router or gateway addresses on Catalyst switches and verifying that redundancy is functioning properly.

- **Chapter 15, "IP Multicast"**—This chapter covers general multicast concepts, routing and switching multicast traffic, and how to verify that multicast routing and switching are functioning properly.

PART IV: Campus Network Services

- **Chapter 16, "IP Telephony"**—This chapter covers how a Catalyst switch can provide power to operate a Cisco IP Phone, how voice traffic can be carried over the links between an IP Phone and a Catalyst switch, QoS for voice traffic, and how to verify that IP Telephony features are functioning properly.

- **Chapter 17, "Securing Switch Access"**—This chapter covers switch Authentication, Authorization, and Accounting (AAA); port security using MAC addresses; port-based security using IEEE 802.1x; DHCP snooping; and dynamic ARP inspection.

- **Chapter 18, "Securing with VLANs"** — This chapter covers how to control traffic within a VLAN using access lists, implementing private VLANs, and monitoring traffic on switch ports for security reasons.

Each chapter in the book uses several features to help you make the best use of your time in that chapter. The features are as follows:

- **Assessment** — Each chapter begins with a "Do I Know This Already?" quiz that helps you determine the amount of time you need to spend studying that chapter. If you intend to read the entire chapter, you can save the quiz for later use. Questions are all multiple-choice, single-answer, to give a quick assessment of your knowledge.

- **Foundation Topics** — This is the core section of each chapter that explains the protocols, concepts, and configuration for the topics in the chapter.

- **Foundation Summary** — At the end of each chapter, a Foundation Summary collects key concepts, facts, and commands into an easy-to-review format. A more lengthy "Q&A" section follows, where many review questions are presented. Questions are mainly open-ended rather than multiple choice, as found on the exams. This is done to focus more on understanding the subject matter than on memorizing details.

- **Scenarios** — Scenarios are collected in the final chapter to allow a much more in-depth examination of a network implementation. Instead of posing a simple question asking for a single fact, the scenarios let you design, configure, and troubleshoot networks (at least on paper) without the clues inherent in a multiple-choice quiz format.

- **CD-based practice exam** — The companion CD-ROM contains two separate test banks — one composed of the questions from the book and an entirely new test bank of questions to reinforce your understanding of the book's concepts. In addition to the multiple-choice questions, you encounter some configuration simulation questions for which you actually perform configurations. This is the best tool for helping you prepare for the actual test-taking process.

How to Use This Book for Study

Retention and recall are the two features of human memory most closely related to performance on tests. This exam-preparation guide focuses on increasing both retention and recall of the topics on the exam. The other human characteristic involved in successfully passing the exam is intelligence; this book does not address that issue!

Adult retention is typically less than that of children. For example, it is common for 4-year-olds to pick up basic language skills in a new country faster than their parents. Children retain facts as an end unto itself; adults typically either need a stronger reason to remember a fact or must have a reason to think about that fact several times to retain it in memory. For these reasons, a student who attends a typical Cisco course and retains 50 percent of the material is actually quite an amazing student.

Memory recall is based on connectors to the information that needs to be recalled—the greater the number of connectors to a piece of information, the better chance and better speed of recall. For example, if the exam asks what VTP stands for, you automatically add information to the question. You know that the topic is switching because of the nature of the test. You might recall the term *VTP domain*, which implies that this is a type of switch domain. You might also remember that it is talking about VLANs. Having read one of the multiple-choice answers "VLAN Trunk Protocol," you might even have the infamous "a-ha" experience, in which you are then sure that your answer is correct—and possibly a brightly lit bulb is hovering over your head. All these added facts and assumptions are the connectors that eventually lead your brain to the fact that needs to be recalled. Of course, recall and retention work together. If you do not retain the knowledge, recalling it will be difficult.

This book is designed with features to help you increase retention and recall. It does this in the following ways:

- By providing succinct and complete methods of helping you decide what you recall easily and what you do not recall at all.

- By giving references to the exact passages in the book that review those concepts you did not recall, so you can quickly be reminded about a fact or concept. Repeating information that connects to another concept helps retention, and describing the same concept in several ways throughout a chapter increases the number of connectors to the same pieces of information.

- By including exercise questions that supply fewer connectors than multiple-choice questions. This helps you exercise recall and avoids giving you a false sense of confidence, as an exercise with only multiple-choice questions might do. For example, fill-in-the-blank questions require you to have better and more complete recall than multiple-choice questions.

- By pulling the entire breadth of subject matter together. A separate chapter (Chapter 19) contains scenarios and several related questions that cover every topic on the exam and gives you the chance to prove that you have gained mastery over the subject matter. This reduces the connectors implied by questions residing in a particular chapter and requires you to exercise other connectors to remember the details.

- Finally, accompanying this book is a CD-ROM that has examlike questions in a variety of formats. These are useful for you to practice taking the exam and to get accustomed to the time restrictions imposed during the exam.

In taking the "Do I Know This Already?" assessment quizzes in each chapter, make sure you treat yourself and your knowledge fairly. If you come across a question that makes you guess at an answer, mark it wrong immediately. This forces you to read through the part of the chapter that relates to that question and forces you to learn it more thoroughly.

If you find that you do well on the assessment quizzes, it still might be wise to quickly skim through each chapter to find sections or topics that do not readily come to mind. Sometimes even reading through the detailed table of contents will reveal topics that are unfamiliar or unclear. If that happens to you, mark those chapters or topics and spend time working through those parts of the book.

Strategies for the Exam

Try to schedule the exam far enough in advance that you have ample time for study. Consider the time of day and even the day of the week so that you choose a time frame that suits your daily routine. Because the exam lasts 90 minutes, you should make sure that the exam time does not coincide with your regular lunchtime or some other part of the day when you are usually tired or trying to wake up. As for the day of the week, your work schedule might prevent you from studying a few days before the exam.

Hopefully, you can find a testing center located nearby. In any event, be sure to familiarize yourself with the driving and parking directions well ahead of time. You do not want to be frantically searching for streets or buildings a few minutes before the exam is scheduled to start. You will need at least one form of picture ID to present at the testing center.

Think about common-sense things, such as eating a nutritious meal before you leave for the exam. You need to be as comfortable as possible for the entire 90-minute exam, so it pays not to be hungry. Limiting the amount of liquids you consume right before test time might also be wise. After the exam begins, the clock does not stop for a restroom break. Also think about taking along a lightweight jacket, in case the exam room feels cold.

During the exam, try to pace yourself by knowing that there are, at most, 70 questions in a 90-minute period. That does not mean that every question should be answered in a little over a minute; it means only that you should try to move along at a regular pace. Be aware that if you are unsure about an answer, you are not allowed to mark the question and return to it later. That was allowed in exams of years past, but not anymore. This might force you into a guessing position on a question, just so you can move along to the others before the time runs out.

At the end of the exam, you receive your final score and news of your passing or failing. If you pass, congratulate yourself and breathe a sigh of relief at not having to study more!

If you fail, remind yourself that you are not a failure. It is never a disgraceful thing to fail a Cisco test, as long as you decide to try it again. Anybody who has ever taken a Cisco exam knows that to be true; just ask the people who have attempted the CCIE lab exam. As soon as you can, schedule to take the same exam again. Allow a few days so that you can study the topics that gave you trouble. The exam score should also break down the entire exam into major topics, each with its respective score. Do not be discouraged about starting over with your studies—the majority is already behind you. Just spend time brushing up on the "low spots" where you lack knowledge or confidence.

CCNP Exam Topics

Carefully consider the exam topics Cisco has posted on its website as you study, particularly for clues to how deeply you should know each topic. Beyond that, you cannot go wrong by developing a broader knowledge of the subject matter. You can do that by reading and studying the topics presented in this book. Remember that it is in your best interest to become proficient in each of the CCNP subjects. When it is time to use what you have learned, being well rounded counts more than being well tested.

Table I-1 shows the official exam topics for the BCMSN exam, as posted on Cisco.com. Note that Cisco has historically changed exam topics without changing the exam number, so do not be alarmed if small changes in the exam topics occur over time. When in doubt, go to cisco.com, click Learning and Events, and select Career Certifications and Paths.

Table I-1   *BCMSN Exam Topics*

Exam Topic	Part of This Book Where Exam Topic Is Covered
Technology	
Describe the Enterprise Composite Model used for designing networks and explain how it addresses enterprise network needs for performance, scalability, and availability	Part I
Describe the physical, data link, and network layer technologies used in a switched network, and identify when to use each	Part I
Explain the role of switches in the various modules of the Enterprise Composite Model (Campus Infrastructure, Server Farm, Enterprise Edge, Network Management)	Part I

Table I-1   *BCMSN Exam Topics (Continued)*

Exam Topic	Part of This Book Where Exam Topic Is Covered
Explain the function of the Switching Database Manager (specifically Content Addressable Memory [CAM] and Ternary Content Addressable Memory [TCAM]) within a Catalyst switch	Part II
Describe the features and operation of VLANs on a switched network	Part II
Describe the features of the VLAN trunking protocols, including 802.1Q, ISL (emphasis on 802.1Q), and Dynamic Trunking Protocol	Part II
Describe the operation and purpose of managed VLAN services	Part II
Describe how VTP versions 1 and 2 operate, including domains, modes, advertisements, and pruning	Part II
Explain the operation and purpose of the Spanning Tree Protocol (STP) on a switched network	Part II
Identify the specific types of Cisco route switch processors, and provide implementation details	Part III
List and describe the operation of the key components required to implement interVLAN routing	Part III
Explain the types of redundancy in a multilayer switched network, including hardware and software redundancy	Part III
Explain how IP multicast operates on a multilayer switched network, including PIM, CGMP, and IGMP	Part III
Describe the quality issues with voice traffic on a switched data network, including jitter and delay	Part IV
Describe the QoS use of a voice VLAN to handle voice traffic	Part IV
Implementation and Operation	
Configure access ports for static and multi-VLAN membership	Part II
Configure and verify 802.1Q trunks	Part II
Configure and verify ISL trunks	Part II
Configure VTP domains in server, client, and transparent modes	Part II
Enable Spanning Tree on ports and VLANs	Part II
Configure Spanning Tree parameters, including port priority, VLAN priority, root bridge, BPDU guard, PortFast, and UplinkFast	Part II
Implement IP technology on a switched network with auxiliary VLANs	Part IV

continues

Table I-1   *BCMSN Exam Topics (Continued)*

Exam Topic	Part of This Book Where Exam Topic Is Covered
Configure and verify router redundancy using HSRP, VRRP, GLBP and SRM	Part III
Configure Fast EtherChannel and Gigabit EtherChannel to increase bandwidth for interswitch connections	Part II
Planning and Design	
Compare end-to-end and local VLANs, determine when to use each	Part I
Design a VLAN configuration with VTP to work for a given specific scenario	Part II
Select multilayer switching architectures, given specific multilayer switching needs	Part III
Describe the general design models when implementing IP telephony in a switched network environment	Part IV
Troubleshoot	
Troubleshoot common VLAN problems on a switched network	Part II
Tune and troubleshoot Spanning Tree Protocol on a multilayer switched network to enhance network performance, prevent network loops, and minimize downtime	Part II
Identify interVLAN routing performance and scalability issues, and propose solutions	Part III
Verify and troubleshoot interVLAN routing on a switched network	Part III
Identify voice VLAN issues at the network access layer	Part IV

For More Information

If you have any comments about the book, you can submit those via the ciscopress.com website. Just go to the website, select Contact Us, and type in your message.

Cisco might make changes that affect the CCNP certification from time to time. You should always check cisco.com for the latest details. Also, you can look to http://www.ciscopress.com/title/ 1587201429, where we will publish any information pertinent to how you might use this book differently in light of Cisco's future changes. For instance, if Cisco decided to remove a major topic from the exam, it might post that on its website; Cisco Press will make an effort to list that information as well.

Overview and Design of a Campus Network

Chapter 1   Campus Network Overview

Chapter 2   Modular Network Design

This part of the book covers the following BCMSN exam topics:

Technology

- Describe the Enterprise Composite Model used for designing networks, and explain how it addresses enterprise network needs for performance, scalability, and availability

- Describe the physical, data link, and network layer technologies used in a switched network, and identify when to use each

- Explain the role of switches in the various modules of the Enterprise Composite Model (Campus Infrastructure, Server Farm, Enterprise Edge, Network Management)

Planning and Design

- Compare end-to-end and local VLANs and determine when to use each

This chapter covers the following topics that you need to master for the CCNP BCMSN exam:

- **Switching Functionality**—This section covers the use of switches in the OSI model layers. You learn about the functions and application of routing and switching in Layers 2, 3, and 4, along with the concept of multilayer switching.

- **Campus Network Models**—This section presents the concept of a campus network, and describes the traditional campus model and models based on traffic patterns. This section also describes the factors that affect a campus network's design.

- **Hierarchical Network Design**—This section details a three-layer, hierarchical structure of campus network designs.

CHAPTER 1

Campus Network Overview

As campus networks have grown and technologies have matured, network engineers and architects have many more options to consider than the hubs, Ethernet switches, and routers traditionally put in place. You can use switches to improve network performance in many ways; however, simply replacing existing shared networks with switched networks is not enough. The switching function alone alleviates congestion and increases bandwidth (in addition to more complex capabilities) if properly placed and designed. Switches themselves have also improved over time. The type of switch, its capabilities, and its location within a network can greatly enhance network performance.

This chapter presents a logical design process that you can use to build a new campus network or to modify and improve an existing network.

"Do I Know This Already?" Quiz

The purpose of the "Do I Know This Already?" quiz is to help you decide whether you need to read the entire chapter. If you intend to read the entire chapter, you do not necessarily need to answer these questions now.

The 12-question quiz, derived from the major sections in the "Foundation Topics" portion of the chapter, helps you determine how to spend your limited study time.

Table 1-1 outlines the major topics discussed in this chapter and the "Do I Know This Already?" quiz questions that correspond to those topics.

Table 1-1   *"Do I Know This Already?" Foundation Topics Section-to-Question Mapping*

Foundation Topics Section	Questions Covered in This Section	Score
Switching Functionality	1–3	
Campus Networks, Traffic Pattern Models	4–7	
Hierarchical Design Model	8–12	
Total Score		

> **CAUTION** The goal of self-assessment is to gauge your mastery of the topics in this chapter. If you do not know the answer to a question or are only partially sure of the answer, you should mark this question wrong. Giving yourself credit for an answer you correctly guess skews your self-assessment results and might provide you with a false sense of security.

You can find the answers to the quiz in Appendix A, "Answers to Chapter 'Do I Know This Already?' Quizzes and Q&A Sections." The suggested choices for your next step are as follows:

- **6 or less overall score**—Read the entire chapter. This includes the "Foundation Topics," "Foundation Summary," and "Q&A" sections.

- **7–9 overall score**—Begin with the "Foundation Summary" section and then follow up with the "Q&A" section at the end of the chapter.

- **10 or more overall score**—If you want more review on these topics, skip to the "Foundation Summary" section and then go to the "Q&A" section at the end of the chapter. Otherwise, move on to Chapter 2, "Modular Network Design."

1. Layer 2 switching uses which of the following values to forward data?

   a. IP address

   b. IPX address

   c. MAC address

   d. RIP address

   e. UDP port

2. Multilayer switching (MLS) forwards packets based on what OSI layers?

   a. Layer 1

   b. Layer 2

   c. Layer 3

   d. Layer 4

   e. b, c, d

   f. a, b, c, d

3. Which of the following does a multilayer switch perform?

   a. Forwarding according to MAC address.

   b. Forwarding according to IP address.

   c. Forwarding according to UDP/TCP port numbers.

   d. All of these answers are correct.

4. What does the 20/80 rule of networking state? (Pick one.)

   a. Only 20 out of 80 packets arrive at the destination.

   b. Twenty percent of the network is used 80 percent of the time.

   c. Twenty percent of the traffic on a network segment travels across the network, while 80 percent of it stays local.

   d. Twenty percent of the traffic on a network segment stays local, while 80 percent of it travels across the network.

5. Where does a collision domain exist in a switched network?

   a. On a single switch port

   b. Across all switch ports

   c. On a single VLAN

   d. Across all VLANs

6. Where does a broadcast domain exist in a switched network?

   a. On a single switch port

   b. Across all switch ports

   c. On a single VLAN

   d. Across all VLANs

7. What is a VLAN primarily used for?

   a. To segment a collision domain

   b. To segment a broadcast domain

   c. To segment an autonomous system

   d. To segment a spanning-tree domain

8. How many layers are recommended in the hierarchical campus network design model?

   a. 1

   b. 2

   c. 3

   d. 4

   e. 7

9. End-user PCs should be connected into which of the following hierarchical layers?

   a. Distribution layer

   b. Common layer

   c. Access layer

   d. Core layer

10. In which OSI layer should devices in the distribution layer typically operate?

   a. Layer 1

   b. Layer 2

   c. Layer 3

   d. Layer 4

11. A hierarchical network's distribution layer aggregates which of the following?

   a. Core switches

   b. Broadcast domains

   c. Routing updates

   d. Access-layer switches

12. In the core layer of a hierarchical network, which of the following are aggregated?

   a. Routing tables

   b. Packet filters

   c. Distribution switches

   d. Access-layer switches

Foundation Topics

Switching Functionality

To understand how switches and routers should be chosen and placed in a network design, you should first understand how to take advantage of data communication at different layers.

The OSI reference model separates data communication into seven layers, as shown in Table 1-2. Each layer has a specific function and a specific protocol so that two devices can exchange data on the same layer. A protocol data unit (PDU) is the generic name for a block of data that a layer on one device exchanges with the same layer on a peer device. A PDU is encapsulated in a layer's protocol before it is made available to a lower-level layer, or unencapsulated before being handed to a higher-level layer.

Table 1-2 *Layers of Data Communications*

OSI Layer	Protocol Data Unit	Mechanism to Process PDU
7 (application)		
6 (presentation)		
5 (session)		
4 (transport)	TCP segment	TCP port
3 (network)	Packet	Router
2 (data link)	Frame	Switch/bridge
1 (physical)		

In Table 1-2, Layers 2, 3, and 4 are represented by the data link, network, and transport layers, respectively, with a PDU frame, packet, and TCP segment. When a TCP segment (Layer 4) needs to be transmitted to another station, the TCP segment is encapsulated as a packet (Layer 3) and further encapsulated as a frame (Layer 2). The receiving station unencapsulates Layers 2 and 3 before processing the original TCP segment.

The layered protocols also apply to networking devices. For example, a Layer 2 device transfers data by looking at the Layer 2 PDU header information. Upper-layer protocols are not looked at or even understood. Layer-specific devices are discussed in detail in the sections that follow.

Layer 2 Switching

Devices that forward frames at Layer 2 involve the following functions:

- MAC addresses are learned from the incoming frames' source addresses.

- A table of MAC addresses and their associated bridge and switch ports is built and maintained.

- Broadcast and multicast frames are flooded out to all ports (except the one that received the frame).

- Frames destined to unknown locations are flooded out to all ports (except the one that received the frame).

- Bridges and switches communicate with each other using the Spanning Tree Protocol to eliminate bridging loops.

A Layer 2 switch performs essentially the same function as a transparent bridge; however, a switch can have many ports and can perform *hardware-based bridging*. Frames are forwarded using specialized hardware, called *application-specific integrated circuits (ASIC)*. This hardware gives switching great scalability, with wire-speed performance, low latency, low cost, and high port density.

As long as Layer 2 frames are being switched between two Layer 1 interfaces of the same media type, such as two Ethernet connections or an Ethernet connection and a Fast Ethernet connection, the frames do not have to be modified. However, if the two interfaces are different media, such as Ethernet and Token Ring or Ethernet and Fiber Distributed Data Interface (FDDI), the Layer 2 switch must translate the frame contents before sending out the Layer 1 interface.

Layer 2 switching is used primarily for workgroup connectivity and network segmentation. You can contain traffic between users and servers in a workgroup within the switch. In addition, the number of stations on a network segment can be reduced with a switch, minimizing the collision domain size.

One drawback to Layer 2 switching is that it cannot be scaled effectively. Switches must forward broadcast frames to all ports, causing large switched networks to become large broadcast domains. In addition, Spanning Tree Protocol (STP) can have a slow convergence time when the switch topology changes. STP also can block certain switch ports, preventing data transfer. (Chapters 9 through 12 discuss STP and its variations in further detail.) Layer 2 switching alone cannot provide an effective, scalable network design.

Layer 3 Routing

Devices involved in Layer 3 routing perform the following functions:

- Packets are forwarded between networks based on Layer 3 addresses.

- An optimal path is determined for a packet to take through a network to the next router.

- Packet forwarding involves a table lookup of the destination network, the next-hop router address, and the router's own outbound interface.

- An optimal path can be chosen from among many possibilities.

- Routers communicate with each other using *routing protocols*.

By nature, routers do not forward broadcast packets and forward only multicast packets to segments with multicast clients. This action provides control over broadcast propagation and offers network *segmentation* into areas of common Layer 3 addressing.

Logical addressing is possible on a network with routers because the Layer 3 (network layer) address uniquely identifies a device only at the network layer of the OSI reference model. Actual frame forwarding occurs using the Layer 2, or data link, address of devices. Therefore, some method must exist to associate a device's data link layer (MAC) address with its network layer (IP) address. A router must also have addresses from both layers assigned to each of its interfaces connected to a network. This assignment gives the router the functionality to support the logical network layer addresses assigned to the physical networks.

In addition, a router must examine each packet's Layer 3 header before making a routing decision. Layer 3 security and control can be implemented on any router interface using the source and destination addresses, protocol, or other Layer 3 attribute to make decisions on whether to limit or forward the packets.

Layer 3 routing is generally performed by microprocessor-based engines, which require CPU cycles to examine each packet's network layer header. The routing table of optimal paths to Layer 3 networks can also be a large table of dynamic values, requiring a finite lookup delay. Although you can place a router anywhere in a network, the router can become a bottleneck because of a latency of packet examination and processing.

Layer 3 Switching

Devices involved in Layer 3 switching perform the following functions:

- Packets are forwarded at Layer 3, just as a router would do.

- Packets are switched using specialized hardware, ASIC, for high speed and low latency.

- Packets can be forwarded with security control and quality of service (QoS) using Layer 3 address information.

Layer 3 switches are designed to examine and forward packets in high-speed LAN environments. Whereas a router might impose a bottleneck to forwarding throughput, a Layer 3 switch can be placed anywhere in the network, with little or no performance penalty.

Layer 4 Switching

Devices involved in Layer 4 switching perform the following functions:

- Packets are forwarded using hardware switching, based on both Layer 3 addressing and Layer 4 application information. (Layer 2 addressing is also inherently used.)

- Layer 4 protocol types (UDP or TCP, for example) in packet headers are examined.

- Layer 4 segment headers are examined to determine application port numbers.

Switching at Layer 4 allows finer control over the movement of information. For example, traffic can be prioritized according to the source and destination port numbers, and QoS can be defined for end users. Therefore, video or voice data can be switched at a higher level of service, with more bandwidth availability than file transfer or HTTP traffic. Layer 4 port numbers for source and destination also can perform traffic accounting.

A Layer 4 switch also must allocate a large amount of memory to its forwarding tables. Layer 2 and Layer 3 devices have forwarding tables based on MAC and network addresses, making those tables only as large as the number of network devices. Layer 4 devices, however, must keep track of application protocols and conversations occurring in the network. Their forwarding tables become proportional to the number of network devices multiplied by the number of applications.

Multilayer Switching

Devices involved in MLS perform the following functions:

- Packets are forwarded in hardware that combines Layer 2, Layer 3, and Layer 4 switching.

- Packets are forwarded at wire speed.

- The traditional Layer 3 routing function is provided using Cisco Express Forwarding (CEF), in which a database of routes to every destination network is maintained and distributed to switching ASICs for very high forwarding performance.

Cisco switches perform multilayer switching at Layer 3 and Layer 4. At Layer 3, the Catalyst family of switches caches traffic flows based on IP addresses. At Layer 4, traffic flows are cached based on source and destination addresses, in addition to source and destination ports. All switching is performed in hardware, providing equal performance at both Layer 3 and Layer 4 switching.

Campus Network Models

A campus network is an enterprise network consisting of many LANs in one or more buildings, all connected and all usually in the same geographic area. A company typically owns the entire campus network as well as the physical wiring. Campus networks commonly consist of Ethernet, 802.11 wireless LANs, higher-speed Fast Ethernet, Fast EtherChannel, and Gigabit Ethernet LANs. Some campus networks also consist of legacy Token Ring and FDDI.

An understanding of traffic flow is a vital part of the campus network design. Although you can leverage high-speed LAN technologies to improve any traffic movement, the emphasis should be on providing an overall design tuned to known, studied, or predicted traffic flows. The network traffic then can be effectively moved and managed, and you can scale the campus network to support future needs.

The next sections present various network models that you can use to classify and design campus networks. Beginning with traditional shared networks, the models build on each other to leverage traffic movement and provide predictable behavior.

Shared Network Model

In the early 1990s, campus networks traditionally were constructed of a single LAN for all users to connect to and use. All devices on the LAN were forced to share the available bandwidth. LAN media such as Ethernet and Token Ring both had distance limitations and limitations on the number of devices that could be connected to a single LAN.

Network availability and performance declined as the number of connected devices increased. For example, an Ethernet LAN required all devices to share the available 10-Mbps half-duplex bandwidth. Ethernet also used the carrier sense multiple access collision detect (CSMA/CD) scheme to determine when a device could transmit data on the shared LAN. If two or more devices tried to transmit at the same time, network collisions occurred, and all devices had to become silent and wait to retransmit their data. This type of LAN is a *collision domain* because all devices are susceptible to collisions. Token Ring LANs are not susceptible to collisions because they are deterministic and allow stations to transmit only when they receive a "token" that passes around the ring.

One solution used to relieve network congestion was to segment, or divide, a LAN into discrete collision domains. This solution used transparent bridges, which forwarded only Layer 2 data frames to the network segment where the destination address was located. Bridges reduced the number of devices on a segment, lessened the probability of collisions on segments, and increased the physical distance limitations by acting as a repeater.

Bridges normally forward frames to the LAN segment where the destination address is located. However, frames containing the broadcast MAC address (ff:ff:ff:ff:ff:ff) must be flooded to all connected segments. Broadcast frames usually are associated with requests for information or services, including network service announcements. IP uses broadcasts for Address Resolution Protocol (ARP) requests to ask what MAC address is associated with a particular IP address. Other broadcast frame examples include Dynamic Host Control Protocol (DHCP) requests, IPX Get Nearest Server (GNS) requests, Service Advertising Protocol (SAP) announcements, Routing Information Protocol (RIP—both IP and IPX) advertisements, and NetBIOS name requests. A broadcast domain is a group of network segments where a broadcast is flooded.

Multicast traffic is traffic destined for a specific set or group of users, regardless of their location on the campus network. Multicast frames must be flooded to all segments because they are a form of broadcast. Although end users must join a multicast group to enable their applications to process and receive the multicast data, a bridge must flood the traffic to all segments because it doesn't know which stations are members of the multicast group. Multicast frames use shared bandwidth on a segment but do not force the use of CPU resources on every connected device. Only CPUs that are registered as multicast group members actually process those frames. Some multicast traffic is sporadic, as in the case of various routing protocol advertisements; other traffic, such as Cisco IP/TV multicast video, can consume most or all network resources with a steady stream of real-time data.

Broadcast traffic presents a two-fold performance problem on a bridged LAN because all broadcast frames flood all bridged network segments. First, as a network grows, the broadcast traffic can grow in proportion and monopolize the available bandwidth. Second, all end-user stations must listen to, decode, and process every broadcast frame. The CPU, which performs this function, must look further into the frame to see which upper-layer protocol the broadcast is associated with. Although today's CPUs are robust and might not show a noticeable degradation from processing broadcasts, forcing unnecessary broadcast loads on every end user is not wise.

NOTE   For a discussion of the Cisco analysis performed on the effects of various protocol broadcasts on CPU performance, refer to Broadcasts in Switched LAN Internetworks, at http://www.cisco.com/univercd/cc/td/doc/cisintwk/idg4/nd20e.htm.

LAN Segmentation Model

Referred to as *network segmentation*, localizing the traffic and effectively reducing the number of stations on a segment is necessary to prevent collisions and broadcasts from reducing a network segment's performance. By reducing the number of stations, the probability of a collision decreases because fewer stations can be transmitting at a given time. For broadcast containment, the idea is to provide a barrier at the edge of a LAN segment so that broadcasts cannot pass outward or be forwarded. The network designer can provide segmentation by using either a router or a switch.

You can use routers to connect the smaller subnetworks and either route Layer 3 packets or bridge Layer 2 packets. You can improve the effect of collisions by placing fewer stations on each segment. A router cannot propagate a collision condition from one segment to another, and broadcasts are not forwarded to other subnets by default unless bridging (or some other specialized feature) is enabled on the router. Figure 1-1 shows an example of how a router physically can segment a campus network. Although broadcasts are contained, the router becomes a potential bottleneck because it must process and route every packet leaving each subnet.

Figure 1-1 *Network Segmentation with a Router*

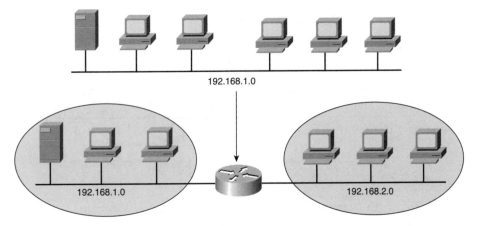

192.168.1.0

192.168.1.0   192.168.2.0

Another option is to replace shared LAN segments with switches. Switches offer greater performance with dedicated bandwidth on each port. Think of a switch as a fast multiport bridge. Each switch port becomes a separate collision domain and does not propagate collisions to any other port. However, broadcast and multicast frames are flooded out all switch ports unless more advanced switch features are invoked. Multicast switch features are covered in Chapter 15, "Multicast."

To contain broadcasts and segment a broadcast domain, you can implement virtual LANs (VLAN) within the switched network. A switch logically can divide its ports into isolated segments (broadcast domains). A VLAN is a group of switch ports (and the end devices to which they are connected) that communicate as if attached to a single shared-media LAN segment. By definition, a VLAN becomes a single broadcast domain. VLAN devices do not have to be physically located on the same switch or in the same building, as long as the VLAN itself is somehow connected between switches end to end. Figure 1-2 shows how you can segment a network into three broadcast and collision domains using three VLANs on a switch. Note that stations on a VLAN cannot communicate with stations on another VLAN in the figure—the VLANs truly are isolated.

By default, all ports on a switch are assigned to a single VLAN. With additional configuration, a switch can assign its ports to many specific VLANs. Although each VLAN is present on the same switch, it effectively is separated from other VLANs. Frames will not be forwarded from one VLAN to another. To communicate between VLANs, a router (or Layer 3 device) is required, as illustrated by Figure 1-3.

Figure 1-2 *Segmentation Using VLANs*

Ports on each switch have been grouped and assigned to one VLAN. A port from each VLAN connects to the router. The router then forwards packets between VLANs through these ports.

To gain the most benefit from routed approaches and VLAN approaches, most campus networks now are built with a combination of Layer 2 switches and routers, or with multilayer switches. Again, the Layer 2 switches generally are placed where the small broadcast domains are located, linked by routers (or multilayer switches) that provide Layer 3 functionality. In this manner, broadcast traffic can be controlled or limited. Users also can be organized and given access to common workgroups, and traffic between workgroups can be interconnected and secured.

Figure 1-3 *Routing Traffic with VLANs*

Figure 1-4 illustrates the structure of a typical routed and switched campus network. Here, the concept of Layer 2 switches and routers has been extended a bit. Each switch in the buildings supports three different VLANs for its users. A single switch port from each connects back to a router. Any switch port normally can carry only one VLAN, so something special must be occurring. These ports have been configured as *trunk links*, carrying multiple VLANs. (Trunking is discussed in Chapter 6, "VLANs and Trunks.")

Figure 1-4 *Typical Campus Network Structure*

Network Traffic Models

To design and build a successful campus network, you must gain a thorough understanding of the traffic generated by applications in use, plus the traffic flow to and from the user communities. All devices on the network will produce data to be transported across the network. Each device can involve many applications that generate data with differing patterns and loads.

Applications such as e-mail, word processing, printing, file transfer, and most web browsers bring about data traffic patterns that are predictable from source to destination. However, newer applications, such as videoconferencing, TV or video broadcasts, and IP telephony, have a more dynamic user base, which makes traffic patterns difficult to predict or model.

Traditionally, users with similar applications or needs have been placed in common workgroups, along with the servers they access most often. Whether these workgroups are logical (VLAN) or physical networks, the idea is to keep the majority of traffic between clients and servers limited to the local network segment. In the case of the switched LANs connected by routers mentioned earlier, both clients and servers would be connected to a Layer 2 switch in the workgroup's proximity. This connection provides good performance while minimizing the traffic load on the routed network backbone.

This concept of network traffic patterns is known as the 80/20 rule. In a properly designed campus network, 80 percent of the traffic on a given network segment is local (switched). No more than 20 percent of the traffic is expected to move across the network backbone (routed).

If the backbone becomes congested, the network administrator will realize that the 80/20 rule no longer is being met. What recourses are available to improve network performance again? Because of expense and complexity, upgrading the campus backbone is not a desirable option. The idea behind the 80/20 rule is to keep traffic off the backbone. Instead, the administrator can implement the following solutions:

- Reassign existing resources to bring the users and servers closer together

- Move applications and files to a different server to stay within a workgroup

- Move users logically (assigned to new VLANs) or physically to stay near their workgroups

- Add more servers, which can bring resources closer to the respective workgroups

Needless to say, conforming modern campus networks to the 80/20 rule has become difficult for the network administrator. Newer applications still use the client/server model, but the servers and their applications have been centralized in most enterprises. For example, databases, Internet access, intranet applications and resources, and e-mail are all available from centralized servers. Not only do these applications involve larger amounts of data, but they also require a greater percentage of traffic to cross a network backbone to reach common destinations—quite a departure from the 80/20 rule.

This new model of campus traffic has become known as the 20/80 rule. Now, only 20 percent of the traffic is local to the workgroup, while at least 80 percent of the traffic is expected to travel off the local network and across the backbone.

This shift in traffic patterns puts a greater burden on the campus backbone's Layer 3 technology. Now, because traffic from anywhere on the network can be destined for any other part of the network, the Layer 3 performance ideally should match the Layer 2 performance. Generally, Layer 3 forwarding involves more processing resources because the data packets must be examined in greater depth. This added computation load can create bottlenecks in the campus network unless carefully designed.

Likewise, a campus network with many VLANs can become difficult to manage. In the past, VLANs were used to logically contain common workgroups and common traffic. With the 20/80 rule, end devices need to communicate with many other VLANs. Measuring traffic patterns and redesigning the campus network become too cumbersome just to keep up with the 20/80 rule model.

Predictable Network Model

Ideally, you should design a network with a predictable behavior in mind to offer low maintenance and high availability. For example, a campus network needs to recover from failures and topology changes quickly and in a predetermined manner. You should scale the network to easily support future expansions and upgrades. With a wide variety of multiprotocol and multicast traffic, the network should be capable of supporting the 20/80 rule from a traffic standpoint. In other words, design the network around traffic flows instead of a particular type of traffic.

Traffic flows in a campus network can be classified as three types, based on where the network service is located in relation to the end user. Table 1-3 lists these types, along with the extent of the campus network that is crossed.

Table 1-3 *Types of Network Services*

Service Type	Location of Service	Extent of Traffic Flow
Local	Same segment/VLAN as user	Access layer only
Remote	Different segment/VLAN as user	Access to distribution layers
Enterprise	Central to all campus users	Access to distribution to core layers

The terms access layer, distribution layer, and core layer are each distinct components of the hierarchical network design model. The network is divided into logical levels, or layers, according to function. These terms and the hierarchical network design are discussed in the next section.

Hierarchical Network Design

You can structure the campus network so that each of the three types of traffic flows or services outlined in Table 1-3 is best supported. Cisco has refined a hierarchical approach to network design that enables network designers to logically create a network by defining and using layers of devices. The resulting network is efficient, intelligent, scalable, and easily managed.

The hierarchical model breaks a campus network into three distinct layers, as illustrated in Figure 1-5.

Figure 1-5 *Hierarchical Network Design*

These layers are the access layer, distribution layer, and core layer. Each layer has attributes that provide both physical and logical network functions at the appropriate point in the campus network. Understanding each layer and its functions or limitations is important to properly apply the layer in the design process.

Access Layer

The access layer is present where the end users are connected to the network. Devices in this layer, sometimes called building access switches, should have the following capabilities:

- Low cost per switch port

- High port density

- Scalable uplinks to higher layers

- User access functions such as VLAN membership, traffic and protocol filtering, and QoS

- Resiliency through multiple uplinks

Distribution Layer

The distribution layer provides interconnection between the campus network's access and core layers. Devices in this layer, sometimes called building distribution switches, should have the following capabilities:

- Aggregation of multiple access-layer devices

- High Layer 3 throughput for packet handling

- Security and policy-based connectivity functions through access lists or packet filters

- QoS features

- Scalable and resilient high-speed links to the core and access layers

In the distribution layer, uplinks from all access-layer devices are aggregated, or come together. The distribution-layer switches must be capable of processing the total volume of traffic from all the connected devices. These switches should have a port density of high-speed links to support the collection of access-layer switches.

VLANs and broadcast domains converge at the distribution layer, requiring routing, filtering, and security. The switches at this layer also must be capable of performing multilayer switching with high throughput.

Core Layer

A campus network's core layer provides connectivity of all distribution-layer devices. The core, sometimes referred to as the backbone, must be capable of switching traffic as efficiently as possible. Core devices, sometimes called campus backbone switches, should have the following attributes:

- Very high throughput at Layer 2 or Layer 3

- No costly or unnecessary packet manipulations (access lists, packet filtering)

- Redundancy and resilience for high availability

- Advanced QoS functions

Devices in a campus network's core layer or backbone should be optimized for high-performance Layer 2 or Layer 3 switching. Because the core layer must handle large amounts of campuswide data (because of the new 20/80 rule of traffic flow), the core layer should be designed with simplicity and efficiency in mind.

Although campus network design is presented as a three-layer approach (access, distribution, and core layers), the hierarchy can be collapsed or simplified in certain cases. For example, small or medium-size campus networks might not have the size, multilayer switching, or volume requirements that would require the functions of all three layers. Here, you could combine the distribution and core layers for simplicity and cost savings. In this case, choose switch products based on the distribution-layer features and access-layer aggregation port densities needed.

Foundation Summary

The Foundation Summary is a collection of tables and figures that provides a convenient review of many key concepts in this chapter. If you are already comfortable with the topics in this chapter, this summary might help you recall a few details. If you just read this chapter, this review should help solidify some key facts. If you are doing your final preparation before the exam, the following tables and figures are a convenient way to review the day before the exam.

Table 1-4   *Layers of Data Communications*

OSI Layer	Protocol Data Unit	Mechanism to Process PDU
7 (application)		
6 (presentation)		
5 (session)		
4 (transport)	TCP segment	TCP port
3 (network)	Packet	Router
2 (data link)	Frame	Switch/bridge
1 (physical)		

Table 1-5   *Types of Network Services*

Service Type	Location of Service	Extent of Traffic Flow
Local	Same segment/VLAN as user	Access layer only
Remote	Different segment/VLAN as user	Access to distribution layers
Enterprise	Central to all campus users	Access to distribution to core layers

Table 1-6   *Comparison of Hierarchical Layers*

Layer	Attributes
Access	High port density to connect to end users, low cost, uplinks to higher layers of the campus network, and Layer 2 services (traffic filtering, VLAN membership, and basic QoS)
Distribution	Aggregation of access-layer devices, high Layer 3 throughput, QoS features, security- and policy-based functions, and scalable and resilient high-speed links into the core and access layers
Core	Fast data transport, no "expensive" Layer 3 processing, redundancy and resiliency for high availability, and advanced QoS

Q&A

The questions and scenarios in this book are more difficult than what you should experience on the actual exam. The questions do not attempt to cover more breadth or depth than the exam; however, they are designed to make sure that you know the answer. Rather than allowing you to derive the answers from clues hidden inside the questions themselves, the questions challenge your understanding and recall of the subject. Hopefully, these questions will help limit the number of exam questions on which you narrow your choices to two options and then guess.

You can find the answers to these questions in Appendix A.

1. For each layer of the OSI model, match the forwarding criteria used by a switch:

_____ Layer 1	A. IP address
_____ Layer 2	B. UDP/TCP port
_____ Layer 3	C. None
_____ Layer 4	D. MAC address

2. What is multilayer switching (MLS)?

3. Fill in the blanks in the following statement:

   In the 20/80 rule of networking, 20 percent of the traffic on a segment usually stays _____, while 80 percent travels _____.

4. What is a collision domain, and where does it exist in a switched LAN?

5. What is a broadcast domain, and where does it exist in a switched LAN?

6. What is a VLAN, and why is it used?

7. At what OSI layers do devices in the distribution layer usually operate?

8. What is network segmentation? When is it necessary, and how is it done in a campus network design?

9. Is it possible to use Layer 2 switches in the distribution layer rather than Layer 3 switches? If so, what are the limitations?

This chapter covers the following topics that you need to master for the CCNP BCMSN exam:

- **Modular Network Design**—This section covers the process of designing a campus network, based on breaking it into functional modules. You also learn how to size and scale the modules in a design.

- **Evaluating an Existing Network**—In this section, you learn about evaluating the structure and operation of an existing network, and redesigning the network according to a robust campus network model.

CHAPTER 2

Modular Network Design

This chapter presents a set of building blocks that can organize and streamline even a large, complex campus network. These building blocks then can be placed using several campus design models to provide maximum efficiency, functionality, and scalability.

"Do I Know This Already?" Quiz

The purpose of the "Do I Know This Already?" quiz is to help you decide whether you need to read the entire chapter. If you already intend to read the entire chapter, you do not necessarily need to answer these questions now.

The 14-question quiz, derived from the major sections in the "Foundation Topics" portion of the chapter, helps you determine how to spend your limited study time.

Table 2-1 outlines the major topics discussed in this chapter and the "Do I Know This Already?" quiz questions that correspond to those topics.

Table 2-1 *"Do I Know This Already?" Foundation Topics Section-to-Question Mapping*

Foundation Topics Section	Questions Covered in This Section	Score
Modular Network Design	1–12	
Evaluating an Existing Network	13–14	
Total Score		

CAUTION The goal of self-assessment is to gauge your mastery of the topics in this chapter. If you do not know the answer to a question or are only partially sure of the answer, you should mark this question wrong. Giving yourself credit for an answer you correctly guess skews your self-assessment results and might provide you with a false sense of security.

You can find the answers to the quiz in Appendix A, "Answers to Chapter 'Do I Know This Already?' Quizzes and Q&A Sections." The suggested choices for your next step are as follows:

- **8 or less overall score**—Read the entire chapter. This includes the "Foundation Topics," "Foundation Summary," and "Q&A" sections.

- **9–10 overall score**—Begin with the "Foundation Summary" section and then follow up with the "Q&A" section at the end of the chapter.

- **12 or more overall score**—If you want more review on these topics, skip to the "Foundation Summary" section and then go to the "Q&A" section at the end of the chapter. Otherwise, move on to Chapter 3, "Switch Operation."

1. What is the purpose of breaking a campus network into a hierarchical design?

   a. To facilitate documentation

   b. To follow political or organizational policies

   c. To make the network predictable and scalable

   d. To make the network more redundant and secure

2. Which of the following are building blocks or modules used to build a scalable campus network? (Check all that apply.)

   a. Access block

   b. Distribution block

   c. Core block

   d. Server farm block

   e. Switch block

3. Which one or more of the following are the components of a typical switch block?

   a. Access-layer switches

   b. Distribution-layer switches

   c. Core-layer switches

   d. E-commerce servers

   e. Service provider switches

4. What are two types of core, or backbone, designs?

   a. Collapsed core

   b. Loop-free core

   c. Dual core

   d. Layered core

5.   In a properly designed hierarchical network, a broadcast from one PC is confined to what?

    a.   One access-layer switch port

    b.   One access-layer switch

    c.   One switch block

    d.   The entire campus network

6.   What is the maximum number of access-layer switches that can connect into a single distribution-layer switch?

    a.   1

    b.   2

    c.   Limited only by the number of ports on the access-layer switch

    d.   Limited only by the number of ports on the distribution-layer switch

    e.   Unlimited

7.   A switch block should be sized according to what?

    a.   The number of access-layer users

    b.   A maximum of 250 access-layer users

    c.   A study of the traffic patterns and flows

    d.   The amount of rack space available

    e.   The number of servers accessed by users

8.   What evidence can be seen when a switch block is too large? (Choose all that apply.)

    a.   IP address space is exhausted.

    b.   You run out of access-layer switch ports.

    c.   Broadcast traffic becomes excessive.

    d.   Traffic is throttled at the distribution-layer switches.

    e.   Network congestion occurs.

9.   How many distribution switches should be built into each switch block?

    a.   1

    b.   2

    c.   4

    d.   8

10. What are the most important aspects to consider when designing the core layer in a large network? (Choose all that apply.)

   a. Low cost

   b. Switches that can efficiently forward traffic, even when every uplink is at 100 percent capacity

   c. High port density of high-speed ports

   d. A low number of Layer 3 routing peers

11. Which services typically are located at the enterprise edge block? (Choose all that apply.)

   a. Network management

   b. Intranet server farms

   c. VPN and remote access

   d. E-commerce servers

   e. End users

12. In a server farm block, where should redundancy be provided? (Choose all that apply.)

   a. Dual connections from each distribution switch to the core.

   b. Dual connections from each access switch to the distribution switches.

   c. Dual connections from each server to the access switches.

   d. No redundancy is necessary.

13. Which of the following protocols can be used as a tool to discover a network topology?

   a. RIP

   b. CDP

   c. STP

   d. ICMP

14. Which one of the following tasks is not an appropriate strategy for migrating an existing network into the Enterprise Composite Model?

   a. Identify groups of end users as switch blocks

   b. Group common resources into switch blocks

   c. Identify distribution switches to connect the switch blocks

   d. Add redundancy between the hierarchical layers

Foundation Topics

Modular Network Design

Recall from Chapter 1, "Campus Network Overview," that a network is best constructed and maintained using a three-tiered hierarchical approach. Making a given network conform to a layered architecture might seem a little confusing.

You can design a campus network in a logical manner, using a modular approach. In this approach, each layer of the hierarchical network model can be broken into basic functional units. These units, or modules, then can be sized appropriately and connected, while allowing for future scalability and expansion.

You can divide enterprise campus networks into the following basic elements:

- **Switch block**—A group of access-layer switches, together with their distribution switches

- **Core block**—The campus network's backbone

Other related elements can exist. Although these elements don't contribute to the campus network's overall function, they can be designed separately and added to the network design. These elements are as follows:

- **Server farm block**—A group of enterprise servers, along with their access and distribution (layer) switches.

- **Management block**—A group of network-management resources, along with their access and distribution switches.

- **Enterprise edge block**—A collection of services related to external network access, along with their access and distribution switches.

- **Service provider edge block**—The external network services contracted or used by the enterprise network. These are the services with which the enterprise edge block interfaces.

The collection of all these elements is also known as the Enterprise Composite Network Model. Figure 2-1 shows a modular campus design's basic structure. Notice how each of the building-block elements can be confined to a certain area or function. Also notice how each is connected into the core block.

Figure 2-1   *Modular Approach to Campus Network Design*

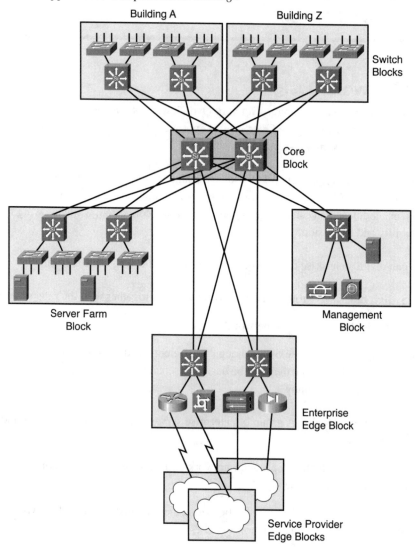

Switch Block

Recall how a campus network is divided into access, distribution, and core layers. The switch block contains switching devices from the access and distribution layers. All switch blocks then connect into the core block, providing end-to-end connectivity across the campus.

Switch blocks contain a balanced mix of Layer 2 and Layer 3 functionality, as might be present in the access and distribution layers. Layer 2 switches located in wiring closets (access layer) connect end users to the campus network. With one end user per switch port, each user receives dedicated bandwidth access.

Upstream, each access-layer switch connects to devices in the distribution layer. Here, Layer 2 functionality transports data among all connected access switches at a central connection point. Layer 3 functionality also can be provided in the form of routing and other networking services (security, quality of service [QoS], and so on). Therefore, a distribution-layer device should be a multilayer switch. Layer 3 functionality is discussed in more detail in Chapter 13, "Multilayer Switching."

The distribution layer also shields the switch block from certain failures or conditions in other parts of the network. For example, broadcasts are not propagated from the switch block into the core and other switch blocks. Therefore, the Spanning Tree Protocol (STP) is confined to each switch block, where a virtual LAN (VLAN) is bounded, keeping the spanning tree domain well defined and controlled.

Access-layer switches can support VLANs by assigning individual ports to specific VLAN numbers. In this way, stations connected to the ports configured for the same VLAN can share the same Layer 3 subnet. However, be aware that a single VLAN can support multiple subnets. Because the switch ports are configured for a VLAN number only (and not a network address), any station connected to a port can present any subnet address range. The VLAN functions as traditional network media and allows any network address to connect.

In this network design model, you should not extend VLANs beyond distribution switches. The distribution layer always should be the boundary of VLANs, subnets, and broadcasts. Although Layer 2 switches can extend VLANs to other switches and other layers of the hierarchy, this activity is discouraged. VLAN traffic should not traverse the network core. (Trunking, or the capability to carry many VLANs over a single connection, is discussed in Chapter 6, "VLANs and Trunks.")

Sizing a Switch Block

Containing access- and distribution-layer devices, the switch block is simple in concept. You should consider several factors, however, to determine an appropriate size for the switch block. The range of available switch devices makes the switch block size very flexible. At the access layer, switch selection usually is based on port density or the number of connected users.

The distribution layer must be sized according to the number of access-layer switches that are collapsed or brought into a distribution device. Consider the following factors:

- Traffic types and patterns

- Amount of Layer 3 switching capacity at the distribution layer

- Number of users connected to the access-layer switches

■   Geographical boundaries of subnets or VLANs

■   Size of spanning-tree domains

Designing a switch block based solely on the number of users or stations contained within the block is usually inaccurate. Usually, no more than 2000 users should be placed within a single switch block. Although this is useful for initially estimating a switch block's size, this idea doesn't take into account the many dynamic processes that occur on a functioning network.

Instead, switch block size should be based primarily on the following:

■   Traffic types and behavior

■   Size and number of common workgroups

Because of the dynamic nature of networks, you can size a switch block too large to handle the load that is placed upon it. Also, the number of users and applications on a network tends to grow over time. A provision to break up or downsize a switch block is necessary. Again, base these decisions on the actual traffic flows and patterns present in the switch block. You can estimate, model, or measure these parameters with network-analysis applications and tools.

> **NOTE**   The actual network-analysis process is beyond the scope of this book. Traffic estimation, modeling, and measurement are complex procedures, each requiring its own dedicated analysis tool.

Generally, a switch block is too large if the following conditions are observed:

■   The routers (multilayer switches) at the distribution layer become traffic bottlenecks. This congestion could be because of the volume of interVLAN traffic, intensive CPU processing, or switching times required by policy or security functions (access lists, queuing, and so on).

■   Broadcast or multicast traffic slows the switches in the switch block. Broadcast and multicast traffic must be replicated and forwarded out many ports. This process requires some overhead in the multilayer switch, which can become too great if significant traffic volumes are present.

Access switches can have one or more redundant links to distribution-layer devices. This situation provides a fault-tolerant environment in which access layer connectivity is preserved on a secondary link if the primary link fails. In fact, because Layer 3 devices are used in the distribution layer, traffic can be load-balanced across both redundant links using redundant gateways.

Generally, you should provide two distribution switches in each switch block for redundancy, with each access-layer switch connecting to the two distribution switches. Then, each Layer 3 distribution switch can load-balance traffic over its redundant links into the core layer (also Layer 3 switches) using routing protocols.

Figure 2-2 shows a typical switch block design. At Layer 3, the two distribution switches can use one of several redundant gateway protocols to provide an active IP gateway and a standby gateway at all times. These protocols are discussed in Chapter 14, "Router Redundancy and Load Balancing."

Figure 2-2 *Typical Switch Block Design*

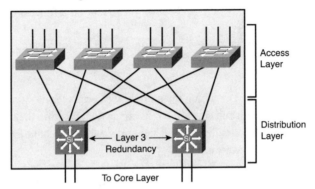

Core Block

A core block is required to connect two or more switch blocks in a campus network. Because all traffic passing to and from all switch blocks, server farm blocks, and the enterprise edge block must cross the core block, the core must be as efficient and resilient as possible. The core is the campus network's basic foundation and carries much more traffic than any other block.

A network core can use any technology (frame, cell, or packet) to transport campus data. Many campus networks use Gigabit and 10-Gigabit Ethernet as a core technology. Ethernet core blocks are reviewed at length here.

Recall that both the distribution and core layers provide Layer 3 functionality. Individual IP subnets connect all distribution and core switches. At least two subnets should be used to provide resiliency and load balancing into the core, although you can use a single VLAN. As VLANs end at the distribution layer, they are routed into the core.

The core block might consist of a single multilayer switch, taking in the two redundant links from the distribution-layer switches. Because of the importance of the core block in a campus network, you should implement two or more identical switches in the core to provide redundancy.

The links between layers also should be designed to carry at least the amount of traffic load handled by the distribution switches. The links between core switches in the same core subnet should be of sufficient size to carry the aggregate amount of traffic coming into the core switch. Consider the average link utilization, but allow for future growth. An Ethernet core allows simple and scalable upgrades of magnitude; consider the progression from Ethernet to Fast Ethernet to Fast EtherChannel to Gigabit Ethernet to Gigabit EtherChannel, and so on.

Two basic core block designs are presented in the following sections, each designed around a campus network's size:

- Collapsed core

- Dual core

Collapsed Core

A collapsed core block is one in which the hierarchy's core layer is collapsed into the distribution layer. Here, both distribution and core functions are provided within the same switch devices. This situation usually is found in smaller campus networks, where a separate core layer (and additional cost or performance) is not warranted.

Figure 2-3 shows the basic collapsed core design. Although the distribution- and core-layer functions are performed in the same device, keeping these functions distinct and properly designed is important. Note also that the collapsed core is not an independent building block but is integrated into the distribution layer of the individual standalone switch blocks.

In the collapsed core design, each access-layer switch has a redundant link to each distribution- and core-layer switch. All Layer 3 subnets present in the access layer terminate at the distribution switches' Layer 3 ports, as in the basic switch block design. The distribution and core switches connect to each other by one or more links, completing a path to use during a redundancy failover.

Figure 2-3 *Collapsed Core Block Design*

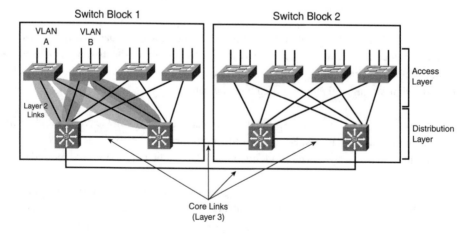

Connectivity between the distribution and core switches is accomplished using Layer 3 links (Layer 3 switch interfaces, with no inherent VLANs). The Layer 3 switches route traffic to and from each other directly. Figure 2-3 shows the extent of two VLANs. Notice that VLAN A and VLAN B each extend only from the access-layer switches where their respective users are located, down to the distribution layer over the Layer 2 uplinks. The VLANs terminate there because the distribution layer uses Layer 3 switching. This is good because it limits the broadcast domains, removes the possibility of Layer 2 bridging loops, and provides fast failover if one uplink fails.

At Layer 3, redundancy is provided through a redundant gateway protocol for IP (covered in Chapter 14). In some of the protocols, the two distribution switches provide a common default gateway address to the access-layer switches, but only one is active at any time. In other protocols, the two switches can both be active, load-balancing traffic. If a distribution and core switch failure occurs, connectivity to the core is maintained because the redundant Layer 3 switch is always available.

Dual Core

A dual core connects two or more switch blocks in a redundant fashion. Although the collapsed core can connect two switch blocks with some redundancy, the core is not scalable when more switch blocks are added. Figure 2-4 illustrates the dual core. Notice that this core appears as an independent module and is not merged into any other block or layer.

Figure 2-4 *Dual Network Core Design*

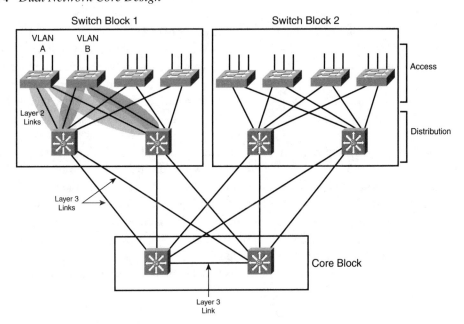

In the past, the dual core usually was built with Layer 2 switches to provide the simplest and most efficient throughput. Layer 3 switching was provided in the distribution layer. Multilayer switches now have become cost-effective and offer high switching performance. Building a dual core with multilayer switches is both possible and recommended. The dual core uses two identical switches to provide redundancy. Redundant links connect each switch block's distribution-layer portion to each of the dual core switches. The two core switches connect by a common link. In a Layer 2 core, the switches cannot be linked to avoid any bridging loops. A Layer 3 core uses routing rather than bridging, so bridging loops are not an issue.

In the dual core, each distribution switch has two equal-cost paths to the core, allowing the available bandwidth of both paths to be used simultaneously. Both paths remain active because the distribution and core layers use Layer 3 devices that can manage equal-cost paths in routing tables. The routing protocol in use determines the availability or loss of a neighboring Layer 3 device. If one switch fails, the routing protocol reroutes traffic using an alternate path through the remaining redundant switch.

Notice again in Figure 2-4 the extent of the access VLANs. Although Layer 3 devices have been added into a separate core layer, VLANs A and B still extend only from the Layer 2 access-layer switches down to the distribution layer. Although the distribution-layer switches use Layer 3 switch interfaces to provide Layer 3 functionality to the access layer, these links actually pass traffic only at Layer 2.

Core Size in a Campus Network

The dual core is made up of redundant switches and is bounded and isolated by Layer 3 devices. Routing protocols determine paths and maintain the core's operation. As with any network, you must pay some attention to the overall design of the routers and routing protocols in the network. Because routing protocols propagate updates throughout the network, network topologies might be undergoing change. The network's size (the number of routers) then affects routing protocol performance as updates are exchanged and network convergence takes place.

Although the network shown previously in Figure 2-4 might look small, with only two switch blocks of two Layer 3 switches (route processors within the distribution-layer switches) each, large campus networks can have many switch blocks connected into the core block. If you think of each multilayer switch as a router, you will recall that each route processor must communicate with and keep information about each of its directly connected peers. Most routing protocols have practical limits on the number of peer routers that can be directly connected on a point-to-point or multiaccess link. In a network with a large number of switch blocks, the number of connected routers can grow quite large. Should you be concerned about a core switch peering with too many distribution switches?

No, because the actual number of directly connected peers is quite small, regardless of the campus network size. Access-layer VLANs terminate at the distribution-layer switches. The only peering routers at that boundary are pairs of distribution switches, each providing routing redundancy for each of the access-layer VLAN subnets. At the distribution and core boundary, each distribution switch connects to only two core switches over Layer 3 switch interfaces. Therefore, only pairs of router peers are formed.

When multilayer switches are used in the distribution and core layers, the routing protocols running in both layers regard each pair of redundant links between layers as equal-cost paths. Traffic is routed across both links in a load-sharing fashion, utilizing the bandwidth of both.

One final core-layer design point is to scale the core switches to match the incoming load. At a minimum, each core switch must handle switching each of its incoming distribution links at 100 percent capacity.

Other Building Blocks

Other resources in the campus network can be identified and pulled into the building block model. For example, a server farm can be made up of servers running applications that users from all across the enterprise access. Most likely, those servers need to be scalable for future expansion, need to be highly accessible, and need to benefit from traffic and security policy control.

To meet these needs, you can group the resources into building blocks that are structured and placed just like regular switch block modules. These blocks should have a distribution layer of switches and redundant uplinks directly into the core layer, and should contain enterprise resources.

A list of the most common examples follows. Refer back to Figure 2-1 to see how each of these is grouped and connected into the campus network. Most of these building blocks are present in medium and large campus networks. Be familiar with the concept of pulling an enterprise function into its own switch block, as well as the structure of that block.

Server Farm Block

Any server or application accessed by most of the enterprise users usually already belongs to a server farm. The entire server farm can be identified as its own switch block and given a layer of access switches uplinked to dual distribution switches (multilayer). Connect these distribution switches into the core layer with redundant high-speed links.

Individual servers can have single network connections to one of the distribution switches. However, this presents a single point of failure. If a redundant server is used, it should connect to the alternate distribution switch. Another more resilient approach is to give each server dual network connections, one going to each distribution switch. This is known as dual-homing the servers.

Examples of enterprise servers include corporate e-mail, intranet services, Enterprise Resource Planning (ERP) applications, and mainframe systems. Notice that each of these is an internal resource that normally would be located inside a firewall or secured perimeter.

Network Management Block

Often campus networks must be monitored through the use of network-management tools so that performance and fault conditions can be measured and detected. You can group the entire suite of network-management applications into a single network management switch block. This is the reverse of a server farm block because the network-management tools are not enterprise resources accessed by most of the users. Instead, these tools go out to access other network devices, application servers, and user activity in all other areas of the campus network.

The network management switch block usually has a distribution layer that connects into the core switches. Because these tools are used to detect equipment and connectivity failures, availability is important. Redundant links and redundant switches should be used.

Examples of network-management resources in this switch block include the following:

- Network-monitoring applications

- System logging (syslog) servers

- Authentication, authorization, and accounting (AAA) servers

- Policy-management applications

- System administration and remote-control services

- Intrusion-detection management applications

> **NOTE**   You can easily gather network-management resources into a single switch block to centralize these functions. Each switch and router in the network must have an IP address assigned for management purposes. In the past, it was easy to "centralize" all these management addresses and traffic into a single "management" VLAN, which extended from one end of the campus to the other.
>
> The end-to-end VLAN concept is now considered a poor practice. VLANs should be isolated, as described in Chapter 1. Therefore, assigning management addresses to as many VLANs or subnets as is practical and appropriate for a campus network is now acceptable.

Enterprise Edge Block

At some point, most campus networks must connect to service providers for access to external resources. This is usually known as the edge of the enterprise or campus network. These resources are available to the entire campus and should be centrally accessible as an independent switch block connected to the network core.

Edge services usually are divided into these categories:

- **Internet access**—Supports outbound traffic to the Internet, as well as inbound traffic to public services, such as e-mail and extranet web servers. This connectivity is provided by one or more Internet service providers (ISP). Network security devices generally are placed here.

- **Remote access and VPN**—Supports inbound dialup access for external or roaming users through the Public Switched Telephone Network (PSTN). If voice traffic is supported over the campus network, Voice over IP (VoIP) gateways connect to the PSTN here. In addition, virtual private network (VPN) devices connected to the Internet support secure tunneled connections to remote locations.

- **E-commerce**—Supports all related web, application, and database servers and applications, as well as firewalls and security devices. This switch block connects to one or more ISPs.

- **WAN access**—Supports all traditional WAN connections to remote sites. This can include Frame Relay, ATM, leased line, ISDN, and so on.

Service Provider Edge Block

Each service provider that connects to an enterprise network must also have a hierarchical network design of its own. A service provider network meets an enterprise at the service provider edge, connecting to the enterprise edge block.

Studying a service provider network's structure isn't necessary because it should follow the same design principles presented here. In other words, a service provider is just another enterprise or campus network itself. Just be familiar with the fact that a campus network has an edge block, where it connects to the edge of each service provider's network.

Can I Use Layer 2 Distribution Switches?

This chapter covers the best practice design that places Layer 3 switches at both the core and distribution layers. What would happen if you could not afford Layer 3 switches at the distribution layer?

Figure 2-5 shows the dual-core campus network with Layer 2 distribution switches. Notice how each access VLAN extends not only throughout the switch block but also into the core. This is because the VLAN terminates at a Layer 3 boundary present only in the core. As an example, VLAN A's propagation is shaded in the figure.

Figure 2-5 *Design Using Layer 2 Distribution Switches*

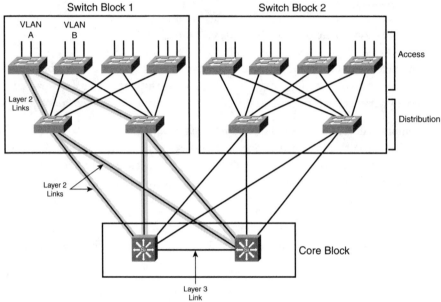

Here are some implications with this design:

- Redundant Layer 3 gateways still can be used in the core.

- Each VLAN propagates across the redundant trunk links from the access to the core layers. Because of this, Layer 2 bridging loops form.

- The STP must run in all layers to prevent Layer 2 loops. This causes traffic on some links to be blocked. As a result, only one of every two access-layer switch uplinks can be used at any time.

- When Layer 2 uplinks go down, the STP can take several seconds to unblock redundant links, causing downtime.

- Access VLANs can propagate from one end of the campus to the other, if necessary.

- Broadcast traffic on any access-layer VLAN also reaches into the core layer. Bandwidth on uplinks and within the core can be wasted unnecessarily.

Evaluating an Existing Network

If you are building an enterprise network from scratch, you might find that it is fairly straightforward to build it in a hierarchical fashion. After all, you can begin with switches in the core layer and fan out into lower layers to meet the users, server farms, and service providers.

In the real world, you might be more likely to find existing networks that need an overhaul to match the hierarchical model. Hopefully, if you are redesigning your own network, you already know its topology and traffic patterns. If you are working on someone else's network, you might not know about its structure.

This section provides some basic information on two tasks:

- Discovering the existing topology

- Planning a migration to a better campus model

Discovering the Network Topology

Whether a diagram of a network is available or not, you should consider tracing out the topology for yourself. For one thing, network documentation tends to become out-of-date or isn't drawn to show the type of information you need.

Some network administrators draw up a diagram that shows only the physical cabling between network devices. That might benefit someone who is working with the cabling, but it might not show any of the logical aspects of the network. After all, switched networks can be cabled together and then configured into many logical topologies.

As you discover or trace out a network, you might end up building several diagrams. One diagram might show all the network devices and only the physical cabling between them. Further diagrams might show Layer 2 virtual LANs (VLANs) and how they extend through the network.

To discover an existing network, you can connect a computer to any switch as a starting point and begin to "walk" the topology. Cisco devices periodically send information about themselves to any neighboring devices. This is done with the Cisco Discovery Protocol (CDP), which is covered in more detail in the "Inter-Switch Communication—Cisco Discovery Protocol" section in Chapter 4, "Switch Configuration."

CDP is enabled by default on all Cisco switches and routers, so, chances are, you will be able to make use of it right away. With CDP, a switch becomes aware of only the devices that are directly connected to it. Therefore, you walk the topology one "hop" at a time: connect to one switch, find its neighbors, and then connect to them one at a time.

Figure 2-6 shows this process being used to discover an example network. (The arrows in the sequence illustrated in Figure 2-6 point out where you are positioned as the topology is discovered.) A laptop PC has been connected to the console connection of an arbitrary switch, Switch-A. Here, Switch-A is a Catalyst 3550, determined either by inspection or from the **show version** command.

Figure 2-6 *Network Discovery with CDP*

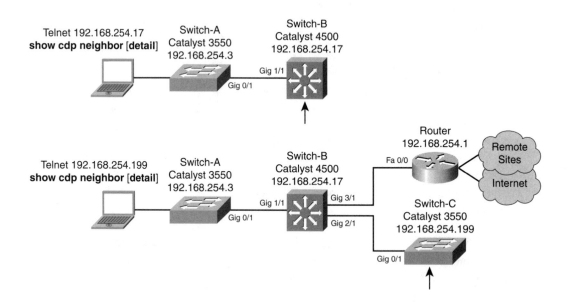

At the top of the figure, you don't know whether Switch-A is in the core, distribution, or access layer. Actually, you don't even know whether this network has been built in layers.

When you are connected and in the privileged EXEC or enable mode, you can begin looking for CDP information by using the **show cdp neighbors** command. At Switch-A, suppose the command had the output in Example 2-1.

Example 2-1 **show cdp neighbors** *Command Output Reveals CDP Information*

```
Switch-A# show cdp neighbors
Capability Codes: R - Router, T - Trans Bridge, B - Source Route Bridge
                  S - Switch, H - Host, I - IGMP, r - Repeater, P - Phone

Device ID       Local Intrfce    Holdtme    Capability  Platform  Port ID
Switch-B        Gig 0/1          152          R S I     WS-C4506  Gig 1/1
Switch-A#
```

Based on the neighbors listed, you should be able to draw the connections to the neighboring switches and detail the names and model of those switches. Notice that the CDP neighbor information shows the local switch interface as well as the neighbor's interface for each connection. This is helpful when you move to a neighbor and need to match the connections from its viewpoint.

From the output in Example 2-1, it's apparent that Switch-A has a neighbor called Switch-B on interface GigabitEthernet 0/1. Switch-B is a Catalyst 4506.

Now you can use a variation of the command to see more detail about each neighbor. The **show cdp neighbors** [**interface** *mod/num*] **detail** command also shows the neighbor's software release, interface settings, and its IP address, as demonstrated in Example 2-2.

Example 2-2   **show cdp neighbors detail** *Command Output Reveals Detailed Information About Neighboring Switches*

```
Switch-A# show cdp neighbors detail
-----------------------
Device ID: Switch-B
Entry address(es): 192.168.254.17
Platform: cisco WS-C4506,  Capabilities: Router Switch IGMP
Interface: GigabitEthernet0/1,  Port ID (outgoing port): GigabitEthernet1/1
Holdtime : 134 sec
Version :
Cisco Internetwork Operating System Software
IOS (tm) Catalyst 4000 L3 Switch Software (cat4000-I9S-M), Version 12.2(18)EW, EARLY
DEPLOYMENT RELEASE SOFTWARE (fc1)
TAC Support: http://www.cisco.com/tac
Copyright  1986-2004 by cisco Systems, Inc.
Compiled Fri 30-Jan-04 02:04 by hqluong
advertisement version: 2
VTP Management Domain: ''
Duplex: full
Management address(es):
Switch-A#
```

When you know the IP address of a neighboring device, you can open a Telnet session from the current switch to the neighboring switch. (This assumes that the neighboring switch has been configured with an IP address and a Telnet password on its vty lines.) Choose a neighbor and use the **telnet** *ip-address* command to move to the neighbor and continue your discovery. At Switch-B (the middle of Figure 2-6), you might see the CDP neighbor output in Example 2-3.

Example 2-3 **show cdp neighbors** *Command Output Display for Switch-B*

```
Switch-B# show cdp neighbors
Capability Codes: R - Router, T - Trans Bridge, B - Source Route Bridge
                  S - Switch, H - Host, I - IGMP, r - Repeater, P - Phone
Device ID        Local Intrfce    Holdtme    Capability  Platform    Port ID
Switch-A         Gig 1/1          105        S I         WS-C3550-4Gig 0/1
Switch-C         Gig 2/1          139        S I         WS-C3550-4Gig 0/1
Router           Gig 3/1          120        R           Cisco 2610Fas 0/0
```

Next, the **show cdp neighbors detail** command reveals that Switch-C has the IP address 192.168.254.199, so you can open a Telnet session there. Switch-C might show only one neighbor (Switch-B), so you have reached the end of the switched network topology. At the bottom portion of Figure 2-6, the physical network has been discovered and drawn.

TIP You should assess the utilization or bandwidth used over various connections in the network. This is especially true of switch-to-switch links—if they are heavily used, you might want to plan for expansion. You also might want to get an idea of the total traffic being passed to and from individual server or user connections.

You can do this by using a network or protocol analyzer that is set up to monitor specific switch interfaces. However, you can get a quick snapshot of average traffic volumes with the **show interfaces** command. A switch maintains a running 5-minute average of traffic rates into and out of each interface. The output from **show interfaces** displays this information along with a host of other interface statistics.

To see only the interfaces that are in use and only the input and output data rates, you can add a filter to that command:

    show interfaces | **include (is up** | **rate)**

This produces output similar to the following:

```
Switch# show interfaces | include (is up | rate)
GigabitEthernet2/1 is up, line protocol is up (connected)
  5 minute input rate 63000 bits/sec, 34 packets/sec
  5 minute output rate 901000 bits/sec, 168 packets/sec
GigabitEthernet2/2 is up, line protocol is up (connected)
  5 minute input rate 0 bits/sec, 0 packets/sec
  5 minute output rate 194000 bits/sec, 80 packets/sec
GigabitEthernet2/3 is up, line protocol is up (connected)
  5 minute input rate 219000 bits/sec, 103 packets/sec
  5 minute output rate 1606000 bits/sec, 265 packets/sec
```

You can discover many more detailed aspects of a network. For example, you might want to know the extent of various VLANs across the switches, which interfaces are acting as trunks, the spanning-tree topology for various VLANs, and so on.

These are all important things to consider in a network design and in troubleshooting a network, but they are beyond the scope of this chapter. These topics and the appropriate commands are presented in later chapters of this book.

Migrating to a Hierarchical Design

After you have discovered the topology of a network, you might find that it doesn't resemble the overall design goals that were presented earlier in this chapter. Perhaps it doesn't have a hierarchical layout with distinct layers. Or maybe you aren't able to see a modular layout with distinct switch blocks.

To move toward the campus hierarchical model, you also need to gather information about the traffic patterns crossing the network. For example, you should try to find answers to these questions:

- Where are the enterprise resources (corporate e-mail, web, and intranet application servers) located?

- Where are the end user communities located?

- Where are the service provider connections to the Internet, remote sites, and VPN users located?

Following the example of Figure 2-6, these have been identified by interviewing system administrators and network staff. Figure 2-7 shows the locations of user groups and server resources. Notice that these seem to be scattered across the entire network and that there is no clear picture of a modular network.

Figure 2-7   *Identifying User and Enterprise Resources*

Now, you should add some structure to the design. Try to identify pieces of the network as specific modules. For example, the end user communities eventually will become switch block modules, containing both distribution- and access-layer switches. Redraw the network with the users and their switches toward the bottom.

Any resources related to connections to service providers, remote sites, or the Internet should be grouped and moved to become a service provider module or switch block. Enterprise servers, such as those in a data center, should be grouped and moved to become server farm switch blocks.

As you do this, a modular structure should begin to appear. Each module will connect into a central core layer, completing the hierarchical design. To see how the example of Figures 2-6 and 2-7 can be transformed, look at Figure 2-8. The existing switches have merely been moved so that they resemble the enterprise composite model. Without adding switches, the existing network has been migrated into the modular structure. Each module shown ultimately will become a switch block.

Figure 2-8 *Migrating an Existing Network into a Modular Structure*

Now, each module should be addressed so that it can be migrated into a proper switch block. Remember that switch blocks always contain the switches necessary to connect a resource (users, servers, and so on) into the core layer. If this is done for the network in Figure 2-8, the network shown in Figure 2-9 might result.

Figure 2-9 *Migrating Network Modules into Switch Blocks*

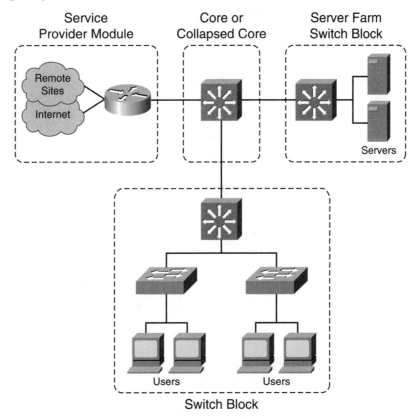

Notice that some additional switches have been added so that there is a distinct distribution layer of switches connecting into the core layer. Here, only single switches and single connections between switches have been shown. At this point, the design doesn't strictly follow the hierarchical model because there is little or no redundancy between layers.

Finally, you should add the redundant components to complete the design. The core should have dual switches. Each switch block should have dual distribution switches and dual links to both the access and core layers. These can be added now, resulting in the network shown in Figure 2-10. This might not be a practical design for a small example network, but a full-fledged hierarchical design stages the example network for growth and stability in the future.

Figure 2-10 *Completing the Hierarchical Campus Design*

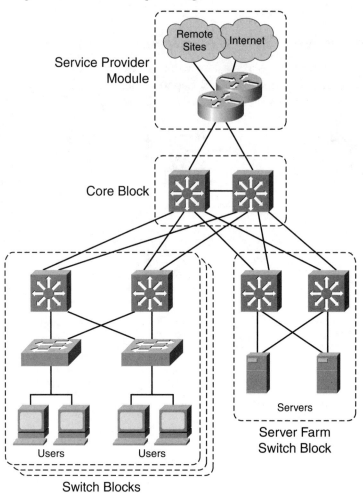

Foundation Summary

The Foundation Summary is a collection of tables, figures, lists, and other information that provides a convenient review of many key concepts in this chapter. If you are already comfortable with the topics in this chapter, this summary might help you recall a few details. If you just read this chapter, this review should help solidify some key facts. If you are doing your final preparation before the exam, the following information is a convenient way to review the day before the exam.

A campus network can be logically divided into these building blocks:

- **Switch block**—A group of access-layer switches, together with their distribution switches.

- **Core block**—The campus network's backbone.

- **Server farm block**—A group of enterprise servers, along with their access- and distribution-layer switches.

- **Management block**—A group of network-management resources, along with their access and distribution switches.

- **Enterprise edge block**—A collection of services related to external network access, along with their access and distribution switches.

- **Service provider edge block**—The external network services contracted or used by the enterprise network. These are the services with which the enterprise edge block interfaces.

Other than the core block, each switch block should have the following characteristics:

- Switches that form an access layer

- Dual distribution switches

- Redundant connections into the access and core layers

The most important factors to consider when choosing a switch block's size are as follows:

- The number of users connected to the access-layer switches

- The extent of the access VLAN or subnet

- Multilayer switching capacity of the distribution switches in the switch block

- The types, patterns, and volume of traffic passing through the switch block

The core layer in a campus network can be designed as follows:

- **Collapsed core**—The distribution- and core-layer switches are combined. This is usually acceptable in a small to medium-size network.

- **Dual core**—The distribution and core layers are separate; the core layer consists of dual or redundant multilayer switches.

Q&A

The questions and scenarios in this book are more difficult than what you should experience on the actual exam. The questions do not attempt to cover more breadth or depth than the exam; however, they are designed to make sure that you know the answer. Rather than allowing you to derive the answers from clues hidden inside the questions themselves, the questions challenge your understanding and recall of the subject. Hopefully, these questions will help limit the number of exam questions on which you narrow your choices to two options and then guess.

You can find the answers to these questions in Appendix A.

1. Where is the most appropriate place to connect a block of enterprise (internal) servers? Why?

2. How can you provide redundancy at the switch and core block layers? (Consider physical means, as well as functional methods using protocols, algorithms, and so on.)

3. What factors should you consider when sizing a switch block?

4. What are the signs of an oversized switch block?

5. What are the attributes and issues of having a collapsed core block?

6. How many switches are sufficient in a core block design?

7. What building blocks are used to build a scalable campus network?

8. What are two types of core, or backbone, designs?

9. Why should links and services provided to remote sites be grouped in a distinct building block?

10. Why should network-management applications and servers be placed in a distinct building block?

Building a Campus Network

This part of the book covers the following BCMSN exam topics:

Technology

- Explain the function of the Switching Database Manager (specifically, Content Addressable Memory [CAM] and Ternary Content Addressable Memory [TCAM]) within a Catalyst switch

- Describe the features and operation of 802.1Q Tunneling (802.1QinQ) within a service provider network

- Describe the operation and purpose of managed VLAN services

- Describe how VTP versions 1 and 2 operate, including domains, modes, advertisements, and pruning

- Explain the operation and purpose of the Spanning Tree Protocol (STP) on a switched network

PART II

Implementation and Operation

- Configure access ports for static and multi-VLAN membership

- Configure and verify 802.1Q trunks

- Configure and verify ISL trunks

- Configure VTP domains in server, client, and transparent modes

- Enable Spanning Tree on ports and VLANs

- Configure Spanning Tree parameters, including port priority, VLAN priority, root bridge, BPDU guard, PortFast, and UplinkFast

- Configure Fast EtherChannel and Gigabit EtherChannel to increase bandwidth for interswitch connections

Planning and Design

- Design a VLAN configuration with VTP to work for a given specific scenario

Troubleshooting

- Troubleshoot common VLAN problems on a switched network

- Tune and troubleshoot STP on a multilayer switched network to enhance network performance, prevent network loops, and minimize downtime

This chapter covers the following topics that you need to master for the CCNP BCMSN exam:

- **Layer 2 Switch Operation**—This section describes the functionality of a switch that forwards Ethernet frames.

- **Multilayer Switch Operation**—This section describes the mechanisms that forward packets at OSI Layers 3 and 4.

- **Tables Used in Switching**—This section explains how tables of information and computation are used to make switching decisions. Coverage focuses on the Content Addressable Memory table involved in Layer 2 forwarding, and the Ternary Content Addressable Memory used in packet-handling decisions at Layers 2 through 4.

- **Troubleshooting Switching Tables**—This section reviews the Catalyst commands that you can use to monitor the switching tables and memory. These commands can be useful when troubleshooting or tracing the sources of data or problems in a switched network.

CHAPTER 3

Switch Operation

To have a good understanding of the many features that you can configure on a Catalyst switch, you first should understand the fundamentals of the switching function itself.

This chapter serves as a primer, describing how an Ethernet switch works. It presents Layer 2 forwarding, along with the hardware functions that make forwarding possible. Multilayer switching also is explained. A considerable portion of the chapter deals with the memory architecture that performs switching at Layers 3 and 4 both flexibly and efficiently. This chapter also provides a brief overview of useful switching table–management commands.

"Do I Know This Already?" Quiz

The purpose of the "Do I Know This Already?" quiz is to help you decide whether you need to read the entire chapter. If you already intend to read the entire chapter, you do not necessarily need to answer these questions now.

The 12-question quiz, derived from the major sections in the "Foundation Topics" portion of the chapter, helps determine how to spend your limited study time.

Table 3-1 outlines the major topics discussed in this chapter and the "Do I Know This Already?" quiz questions that correspond to those topics.

Table 3-1 *"Do I Know This Already?" Foundation Topics Section-to-Question Mapping*

Foundation Topics Section	Questions Covered in This Section	Score
Layer 2 Switch Operation	1–5	
Multilayer Switch Operation	6–9	
Switching Tables	10–11	
Troubleshooting Switching Tables	12	
Total Score		

> **CAUTION** The goal of self-assessment is to gauge your mastery of the topics in this chapter. If you do not know the answer to a question or are only partially sure of the answer, you should mark this question wrong. Giving yourself credit for an answer you correctly guess skews your self- assessment results and might provide you with a false sense of security.

You can find the answers to the quiz in Appendix A, "Answers to Chapter 'Do I Know This Already?' Quizzes and Q&A Sections." The suggested choices for your next step are as follows:

- **7 or less overall score**—Read the entire chapter. This includes the "Foundation Topics," "Foundation Summary," and "Q&A" sections.

- **8–10 overall score**—Begin with the "Foundation Summary" section and then follow up with the "Q&A" section at the end of the chapter.

- **11 or more overall score**—If you want more review on these topics, skip to the "Foundation Summary" section and then go to the "Q&A" section at the end of the chapter. Otherwise, move on to Chapter 4, "Switch Configuration."

1. Which of the following devices performs transparent bridging?

    a. Ethernet hub

    b. Layer 2 switch

    c. Layer 3 switch

    d. Router

2. When a PC is connected to a Layer 2 switch port, how far does the collision domain spread?

    a. No collision domain exists.

    b. One switch port.

    c. One VLAN.

    d. All ports on the switch.

3. What information is used to forward frames in a Layer 2 switch?

    a. Source MAC address

    b. Destination MAC address

    c. Source switch port

    d. IP addresses

4. What does a switch do if a MAC address cannot be found in the CAM table?

  a. The frame is forwarded to the default port.

  b. The switch generates an ARP request for the address.

  c. The switch floods the frame out all ports (except the receiving port).

  d. The switch drops the frame.

5. In the Catalyst 6500, frames can be filtered with access lists for security and QoS purposes. This filtering occurs according to which of the following?

  a. Before a CAM table lookup

  b. After a CAM table lookup

  c. Simultaneously with a CAM table lookup

  d. According to how the access lists are configured

6. Access list contents can be merged into which of the following?

  a. A CAM table

  b. A TCAM table

  c. A FIB table

  d. An ARP table

7. Multilayer switches using CEF are based on which of these techniques?

  a. Route caching

  b. Netflow switching

  c. Topology-based switching

  d. Demand-based switching

8. Which answer describes multilayer switching with CEF?

  a. The first packet is routed and then the flow is cached.

  b. The switch supervisor CPU forwards each packet.

  c. The switching hardware learns station addresses and builds a routing database.

  d. A single database of routing information is built for the switching hardware.

9. In a switch, frames are placed in which buffer after forwarding decisions are made?

  a. Ingress queues

  b. Egress queues

  c. CAM table

  d. TCAM

10. What size are the mask and pattern fields in a TCAM entry?

   a. 64 bits

   b. 128 bits

   c. 134 bits

   d. 168 bits

11. Access list rules are compiled as TCAM entries. When a packet is matched against an access list, in what order are the TCAM entries evaluated?

   a. Sequentially in the order of the original access list.

   b. Numerically by the access list number.

   c. Alphabetically by the access list name.

   d. All entries are evaluated in parallel.

12. Which Catalyst IOS command can you use to display the addresses in the CAM table?

   a. **show cam**

   b. **show mac address-table**

   c. **show mac**

   d. **show cam address-table**

Foundation Topics

Layer 2 Switch Operation

Recall that with shared Ethernet networks using hubs, many hosts are connected to a single broadcast and collision domain. In other words, shared Ethernet media operate at OSI Layer 1.

Each host must share the available bandwidth with every other connected host. When more than one host tries to talk at one time, a collision occurs, and everyone must back off and wait to talk again. This forces every host to operate in half-duplex mode, by either talking *or* listening at any given time. In addition, when one host sends a frame, all connected hosts hear it. When one host generates a frame with errors, everyone hears that, too.

At its most basic level, an Ethernet switch provides isolation from other connected hosts in several ways:

- The collision domain's scope is severely limited. On each switch port, the collision domain consists of the switch port itself and the devices directly connected to that port—either a single host or, if a shared-media hub is connected, the set of hosts connected to the hub.

- Host connections can operate in full-duplex mode because there is no contention on the media. Hosts can talk *and* listen at the same time.

- Bandwidth is no longer shared. Instead, each switch port offers dedicated bandwidth across a switching fabric to another switch port. (These connections change dynamically.)

- Errors in frames are not propagated. Each frame received on a switch port is checked for errors. Good frames are regenerated when they are forwarded or transmitted. This is known as *store-and-forward* switching technology: Packets are received, stored for inspection, and then forwarded.

- You can limit broadcast traffic to a volume threshold.

- Other types of intelligent filtering or forwarding become possible.

Transparent Bridging

A Layer 2 switch is basically a multiport transparent bridge, where each switch port is its own Ethernet LAN segment, isolated from the others. Frame forwarding is based completely on the MAC addresses contained in each frame, such that the switch will not forward a frame unless it knows the destination's location. (When the switch does not know where the destination is, it makes some safe assumptions.) Figure 3-1 shows the progression from a two-port to a multiport transparent bridge, and then to a switch.

Figure 3-1   *A Comparison of Transparent Bridges and Switches*

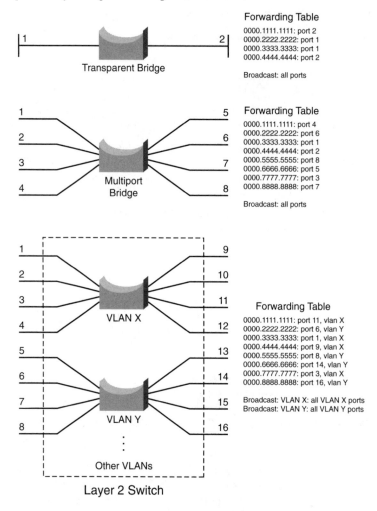

The entire process of forwarding Ethernet frames then becomes figuring out what MAC addresses connect to which switch ports. A switch either must be told explicitly where hosts are located or must learn this information for itself. You can configure MAC address locations through a switch's command-line interface, but this quickly gets out of control when there are many stations on the network or when stations move around.

To dynamically learn about station locations, a switch listens to incoming frames and keeps a table of address information. As a frame is received on a switch port, the switch inspects the source MAC address. If that address is not in the address table already, the MAC address, switch port, and virtual LAN (VLAN) on which it arrived are recorded in the table. Learning the address locations of the incoming packets is easy and straightforward.

Incoming frames also include the destination MAC address. Again, the switch looks up this address in the address table, hoping to find the switch port and VLAN where the address is attached. If it is found, the frame can be forwarded out that switch port. If the address is not found in the table, the switch must take more drastic action—the frame is forwarded in a "best effort" fashion by *flooding* it out all switch ports assigned to the source VLAN. This is known as *unknown unicast flooding*, with the unicast destination location unknown. Figure 3-2 illustrates this process, using only a single VLAN for simplification.

A switch constantly listens to incoming frames on each of its ports, learning source MAC addresses. However, be aware that the learning process is allowed only when the Spanning Tree Protocol (STP) algorithm has decided that a port is stable for normal use. STP is concerned only with maintaining a loop-free network, where frames will not be forwarded recursively. If a loop formed, a flooded frame could follow the looped path, where it would be flooded again and again.

In a similar manner, frames containing a broadcast or multicast destination address also are flooded. These destination addresses are not unknown—the switch knows them well. They are destined for multiple locations, so they must be flooded by definition. In the case of multicast addresses, flooding is performed by default. Other more elegant means of determining the destination locations are available and are discussed in Chapter 15, "IP Multicast."

Follow That Frame!

You should have a basic understanding of the operations that a frame undergoes as it passes through a Layer 2 switch. This helps you get a firm grasp on how to configure the switch for complex functions. Figure 3-3 shows a typical Layer 2 Catalyst switch and the decision processes that take place to forward each frame.

Figure 3-2 *Unknown Unicast Flooding*

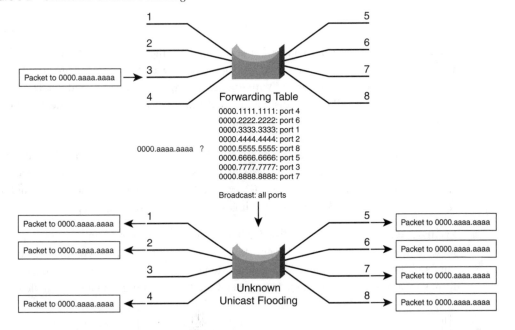

When a frame arrives at a switch port, it is placed into one of the port's ingress queues. The queues each can contain frames to be forwarded, with each queue having a different priority or service level. The switch port then can be fine-tuned so that important frames get processed and forwarded before less important frames. This can prevent time-critical data from being "lost in the shuffle" during a flurry of incoming traffic.

Figure 3-3 *Operations Within a Layer 2 Catalyst Switch*

As the ingress queues are serviced and a frame is pulled off, the switch must figure out not only *where* to forward the frame, but also *whether* it should be forwarded and *how*. Three fundamental decisions must be made: one concerned with finding the egress switch port, and two concerned with forwarding policies. All these decisions are made *simultaneously* by independent portions of switching hardware and can be described as follows:

- **L2 forwarding table**—The frame's destination MAC address is used as an index, or key, into the Content Addressable Memory (CAM), or address, table. If the address is found, the egress switch port and the appropriate VLAN ID are read from the table. (If the address is not found, the frame is marked for flooding so that it is forwarded out every switch port in the VLAN.)

- **Security ACLs**—Access control lists (ACL) can be used to identify frames according to their MAC addresses, protocol types (for non-IP frames), IP addresses, protocols, and Layer 4 port numbers. The Ternary Content Addressable Memory (TCAM) contains ACLs in a compiled form so that a decision can be made on whether to forward a frame in a single table lookup.

- **QoS ACLs**—Other ACLs can classify incoming frames according to quality of service (QoS) parameters, to police or control the rate of traffic flows, and to mark QoS parameters in outbound frames. The TCAM also is used to make these decisions in a single table lookup.

The CAM and TCAM tables are discussed in greater detail in the "Content Addressable Memory" and "Ternary Content Addressable Memory" sections, later in this chapter. After the CAM and TCAM table lookups have occurred, the frame is placed into the appropriate egress queue on the appropriate outbound switch port. The egress queue is determined by QoS values either contained in the frame or passed along with the frame. Like the ingress queues, the egress queues are serviced according to importance or time criticality; frames are sent out without being delayed by other outbound traffic.

Multilayer Switch Operation

Catalyst switches, such as the 3560 (with the appropriate Cisco IOS Software image), 4500, and 6500, also can forward frames based on Layer 3 and 4 information contained in packets. This is known as *multilayer switching (MLS)*. Naturally, Layer 2 switching is performed at the same time because even the higher-layer encapsulations still are contained in Ethernet frames.

Types of Multilayer Switching

Catalyst switches have supported two basic generations or types of MLS: route caching (first generation MLS) and topology based (second-generation MLS). This section presents an overview of both, although only the second generation is supported in the Cisco IOS Software–based switch families, such as the Catalyst 3560, 4500, and 6500. You should understand the two types and the differences between them:

- **Route caching**—The first generation of MLS, requiring a route processor (RP) and a switch engine (SE). The RP must process a traffic flow's first packet to determine the destination. The SE listens to the first packet and to the resulting destination, and sets up a "shortcut" entry in its MLS cache. The SE forwards subsequent packets in the same traffic flow based on shortcut entries in its cache.

    This type of MLS also is known by the names Netflow LAN switching, flow-based or demand-based switching, and "route once, switch many." Even if this isn't used to forward packets in Cisco IOS–based Catalyst switches, the technique generates traffic flow information and statistics.

- **Topology-based**—The second generation of MLS, utilizing specialized hardware. Layer 3 routing information builds and prepopulates a single database of the entire network topology. This database, an efficient table lookup in hardware, is consulted so that packets can be forwarded at high rates. The longest match found in the database is used as the correct Layer 3 destination. As the routing topology changes over time, the database contained in the hardware can be updated dynamically with no performance penalty.

This type of MLS is known as *Cisco Express Forwarding (CEF)*. A routing process running on the switch downloads the current routing table database into the *Forwarding Information Base (FIB)* area of hardware. CEF is discussed in greater detail in Chapter 13, "Multilayer Switching."

Follow That Packet!

The path that a Layer 3 packet follows through a multilayer switch is similar to that of a Layer 2 switch. Obviously, some means of making a Layer 3 forwarding decision must be added. Beyond that, several, sometimes unexpected, things can happen to packets as they are forwarded. Figure 3-4 shows a typical multilayer switch and the decision processes that must occur. Packets arriving on a switch port are placed in the appropriate ingress queue, just as in a Layer 2 switch.

Each packet is pulled off an ingress queue and inspected for both Layer 2 and Layer 3 destination addresses. Now, the decision of *where* to forward the packet is based on two address tables, whereas the decision of *how* to forward the packet still is based on access list results. As in Layer 2 switching, all these multilayer decisions are performed simultaneously in hardware:

- **L2 forwarding table**—The destination MAC address is used as an index to the CAM table. If the frame contains a Layer 3 packet to be forwarded, the destination MAC address is that of a Layer 3 port on the switch. In this case, the CAM table results are used only to decide that the frame should be processed at Layer 3.

- **L3 forwarding table**—The FIB table is consulted, using the destination IP address as an index. The longest match in the table is found (both address and mask), and the resulting next-hop Layer 3 address is obtained. The FIB also contains each next-hop entry's Layer 2 MAC address and the egress switch port (and VLAN ID) so that further table lookups are not necessary.

- **Security ACLs**—Inbound and outbound access lists are compiled into TCAM entries so that decisions of whether to forward a packet can be determined as a single table lookup.

- **QoS ACLs**—Packet classification, policing, and marking all can be performed as single table lookups in the QoS TCAM.

Figure 3-4 *Operations Within a Multilayer Catalyst Switch*

As with Layer 2 switching, the packet finally must be placed in the appropriate egress queue on the appropriate egress switch port.

However, recall that during the multilayer switching process, the next-hop destination was obtained from the FIB table, just as a router would do. The Layer 3 address identified the next hop and found its Layer 2 address. Only the Layer 2 address would be used, so the Layer 2 frames could be sent on.

The next-hop Layer 2 address must be put into the frame in place of the original destination address (the multilayer switch). The frame's Layer 2 source address also must become that of the multilayer switch before it is sent on to the next hop. As any good router must do, the Time-To-Live (TTL) value in the Layer 3 packet must be decremented by one.

Because the contents of the Layer 3 packet (the TTL value) have changed, the Layer 3 header checksum must be recalculated. And because both Layer 2 and 3 contents have changed, the Layer 2 checksum must be recalculated. In other words, the entire Ethernet frame must be rewritten before it goes into the egress queue. This also is accomplished efficiently in hardware.

Multilayer Switching Exceptions

To forward packets using the simultaneous decision processes described in the preceding section, the packet must be "MLS-ready" and must require no additional decisions. For example, CEF directly can forward most IP packets between hosts. This occurs when the source and destination addresses (both MAC and IP) are known already and no other IP parameters must be manipulated.

Other packets cannot be directly forwarded by CEF and must be handled in more detail. This is done by a quick inspection during the forwarding decisions. If a packet meets criteria such as the following, it is flagged for further processing and sent to the switch CPU for *process switching*:

■   ARP requests and replies

■   IP packets requiring a response from a router (TTL has expired, MTU is exceeded, fragmentation is needed, and so on)

■   IP broadcasts that will be relayed as unicast (DHCP requests, IP helper-address functions)

■   Routing protocol updates

■   Cisco Discovery Protocol packets

■   IPX routing protocol and service advertisements

■   Packets needing encryption

■   Packets triggering Network Address Translation (NAT)

■   Other non-IP and non-IPX protocol packets (AppleTalk, DECnet, and so on)

NOTE   On the Catalyst 6500, both IP and IPX packets are CEF-switched in hardware. All other protocols are handled by process switching on the MSFC module (the routing CPU). On the Catalyst 4500, only IP packets are CEF-switched in hardware. All other routable protocols, including IPX, are flagged for process switching by the switch CPU.

With the Catalyst 3560, only IP is CEF-switched in hardware. Other non-IP protocols are not routed at all. Instead, they are flagged for *fallback bridging*, where they are treated as transparently bridged (Layer 2 switched) packets. An external router or multilayer switch must handle any routing that still is needed during fallback bridging.

Tables Used in Switching

Catalyst switches maintain several types of tables to be used in the switching process. The tables are tailored for Layer 2 switching or MLS and are kept in very fast memory so that many fields within a frame or packet can be compared in parallel.

Content Addressable Memory

All Catalyst switch models use a Content Addressable Memory (CAM) table for Layer 2 switching. As frames arrive on switch ports, the source MAC addresses are learned and recorded in the CAM table. The port of arrival and the VLAN both are recorded in the table, along with a time stamp. If a MAC address learned on one switch port has moved to a different port, the MAC address and time stamp are recorded for the most recent arrival port. Then, the previous entry is deleted. If a MAC address is found already present in the table for the correct arrival port, only its time stamp is updated.

Switches generally have large CAM tables so that many addresses can be looked up for frame forwarding. However, there is not enough table space to hold every possible address on large networks. To manage the CAM table space, *stale entries* (addresses that have not been heard from for a period of time) are aged out. By default, idle CAM table entries are kept for 300 seconds before they are deleted. You can change the default setting using the following configuration command:

```
Switch(config)# mac address-table aging-time seconds
```

By default, MAC addresses are learned dynamically from incoming frames. You also can configure static CAM table entries that contain MAC addresses that might not be learned otherwise. To do this, use the following configuration command:

```
Switch(config)# mac address-table static mac-address vlan vlan-id interface type
    mod/num
```

Here, the MAC address (in dotted triplet hex format) is identified with the switch port and VLAN where it appears.

> **NOTE**   You should be aware that there is a slight discrepancy in the CAM table command syntax. Until Catalyst IOS version 12.1(11)EA1, the syntax for CAM table commands used the keywords **mac-address-table**. In more recent Cisco IOS versions, the syntax has changed to use the keywords **mac address-table** (first hyphen omitted). The Catalyst 4500 and 6500 IOS Software are exceptions, however, and continue to use the **mac-address-table** keyword form.

What happens when a host's MAC address is learned on one switch port, and then the host moves so that it appears on a different switch port? Ordinarily, the host's original CAM table entry would have to age out after 300 seconds, while its address was learned on the new port. To avoid having duplicate CAM table entries, a switch purges any existing entries for a MAC address that has just been learned on a different switch port. This is a safe assumption because MAC addresses are unique, and a single host should never be seen on more than one switch port unless problems exist in the network. If a switch notices that a MAC address is being learned on alternating switch ports, it generates an error message that flags the MAC address as "flapping" between interfaces.

Ternary Content Addressable Memory

In traditional routing, ACLs can match, filter, or control specific traffic. Access lists are made up of one or more access control entities (ACE), or matching statements that are evaluated in sequential order. Evaluating an access list can take up additional time, adding to the latency of forwarding packets.

In multilayer switches, however, all the matching process that ACLs provide is implemented in hardware. TCAM allows a packet to be evaluated against an entire access list in a single table lookup. Most switches have multiple TCAMs so that both inbound and outbound security and QoS ACLs can be evaluated simultaneously, or entirely in parallel with a Layer 2 or Layer 3 forwarding decision.

The Catalyst IOS Software has two components that are part of the TCAM operation:

- **Feature Manager (FM)**—After an access list has been created or configured, the Feature Manager software compiles, or merges, the ACEs into entries in the TCAM table. The TCAM then can be consulted at full frame-forwarding speed.

- **Switching Database Manager (SDM)**—You can partition the TCAM on some Catalyst switches into areas for different functions. The SDM software configures or tunes the TCAM partitions, if needed. (The TCAM is fixed on Catalyst 4500 and 6500 platforms, and cannot be repartitioned.)

TCAM Structure

The TCAM is an extension of the CAM table concept. Recall that a CAM table takes in an index or key value (usually a MAC address) and looks up the resulting value (usually a switch port or VLAN ID). Table lookup is fast and always based on an exact key match consisting of two input values: 0 and 1 bits.

TCAM also uses a table-lookup operation but is greatly enhanced to allow a more abstract operation. For example, binary values (0s and 1s) make up a key into the table, but a mask value also is used to decide which bits of the key are actually relevant. This effectively makes a key consisting of three input values: 0, 1, and X (don't care) bit values—a three-fold or *ternary* combination.

TCAM entries are composed of Value, Mask, and Result (VMR) combinations. Fields from frame or packet headers are fed into the TCAM, where they are matched against the value and mask pairs to yield a result. As a quick reference, these can be described as follows:

■ **Values** are always 134-bit quantities, consisting of source and destination addresses and other relevant protocol information—all patterns to be matched. The information concatenated to form the value depends on the type of access list, as shown in Table 3-2. Values in the TCAM come directly from any address, port, or other protocol information given in an ACE.

■ **Masks** are also 134-bit quantities, in exactly the same format, or bit order, as the values. Masks select only the value bits of interest; a mask bit is set to exactly match a value bit, or is not set for value bits that do not matter. The masks used in the TCAM stem from address or bit masks in ACEs.

■ **Results** are numerical values that represent what action to take after the TCAM lookup occurs. Whereas traditional access lists offer only a *permit* or *deny* result, TCAM lookups offer a number of possible results or actions. For example, the result can be a permit or deny decision, an index value to a QoS policer, a pointer to a next-hop routing table, and so on.

Table 3-2   *TCAM Value Pattern Components*

Access List Type	Value and Mask Components, 134-Bits Wide (Number of Bits)
Ethernet	Source MAC (48), destination MAC (48), Ethertype (16)
ICMP	Source IP (32), destination IP (32), protocol (16), ICMP code (8), ICMP type (4), IP type of service (ToS) (8)
Extended IP using TCP/UDP	Source IP (32), destination IP (32), protocol (16), IP ToS (8), source port (16), source operator (4), destination port (16), destination operator (4)
Other IP	Source IP (32), destination IP (32), protocol (16), IP ToS (8)
IGMP	Source IP (32), destination IP (32), protocol (16), IP ToS (8), IGMP message type (8)
IPX	Source IPX network (32), destination IPX network (32), destination node (48), IPX packet type (16)

The TCAM always is organized by masks, where each unique mask has eight value patterns associated with it. For example, the Catalyst 6500 TCAM (one for security ACLs and one for QoS ACLs) holds up to 4096 masks and 32,768 value patterns. The trick is that each of the mask-value pairs is evaluated *simultaneously,* or in parallel, revealing the best or longest match in a single table lookup.

TCAM Example

Figure 3-5 shows how the TCAM is built and used. This is a simple example and might or might not be identical to the results that the Feature Manager produces because the ACEs might need to be optimized or rewritten to achieve certain TCAM algorithm requirements.

Figure 3-5 *How an Access List Is Merged into TCAM*

```
access-list 100 permit tcp host 192.168.199.14 10.41.0.0 0.0.255.255 eq telnet
access-list 100 permit ip any 192.168.100.0 0.0.0.255
access-list 100 deny udp any 192.168.5.0 0.0.0.255 gt 1024
access-list 100 deny udp any 192.168.199.0 0.0.0.255 range 1024 2047
```

The example access list 100 (extended IP) is configured and merged into TCAM entries. First, the mask values must be identified in the access list. When an address value and a corresponding address mask are specified in an ACE, those mask bits must be set for matching. All other mask bits can remain in the "don't care" state. The access list contains only three unique masks: one that matches all 32 bits of the source IP address (found with an address mask of 0.0.0.0 or the keyword **host**), one that matches 16 bits of the destination address (found with an address mask of

0.0.255.255), and one that matches only 24 bits of the destination address (found with an address mask of 0.0.0.255). The keyword **any** in the ACEs means "match anything" or "don't care."

The unique masks are placed into the TCAM. Then, for each mask, all possible value patterns are identified. For example, a 32-bit source IP mask (Mask 1) can be found only in ACEs with a source IP address of 192.168.199.14 and a destination of 10.41.0.0. (The rest of Mask 1 is the destination address mask 0.0.255.255.) Those address values are placed into the first value pattern slot associated with Mask 1. Mask 2 has three value patterns: destination addresses 192.168.100.0, 192.168.5.0, and 192.168.199.0. Each of these is placed in the three pattern positions of Mask 2. This process continues until all ACEs have been merged.

When a mask's eighth pattern position has been filled, the next pattern with the same mask must be placed under a new mask. A bit of a balancing act occurs to try to fit all ACEs into the available mask and pattern entries without an overflow.

Port Operations in TCAM

You might have noticed that matching strictly based on values and masks covers only ACE statements that involve exact matches (either the **eq** port operation keyword or no Layer 4 port operations). For example, ACEs such as the following involve specific address values, address masks, and port numbers:

```
access-list test permit ip 192.168.254.0 0.0.0.255 any
access-list test permit tcp any host 192.168.199.10 eq www
```

What about ACEs that use port operators, where a comparison must be made? Consider the following:

```
access-list test permit udp any host 192.168.199.50 gt 1024
access-list test permit tcp any any range 2000 2002
```

A simple logical operation between a mask and a pattern cannot generate the desired result. The TCAM also provides a mechanism for performing a Layer 4 operation or comparison, also done during the single table lookup. If an ACE has a port operator, such as **gt**, **lt**, **neq**, or **range**, the Feature Manager software compiles the TCAM entry to include the use of the operator and the operand in a Logical Operation Unit (LOU) register. Only a limited number of LOUs are available in the TCAM. If there are more ACEs with comparison operators than there are LOUs, the Feature Manager must break up the ACEs into multiple ACEs with only regular matching (using the **eq** operator).

In Figure 3-5, two ACEs require a Layer 4 operation:

■ One that checks for UDP destination ports greater than 1024

■ One that looks for the UDP destination port range 1024 to 2047

The Feature Manager checks all ACEs for Layer 4 operation and places these into Logical Operation Unit (LOU) register pairs. These can be loaded with operations, independent of any other ACE parameters. The LOU contents can be reused if other ACEs need the same comparisons and values. After the LOUs are loaded, they are referenced in the TCAM entries that need them. This is shown by LOUs A1 and the B1:2 pair. A finite number (actually, a rather small number) of LOUs are available in the TCAM, so the Feature Manager software must use them carefully.

Troubleshooting Switching Tables

If you see strange behavior in a Catalyst switch, it might be useful to examine the contents of the various switching tables. In any event, you might sometimes need to find out on which switch port a specific MAC address has been learned.

CAM Table Operation

To view the contents of the CAM table, you can use the following form of the **show mac address-table** EXEC command:

```
Switch# show mac address-table dynamic [address mac-address | interface type mod/num |
    vlan vlan-id]
```

The entries that have been learned dynamically will be shown. You can add the **address** keyword to specify a single MAC address, or the **interface** or **vlan** keywords to see addresses that have been learned on a specific interface or VLAN.

For example, assume that you need to find the learned location of the host with MAC address 0050.8b11.54da. The **show mac address-table dynamic address 0050.8b11.54da** command might produce the output in Example 3-1.

Example 3-1 *Determining Host Location by MAC Address*

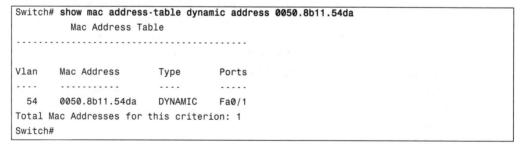

```
Switch# show mac address-table dynamic address 0050.8b11.54da
          Mac Address Table
-------------------------------------------

Vlan    Mac Address       Type       Ports
----    -----------       ----       -----
  54    0050.8b11.54da    DYNAMIC    Fa0/1
Total Mac Addresses for this criterion: 1
Switch#
```

From this, you can see that the host somehow is connected to interface FastEthernet 0/1, on VLAN 54.

> **TIP** If your Catalyst IOS switch is not accepting commands of the form **mac address-table**, try adding a hyphen between the keywords. For example, the Catalyst 4500 and 6500 most likely will accept **show mac-address-table** instead.

Suppose that this same command produced no output for the interface and VLAN. What might that mean? Either the host has not sent a frame that the switch can use for learning its location, or something odd is going on. Perhaps, the host is using two network interface cards (NICs) to load-balance traffic; one NIC is only receiving traffic, while the other is only sending. Therefore, the switch never hears and learns the receiving—only NIC address.

To see the CAM table's size, use the **show mac address-table count** command. MAC address totals are shown for each active VLAN on the switch. This can give you a good idea of the size of the CAM table and how many hosts are using the network. Be aware that many MAC addresses can be learned on a switch's uplink ports.

CAM table entries can be cleared manually, if needed, by using the following EXEC command:

```
Switch# clear mac address-table dynamic [address mac-address | interface type
    mod/num | vlan vlan-id]
```

Frequently, you need to know where a user with a certain MAC address is connected. In a large network, discerning at which switch and switch port a MAC address can be found might be difficult. Start at the network's center, or core, and display the CAM table entry for the MAC address. Look at the switch port shown in the entry and move to the neighboring switch connected to that port. Then, repeat the CAM table process. Keep moving from switch to switch until you reach the edge of the network where the MAC address connects.

TCAM Operation

The TCAM in a switch is more or less self-sufficient. Access lists are compiled or merged automatically into the TCAM, so there is nothing to configure. The only concept you need to be aware of is how the TCAM resources are being used.

TCAMs have a limited number of usable mask, value pattern, and LOU entries. If access lists grow to be large or many Layer 4 operations are needed, the TCAM tables and registers can overflow. If that happens while you are configuring an ACL, the switch will generate syslog messages that flag the TCAM overflow situation as it tries to compile the ACL into TCAM entries.

Foundation Summary

The Foundation Summary is a collection of tables, lists, and other information that provides a convenient review of many key concepts in this chapter. If you are already comfortable with the topics in this chapter, this summary might help you recall a few details. If you just read this chapter, this review should help solidify some key facts. If you are doing your final prep before the exam, the following information is a convenient way to review the day before the exam:

- Layer 2 switches learn incoming MAC addresses and record their locations based on the inbound switch ports.

- Layer 2 switching information is stored in the Content Addressable Memory (CAM) table. The CAM is consulted to find the outbound switch port when forwarding frames.

- Multilayer switching looks at the Layer 2 addresses, along with Layers 3 and 4 address and port information, to forward packets.

- Multilayer switching is performed in hardware using the Cisco Express Forwarding (CEF) method.

- CEF builds Layer 3 destination information from routing tables and Layer 2 data. This information is stored in hardware as a Forwarding Information Base (FIB) table.

- Multilayer switches can make many policy decisions in parallel, using the Ternary Content Addressable Memory (TCAM) contents.

- TCAM combines a 134-bit value, or pattern (made up of addresses, port numbers, or other appropriate fields), with a 134-bit mask to yield a result value. The result instructs the switch hardware on how to finish forwarding the packet.

- Access lists for security (traditional router ACLs and VLAN ACLs) and QoS ACLs are compiled or merged into TCAM entries. These access lists then can be processed on each packet that passes through the switch, as a single table lookup.

- As a packet exits a multilayer switch, it must be rewritten so that its header and checksum values are valid. The fields in the original packet that the switch updates are as follows:

  — The source MAC address becomes the Layer 3 switch MAC address.

  — The destination MAC address becomes the next-hop MAC address.

  — The IP TTL value is decremented by one.

  — The IP checksum is recomputed.

  — The Ethernet frame checksum is recomputed.

Table 3-3 *Switching Table Commands*

Task	Command Syntax
Set the CAM table aging time.	**mac address-table aging-time** *seconds*
Configure a static CAM entry.	**mac address-table static** *mac-address* **vlan** *vlan-id* **interface** *type mod/num*
Clear a CAM table entry.	**clear mac address-table dynamic** [**address** *mac-address* ∣ **interface** *type mod/num* ∣ **vlan** *vlan-id*]
View the CAM table.	**show mac address-table dynamic** [**address** *mac-address* ∣ **interface** *type mod/num* ∣ **vlan** *vlan-id*]
View the CAM table size.	**show mac address-table count**

Q&A

The questions and scenarios in this book are more difficult than what you should experience on the actual exam. The questions do not attempt to cover more breadth or depth than the exam; however, they are designed to make sure that you know the answer. Rather than allowing you to derive the answers from clues hidden inside the questions themselves, the questions challenge your understanding and recall of the subject. Hopefully, these questions will help limit the number of exam questions on which you narrow your choices to two options and then guess.

You can find the answers to these questions in Appendix A.

1. By default, how long are CAM table entries kept before they are aged out?

2. A TCAM lookup involves which values?

3. How many table lookups are required to find a MAC address in the CAM table?

4. How many table lookups are required to match a packet against an access list that has been compiled into 10 TCAM entries?

5. How many value patterns can a TCAM store for each mask?

6. Can all packets be switched in hardware by a multilayer switch?

7. Multilayer switches must rewrite which portions of an Ethernet frame?

8. If a station receives only Ethernet frames and doesn't transmit anything, how will a switch learn of its location?

9. What is a TCAM's main purpose?

10. Why do the TCAM mask and pattern fields consist of so many bits?

11. In a multilayer switch with a TCAM, a longer access list (more ACEs or statements) takes longer to process for each frame. True or false?

12. A multilayer switch receives a packet with a certain destination IP address. Suppose that the switch has that IP address in its Layer 3 forwarding table but has no corresponding Layer 2 address. What happens to the packet next?

13. Suppose that a multilayer switch can't support a protocol with CEF, and it relies on *fallback bridging*. Can the switch still route that traffic?

14. To configure a static CAM table entry, the **mac address-table static** *mac-address* command is used. Which two other parameters also must be given?

15. As a network administrator, what aspects of a switch TCAM should you be concerned with?

16. What portion of the TCAM is used to evaluate port number comparisons in an access list?

17. Someone has asked you where the host with MAC address 00-10-20-30-40-50 is located. Assuming that you already know the switch it is connected to, what command can you use to find it?

18. Complete this command to display the size of the CAM table: **show mac** _____.

19. What protocol is used to advertise CAM table entries among neighboring switches?

20. Suppose that a host uses one MAC address to send frames and another to receive them. In other words, one address will always be the source address sent in frames, and the other is used only as a destination address in incoming frames. Is it possible for that host to communicate with others through a Layer 2 switch? If so, how?

This chapter covers the following topics that you need to master for the CCNP BCMSN exam:

- **Switch Management**—This section describes the software operating systems that are available on Cisco Catalyst switches, along with the command-line interface (CLI) that is used for configuration and troubleshooting. In addition, this section covers the basic Catalyst switch configuration and administration commands and techniques for interswitch communication.

- **Switch File Management**—This section explains the various files and file systems used in a Catalyst switch, along with the commands necessary to manage them.

- **Troubleshooting from the Operating System**—This section presents a brief overview of the commands that you can use to verify or troubleshoot basic switch operation.

CHAPTER 4

Switch Configuration

Chapter 3, "Switch Operation," covers the topic of switch operation from the ground up. This chapter adds to that by reviewing the Catalyst operating systems—the mechanisms by which you can connect to a switch to configure and monitor how it works. Catalyst file systems are explained, along with the files needed to make a switch functional.

This chapter also covers the configuration steps for switch management. Management functions include the methods used to connect to a switch, how to configure switch identification, user authentication, interswitch communication, and file management. A brief overview of useful troubleshooting commands also is given.

"Do I Know This Already?" Quiz

The purpose of the "Do I Know This Already?" quiz is to help you decide whether you need to read the entire chapter. If you already intend to read the entire chapter, you do not necessarily need to answer these questions now.

The 12-question quiz, derived from the major sections in the "Foundation Topics" portion of the chapter, helps you determine how to spend your limited study time.

Table 4-1 outlines the major topics discussed in this chapter and the "Do I Know This Already?" quiz questions that correspond to those topics.

Table 4-1 *"Do I Know This Already?" Foundation Topics Section-to-Question Mapping*

Foundation Topics Section	Questions Covered in This Section	Score
Switch Management	1–7	
Switch File Management	8–10	
Troubleshooting from the Operating System	11–12	
Total Score		

> **CAUTION** The goal of self-assessment is to gauge your mastery of the topics in this chapter. If you do not know the answer to a question or are only partially sure of the answer, you should mark this question wrong. Giving yourself credit for an answer you correctly guess skews your self- assessment results and might provide you with a false sense of security.

1. Which of the following is an operating system available on Cisco Catalyst 3750, 4500, and 6500 family switches?

    a. Catalyst OS

    b. Cisco IOS Software

    c. SNMP

    d. QoS

2. Which of the following is *not* a valid way to connect to a Catalyst switch?

    a. Telnet

    b. rsh

    c. Async serial

    d. rlogin

3. Which user interface mode allows the greatest authority for making configuration changes?

    a. User EXEC mode

    b. Privileged EXEC (enable) mode

    c. Telnet mode

    d. Root mode

4. To configure a password for Telnet access to a switch, which one of the following must the password be applied to?

    a. **interface vlan 1**

    b. **line con 0**

    c. **line vty 0 15**

    d. **hostname**

5. Which of the following is not required to set up Telnet access to a switch?

    a. Password on vty

    b. IP address

    c. Default gateway or route

    d. Enable password

6. Which protocol is used to exchange information between connected Cisco neighbors?

   a. SNMP

   b. VTP

   c. CDP

   d. STP

7. Cisco Discovery Protocol is sent over which OSI layer?

   a. Layer 1

   b. Layer 2

   c. Layer 3

   d. Layer 4

8. Which Catalyst file system contains the Cisco IOS Software image?

   a. Running-config

   b. RAM

   c. Flash

   d. NVRAM

9. Which command saves newly made configuration changes so that they will be used automatically after the next switch reload?

   a. **save all**

   b. **copy running-config flash:**

   c. **copy startup-config running-config**

   d. **copy running-config startup-config**

10. If the **erase flash:** command is given, what is the next logical step?

   a. **copy tftp: flash:**

   b. **copy running-config startup-config**

   c. **erase startup-config**

   d. **copy startup-config flash:**

11. What command can you use to examine the Gigabit Ethernet 3/1 interface's current configuration?

   a. **show interface gigabitethernet 3/1**

   b. **show gigabit ethernet 3/1**

   c. **show startup-config interface gig 3/1**

   d. **show running-config interface gig 3/1**

12.   What command can you use to view information received from a neighboring Cisco switch, including its version of Cisco IOS Software?

   a. **show neighbors**

   b. **show cdp neighbors all**

   c. **show all neighbors**

   d. **show cdp neighbors detail**

You can find the answers to the quiz in Appendix A, "Answers to Chapter 'Do I Know This Already?' Quizzes and Q&A Sections." The suggested choices for your next step are as follows:

- **7 or less overall score**—Read the entire chapter. This section includes the "Foundation Topics," "Foundation Summary," and "Q&A" sections.

- **8–10 overall score**—Begin with the "Foundation Summary" section and then go to the "Q&A" section at the end of the chapter.

- **11 or more overall score**—If you want more review on these topics, skip to the "Foundation Summary" section and then go to the "Q&A" section at the end of the chapter. Otherwise, move to Chapter 5, "Switch Port Configuration."

Foundation Topics

Switch Management

Managing a Catalyst switch can be broken up into several topics. A switch runs an operating system, which provides a user interface and controls all processes that are used to forward packets. The following sections address all these topics.

Operating Systems

You can configure Cisco Catalyst switch devices to support many different requirements and features. When a PC is connected to the serial console port, configuration generally is done with a terminal emulator application on the PC. You can perform further configurations through a Telnet session across the LAN or through a web-based interface. These topics are covered in later sections.

Catalyst switches support one of two operating systems, each with a different type of user interface for configuration:

■ **Cisco IOS Software**—The user interface is identical to that of Cisco routers, having an EXEC mode for session and monitoring commands, and a hierarchical configuration mode for switch configuration commands.

Cisco IOS Software is supported on all current Catalyst platforms, such as the 2970, 3750, 4500 (with Supervisors III and above), and 6500 (with Supervisor II and MSFC "Supervisor IOS," also known as "native" code, and Supervisor 720). This operating system can support Layer 2–only switching or Layer 2and Layer 3 operation, depending on the software license.

■ **Catalyst OS (CatOS or COS, also called XDI)**—This user interface allows session and monitoring commands to be intermingled with set-based (using the **set** and **clear** commands) configuration commands.

CatOS is supported on legacy switch families, such as the Catalyst 4000 (Supervisor I or II), Catalyst 5000, Catalyst 5500, and Catalyst 6500 (any Supervisor module, known as "hybrid" code). This operating system can support only Layer 2 switching.

> **NOTE** The Catalyst OS is mentioned here only for comparison. It is not covered in detail in the BCMSN 3.0 course; therefore, it is not covered in this text. For more information about Catalyst OS comparisons and side-by-side configuration commands, refer to these sources:
>
> *Cisco Field Manual: Catalyst Switch Configuration*, by David Hucaby and Steve McQuerry, Cisco Press, ISBN 1-58705-043-9
>
> Comparison of the Cisco Catalyst and Cisco IOS Operating Systems for the Cisco Catalyst 6500 Series Switch, at http://www.cisco.com/en/US/products/hw/switches/ps708/products_white_paper09186a00800c8441.shtml

Generally, you are provided with an interface where you can issue commands, such as **show**, to display many different types of information about the switch, its configuration, and dynamic operation. This is called *user EXEC* mode. Users are given access to various commands, according to their privilege level, ranging from Level 1 through Level 15. By default, a user is given Level 1. To make any configuration changes, a user must enter a higher level, such as Level 15, through the **enable** command.

When in the *privileged EXEC* or *enable* mode, you can make configuration changes using the **config** command. Configuration is performed in layers, starting with the *global configuration*. Each time you select a specific item to configure in global configuration mode, you are moved into that respective configuration mode.

The switch prompt changes to give you a clue about your current mode. For example, *normal* or user EXEC mode generally is shown with the name of the switch followed by a greater-than (>) character. Privileged EXEC (enable) mode replaces the > with a hash or pound sign (#). Global configuration is shown as the switch name followed by **(config)**. If you select an interface to configure, you enter *interface configuration* mode, signified by **(config-if)**.

Basically, if you are familiar with router EXEC and configuration commands and the IOS user interface, you will be comfortable working with the Catalyst IOS Software.

Identifying the Switch

All switches come from the factory with a default configuration and a default system name or prompt. You can change this name so that each switch in a campus network has a unique identity. This option is useful when you are using Telnet to move from switch to switch in a network.

To change the host or system name, enter the following command in configuration mode:

```
Switch(config)# hostname hostname
```

The host name is a string of 1 to 255 alphanumeric characters. As soon as this command is executed, the system prompt changes to reflect the new host name.

> **NOTE** Configuration changes made on Cisco IOS-based switches apply only to the active *running configuration*, stored in RAM. To make the changes permanent, in effect even after a power cycle, remember to copy the switch configuration into the *startup configuration*, stored in NVRAM. This is discussed in the "Switch File Management" section of this chapter.

Passwords and User Access

Normally, a network device should be configured to secure it from unauthorized access. Administrative users can connect to Catalyst switches through an asynchronous serial console port, Telnet sessions, rlogin (remote login), and SSH (secure shell). Catalyst switches offer a simple form of security by setting passwords to restrict who can log in to the user interface. Two levels of user access are available: regular login, or *user EXEC mode*, and enable login, or *privileged EXEC mode*. User EXEC mode is the first level of access, which gives access to the basic user interface through any line or the console port. Privileged EXEC mode requires a second password and gives access to set or change switch operating parameters or configurations.

Cisco offers various methods for providing device security and user authentication. Many of these methods are more secure and robust than using the login passwords. Chapter 17, "Securing Switch Access," describes these features in greater detail.

To set the login passwords for user EXEC mode, enter the following commands in global configuration mode:

```
Switch(config)# line con 0
Switch(config-line)# password password
Switch(config-line)# login
Switch(config)# line vty 0 15
Switch(config-line)# password password
Switch(config-line)# login
Switch(config)# enable secret enable-password
```

Here, the user EXEC mode password is set on the console (**line con 0**) and on all the virtual terminal (**line vty 0 15**) lines used for Telnet access. The enable mode password (**enable secret**), which automatically is encrypted when set, is a global value for all users. The user EXEC password is a string of 1 to 80 alphanumeric characters. The enable secret password is a string of 1 to 25 alphanumeric characters. All passwords are case sensitive.

You can change the passwords by reconfiguring the passwords with different strings. To completely remove a password, use the **no password** or **no enable secret** command in the appropriate line-configuration mode.

Password Recovery

After the EXEC and enable passwords are configured, there is always a chance that you could forget them. You also might inherit a switch that has its passwords set to unknown values. In this case, you must take the switch through a password-recovery procedure. The procedure varies among the different Catalyst switch families. Refer to the following documents:

- **Catalyst 2970 and 3750**—http://www.cisco.com/warp/public/474/pswdrec_2900xl.html

- **Catalyst 4000 and 4500 (Supervisor III and above)**—http://www.cisco.com/warp/public/ 474/ pswdrec_cat4000_supiii_21229.html

- **Catalyst 6500 (Supervisor IOS)**—http://www.cisco.com/warp/public/474/ pswdrec_6000IOS.html

For a complete list of password-recovery procedures for any model of Cisco equipment, refer to the handy *Password Recovery Procedures* technical tip at http://www.cisco.com/warp/public/474/.

> **TIP** Although password recovery is not covered explicitly in the BCMSN course (nor is likely in the CCNP BCMSN exam), you should be aware of the concepts needed to regain access to a switch.

Remote Access

By default, the switch allows user access only via the console port. To use Telnet to access a switch from within the campus network, to use **ping** to test a switch's reachability, or to monitor a switch by SNMP, you must configure for remote access.

Even if a switch operates at Layer 2, the switch supervisor processor must maintain an IP stack at Layer 3 for administrative purposes. An IP address and subnet mask then can be assigned to the switch so that remote communications with the switch supervisor are possible.

By default, all ports on a switch are assigned to the same virtual LAN (VLAN) or broadcast domain. The switch supervisor and its IP stack must be assigned to a VLAN before remote Telnet and ping sessions will be supported. VLANs are discussed further in Chapter 6, "VLANs and Trunks."

You can assign an IP address to the management VLAN (default is VLAN 1) with the following commands in global configuration mode:

```
Switch(config)# interface vlan vlan-id
Switch(config-if)# ip address ip-address netmask
Switch(config-if)# ip default-gateway ip-address
Switch(config-if)# no shutdown
```

As demonstrated by the preceding command syntax, an IP address and subnet mask are assigned to the VLAN "interface," which is really the switch supervisor's IP stack listening on VLAN number *vlan-id*. Any VLAN number can be used, as long as the VLAN has been defined and is active (in use on a physical switch interface).

To send packets off that local VLAN subnet, a default gateway IP address also must be assigned. This default gateway has nothing to do with processing packets that are passed through the switch; the default gateway is used only to forward traffic between a user and the switch supervisor for management purposes. (This concept can be expanded greatly on a Layer 3 switch, which can perform its own "routing" functions and can use dynamic routing protocols.)

Interswitch Communication: Cisco Discovery Protocol

Because switch devices usually are interconnected, management is simplified if the switches can communicate on some level to become aware of each other. Cisco has implemented protocols on its devices so that neighboring Cisco equipment can be found and identified.

Cisco uses a proprietary protocol on both switches and routers to discover neighboring devices. You can enable the Cisco Discovery Protocol (CDP) on interfaces to periodically advertise the existence of a device and exchange basic information with directly connected neighbors. The information exchanged in CDP messages includes the device type, software version, links between devices, and number of ports within each device.

By default, CDP runs on each port of a Catalyst switch, and CDP advertisements occur every 60 seconds. CDP communication occurs at the data link layer so that it is independent of any network layer protocol that might be running on a network segment. This means that CDP can be sent and received using only *Layer 2 functionality*. CDP frames are sent as multicasts, using a destination MAC address of 01:00:0c:cc:cc:cc.

Cisco Catalyst switches regard the CDP address as a special address designating a multicast frame that should *not* be forwarded. Instead, CDP multicast frames are redirected to the switch's management port and are processed by the switch supervisor alone. Cisco switches become aware only of other directly connected Cisco devices.

CDP is enabled by default on all switch interfaces. To manually enable or disable CDP on an interface, use the following interface-configuration command:

```
Switch(config-if)# [no] cdp enable
```

If a switch port connects to a non-Cisco device or to a network outside your administrative control, consider disabling CDP on that port. Add the **no** keyword to disable CDP.

Switch File Management

A Catalyst switch uses several types of files while it is operating. To manage a switch, you should understand what type of file is used for what purpose, how to move these files, and how to upgrade them.

The following files typically are used in a Catalyst switch:

- **IOS image files**—The software or code that the switch CPU executes. Image files are compiled and tailored for specific switch hardware models.

- **Configuration files**—Text files containing all configuration commands needed to operate a switch in a network.

All Catalyst files can be stored in various file systems so that they can be accessed and used by the switch hardware. Files also can be stored in file systems external to the switch, either as backup copies or as downloadable upgrades.

The typical file systems available to a Catalyst switch are as follows:

- **Flash memory**—Nonvolatile memory present in the switch; files stored here remain intact even after a power cycle.

- **Network servers**—Systems apart from the switch that are connected to the network and provide TFTP, FTP, or remote copy program (rcp) file-transfer services.

- **NVRAM**—Nonvolatile memory that contains the switch configuration used during bootup. On many switches, the NVRAM file system actually is emulated in Flash memory.

- **RAM**—Volatile memory available to the switch for a variety of purposes. The switch configuration used during runtime and altered by configuration commands is stored here.

OS Image Files

The Catalyst IOS Software is packaged as an IOS image file, just as it is for routers. IOS image files are stored in the Flash memory on a switch. Only one image file can be executed while the switch is running, but more than one image file can be stored on the switch.

Switches such as the Catalyst 2970 and 3750 have one Flash area where images are stored. This is always named flash:. Larger, more modular switches can have several Flash file systems. For example, a Catalyst 4500 has one named cat4000_flash: that contains the VLAN database file and another called bootflash: that contains the IOS image and bootstrap image files. Flash memory also can be present in the form of a PCMCIA card, so stored files can be swapped out by replacing the Flash card. These cards are named slot0:, slot1:, and so on.

You can copy IOS image files from one file system to another or to an external location. This allows an image file to be backed up in case of a switch failure. Image files also can be copied into the switch Flash file system so that the software version can be upgraded.

Filename Conventions

IOS image files are named according to a predefined format. The filenames follow this basic template:

mmmmm-fffff-mm.vvvv.bin

- *mmmmm* represents the Catalyst switch model (for example, c3750 corresponds to Catalyst 3750, cat4000 to Catalyst 4000 or 4500, c6k222 to Catalyst 6500 Supervisor II, and s72033 to Catalyst 6500 Supervisor 720).

- *fffff* represents the feature sets included in the image—generally, *i* followed by anything denotes an IP feature set, *s* is the IP "Plus," *k* denotes a cryptographic feature set (Data Encryption Standard [DES] or 3DES), *j* is the enterprise set, *p* is for service providers, and *d* is the desktop (IP, IPX, AppleTalk, DECnet) feature set.

- *mm* denotes the file format: The first letter is *m* if the image runs in RAM, and the second letter is *z* if the image is Zip compressed.

- *vvvv* represents the IOS version, in the format *vvv-mmm.bbb*; the major release (*vvv*) is given first and followed by a dash; then the maintenance release (*mmm*) is given and followed by a period. The build level (*bbb*) is given using one or more letters and a number. The first letter denotes the type of build: *E* means an early deployment of features. The next letter is the interim build level, where *A* means the first build, and so on. The number following denotes the number of times the interim build has been released incrementally.

  Therefore, 122-20.EWA means version 12.2(20)EWA, or early deployment build WA of the 12.2(20) code.

- *.bin* flags the image file as a binary executable (not readable text).

Configuration Files

The switch configuration is a file containing all the commands needed to configure each switch feature and function. Here are three of the most common configuration files:

- **startup-config**—When a switch first boots up, the startup-config file is read, parsed, and executed. The startup-config is stored in NVRAM (actually, the nvram: file system), so it survives power failures.

■ **running-config**—While a switch is running, this contains a copy of the current state of every command in use. This file is dynamic, so it is updated with each configuration command entered.

The running-config contents are volatile, causing all commands in it to be lost during a power failure or a switch reload. (To preserve the running-config, it must be copied into the startup-config before the next switch reload.)

■ **vlan.dat**—As VLANs are defined or changed, their configurations are entered into the VLAN database file, vlan.dat. This file is updated as you make configuration changes to the VLAN database on a switch and as any VLAN Trunking Protocol (VTP) updates occur.

The VLAN database (vlan.dat) is stored in Flash memory (or the const_nvram: filesystem on a Catalyst 6500). The contents of the VLAN database are preserved across a power failure or reload.

Other Catalyst Switch Files

You can find several other files stored in the file systems on a Catalyst switch. Most of the time, you will not need to do anything with them. They are mentioned here for your understanding and in case you need to access the information they contain. These files can include the following:

■ **system_env_vars**—A text file containing system variables such as the MAC address, model number, serial number, and various module information. This file is consulted to get the system information displayed by the **show version** command.

■ **crashinfo**—A file or directory containing text output from previous switch crashes. This normally is stored and accessed as flash:crashinfo (a file) or crashinfo: (a directory).

Moving Catalyst Switch Files

A switch can copy files to and from various locations, including those in Table 4-2.

Table 4-2 *Locations of Catalyst Switch Files*

FileSystemName	Function
flash:	Flash memory, usually containing bootable IOS image files (some models emulate nvram: here)
bootflash:	Flash memory, usually containing bootable IOS image files
slot0:	Optional removable Flash card memory; can store any type of files
nvram:	NVRAM area, usually containing the startup-config file
system:	RAM area; contains the running-config file and a directory of all dynamic switch memory areas

Table 4-2   *Locations of Catalyst Switch Files (Continued)*

FileSystemName	Function
tftp:	An external TFTP server where any type of switch file can be stored or retrieved; no user authentication needed
ftp:	An external FTP server where any type of switch file can be stored or retrieved; user authentication required
rcp:	An external rcp server where any type of switch file can be stored or retrieved; user authentication required

Cisco IOS Software allows you to navigate and manipulate the Flash file system in much the same way other operating systems, such as UNIX and DOS, do. In Flash memory, you can find plain-text files, binary executable files, and directories. You are free to "move" up and down into directories. You also can copy, rename, or delete files.

In the EXEC mode, you always are positioned in the "root" directory, flash:, by default. To perform a function in the Flash file system, use one of the following commands:

- **dir** [**flash:**[*directory*]]—Shows a list of all files in the current Flash directory or the directory given.

- **cd flash:***directory*—Changes the directory to the directory given.

- **cd ..**—Changes the directory one level up.

- **cd**—Changes the directory to the home or root Flash directory.

- **copy flash:**[*filename*] **tftp:**—Copies the file *filename* from Flash to a TFTP server. The server address and destination filename are prompted.

- **copy tftp: flash:**[*filename*]—Copies a file from the TFTP server into Flash memory. The TFTP server address and any unresolved filenames are prompted.

- **delete flash:***filename*—The file *filename* is deleted from Flash memory.

- **erase flash:**—All files in Flash memory are erased in one command.

- **format flash:**—The Flash file system is reformatted, destroying all existing files. Formatting is appropriate when the Flash memory has been corrupted.

You also can manipulate the switch-configuration files from privileged EXEC (enable) mode. Remember that two configuration files exist at all times—running-config and startup-config. Any configuration changes that you make to a switch are applied immediately to the running-config file. The only way to update the startup-config is by manually copying another file to it.

Cisco IOS Software allows the following commands to manipulate the configuration files:

- **copy running-config startup-config**—The contents of the running-config are copied into the startup-config, replacing any similar commands there. After this is done, any dynamic configuration changes are saved and are preserved across power failures or switch reloads. (This command should be used regularly to save any new configuration changes. Use it prudently if you need to back out a large number of changes.)

- **copy startup-config running-config**—The permanent contents of the startup-config file are copied into the running-config, replacing any similar commands there. The entire running-config is not simply overwritten; the **startup-config** commands are copied over while any other existing **running-config** commands are kept active. This operation is performed as a switch boots up. (This command quickly can restore a misconfigured switch to a known state.)

- **copy running-config tftp:**—A switch's current running configuration is copied to a TFTP server. The server address and destination filename are prompted. Use this command to store a backup snapshot copy of the switch configuration.

- **copy tftp: startup-config**—When a switch configuration is lost or needs to be restored to a known state, a backup copy of the configuration is copied from a TFTP server to the startup-config file. The new changes do not take effect until the switch is reloaded or until the startup-config is copied to the running-config. (You also could use **copy tftp: running-config**, but this would make immediate configuration changes as commands from the TFTP file are copied over. Use caution so that your configuration changes occur under controlled circumstances.)

- **erase startup-config**—The entire contents of the startup-config file are erased. Use this command when a switch has been retired from one function and needs to be relocated or completely reconfigured.

Troubleshooting from the Operating System

The Cisco Catalyst IOS Software provides many commands that can verify or troubleshoot a switch in its current environment. Sometimes you might wonder what software image or configuration commands are being used by a switch. A switch also can produce real-time debugging information about a feature or condition to aid in troubleshooting. Information is also available to help identify other neighboring Cisco devices in a network. This section explains each of these tasks and how to accomplish them using the relevant commands.

Displaying Configuration and File Contents

Cisco IOS Software offers many commands that you can use from the EXEC mode command line to display the contents of files, current configuration states, and values for troubleshooting. You can use the following commands to view and troubleshoot switch files and file systems:

- **show version**—Displays the current version of Cisco IOS Software running in a switch, along with many details about available hardware, RAM and Flash memory, switch uptime, the current running IOS image file, the reason for the last reload, and the configuration register's contents.

- **show running-config [interface** *type mod/num* | **vlan** *vlan-id* | **module** *mod*]—Displays the contents of the running-config configuration file. You can jump to the relevant configuration of a specific interface, VLAN, or switch module, if desired.

- **show startup-config**—Displays the startup-config configuration file contents.

- **show tech-support**—Provides information to Cisco TAC support personnel; almost every known bit of information about the switch is displayed. Be sure to configure your terminal emulator to capture text to a file before issuing this command.

- **verify flash:***filename*—Verifies the checksum of the Flash file *filename.* This can ensure that an IOS image is not corrupted after it has been copied into Flash memory. (During the actual copy process, the checksum automatically is verified. You can use the **verify** command to make sure that the file has not become corrupted since it was copied originally.)

- **more** *filesystem:filename*—Displays the contents of a plain-text file from the command line. This can be useful when you need to read configuration files that have been stored in a Flash file system. You also can view text files that are stored on a remote TFTP server—from the IOS command line.

> **NOTE**   You can filter the output of any **show** command so that you see only lines containing specific keywords. Append the "pipe" symbol (|) to the command line, followed by one of these keywords: **begin** *text* (start the output with the line containing *text*), **include** *text* (display only lines that contain *text*), or **exclude** *text* (display only lines that don't contain *text*).
>
> When a large amount of output is displayed, the switch usually shows a page at a time, pausing with a "-More-" prompt. You can press either the Space key to display the next page, the Return (Enter) key to display the next line, or */text* to search forward and begin the page of output at the line containing *text*. Using the slash key allows a quick search within the context of the entire output.

Debugging Output

For more focused and real-time information about a certain switch feature, you can use the **debug** EXEC command. Debug output is not used normally, unless you suspect a problem with a feature or an interaction with other switches in the network.

You can use many options with the **debug** command, each pertaining to a switch feature or a specific activity. Type the **debug** command followed by **?** to get context-based help on all the supported debugging commands and keywords.

After you enable a **debug** command, you can see the debug output listed as events occur on the switch.

> **CAUTION**   Use the **debug** commands cautiously because they can generate a tremendous amount of output. Not only can this display slowly on a serial console connection, but the debug process itself also can bog down the switch CPU to the point that it severely impacts traffic forwarding.

Always be sure to turn off any debugging commands when you finish with them by using the **no debug** *options* command, where the *options* keywords match the ones you used to enable debugging. To quickly disable *all* active debugging commands, use the **no debug all** or **undebug all** commands.

Viewing CDP Information

To view information learned from CDP advertisements of neighboring Cisco devices, use one of the following commands:

```
Switch# show cdp interface [type mod/num]
Switch# show cdp neighbors [type mod/num | vlan vlan-id] [detail]
```

The first command displays CDP information pertaining to a specific interface. If the type, module, and port information is omitted, CDP information from all interfaces is listed. The second command displays CDP information about neighboring Cisco devices. A specific interface or VLAN can be given to display only neighbors connected to it. Using the **detail** keyword results in the display of all possible CDP information about each neighbor.

Recall that CDP messages are sent out every 60 seconds, and all entries received are placed in a cache. The cache is updated with new entries, and stale entries are aged out after a hold time of 180 seconds. If you suspect a problem with a neighboring switch, you might want to clear the CDP cache of all potentially stale information to see what new information is being received from neighbors. Do this with the **clear cdp table** command.

As demonstrated in Example 4-1, the **show cdp neighbors** and the **show cdp neighbors detail** commands can be useful when you are connected to a switch and need to know more about what other switches are nearby in a network. Particularly useful are the IP address entries, allowing Telnet access to previously unknown switches. To see a brief listing of only the neighbor switch names and their management IP addresses, use the **show cdp entry * protocol** command.

Example 4-1 *Displaying CDP Information for Neighboring Devices*

```
Switch# show cdp neighbors
Capability Codes: R - Router, T - Trans Bridge, B - Source Route Bridge
                  S - Switch, H - Host, I - IGMP, r - Repeater

Device ID        Local Intrfce    Holdtme    Capability  Platform  Port ID
BuildingA-1      Gig 2/1             158        S I       WS-C3550-4Gig 0/1
CoreSwitch-1     Gig 1/1             158        T S       Cat 6000  Gig 3/1
Switch# show cdp neighbors gig 1/1 detail
-----------------------
Device ID: CoreSwitch-1
Entry address(es):
  IP address: 192.168.199.9
Platform: cisco Catalyst 6000,  Capabilities: Router Switch IGMP
Interface: GigabitEthernet1/1,  Port ID (outgoing port): GigabitEthernet3/1
Holdtime : 136 sec

Version :
Cisco Internetwork Operating System Software
IOS (tm) c6sup2_rp Software (c6sup2_rp-JK9SV-M), Version 12.2(14)SY4, EARLY DEPLOYMENT
RELEASE SOFTWARE (fc1)
Technical Support: http://www.cisco.com/techsupport
Copyright  1986-2004 by cisco Systems, Inc.
Compiled Wed 31-Mar-04 10:50 by kellmill

Switch# show cdp entry * protocol
Protocol information for BuildingA-1 :
  IP address: 192.168.199.107
Protocol information for CoreSwitch-1 :
  IP address: 192.168.199.9
Switch#
```

Foundation Summary

The Foundation Summary is a collection of tables that provides a convenient review of many key concepts in this chapter. If you are already comfortable with the topics in this chapter, this summary can help you recall a few details. If you just read this chapter, this review should help solidify some key facts. If you are doing your final preparation before the exam, the following tables are a convenient way to review the day before the exam.

Table 4-3 *Switch-Management Configuration Commands*

Task	Command Syntax
Identify switch	**hostname** *hostname*
Set EXEC-level password	**line** *type number*
	password *password*
Set privileged-level password	**enable secret** *password*
Set IP address	**interface vlan** *vlan-id*
	ip address *ip-address netmask*
	ip default-gateway *ip-address*
CDP (enabled by default on every switch port)	**cdp enable**

Table 4-4 *File-Management Commands*

Task	Command Syntax
Navigate to the directory of Flash	**dir** [**flash:**[*directory*]]
Change directory	**cd flash:***directory*
Copy a file between Flash and a TFTP server	**copy flash:**[*filename*] **tftp:**
	or
	copy tftp: flash:[*filename*]
Delete a file in Flash	**delete flash:***filename*
Clear Flash contents	**erase flash:**
	or
	format flash:

Table 4-4 *File-Management Commands (Continued)*

Task	Command Syntax
Save the running configuration	**copy running-config startup-config** or **copy running-config tftp:**
Overwrite the running configuration	**copy startup-config running-config**
Overwrite the permanent configuration	**copy tftp: startup-config** or **erase startup-config**

Table 4-5 *Troubleshooting Commands*

Task	Command Syntax
Display the current running environment and IOS version	**show version**
Display the running configuration	**show running-config [interface** *type mod/num* I **vlan** *vlan-id* I **module** *mod*]
Display the permanent configuration	**show startup-config** or **show config**
Display all technical support information	**show tech-support**
Verify an image checksum	**verify flash:***filename*
Enable or disable debugging	**debug** *keywords* **no debug** *keywords* or **no debug all** or **undebug all**
Display CDP information	**show cdp interface** [*type mod/num*] or **show cdp neighbors** [*type mod/num* I **vlan** *vlan-id*] [**detail**] or **show cdp entry * protocol**

Q&A

The questions and scenarios in this book are more difficult than what you should experience on the actual exam. The questions do not attempt to cover more breadth or depth than the exam; however, they are designed to make sure that you know the answer. Rather than allowing you to derive the answer from clues hidden inside the questions themselves, the questions challenge your understanding and recall of the subject. Hopefully, these questions will help limit the number of exam questions on which you narrow your choices to two options and then guess.

You can find the answers to these questions in Appendix A.

1. When Cisco IOS Software is used on a Catalyst switch, the switch must perform routing. True or false?

2. What is the major difference between the Cisco IOS Software and CatOS command sets?

3. What switch command will enter privileged EXEC or "enable" mode on a Catalyst 4500?

4. Match these default command-line prompts with their respective modes:

   a. Switch#   _____Normal user EXEC mode

   b. Switch(config)   _____Privileged EXEC or enable

   c. Switch(config-if)# _____Global configuration

   d. Switch>   _____Interface configuration

5. With the command-line prompt **testlab#**, what command has been used to customize the prompt?

6. The following commands have just been entered, assuming that interface VLAN 10 did not previously exist:

   ```
   interface vlan 10
   ip address 192.168.199.10 255.255.255.0
   no shutdown
   ```

   Suddenly, the power cord is pulled out of the switch. What will happen when the power is restored?

7. Can you configure an enable secret password (**enable secret** *password*) for the switch console and a different enable secret password for Telnet access?

8. When you configure an IP address and subnet mask on a Layer 2 switch for management purposes, which VLAN are you required to use?

  a. VLAN 1.

  b. VLAN 0.

  c. VLAN 1001.

  d. Any VLAN that is appropriate.

  e. You cannot assign an IP address to a VLAN.

9. What commands will allow Telnet and ping access to a switch-management interface at 192.168.200.10, subnet mask 255.255.255.0, on VLAN 5? A router is available at address 192.168.200.1.

10. CDP advertisements occur every _____ seconds.

11. When a Cisco Catalyst switch receives a CDP multicast frame, it relays it to neighboring switches. True or false?

12. Eight access-layer switches connect to a central distribution-layer switch using Gigabit Ethernet connections. Each connection is assigned to VLAN 1 so that no link is in trunking mode. On one of the access switches, how many neighboring switches will be shown by the **show cdp neighbor gigabit 0/1**?

13. Which Cisco IOS Software image file is more recent:

c3550-i5q3l2-mz.121-12c.EA1.bin

or

c3550-i9q3l2-mz.121-11c.EA1.bin?

14. A new switch has just been configured with 100 command lines from the console. You realize the need to save the new configuration and type **copy start run**. Where will your configuration be stored?

15. What command can you use to see what Cisco IOS Software version currently is running on a switch?

16. Complete this command so that the output is displayed starting with the configuration for interface VLAN 100:

show run _____

17. The **debug spanning-tree all** command has been given from the EXEC mode command line. What commands can you use to stop or disable the debugging output?

18. What command can you use to verify CDP configuration on switch port GigabitEthernet 3/1?

This chapter covers the following topics that you need to master for the CCNP BCMSN exam:

- **Ethernet Concepts**—This section discusses the concepts and technology behind various forms of Ethernet media.

- **Connectivity with Scalable Ethernet**—This section covers the configuration steps and commands needed to use Catalyst Ethernet, Fast Ethernet, and Gigabit and 10-Gigabit Ethernet switch ports in a network.

- **Connecting Switch Block Devices**—This section discusses the physical cabling and connectivity used with Catalyst switches, including console and Ethernet interfaces.

- **Troubleshooting Port Connectivity**—This section covers some of the symptoms, methods, and switch commands that you can use to diagnose problems with Ethernet switch connections.

CHAPTER 5

Switch Port Configuration

Chapters 1, "Campus Network Overview," and 2, "Modular Network Design," dealt with the logical processes that you can use to design a campus network. Connections between switch blocks were discussed so that traffic can be transported efficiently across the campus. Single connections, load balancing, and redundant paths connected switches in modular blocks for complete connectivity. However, these paths were only functional paths—no specifics were presented about how much traffic the network could handle or what physical capabilities were supported. These topics become important when you begin to size traffic loads and actually connect Cisco switch devices.

This chapter presents the various Ethernet network technologies used to establish switched connections within the campus network. The chapter also details the switch commands required for configuring and troubleshooting Ethernet LAN ports.

"Do I Know This Already?" Quiz

The purpose of the "Do I Know This Already?" quiz is to help you decide whether you need to read the entire chapter. If you already intend to read the entire chapter, you do not necessarily need to answer these questions now.

The 11-question quiz, derived from the major sections in the "Foundation Topics" portion of the chapter, helps you determine how to spend your limited study time.

Table 5-1 outlines the major topics discussed in this chapter and the "Do I Know This Already?" quiz questions that correspond to those topics.

Table 5-1 *"Do I Know This Already?" Foundation Topics Section-to-Question Mapping*

Foundation Topics Section	Questions Covered in This Section	Score
Ethernet Concepts	1–6	
Connecting Switch Block Devices	7–8	
Switch Port Configuration	9	

Table 5-1 *"Do I Know This Already?" Foundation Topics Section-to-Question Mapping (Continued)*

Foundation Topics Section	Questions Covered in This Section	Score
Troubleshooting Port Connectivity	10–11	
Total Score		

CAUTION The goal of self-assessment is to gauge your mastery of the topics in this chapter. If you do not know the answer to a question or are only partially sure of the answer, you should mark this question wrong. Giving yourself credit for an answer you correctly guess skews your self- assessment results and might provide you with a false sense of security.

1. What does the IEEE 802.3 standard define?

   a. Spanning Tree Protocol

   b. Token Ring

   c. Ethernet

   d. Switched Ethernet

2. At what layer are traditional 10-Mbps Ethernet, Fast Ethernet, and Gigabit Ethernet the same?

   a. Layer 1

   b. Layer 2

   c. Layer 3

   d. Layer 4

3. At what layer are traditional 10-Mbps Ethernet, Fast Ethernet, and Gigabit Ethernet different?

   a. Layer 1

   b. Layer 2

   c. Layer 3

   d. Layer 4

4. What is the maximum cable distance for a Category 5 100BASE-TX connection?

   a. 100 feet

   b. 100 m

   c. 328 m

   d. 500 m

5. Ethernet autonegotiation determines which of the following?

    a. Spanning Tree mode

    b. Duplex mode

    c. Quality of service mode

    d. Error threshold

6. Which of the following cannot be determined if the far end of a connection doesn't support autonegotiation?

    a. Link speed

    b. Link duplex mode

    c. Link media type

    d. MAC address

7. Which of these is not a standard type of Gigabit Interface Converter (GBIC) or small form factor pluggable (SFP) module?

    a. 1000BASE-LX/LH

    b. 1000BASE-T

    c. 1000BASE-FX

    d. 1000BASE-ZX

8. What type of cable should you use to connect two switches back to back using their FastEthernet 10/100 ports?

    a. Rollover cable

    b. Transfer cable

    c. Crossover cable

    d. Straight-through cable

9. Assume you have just entered the **configure terminal** command. To configure the speed of the first FastEthernet interface on a Cisco IOS Software–based Catalyst switch to 100 Mbps, which one of these commands should you enter first?

    a. **speed 100 mbps**

    b. **speed 100**

    c. **interface fastethernet 0/1**

    d. **interface fast ethernet 0/1**

10. If a switch port is in the errdisable state, what is the first thing you should do?

    a. Reload the switch.

    b. Use the **clear errdisable port** command.

    c. Use the **shut** and **no shut** interface-configuration commands.

    d. Determine the cause of the problem.

11. Which of the following **show interface** output information can you use to diagnose a switch port problem?

    a. Port state.

    b. Port speed.

    c. Input errors.

    d. Collisions.

    e. All of these answers are correct.

You can find the answers to the quiz in Appendix A, "Answers to Chapter 'Do I Know This Already?' Quizzes and Q&A Sections." The suggested choices for your next step are as follows:

- **7 or less overall score**—Read the entire chapter. This includes the "Foundation Topics," "Foundation Summary," and "Q&A" sections.

- **8–9 overall score**—Begin with the "Foundation Summary" section and follow up with the "Q&A" section at the end of the chapter.

- **10 or more overall score**—If you want more review on these topics, skip to the "Foundation Summary" section and then go to the "Q&A" section at the end of the chapter. Otherwise, move to Chapter 6, "VLANs and Trunks."

Foundation Topics

Ethernet Concepts

This section reviews the varieties of Ethernet and their application in a campus network. Recall how the bandwidth requirements for each network segment are determined by the types of applications in use, the traffic flows within the network, and the size of the user community served. Ethernet scales to support increasing bandwidths and should be chosen to match the need at each point in the campus network. As network bandwidth requirements grow, you can scale the links between access, distribution, and core layers to match the load.

Other network media technologies available include Fiber Distribution Data Interface (FDDI), Copper Distribution Data Interface (CDDI), Token Ring, and Asynchronous Transfer Mode (ATM). Although some networks still use these media, Ethernet has emerged as the most popular choice in installed networks. Ethernet is chosen because of its low cost, market availability, and scalability to higher bandwidths.

Ethernet (10 Mbps)

Ethernet is a LAN technology based on the Institute of Electrical and Electronics Engineers (IEEE) 802.3 standard. Ethernet (in contrast to Fast Ethernet and later versions) offers a bandwidth of 10 Mbps between end users. In its most basic form, Ethernet is a shared medium that becomes both a collision and a broadcast domain. As the number of users on the shared media increases, so does the probability that a user is trying to transmit data at any given time. When one user transmits at about the same time as another, a *collision* occurs. In other words, both users can't transmit data at the same time if they both are sharing the same network media.

Ethernet is based on the *carrier sense multiple access collision detect (CSMA/CD)* technology, which requires that transmitting stations back off for a random period of time when a collision occurs. If a station must wait its turn to transmit, it cannot transmit and receive at the same time. This is called *half-duplex* operation.

The more crowded an Ethernet segment becomes, the number of stations likely to be transmitting at a given time increases. Imagine standing in a crowded room trying to tell a story. Instead of attempting to talk over the crowd, you stop and politely wait while other people talk. The more people there are in the room, the more difficult talking becomes. Likewise, as an Ethernet segment becomes more crowded, it becomes more inefficient.

Ethernet switching addresses this problem by dynamically allocating a dedicated 10-Mbps bandwidth to each of its ports. The resulting increased network performance occurs by reducing the number of users connected to an Ethernet segment. In effect, collisions are less probable and the collision domain is reduced in size.

Although switched Ethernet's job is to offer fully dedicated bandwidth to each connected device, assuming that network performance will improve across the board when switching is introduced is a common mistake. For example, consider a workgroup of users connected by a shared-media Ethernet hub. These users regularly access an enterprise server located elsewhere in the campus network. To improve performance, the decision is made to replace the hub with an Ethernet switch so that all users get dedicated 10-Mbps connections. Because the switch offers dedicated bandwidth for connections between the end-user devices connected to its ports, any user-to-user traffic probably would see improved performance. However, the enterprise server still is located elsewhere in the network, and all the switched users still must share available bandwidth across the campus to reach it. As discussed in Chapter 1, instead of throwing raw bandwidth at a problem, a design based on careful observation of traffic patterns and flows offers a better solution.

Because switched Ethernet can remove the possibility of collisions, stations do not have to listen to each other to take a turn transmitting on the wire. Instead, stations can operate in *full-duplex* mode—transmitting and receiving simultaneously. Full-duplex mode further increases network performance, with a net throughput of 10 Mbps in each direction, or 20 Mbps total throughput on each port.

Another consideration when dealing with 10-Mbps Ethernet is the physical cabling. Ethernet cabling involves the use of unshielded twisted-pair (UTP) wiring (10BASE-T Ethernet), usually restricted to an end-to-end distance of 100 m (328 feet) between active devices. Keeping cable lengths as short as possible in the wiring closet also reduces noise and crosstalk when many cables are bundled together.

In a campus network environment, Ethernet usually is used in the access layer, between end user devices and the access-layer switch. Many networks still use Ethernet to connect end users to shared-media hubs, which then connect to access-layer switches. Ethernet typically is not used at either the distribution or the core layer.

> **NOTE**   Ethernet applications (10BASE2, 10BASE5, 10BASE-F, and so on) use other cabling technologies, although they are not discussed here. For the most part, 10BASE-T with UTP wiring is the most commonly used. A useful website for further reading about Ethernet technology is Charles Spurgeon's Ethernet Web Site, at http://www.ethermanage.com/ethernet/.

Fast Ethernet

Instead of requiring campuses to invest in a completely new technology to gain increased bandwidth, the networking industry developed a higher-speed Ethernet based on existing Ethernet standards. Fast Ethernet operates at 100 Mbps and is defined in the IEEE 802.3u standard. The Ethernet cabling schemes, CSMA/CD operation, and all upper-layer protocol operations are maintained with Fast Ethernet. The net result is the same data link Media Access Control (MAC) layer merged with a new physical layer.

The campus network can use Fast Ethernet to link access- and distribution-layer switches, if no higher-speed links are available. These links can support the aggregate traffic from multiple Ethernet segments in the access layer. Fast Ethernet generally is used to connect end-user workstations to the access-layer switch and to provide improved connectivity to enterprise servers.

Cabling for Fast Ethernet can involve either UTP or fiber. Table 5-2 lists the specifications for Fast Ethernet that define the media types and distances.

Table 5-2   *Cabling Specifications for Fast Ethernet*

Technology	Wiring Type	Pairs	Cable Length
100BASE-TX	EIA/TIA Category 5 UTP	2	100 m
100BASE-T2	EIA/TIA Category 3, 4, 5 UTP	2	100 m
100BASE-T4	EIA/TIA Category 3, 4, 5 UTP	4	100 m
100BASE-FX	Multimode fiber (MMF); 62.5-micron core, 125-micron outer cladding (62.5/125)	1	400 m half duplex or 2000 m full duplex
	Single-mode fiber (SMF)	1	10 km

Full-Duplex Fast Ethernet

As with traditional Ethernet, the natural progression to improve performance is to use full-duplex operation. Fast Ethernet can provide up to 100 Mbps in each direction on a switched connection, for 200 Mbps total throughput.

This maximum throughput is possible only when one device (a workstation, server, router, or another switch) is connected directly to a switch port. In addition, the devices at each end of the link must both support full-duplex operation, allowing each to transmit at will without having to detect and recover from collisions.

The Fast Ethernet specification also offers backward-compatibility to support traditional 10-Mbps Ethernet. In the case of 100BASE-TX, switch ports often are called "10/100" ports, to denote the dual speed. To provide this support, the two devices at each end of a network connection automatically can negotiate link capabilities so that they both can operate at a maximum common level. This negotiation involves detecting and selecting the highest physical layer technology (available bandwidth) and half-duplex or full-duplex operation. To properly negotiate a connection, *both* ends should be configured for autonegotiation.

The link speed is determined by electrical signaling so that either end of a link can determine what speed the other end is trying to use. If both ends of the link are configured to autonegotiate, they will use the highest speed that is common to them.

A link's duplex mode, however, is negotiated through an exchange of information. This means that for one end to successfully autonegotiate the duplex mode, the other end also must be set to autonegotiate. Otherwise, one end never will see duplex information from the other end and won't be capable of determining the correct mode to use. If duplex autonegotiation fails, a switch port always falls back to its default setting—half-duplex.

> **CAUTION** Beware of a duplex mismatch when both ends of a link are not set for autonegotiation. During a mismatch, one end uses full duplex while the other end uses half duplex. The result is that the half-duplex station will detect a collision when both ends transmit; it will back off appropriately. The full-duplex station, however, will assume that it has the right to transmit at any time. It will not stop and wait for any reason. This can cause errors on the link and poor response times between the stations.

Autonegotiation uses the priorities shown in Table 5-3 for each mode of Ethernet to determine which technology to agree upon. If both devices can support more than one technology, the technology with the highest priority is used. For example, if two devices can support both 10BASE-T and 100BASE-TX, both devices will use the higher-priority 100BASE-TX mode.

Table 5-3 *Autonegotiation Selection Priorities*

Priority	Ethernet Mode
7	100BASE-T2 (full duplex)
6	100BASE-TX (full duplex)
5	100BASE-T2 (half duplex)
4	100BASE-T4
3	100BASE-TX
2	10BASE-T (full duplex)
1	10BASE-T

To ensure proper configuration at both ends of a link, Cisco recommends that the appropriate values for transmission speed and duplex mode be configured manually on switch ports. This precludes any possibility that one end of the link will change its settings, resulting in an unusable connection. If you manually set the switch port, don't forget to manually set the device on the other end of the link accordingly. Otherwise, a speed or duplex mismatch between the two devices might occur.

Cisco provides one additional capability to Fast Ethernet, which allows several Fast Ethernet links to be bundled together for increased throughput. *Fast EtherChannel (FEC)* allows two to eight full-duplex Fast Ethernet links to act as a single physical link, for 400- to 1600-Mbps duplex bandwidth. This technology is described in greater detail in Chapter 8, "Aggregating Switch Links."

For further reading about Fast Ethernet technology, refer to the article "Fast Ethernet 100-Mbps Solutions," at Cisco.com:

> http://www.cisco.com/en/US/netsol/ns340/ns394/ns147/
> networking_solutions_white_paper09186a00800a4a29.shtml.

Gigabit Ethernet

You can scale Fast Ethernet by an additional order of magnitude with Gigabit Ethernet (which supports 1000 Mbps or 1 Gbps) using the same IEEE 802.3 Ethernet frame format as before. This scalability allows network designers and managers to leverage existing knowledge and technologies to install, migrate, manage, and maintain Gigabit Ethernet networks.

However, the physical layer has been modified to increase data-transmission speeds. Two technologies were merged to gain the benefits of each: the IEEE 802.3 Ethernet standard and the American National Standards Institute (ANSI) X3T11 FibreChannel. IEEE 802.3 provided the foundation of frame format, CSMA/CD, full duplex, and other Ethernet characteristics. FibreChannel provided a base of high-speed ASICs, optical components, and encoding/decoding and serialization mechanisms. The resulting protocol is termed IEEE 802.3z Gigabit Ethernet.

Gigabit Ethernet supports several cabling types, referred to as *1000BASE-X*. Table 5-4 lists the cabling specifications for each type.

In a campus network, you can use Gigabit Ethernet in the switch block, core block, and server block. In the switch block, it can connect access-layer switches to distribution-layer switches. In the core block, it can connect the distribution layer to the core switches and interconnects the core devices. In a server block, a Gigabit Ethernet switch can provide high-speed connections to individual servers.

Table 5-4 *Gigabit Ethernet Cabling and Distance Limitations*

GE Type	Wiring Type	Pairs	Cable Length
1000BASE-CX	Shielded twisted pair (STP)	1	25 m
1000BASE-T	EIA/TIA Category 5 UTP	4	100 m

continues

Table 5-4 *Gigabit Ethernet Cabling and Distance Limitations (Continued)*

GE Type	Wiring Type	Pairs	Cable Length
1000BASE-SX	Multimode fiber (MMF) with 62.5-micron core; 850-nm laser	1	275 m
	MMF with 50-micron core; 850-nm laser	1	550 m
1000BASE-LX/LH	MMF with 62.5-micron core; 1300-nm laser	1	550 m
	Single-mode fiber (SMF) with 50-micron core; 1300-nm laser	1	550 m
	SMF with 9-micron core; 1300-nm laser	1	10 km
1000BASE-ZX	SMF with 9-micron core; 1550-nm laser	1	70 km
	SMF with 8-micron core; 1550-nm laser	1	100 km

The "Gigabit over copper" solution that the 1000BASE-T media provides is based on the IEEE 802.3ab standard. Most Gigabit Ethernet switch ports used between switches are fixed at 1000 Mbps. However, other switch ports can support a fallback to Fast or Legacy Ethernet speeds. Here, speed can be autonegotiated between end nodes to the highest common speed—10 Mbps, 100 Mbps, or 1000 Mbps. These ports are often called "10/100/1000" ports to denote the triple speed. Here, the autonegotiation supports the same priority scheme as Fast Ethernet, although 1000BASE-T full duplex becomes the highest priority, followed by 1000BASE-T half duplex. Gigabit Ethernet's port duplex mode always is set to full duplex on Cisco switches, so duplex autonegotiation is not possible.

Finally, Cisco has extended the concept of Fast EtherChannel to bundle several Gigabit Ethernet links to act as a single physical connection. With *Gigabit EtherChannel (GEC)*, two to eight full-duplex Gigabit Ethernet connections can be aggregated, for a single logical link of up to 16 Gbps throughput. Port aggregation and the EtherChannel technology are described further in Chapter 8.

> **NOTE**   The 10-Gigabit Ethernet Alliance offers further reading about Gigabit Ethernet and its operation, migration, and standards. Refer to the "Archive White Papers" section on its website at http://www.10gea.org.

10-Gigabit Ethernet

Ethernet scales by orders of magnitude, beginning with 10 Mbps, progressing to 100 Mbps, and then to 1000 Mbps. To meet the demand for aggregating many Gigabit Ethernet links over a single connection, 10-Gigabit Ethernet was developed. Again, the Layer 2 characteristics of Ethernet have been preserved; the familiar 802.3 frame format and size, along with the MAC protocol, remain unchanged.

The 10-Gigabit Ethernet, also known as *10GbE,* and the IEEE 802.3ae standard differ from their predecessors only at the physical layer (PHY); 10GbE operates only at full duplex. The standard defines several different transceivers that can be used as Physical Media Dependent (PMD) interfaces. These are classified into the following:

- **LAN PHY**—Interconnects switches in a campus network, predominantly in the core layer

- **WAN PHY**—Interfaces with existing synchronous optical network (SONET) or synchronous digital hierarchy (SDH) networks typically found in metropolitan-area networks (MAN)

The PMD interfaces also have a common labeling scheme, much as Gigabit Ethernet does. Where Gigabit Ethernet uses 1000BASE-X to indicate the media type, 10-Gigabit Ethernet uses 10GBASE-X. Table 5-5 lists the different PMDs defined in the standard, along with the type of fiber and distance limitations. All the fiber-optic PMDs can be used as either a LAN or a WAN PHY, except for the 10GBASE-LX4, which is only a LAN PHY. Be aware that the long-wavelength PMDs carry a significantly greater expense than the others.

At press time, the Cisco Catalyst 6500, 4500 (Supervisor VI), and 3750 switches supported 10-Gigabit Ethernet PMDs in the form of XENPAK transceivers, beginning with a minimum software release.

For the most current switch compatibility listing, refer to the "Cisco 10-Gigabit Ethernet Transceiver Modules Compatibility Matrix" document at http://www.cisco.com/en/US/products/hw/modules/ps5251/products_device_support_table09186a00803857e7.html.

Table 5-5 *10-Gigabit Ethernet PMD Types and Characteristics*

PMD Type [*]	Fiber Medium	Maximum Distance
10GBASE-SR/SW (850 nm serial)	MMF: 50 micron	66 m
	MMF: 50 micron (2GHz * km modal bandwidth)	300 m
	MMF: 62.5 micron	33 m
10GBASE-LR/LW (1310 nm serial)	SMF: 9 micron	10 km
10GBASE-ER/EW (1550 nm serial)	SMF: 9 micron	40 km
10GBASE-LX4/LW4 (1310 nm WWDM)	MMF: 50 micron	300 m
	MMF: 62.5 micron	300 m
	SMF: 9 micron	10 km
10GBASE-CX4	Copper: CX4 with Infiniband connectors	15 m

*Transceiver types are denoted by a two-letter suffix. The first letter specifies the wavelength used: S = short, L = long, E = extra-long wavelength. The second letter specifies the PHY type: R = LAN PHY, W = WAN PHY. In the case of LX4 and LW4, L refers to a long wavelength, X and W refer to the coding used, and 4 refers to the number of wavelengths transmitted. WWDM is wide-wavelength division multiplexing.

Connecting Switch Block Devices

Switch deployment in a network involves two steps: physical connectivity and switch configuration. This section describes the connections and cabling requirements for devices in a switch block. Cable connections must be made to a switch's console port to make initial configurations. Physical connectivity between switches and end users involves cabling for the various types of LAN ports.

Console Port Cables/Connectors

A terminal-emulation program on a PC usually is required to interface with the console port on a switch. Various types of console cables and console connectors are associated with each Cisco switch family.

All Catalyst switch families use an RJ-45-to-RJ-45 *rollover cable* to make the console connection between a PC (or terminal or modem) and the console port. A rollover cable is made so that pin 1 on one RJ-45 connector goes to pin 8 on the other RJ-45 connector, pin 2 goes to pin 7, and so forth. In other words, the cable remains flat while the two RJ-45 connectors point in opposite directions.

To connect the PC end, the rollover cable plugs into an RJ-45 to DB-9 or DB-25 "terminal" adapter (or a DB-25 "modem" adapter for a modem connection). At the switch end, the rollover cable plugs directly into the console port's RJ-45 jack.

After the console port is cabled to the PC, terminal, or modem, a terminal-emulation program can be started or a user connection can be made. The console ports on all switch families require an asynchronous serial connection at 9600 baud, 8 data bits, no parity, 1 stop bit, and no flow control.

Ethernet Port Cables and Connectors

Catalyst switches support a variety of network connections, including all forms of Ethernet. In addition, Catalyst switches support several types of cabling, including UTP and optical fiber.

Fast Ethernet (100BASE-FX) ports use two-strand multimode fiber (MMF) with MT-RJ or SC connectors to provide connectivity. The MT-RJ connectors are small and modular, each containing a pair of fiber-optic strands. The connector snaps into position, but you must press a tab to remove it. The SC connectors on the fiber cables are square in shape. These connectors snap in and out of the switch port connector as the connector is pushed in or pulled out. One fiber strand is used as a transmit path and the other as a receive path. The transmit fiber on one switch device should connect to the receive fiber on the other end.

All Catalyst switch families support 10/100 autosensing (using Fast Ethernet autonegotiation) and 10/100/1000 autosensing for Gigabit Ethernet. These ports use RJ-45 connectors on Category 5

UTP cabling to complete the connections. These ports can connect to other UTP-based Ethernet autosensing devices. UTP cabling is arranged so that RJ-45 pins 1,2 and 3,6 form two twisted pairs. These pairs connect straight through to the far end.

To connect two 10/100 switch ports back to back, as in an access-layer to distribution-layer link, you must use a Category 5 UTP crossover cable. In this case, RJ-45 pins 1,2 and 3,6 are still twisted pairs, but 1,2 on one end connects to 3,6 on the other end, and 3,6 on one end connects to 1,2 on the other end.

> **NOTE**   Because UTP Ethernet connections use only pairs 1,2 and 3,6, some cable plant installers connect only these pairs and leave the remaining two pair positions empty. Although this move provides Ethernet connectivity, it is not good practice for future needs. Instead, all four RJ-45 connector pairs should be connected end to end. For example, a full four-pair UTP cable plant can be used for either Ethernet or Token Ring connectivity, without rewiring. (Token Ring UTP connections use pairs 3,6 and 4,5.)
>
> Also, to be compatible with the new IEEE 802.3ab standard for Gigabit Ethernet over copper (1000BASE-T), you must use all four pairs end to end.

Gigabit Ethernet Port Cables and Connectors

Gigabit Ethernet connections take a different approach by providing modular connectivity options. Catalyst switches with Gigabit Ethernet ports have standardized rectangular openings that can accept GBIC or SFP modules. The Gigabit Interface Converter (GBIC) and small form factor pluggable (SFP) modules provide the media personality for the port so that various cable media can connect. In this way, the switch chassis is completely modular and requires no major change to accept a new media type. Instead, the appropriate module is hot-swappable and is plugged into the switch to support the new media. GBIC modules can use SC fiber-optic and RJ-45 UTP connectors. SFP modules can use LC and MT-RJ fiber-optic and RJ-45 UTP connectors. GBIC and SFP modules are available for the following Gigabit Ethernet media:

- **1000BASE-SX**—Short-wavelength connectivity using SC fiber connectors and MMF for distances up to 550 m (1804 feet).

- **1000BASE-LX/LH**—Long-wavelength/long-haul connectivity using SC fiber connectors and either MMF or single-mode fiber (SMF); MMF can be used for distances up to 550 m (1804 feet), and SMF can be used for distances up to 10 km (32,810 feet). MMF requires a special mode-conditioning cable for fiber distances less than 100 m (328 feet) or greater than 300 m (984 feet). This keeps the GBIC from overdriving the far-end receiver on a short cable and lessens the effect of differential mode delay on a long cable.

- **1000BASE-ZX**—Extended-distance connectivity using SC fiber connectors and SMF; works for distances up to 70 km, and even to 100 km when used with premium-grade SMF.

■ **GigaStack**—Uses a proprietary connector with a high-data-rate copper cable with enhanced signal integrity and electromagnetic interference (EMI) performance; provides a GBIC-to-GBIC connection between stacking Catalyst switches or between any two Gigabit switch ports over a short distance. The connection is full duplex if only one of the two stacking connectors is used; if both connectors are used, they each become half duplex over a shared bus.

■ **1000BASE-T**—Sports an RJ-45 connector for four-pair UTP cabling; works for distances up to 100 m (328 feet).

> **NOTE** You must use a four-pair Category 5 UTP crossover cable to connect two 1000BASE-T switch ports back to back. In this case, RJ-45 pins 1,2, 3,6, 4,5, and 7,8 are still twisted pairs on one end, connecting to pins 3,6, 1,2, 7,8, and 4,5 respectively on the other end.

> **CAUTION** The fiber-based modules always have the receive fiber on the left connector and the transmit fiber on the right connector, as you face the connectors. These modules could produce invisible laser radiation from the transmit connector. Therefore, always keep unused connectors covered with the rubber plugs, and don't ever look directly into the connectors.

Switch Port Configuration

You can configure the individual ports on a switch with various information and settings, as detailed in the following sections.

Selecting Ports to Configure

Before you can modify port settings, you must select one or more switch ports. Catalyst switches running the Catalyst operating system (CatOS) refer to these as *ports*, whereas switches running the Cisco IOS Software refer to them as *interfaces*. The BCMSN exam is based on IOS-based switches only.

To select a single switch port, enter the following command in global configuration mode:

```
Switch(config)# interface type module/number
```

The port is identified by its Ethernet type (**fastethernet**, **gigabitethernet**, **tengigabitethernet**, or **vlan**), the physical module or "blade" where it is located, and the port number within the module. Some switches, such as the Catalyst 2950 and 3550, don't have multiple modules. For those models, ports have a module number of 0 (zero). As an example, the FastEthernet 0/14 interface is selected for configuration using the following command:

```
Switch(config)# interface fastethernet 0/14
```

The Catalyst 3750 is also a fixed-configuration switch, but it can be stacked with other switches in the 3750 family. Interfaces are referenced by module and port number, where the module number represents the switch position in the stack. For example, port 24 on the switch at position 2 in the stack would be referenced as FastEthernet 2/24.

Naturally, you can select and configure multiple interfaces in this fashion, one at a time. If you need to make many configuration changes for each interface, however, this can get very tedious. The Catalyst IOS Software also allows multiple interfaces to be selected in a single pass, through the **interface range** configuration command. After you select the range, any interface configuration commands entered are applied to each of the interfaces in the range.

To select several arbitrary ports for a common configuration setting, you can identify them as a "range" entered as a list. Port numbers and the commas that separate them all must be separated with spaces. Use the following command in global configuration mode:

```
Switch(config)# interface range type module/number [, type module/number ...]
```

For example, to select interfaces FastEthernet 0/3, 0/7, 0/9, and 0/48 for configuration, you could use this command:

```
Switch(config)# interface range fastethernet 0/3 , fastethernet 0/7 , fastethernet
  0/9 , fastethernet 0/48
```

You also can select a continuous range of ports, from a beginning interface to an ending interface. Enter the interface type and module, followed by the beginning and ending port number separated by a dash with spaces. Use this command in global configuration mode:

```
Switch(config)# interface range type module/first-number - last-number
```

For example, you could select all 48 FastEthernet interfaces on module 1 with the following command:

```
Switch(config)# interface range fastethernet 1/0 - 48
```

Finally, you sometimes need to make configuration changes to several groups or ranges of ports at the same time. You can define a macro that contains a list of interfaces or ranges of interfaces or both. Then, you can invoke the interface-range macro just before configuring the port settings. This applies the port settings to each interface that is identified by the macro. The steps for defining and applying this macro are as follows:

Step 1   Define the macro name and specify as many lists and ranges of interfaces as needed. The command syntax is open ended but follows the list and range syntax of the **interface range** commands defined previously:

```
Switch(config)# define interface-range macro-name type module/number [,
  type module/ number ...] [type module/first-number - last-number] [...]
```

Step 2   Invoke the macro called *macro-name* just as you would with a regular interface, just before entering any interface-configuration commands:

```
Switch(config)# interface range macro macro-name
```

As an example, suppose you need to configure GigabitEthernet 2/1, 2/3 through 2/5, 3/1, 3/10, and 3/32 through 3/48 with a set of identical interface configurations. You could use the following commands to define and apply a macro, respectively:

```
Switch(config)# define interface-range MyGroup gig 2/1 , gig 2/3 - 2/5 , gig 3/1 , gig
  3/10, gig 3/32 - 3/48
Switch(config)# interface range macro MyGroup
```

Remember to surround any commas and hyphens with spaces when you enter interface range commands.

Identifying Ports

You can add a text description to a switch port's configuration to help identify it. This description is meant as a comment field only, as a record of port use or other unique information. The port description is included when displaying the switch configuration and interface information.

To assign a comment or description to a port, enter the following command in interface configuration mode:

```
Switch(config-if)# description description-string
```

The description string can have embedded spaces between words, if needed. To remove a description, use the **no description** interface-configuration command.

As an example, interface FastEthernet 0/11 is labeled with "Printer in Bldg A, room 213":

```
Switch(config)# interface fast 0/11
Switch(config-if)# description Printer in Bldg A, room 213
```

Port Speed

You can assign a specific speed to switch ports through switch-configuration commands. Fast Ethernet 10/100 ports can be set to speeds of 10, 100, and Auto (the default) for autonegotiate mode. Gigabit Ethernet GBIC ports always are set to a speed of 1000, while 1000BASE-T ports can be set to speeds of 10, 100, 1000, and Auto (the default).

NOTE   If a 10/100 or a 10/100/1000 port is assigned a speed of Auto, both its speed and duplex mode will be negotiated.

To specify the port speed on a particular Ethernet port, use the following interface-configuration command:

```
Switch(config-if)# speed {10 | 100 | 1000 | auto}
```

Port Duplex Mode

You also can assign a specific link mode to Ethernet-based switch ports. Therefore, the port operates in half-duplex, full-duplex, or autonegotiated mode. Autonegotiation is allowed only on UTP Fast Ethernet and Gigabit Ethernet ports. In this mode, the port *participates* in a negotiation by attempting full-duplex operation first and then half-duplex operation if full duplex is not successful. The autonegotiation process repeats whenever the link status changes. Be sure to set both ends of a link to the same speed and duplex settings, to eliminate any chance that the two ends will be mismatched.

> **NOTE**   A 10-Mbps Ethernet link (fixed speed) defaults to half duplex, whereas a 100-Mbps Fast Ethernet (dual speed 10/100) link defaults to full duplex. Multispeed links default to autonegotiate the duplex mode.

To set the link mode on a switch port, enter the following command in interface configuration mode:

```
Switch(config-if)# duplex {auto | full | half}
```

For instance, you could use the commands in Example 5-1 to configure 10/100/1000 interfaces GigabitEthernet 3/1 for autonegotiation and 3/2 for 100-Mbps full duplex (no autonegotiation).

Example 5-1   *Configuring the Link Mode on a Switch Port*

```
Switch(config)# interface gig 3/1
Switch(config-if)# speed auto
Switch(config-if)# duplex auto
Switch(config-if)# interface gig 3/2
Switch(config-if)# speed 100
Switch(config-if)# duplex full
```

Managing Error Conditions on a Switch Port

Traditionally, a network-management application was used to detect a serious error condition on a switch port. A switch periodically was polled and switch port error counters were examined to see if an error condition had occurred. If so, an alert was issued so that someone could take action to correct the problem.

Catalyst switches can detect error conditions automatically, without any further help. If a serious error occurs on a switch port, that port can be shut down automatically until someone manually enables the port again, or until a predetermined time has elapsed.

Detecting Error Conditions

By default, a Catalyst switch detects an error condition on every switch port for every possible cause. If an error condition is detected, the switch port is put into the errdisable state and is disabled. You can tune this behavior on a global basis so that only certain causes trigger any port being disabled. Use the following command in global configuration mode, where the **no** keyword is added to disable the specified cause:

```
Switch(config)# [no] errdisable detect cause [all | cause-name]
```

You can repeat this command to enable or disable more than one cause. One of the following causes triggers the errdisable state:

- **all**—Detects every possible cause

- **arp-inspection**—Detects errors with dynamic ARP inspection

- **bpduguard**—Detects when a spanning-tree bridge protocol data unit (BPDU) is received on a port configured for STP portfast

- **channel-misconfig**—Detects an error with an EtherChannel bundle

- **dhcp-rate-limit**—Detects an error with DHCP snooping

- **dtp-flap**—Detects when trunking encapsulation is changing from one type to another

- **gbic-invalid**—Detects the presence of an invalid GBIC or SFP module

- **ilpower**—Detects an error with offering inline power

- **l2ptguard**—Detects an error with Layer 2 Protocol Tunneling

- **link-flap**—Detects when the port link state is "flapping" between the up and down states

- **loopback**—Detects when an interface has been looped back

- **pagp-flap**—Detects when an EtherChannel bundle's ports no longer have consistent configurations

- **psecure-violation**—Detects conditions that trigger port security configured on a port

- **rootguard**—Detects when an STP BPDU is received from the root bridge on an unexpected port

- **security-violation**—Detects errors related to port security

- **storm-control**—Detects when a storm control threshold has been exceeded on a port

- **udld**—Detects when a link is seen to be unidirectional (data passing in only one direction)

- **unicast-flood**—Detects conditions that trigger unicast flood blocking on a port

- **vmps**—Detects errors when assigning a port to a dynamic VLAN through VLAN membership policy server (VMPS)

Automatically Recover from Error Conditions

By default, ports put into the errdisable state must be re-enabled manually. This is done by issuing the **shutdown** command in interface configuration mode, followed by the **no shutdown** command. Before you re-enable a port from the errdisable condition, you always should determine the cause of the problem so that the errdisable condition doesn't occur again.

You can decide to have a switch automatically re-enable an errdisabled port if it is more important to keep the link up until the problem can be resolved. To automatically re-enable an errdisabled port, you first must specify the errdisable causes that can be re-enabled. Use this command in global configuration mode, with a *cause-name* from the preceding list:

```
Switch(config)# errdisable recovery cause [all | cause-name]
```

If any errdisable causes are configured for automatic recovery, the errdisabled port stays down for 300 seconds, by default. To change the recovery timer, use the following command in global configuration mode:

```
Switch(config)# errdisable recovery interval seconds
```

You can set the interval from 30 to 86,400 seconds (24 hours).

As an example, you could use the following commands to configure all switch ports to be re-enabled automatically in 1 hour after a port security violation has been detected:

```
Switch(config)# errdisable recovery cause psecurity-violation
Switch(config)# errdisable recovery interval 3600
```

Remember that the errdisable causes and automatic recovery are configured globally—the settings apply to all switch ports.

Enable and Use the Switch Port

If the port is not enabled or activated automatically, use the **no shutdown** interface-configuration command. To view a port's current speed and duplex state, use the **show interface** command. You can see a brief summary of all interface states with the **show interfaces status** command.

Troubleshooting Port Connectivity

Suppose you are experiencing problems with a switch port. How would you troubleshoot it? The following sections cover a few common troubleshooting techniques.

Looking for the Port State

Use the **show interfaces** EXEC command to see complete information about the switch port. The port's current state is given in the first line of output, as in Example 5-2.

Example 5-2 *Determining Port State Information*

```
Switch# show interfaces fastethernet 0/1
FastEthernet0/1 is up, line protocol is up
  Hardware is Fast Ethernet, address is 0009.b7ee.9801 (bia 0009.b7ee.9801)
  MTU 1500 bytes, BW 100000 Kbit, DLY 100 usec,
     reliability 255/255, txload 1/255, rxload 1/255
```

The first **up** tells the state of the port's physical or data link layer. If this is shown as **down**, the link is physically disconnected or a link cannot be detected. The second state, given as **line protocol is up**, shows the Layer 2 status. If the state is given as **errdisable**, the switch has detected a serious error condition on this port and automatically has disabled it.

To quickly see a list of states for all switch ports, use the **show interface status** EXEC command. Likewise, you can see a list of all ports in the errdisable state (as well as the cause) by using the **show interface status err-disabled** EXEC command.

Looking for Speed and Duplex Mismatches

If a user notices slow response time or low throughput on a 10/100 or 10/100/1000 switch port, the problem could be a mismatch of the port speed or duplex mode between the switch and the host. This is particularly common when one end of the link is set to autonegotiate the link settings and the other end is not.

Use the **show interface** command for a specific interface and look for any error counts that are greater than 0. For example, in the following output in Example 5-3, the switch port is set to autonegotiate the speed and duplex mode. It has decided on 100 Mbps at half duplex. Notice that there are many *runts* (packets that were truncated before they were fully received) and input errors. These are symptoms that a setting mismatch exists between the two ends of the link.

Example 5-3 *Determining Link Speed and Duplex Mode*

```
Switch# show interfaces fastethernet 0/13
FastEthernet0/13 is up, line protocol is up
  Hardware is Fast Ethernet, address is 00d0.589c.3e8d (bia 00d0.589c.3e8d)
  MTU 1500 bytes, BW 10000 Kbit, DLY 1000 usec,
     reliability 255/255, txload 2/255, rxload 1/255
  Encapsulation ARPA, loopback not set
  Keepalive not set
 Auto-duplex (Half), Auto Speed (100), 100BASETX/FX  ARP type: ARPA, ARP
     Timeout 04:00:00
Last input never, output 00:00:01, output hang never
 Last clearing of "show interface" counters never
 Queueing strategy: fifo
 Output queue 0/40, 0 drops; input queue 0/75, 0 drops
 5 minute input rate 0 bits/sec, 0 packets/sec
 5 minute output rate 81000 bits/sec, 49 packets/sec
    500867 packets input, 89215950 bytes
    Received 12912 broadcasts, 374879 runts, 0 giants, 0 throttles
    374879 input errors, 0 CRC, 0 frame, 0 overrun, 0 ignored
    0 watchdog, 0 multicast
    0 input packets with dribble condition detected
    89672388 packets output, 2205443729 bytes, 0 underruns
    0 output errors, 0 collisions, 3 interface resets
    0 babbles, 0 late collision, 0 deferred
    0 lost carrier, 0 no carrier
    0 output buffer failures, 0 output buffers swapped out
```

Because this port is autonegotiating the link speed, it must have detected an electrical signal that indicated 100 Mbps in common with the host. However, the host most likely was configured for 100 Mbps at full duplex (not autonegotiating). The switch was incapable of exchanging duplex information, so it fell back to its default of half duplex. Again, always make sure both ends of a connection are set to the same speed and duplex.

Foundation Summary

The Foundation Summary is a collection of tables that provides a convenient review of many key concepts in this chapter. If you are already comfortable with the topics in this chapter, this summary might help you recall a few details. If you just read this chapter, this review should help solidify some key facts. If you are doing your final prep before the exam, the following tables are a convenient way to review the day before the exam.

Table 5-6 *Ethernet Standards*

Ethernet Type	Media Name	Standard Name
10-Mbps Ethernet	10BASE-X	IEEE 802.3
Fast Ethernet	100BASE-X	IEEE 802.3u
Gigabit Ethernet	1000BASE-X	IEEE 802.3z (fiber) IEEE 802.3ab (UTP)
10-Gigabit Ethernet	10GBASE-X	IEEE 802.3ae

Table 5-7 *Ethernet Cabling Specifications*

Technology	Wiring Type	Pairs	Cable Length
10BASE-T	EIA/TIA Category 5 UTP	2	100 m
100BASE-TX	EIA/TIA Category 5 UTP	2	100 m
100BASE-T2	EIA/TIA Category 3, 4, 5 UTP	2	100 m
100BASE-T4	EIA/TIA Category 3, 4, 5 UTP	4	100 m
100BASE-FX	Multimode fiber (MMF); 62.5-micron core, 125-micron outer cladding (62.5/125)	1	400 m half duplex 2000 m full duplex
	Single-mode fiber (SMF)	1	10 km
1000BASE-CX	Shielded twisted pair (STP)	1	25 m
1000BASE-T	EIA/TIA Category 5 UTP	4	100 m
1000BASE-SX	MMF with 62.5-micron core; 850-nm laser	1	275 m
	MMF with 50-micron core; 850-nm laser	1	550 m

Table 5-7 *Ethernet Cabling Specifications (Continued)*

Technology	Wiring Type	Pairs	Cable Length
1000BASE-LX/LH	MMF with 62.5-micron core; 1300-nm laser	1	550 m
	SMF with 50-micron core; 1300-nm laser	1	550 m
	SMF with 9-micron core; 1300-nm laser	1	10 km
1000BASE-ZX	SMF with 9-micron core; 1550-nm laser	1	70 km
	SMF with 8-micron core; 1550-nm laser	1	100 km
10GBASE-SR/SW (850 nm serial)	MMF: 50 micron	1	66 m
	MMF: 62.5 micron	1	33 m
10GBASE-LR/LW (1310 nm serial)	SMF: 9 micron	1	10 km
10GBASE-ER/EW (1550 nm serial)	SMF: 9 micron	1	40 km
10GBASE-LX4 (1310 nm WWDM)	MMF: 50 micron	1	300 m
	MMF: 62.5 micron	1	300 m
	SMF: 9 micron	1	10 km

Table 5-8 *Switch Port Configuration Commands*

Task	Command Syntax
Select a port	**interface** type module/number
Select multiple ports	**interface range** type module/number [, type module/ number ...] or **interface range** type module/first-number – last-number
Define an interface macro	**define interface-range** macro-name type module/number [, type module/number ...] [type module/first-number – last-number] [...] **interface range macro** macro-name
Identify port	**description** description-string

continues

Table 5-8 *Switch Port Configuration Commands (Continued)*

Task	Command Syntax
Set port speed	**speed {10 ❙ 100 ❙ 1000 ❙ auto}**
Set port mode	**duplex {auto ❙ full ❙ half}**
Detect port error conditions	**errdisable detect cause** [**all** ❙ *cause-name*]
Automatically recover from errdisable	**errdisable recovery cause** [**all** ❙ *cause-name*] **errdisable recovery interval** *seconds*
Manually recover from errdisable	**shutdown** **no shutdown**

Q&A

The questions and scenarios in this book are more difficult than what you should experience on the actual exam. The questions do not attempt to cover more breadth or depth than the exam; however, they are designed to make sure that you know the answer. Rather than allowing you to derive the answers from clues hidden inside the questions themselves, the questions challenge your understanding and recall of the subject. Hopefully, these questions will help limit the number of exam questions on which you narrow your choices to two options and then guess.

You can find the answers to these questions in Appendix A.

1. Put the following Ethernet standards in order of increasing bandwidth:

   a. 802.3z

   b. 802.3ae

   c. 802.3

   d. 802.3u

2. What benefits does switched Ethernet have over shared Ethernet?

3. When a 10/100 Ethernet link is autonegotiating, which will be chosen if both stations can support the same capabilities—10BASE-T full duplex, 100BASE-TX half duplex, or 100BASE-TX full duplex?

4. How many pairs of copper wires does a 1000BASE-T connection need?

5. A switch port is being configured as shown here. What command is needed next to set the port to full-duplex mode?

   ```
   Switch(config)# interface fastethernet 0/13
   Switch(config-if)#
   ```

6. If a full-duplex Gigabit Ethernet connection offers 2 Gbps throughput, can a single host send data at 2 Gbps?

7. Which GBIC would you use for a connection over multimode fiber (MMF)?

8. A Category 5 cable having only pins 1,2 and 3,6 has been installed and used for a Fast Ethernet link. Can this same cable be used for a migration to Gigabit Ethernet using 1000BASE-T GBICs, assuming that the length is less than 100 m?

9. A Catalyst 3560 switch port has been configured for 100 Mbps full-duplex mode, but a link cannot be established. What are some commands that you could use to investigate and correct the problem?

10. The 10-Gigabit Ethernet is backward-compatible with other forms of Ethernet at Layer _____ but not at Layer _____.

11. What one switch command will select Fast Ethernet interfaces 4/1 through 48 for a common configuration?

12. What is the purpose of a GBIC?

13. Suppose you need to apply several different common configurations to Fast Ethernet interfaces 3/1 through 12, 3/34, 3/48, and 5/14 through 48. What commands are needed to create an interface macro to accomplish this, and what command would apply the macro?

14. If a switch port is configured with the **speed 100** and **duplex full** commands, what will happen if the PC connected to it is set for autonegotiated speed and duplex? Now reverse the roles. (The switch will autonegotiate, but the PC won't.) What will happen?

15. By default, what will a switch do if one of its ports has a serious error condition, and how can you tell when this has happened?

16. What port speeds can you assign to a UTP Gigabit Ethernet switch port? Consider both 1000BASE-T GBIC and native RJ-45 copper switch module ports.

17. What command can you use to make sure that no switch ports automatically are shut down in an errdisable state for any reason?

18. Suppose you commonly find that switch ports are being shut down in errdisable because users are making their connections go up and down too often. Thinking that this might be the result of odd PC behavior, you would like to visit each user to troubleshoot the problem; however, this is a minor error and you don't want to inconvenience the end users too much. What commands can you use to have the switch automatically re-enable the ports after 10 minutes? Make sure a flapping link will be recovered automatically in this time frame.

19.   Look at the following **show interfaces** output. Does the high number of collisions indicate a problem? Why or why not?

```
FastEthernet0/6 is up, line protocol is up
  Hardware is Fast Ethernet, address is 000a.f4d2.5506 (bia 000a.f4d2.5506)
  Description: Front Office PC
  MTU 1500 bytes, BW 10000 Kbit, DLY 1000 usec,
     reliability 255/255, txload 1/255, rxload 1/255
  Encapsulation ARPA, loopback not set
  Keepalive set (10 sec)
  Half-duplex, 10Mb/s
  input flow-control is off, output flow-control is off
  ARP type: ARPA, ARP Timeout 04:00:00
  Last input never, output 00:00:00, output hang never
  Last clearing of "show interface" counters never
  Input queue: 0/75/0/0 (size/max/drops/flushes); Total output drops: 0
  Queueing strategy: fifo
  Output queue :0/40 (size/max)
  5 minute input rate 0 bits/sec, 0 packets/sec
  5 minute output rate 0 bits/sec, 0 packets/sec
     1321140 packets input, 227738894 bytes, 0 no buffer
     Received 13786 broadcasts, 0 runts, 0 giants, 0 throttles
     1 input errors, 1 CRC, 0 frame, 0 overrun, 0 ignored
     0 watchdog, 42 multicast, 0 pause input
     0 input packets with dribble condition detected
     87798820 packets output, 2662785561 bytes, 1316 underruns
     6 output errors, 406870 collisions, 3 interface resets
     0 babbles, 0 late collision, 19458 deferred
     0 lost carrier, 0 no carrier, 0 PAUSE output
     1316 output buffer failures, 0 output buffers swapped out
```

This chapter covers the following topics that you need to master for the CCNP BCMSN exam:

- **Virtual LANs**—This section reviews VLANs, VLAN membership, and VLAN configuration on a Catalyst switch.

- **VLAN Trunks**—This section covers transporting multiple VLANs over single links and VLAN trunking with Ethernet.

- **VLAN Trunk Configuration**—This section outlines the Catalyst switch commands that configure VLAN trunks.

- **Troubleshooting VLANs and Trunks**—This section provides commands to use when a VLAN or trunk is not operating properly.

CHAPTER 6

VLANs and Trunks

Switched campus networks can be broken up into distinct broadcast domains or virtual LANs (VLAN). A flat network topology, or a network with a single broadcast domain, can be simple to implement and manage. However, flat network topology is not scalable. Instead, the campus can be divided into segments using VLANs, while Layer 3 routing protocols manage interVLAN communication.

This chapter details the process of defining common workgroups within a group of switches. It covers switch configuration for VLANs, along with the method of identifying and transporting VLANs on various types of links.

"Do I Know This Already?" Quiz

The purpose of the "Do I Know This Already?" quiz is to help you decide whether you need to read the entire chapter. If you already intend to read the entire chapter, you do not necessarily need to answer these questions now.

The 12-question quiz, derived from the major sections in the "Foundation Topics" portion of the chapter, helps you determine how to spend your limited study time.

Table 6-1 outlines the major topics discussed in this chapter and the "Do I Know This Already?" quiz questions that correspond to those topics.

Table 6-1   *"Do I Know This Already?" Foundation Topics Section-to-Question Mapping*

Foundation Topics Section	Questions Covered in This Section	Score
Virtual LANs	1–4	
VLAN Trunks	5–12	
VLAN Trunk Configuration		
Total Score		

CAUTION   The goal of self-assessment is to gauge your mastery of the topics in this chapter. If you do not know the answer to a question or are only partially sure of the answer, you should mark this question wrong. Giving yourself credit for an answer you correctly guess skews your self-assessment results and might give you a false sense of security.

1. A VLAN is which of the following?

    a. Collision domain

    b. Spanning-tree domain

    c. Broadcast domain

    d. VTP domain

2. Switches provide VLAN connectivity at which layer of the OSI model?

    a. Layer 1

    b. Layer 2

    c. Layer 3

    d. Layer 4

3. Which one of the following is needed to pass data between two PCs, each connected to a different VLAN?

    a. Layer 2 switch

    b. Layer 3 switch

    c. Trunk

    d. Tunnel

4. Which Catalyst IOS switch command is used to assign a port to a VLAN?

    a. **access vlan** *vlan-id*

    b. **switchport access vlan** *vlan-id*

    c. **vlan** *vlan-id*

    d. **set port vlan** *vlan-id*

5. Which of the following is a standardized method of trunk encapsulation?

    a. 802.1d

    b. 802.1Q

    c. 802.3z

    d. 802.1a

6. What is the Cisco proprietary method for trunk encapsulation?

   a. CDP

   b. EIGRP

   c. ISL

   d. DSL

7. Which of these protocols dynamically negotiates trunking parameters?

   a. PAgP

   b. STP

   c. CDP

   d. DTP

8. How many different VLANs can an 802.1Q trunk support?

   a. 256

   b. 1024

   c. 4096

   d. 32,768

   e. 65,536

9. Which of the following incorrectly describes a native VLAN?

   a. Frames are untagged on an 802.1Q trunk.

   b. Frames are untagged on an ISL trunk.

   c. Frames can be interpreted by a nontrunking host.

   d. The native VLAN can be configured for each trunking port.

10. If two switches each support all types of trunk encapsulation on a link between them, which one will be negotiated?

   a. ISL

   b. 802.1Q

   c. DTP

   d. VTP

11. Which VLANs are allowed on a trunk link by default?

   a. None

   b. Only the native VLAN

   c. All active VLANs

   d. Only negotiated VLANs

12.   Which command configures a switch port to form a trunk without using negotiation?

a. **switch mode trunk**

b. **switch mode trunk nonegotiate**

c. **switch mode dynamic auto**

d. **switch mode dynamic desirable**

The answers to the quiz are found in Appendix A, "Answers to Chapter 'Do I Know This Already?' Quizzes and Q&A Sections." The suggested choices for your next step are as follows:

■   **6 or less overall score**—Read the entire chapter. This includes the "Foundation Topics," "Foundation Summary," and "Q&A" sections.

■   **7–9 overall score**—Begin with the "Foundation Summary" section and then follow with the "Q&A" section at the end of the chapter.

■   **10 or more overall score**—If you want more review on these topics, skip to the "Foundation Summary" section and then go to the "Q&A" section at the end of the chapter. Otherwise, move on to Chapter 7, "VLAN Trunking Protocol."

Foundation Topics

Virtual LANs

Consider a network design that consists of Layer 2 devices only. For example, this design could be a single Ethernet segment, an Ethernet switch with many ports, or a network with several interconnected Ethernet switches. A full Layer 2–only switched network is referred to as a *flat network topology*. A flat network is a single broadcast domain, such that every connected device sees every broadcast packet that is transmitted. As the number of stations on the network increases, so does the number of broadcasts.

Because of the Layer 2 foundation, flat networks cannot contain redundant paths for load balancing or fault tolerance. The reason for this is explained in Chapters 9, "Traditional Spanning Tree Protocol," through 12, "Advanced Spanning Tree Protocol." To gain any advantage from additional paths to a destination, Layer 3 routing functions must be introduced.

A switched environment offers the technology to overcome flat network limitations. Switched networks can be subdivided into VLANs. By definition, a VLAN is a single broadcast domain. All devices connected to the VLAN receive broadcasts sent by any other VLAN members. However, devices connected to a different VLAN will not receive those same broadcasts. (Naturally, VLAN members also receive unicast packets directed toward them from other VLAN members.)

A VLAN consists of hosts defined as members, communicating as a *logical* network segment. In contrast, a physical segment consists of devices that must be connected to a physical cable segment. A VLAN can have connected members located anywhere in the campus network, as long as VLAN connectivity is provided among all members. Layer 2 switches are configured with a VLAN mapping and provide the logical connectivity among the VLAN members.

Figure 6-1 shows how a VLAN can provide logical connectivity between switch ports. Two workstations on the left Catalyst switch are assigned to VLAN 1, while a third workstation is assigned to VLAN 100. In this example, no communication can occur between VLAN 1 and VLAN 100. Both ends of the link between the Catalysts are assigned to VLAN 1. One workstation on the right Catalyst also is assigned to VLAN 1. Because there is end-to-end connectivity of VLAN 1, any of the workstations on VLAN 1 can communicate as if they were connected to a physical network segment.

Figure 6-1 *VLAN Functionality*

VLAN Membership

When a VLAN is provided at an access-layer switch, an end user must have some means of gaining membership to it. Two membership methods exist on Cisco Catalyst switches:

■ Static VLAN configuration

■ Dynamic VLAN assignment

Static VLANs

Static VLANs offer *port-based* membership, in which switch ports are assigned to specific VLANs. End-user devices become members in a VLAN based on the physical switch port to which they are connected. No handshaking or unique VLAN membership protocol is needed for the end devices; they automatically assume VLAN connectivity when they connect to a port. Normally, the end device is not even aware that the VLAN exists. The switch port and its VLAN simply are viewed and used as any other network segment, with other "locally attached" members on the wire.

Switch ports are assigned to VLANs by the manual intervention of the network administrator, hence the static nature. Each port receives a Port VLAN ID (PVID) that associates it with a VLAN number. The ports on a single switch can be assigned and grouped into many VLANs. Even though two devices are connected to the same switch, traffic will not pass between them if they are connected to ports on different VLANs. To perform this function, you could use either a Layer 3 device to route packets or an external Layer 2 device to bridge packets between the two VLANs.

The static port-to-VLAN membership normally is handled in hardware with application-specific integrated circuits (ASIC) in the switch. This membership provides good performance because all port mappings are done at the hardware level, with no complex table lookups needed.

Configuring Static VLANs

This section describes the switch commands needed to configure static VLANs. By default, all switch ports are assigned to VLAN 1, are set to be a VLAN type of Ethernet, and have a maximum transmission unit (MTU) size of 1500 bytes.

First, the VLAN must be created on the switch, if it does not already exist. Then, the VLAN must be assigned to specific switch ports. VLANs always are referenced by a VLAN number, which can range from 1 to 1005. VLANs 1 and 1002 through 1005 automatically are created and are set aside for special uses. For example, VLAN 1 is the default VLAN for every switch port. VLANs 1002 to 1005 are reserved for legacy functions related to Token Ring and FDDI switching.

Catalyst IOS switches also can support extended-range VLANs, in which the VLAN number can be 1 to 4094, for compatibility with the IEEE 802.1Q standard. The extended range is enabled only when the switch is configured for VTP transparent mode with the **vtp mode transparent** global configuration command. This is because of limitations with VTP versions 1 and 2. VTP version 3 does allow extended range VLANs to be used and advertised, but this version is not available in any IOS-based Catalyst switches at press time. (VTP is covered in Chapter 7).

> **TIP**   Although the extended range of VLAN numbers enables you to support more VLANs in your network, some limitations exist. For example, a switch normally maintains VLAN definitions in a special database file, separate from the switch configuration. The VLAN Trunking Protocol (VTP) uses the VLAN database so that VLAN definitions can be advertised and shared between switches over trunk links. When extended-range VLANs are created, they are not stored in the VLAN database file.
>
> Why does this matter? As long as the switch remains in VTP transparent mode, the extended VLANs can be used. However, if the switch later is configured to participate in VTP as either a server or a client, you must manually delete the extended VLANs. For any switch ports that were assigned to the extended VLANs, you also must reconfigure them for VLAN membership within the normal VLAN range.

To configure static VLANs, you first can define the VLAN with the following command in global configuration mode:

```
Switch(config)# vlan vlan-num
Switch(config-vlan)# name vlan-name
```

The VLAN numbered *vlan-num* immediately is created and stored in the database, along with a descriptive text string defined by *vlan-name* (up to 32 characters with no embedded spaces). The **name** command is optional; if it is not used, the default VLAN name is of the form **VLAN***XXX*, where *XXX* represents the VLAN number. If you need to include spaces to separate words in the VLAN name, use underscore characters instead.

As an example, you can use the following commands to create VLANs 2 and 101:

```
Switch(config)# vlan 2
Switch(config-vlan)# name Engineering
Switch(config-vlan)# vlan 101
Switch(config-vlan)# name Marketing
```

To delete a VLAN from the switch configuration, you can use the **no vlan** *vlan-num* command.

Next, you should assign one or more switch ports to the VLAN. Use the following configuration commands:

```
Switch(config)# interface type module/number
Switch(config-if)# switchport
Switch(config-if)# switchport mode access
Switch(config-if)# switchport access vlan vlan-num
```

The initial **switchport** command configures the port for Layer 2 operation. By default, every Catalyst IOS switch port is ready for Layer 3 operation, something that doesn't coexist with Layer 2 VLANs.

The **switchport mode access** command forces the port to be assigned to only a single VLAN, providing VLAN connectivity to the access layer or end user. The port is given a static VLAN membership by the **switchport access vlan** command. Here, the logical VLAN is referenced by the *vlan-num* setting (1 to 1005 or 1 to 4094).

To verify VLAN configuration, use the **show vlan** command to output a list of all VLANs defined in the switch, along with the ports that are assigned to each VLAN. Example 6-1 shows some sample output from the **show vlan** command.

Example 6-1 *Verifying VLAN Configuration with **show vlan** Command*

```
Switch# show vlan
VLAN Name                             Status    Ports
---- -------------------------------- --------- -------------------------------
1    default                          active    Gi1/1, Gi1/2, Gi3/20, Gi4/20
2    Engineering                      active    Gi4/2, Gi4/3, Gi4/4, Gi4/5
```

Example 6-1 *Verifying VLAN Configuration with **show vlan** Command (Continued)*

```
                                        Gi4/6, Gi4/7, Gi4/8, Gi4/9
                                        Gi4/10, Gi4/11, Gi4/12
101  Marketing                 active   Gi2/5, Gi2/6, Gi2/7, Gi2/8
                                        Gi2/9, Gi2/10, Gi2/11, Gi2/12
                                        Gi2/13, Gi2/14, Gi2/15, Gi2/16
                                        Gi2/17, Gi2/18
```

Dynamic VLANs

Dynamic VLANs provide membership based on the MAC address of an end-user device. When a device is connected to a switch port, the switch must, in effect, query a database to establish VLAN membership. A network administrator also must assign the user's MAC address to a VLAN in the database of a VLAN Membership Policy Server (VMPS).

With Cisco switches, dynamic VLANs are created and managed using network-management tools such as CiscoWorks 2000. Dynamic VLANs allow a great deal of flexibility and mobility for end users but require more administrative overhead.

> **NOTE**   Dynamic VLANs are not covered in this text or in the BCMSN course or exam (at press time). For more information, refer to "Configuring VMPS" at http://www.cisco.com/univercd/cc/td/doc/product/lan/c3550/12112cea/3550scg/swvlan.htm#xtocid35.

Deploying VLANs

To implement VLANs, you must consider the number of VLANs you need and how best to place them. As usual, the number of VLANs depends on traffic patterns, application types, segmentation of common workgroups, and network-management requirements.

An important factor to consider is the relationship between VLANs and the IP addressing schemes used. Cisco recommends a one-to-one correspondence between VLANs and IP subnets. This recommendation means that if a subnet with a 24-bit mask (255.255.255.0) is used for a VLAN, no more than 254 devices should be in the VLAN. In addition, you should not allow VLANs to extend beyond the Layer 2 domain of the distribution switch. In other words, the VLAN should not reach across a network's core and into another switch block. The idea again is to keep broadcasts and unnecessary traffic movement out of the core block.

VLANs can be scaled in the switch block by using two basic methods:

- End-to-end VLANs

- Local VLANs

End-to-End VLANs

End-to-end VLANs, also called *campus-wide VLANs*, span the entire switch fabric of a network. They are positioned to support maximum flexibility and mobility of end devices. Users can be assigned to VLANs regardless of their physical location. As a user moves around the campus, that user's VLAN membership stays the same. This means that each VLAN must be made available at the access layer in every switch block.

End-to-end VLANs should group users according to common requirements. All users in a VLAN should have roughly the same traffic flow patterns, following the 80/20 rule. Recall that this rule estimates that 80 percent of user traffic stays within the local workgroup, while 20 percent is destined for a remote resource in the campus network. Although only 20 percent of the traffic in a VLAN is expected to cross the network core, end-to-end VLANs make it possible for 100 percent of the traffic within a single VLAN to cross the core.

Because all VLANs must be available at each access-layer switch, VLAN trunking must be used to carry all VLANs between the access- and distribution-layer switches.

> **TIP** End-to-end VLANs are not recommended in an enterprise network, unless there is a good reason. In an end-to-end VLAN, broadcast traffic is carried over from one end of the network to the other, creating the possibility for a broadcast storm or Layer 2 bridging loop to spread across the whole extent of a VLAN. This can exhaust the bandwidth of distribution- and core-layer links, as well as switch CPU resources. Now the storm or loop has disrupted users on the end-to-end VLAN, in addition to users on other VLANs that might be crossing the core.
>
> When such a problem occurs, troubleshooting becomes more difficult. In other words, the risks of end-to-end VLANs outweigh the convenience and benefits.

Local VLANs

Because most enterprise networks have moved toward the 20/80 rule (where server and intranet/Internet resources are centralized), end-to-end VLANs have become cumbersome and difficult to maintain. The 20/80 rule reverses the traffic pattern of the end-to-end VLAN: Only 20 percent of traffic is local, while 80 percent is destined to a remote resource across the core layer. End users usually require access to central resources outside their VLAN. Users must cross into the network core more frequently. In this type of network, VLANs should be designed to contain user communities based on geographic boundaries, with little regard to the amount of traffic leaving the VLAN.

Local or geographic VLANs range in size from a single switch in a wiring closet to an entire building. Arranging VLANs in this fashion enables the Layer 3 function in the campus network to intelligently handle the interVLAN traffic loads, where traffic passes into the core. This scenario provides maximum availability by using multiple paths to destinations, maximum scalability by keeping the VLAN within a switch block, and maximum manageability.

VLAN Trunks

At the access layer, end-user devices connect to switch ports that provide simple connectivity to a single VLAN each. The attached devices are unaware of any VLAN structure and simply attach to what appears to be a normal physical network segment. Remember, sending information from an access link on one VLAN to another VLAN is not possible without the intervention of an additional device—either a Layer 3 router or an external Layer 2 bridge.

Note that a single switch port can support more than one IP subnet for the devices attached to it. For example, consider a shared Ethernet hub that is connected to a single Ethernet switch port. One user device on the hub might be configured for 192.168.1.1 255.255.255.0, while another is assigned 192.168.17.1 255.255.255.0. Although these subnets are discontiguous and unique, and both are communicating on one switch port, they cannot be considered separate VLANs. The switch port supports one VLAN, but multiple subnets can exist on that single VLAN.

A *trunk link*, however, can transport more than one VLAN through a single switch port. Trunk links are most beneficial when switches are connected to other switches or switches are connected to routers. A trunk link is not assigned to a specific VLAN. Instead, one, many, or all active VLANs can be transported between switches using a single physical trunk link.

Connecting two switches with separate physical links for each VLAN is possible. The top half of Figure 6-2 shows how two switches might be connected in this fashion.

Figure 6-2 *Passing VLAN Traffic Using Single Links Versus Trunk Links*

As VLANs are added to a network, the number of links can grow quickly. A more efficient use of physical interfaces and cabling involves the use of trunking. The bottom half of the figure shows how one trunk link can replace many individual VLAN links.

Cisco supports trunking on both Fast Ethernet and Gigabit Ethernet switch links, as well as aggregated Fast and Gigabit EtherChannel links. To distinguish between traffic belonging to different VLANs on a trunk link, the switch must have a method of identifying each frame with the appropriate VLAN. In fact, the switches on *each end* of a trunk link both must have the same method for correlating frames with VLAN numbers. The next section covers several available identification methods.

VLAN Frame Identification

Because a trunk link can transport many VLANs, a switch must identify frames with their respective VLANs as they are sent and received over a trunk link. Frame identification, or *tagging*, assigns a unique user-defined ID to each frame transported on a trunk link. Think of this ID as the VLAN number or VLAN "color," as if each VLAN was drawn on a network diagram in a unique color.

VLAN frame identification was developed for switched networks. As each frame is transmitted over a trunk link, a unique identifier is placed in the frame header. As each switch along the way receives these frames, the identifier is examined to determine to which VLAN the frames belong and then is removed.

If frames must be transported out another trunk link, the VLAN identifier is added back into the frame header. Otherwise, if frames are destined out an access (nontrunk) link, the switch removes the VLAN identifier before transmitting the frames to the end station. Therefore, all traces of VLAN association are hidden from the end station.

VLAN identification can be performed using two methods, each using a different frame identifier mechanism:

■   Inter-Switch Link (ISL) protocol

■   IEEE 802.1Q protocol

These methods are described in the sections that follow.

Inter-Switch Link Protocol

The Inter-Switch Link (ISL) protocol is a Cisco-proprietary method for preserving the source VLAN identification of frames passing over a trunk link. ISL performs frame identification in Layer 2 by encapsulating each frame between a header and a trailer. Any Cisco switch or router device configured for ISL can process and understand the ISL VLAN information. ISL primarily is used for Ethernet media, although Cisco has included provisions to carry Token Ring, FDDI, and ATM frames over Ethernet ISL. (A Frame-Type field in the ISL header indicates the source frame type.)

When a frame is destined out a trunk link to another switch or router, ISL adds a 26-byte header and a 4-byte trailer to the frame. The source VLAN is identified with a 15-bit VLAN ID field in the header. The trailer contains a cyclic redundancy check (CRC) value to ensure the data integrity of the new encapsulated frame. Figure 6-3 shows how Ethernet frames are encapsulated and forwarded out a trunk link. Because tagging information is added at the beginning and end of each frame, ISL sometimes is referred to as *double tagging*.

Figure 6-3 *ISL Frame Identification*

If a frame is destined for an access link, the ISL encapsulation (both header and trailer) is not rewritten into the frame before transmission. This removal preserves ISL information only for trunk links and devices that can understand the protocol.

> **TIP** The ISL method of VLAN identification or trunking encapsulation no longer is supported across all Cisco Catalyst switch platforms. Even so, you should still be familiar with it and know how it compares to the standards-based IEEE 802.1Q method.

IEEE 802.1Q Protocol

The IEEE 802.1Q protocol also can carry VLAN associations over trunk links. However, this frame-identification method is standardized, allowing VLAN trunks to exist and operate between equipment from multiple vendors.

In particular, the IEEE 802.1Q standard defines an architecture for VLAN use, services provided with VLANs, and protocols and algorithms used to provide VLAN services. You can find further information about the 802.1Q standard at http://grouper.ieee.org/groups/802/1/pages/802.1Q.html.

As with Cisco ISL, IEEE 802.1Q can be used for VLAN identification with Ethernet trunks. However, instead of encapsulating each frame with a VLAN ID header and trailer, 802.1Q embeds its tagging information within the Layer 2 frame. This method is referred to as *single-tagging* or *internal tagging*.

802.1Q also introduces the concept of a *native VLAN* on a trunk. Frames belonging to this VLAN are *not* encapsulated with any tagging information. If an end station is connected to an 802.1Q trunk link, the end station can receive and understand only the native VLAN frames. This provides a simple way to offer full trunk encapsulation to the devices that can understand it, while giving normal-access stations some inherent connectivity over the trunk.

In an Ethernet frame, 802.1Q adds a 4-byte tag just after the source address field, as shown in Figure 6-4.

Figure 6-4   *IEEE 802.1Q Frame-Tagging Standard*

The first 2 bytes are used as a Tag Protocol Identifier (TPID) and always have a value of 0x8100 to signify an 802.1Q tag. The remaining 2 bytes are used as a Tag Control Information (TCI) field. The TCI information contains a 3-bit Priority field, which is used to implement class-of-service (CoS) functions in the accompanying 802.1Q/802.1p prioritization standard. One bit of the TCI is a Canonical Format Indicator (CFI), flagging whether the MAC addresses are in Ethernet or Token Ring format. (This also is known as *canonical format*, or little-endian or big-endian format.)

The last 12 bits are used as a VLAN Identifier (VID) to indicate the source VLAN for the frame. The VID can have values from 0 to 4095, but VLANs 0, 1, and 4095 are reserved.

Note that both ISL and 802.1Q tagging methods have one implication—they add to the length of an existing Ethernet frame. ISL adds a total of 30 bytes to each frame, whereas 802.1Q adds 4 bytes. Because Ethernet frames cannot exceed 1518 bytes, the additional VLAN tagging information can cause the frame to become too large. Frames that barely exceed the MTU size are called *baby giant frames*. Switches usually report these frames as Ethernet errors or oversize frames.

NOTE   Baby giant, or oversize, frames can exceed the frame size set in various standards. To properly handle and forward them anyway, Catalyst switches use proprietary hardware with the ISL encapsulation method. In the case of 802.1Q encapsulation, switches can comply with the IEEE 802.3ac standard, which extends the maximum frame length to 1522 bytes.

Dynamic Trunking Protocol

You manually can configure trunk links on Catalyst switches for either ISL or 802.1Q mode. In addition, Cisco has implemented a proprietary, point-to-point protocol called *Dynamic Trunking Protocol (DTP)* that negotiates a common trunking mode between two switches. The negotiation covers the encapsulation (ISL or 802.1Q) and whether the link becomes a trunk at all. This allows trunk links to be used without a great deal of manual configuration or administration. The use of DTP is explained in the next section.

> **TIP**   You should disable DTP negotiation if a switch has a trunk link connected to a nontrunking router or firewall interface because those devices cannot participate in DTP negotiation. A trunk link can be negotiated between two switches only if both switches belong to the same VLAN Trunking Protocol (VTP) management domain or if one or both switches have not defined their VTP domain (that is, the NULL domain). VTP is discussed in Chapter 7.
>
> If the two switches are in different VTP domains and trunking is desired between them, you must set the trunk links to on mode or nonegotiate mode. This setting forces the trunk to be established. These options are explained in the next section.

VLAN Trunk Configuration

By default, all switch ports in Layer 2 mode are nontrunking and operate as access links until some intervention changes the mode. Specifically, ports actively try to become trunks as long as the far end agrees. In that case, a common encapsulation is chosen, favoring ISL if both support it. The sections that follow demonstrate the commands necessary to configure VLAN trunks.

VLAN Trunk Configuration

Use the following commands to create a VLAN trunk link:

```
Switch(config)# interface type mod/port
Switch(config-if)# switchport
Switch(config-if)# switchport trunk encapsulation {isl | dot1q | negotiate}
Switch(config-if)# switchport trunk native vlan vlan-id
Switch(config-if)# switchport trunk allowed vlan {vlan-list | all |
  {add | except | remove} vlan-list}
Switch(config-if)# switchport mode {trunk | dynamic {desirable | auto}}
```

A switch port must be in Layer 2 mode before it can support a trunk. To accomplish this, you use the **switchport** command with no other keywords. You then can configure the trunk encapsulation with the **switchport trunk encapsulation** command, as one of the following:

- **isl**—VLANs are tagged by encapsulating each frame using the Cisco ISL protocol.

- **dot1q**—VLANs are tagged in each frame using the IEEE 802.1Q standard protocol. The only exception is the native VLAN, which is sent normally and is not tagged.

- **negotiate** (the default)—The encapsulation is negotiated to select either ISL or IEEE 802.1Q, whichever both ends of the trunk support. If both ends support both types, ISL is favored. (The Catalyst 2950 switch does not support ISL encapsulation.)

In the case of an IEEE 802.1Q trunk, you should configure the native VLAN with the **switchport trunk native vlan** command, identifying the untagged or native VLAN number as *vlan-id* (1 to

4094). By default, an 802.1Q trunk uses VLAN 1 as the native VLAN. In the case of an ISL trunk, using this command has no effect because ISL doesn't support an untagged VLAN.

The last command, **switchport trunk allowed vlan**, defines which VLANs can be trunked over the link. By default, a switch transports all active VLANs (1 to 4094) over a trunk link. An active VLAN is one that has been defined on the switch and has ports assigned to carry it.

There might be times when the trunk link should not carry all VLANs. For example, broadcasts are forwarded to every switch port on a VLAN—including the trunk link because it, too, is a member of the VLAN. If the VLAN does not extend past the far end of the trunk link, propagating broadcasts across the trunk makes no sense.

You can tailor the list of allowed VLANs on the trunk by using the **switchport trunk allowed vlan** command with one of the following:

- *vlan-list*—An explicit list of VLAN numbers, separated by commas or dashes.

- **all**—All active VLANs (1 to 4094) will be allowed.

- **add** *vlan-list*—A list of VLAN numbers will be added to the already configured list; this is a shortcut to keep from typing a long list of numbers.

- **except** *vlan-list*—All VLANs (1 to 4094) will be allowed, except for the VLAN numbers listed; this is a shortcut to keep from typing a long list of numbers.

- **remove** *vlan-list*—A list of VLAN numbers will be removed from the already configured list; this is a shortcut to keep from typing a long list of numbers.

In the **switchport mode** command, you can set the trunking mode to any of the following:

- **trunk**—This setting places the port in permanent trunking mode. DTP is still operational, so if the far-end switch port is configured to trunk, dynamic desirable, or dynamic auto mode, trunking will be negotiated successfully.

  The trunk mode is usually used to establish an unconditional trunk. Therefore, the corresponding switch port at the other end of the trunk should be configured similarly. In this way, both switches always expect the trunk link to be operational without any negotiation. You also should manually configure the encapsulation mode to eliminate its negotiation.

- **dynamic desirable (the default)**—The port actively attempts to convert the link into trunking mode. In other words, it "asks" the far-end switch to bring up a trunk. If the far-end switch port is configured to trunk, dynamic desirable, or dynamic auto mode, trunking is negotiated successfully.

■ **dynamic auto**—The port can be converted into a trunk link, but only if the far-end switch actively requests it. Therefore, if the far-end switch port is configured to trunk or dynamic desirable mode, trunking is negotiated. Because of the passive negotiation behavior, the link never becomes a trunk if both ends of the link are left to the dynamic auto default.

> **TIP** In all these modes, DTP frames are sent out every 30 seconds to keep neighboring switch ports informed of the link's mode. On critical trunk links in a network, manually configuring the trunking mode on both ends is best so that the link never can be negotiated to any other state.
>
> If you decide to configure *both ends* of a trunk link as a fixed trunk (**switchport mode trunk**), you can disable DTP completely so that these frames are not exchanged. To do this, add the **switchport nonegotiate** command to the interface configuration. Be aware that after DTP frames are disabled, no future negotiation is possible until this configuration is reversed.

To view the trunking status on a switch port, use the **show interface** *type mod/port* **trunk** command, as demonstrated in Example 6-2.

Example 6-2 *Determining Switch Port Trunking Status*

```
Switch# show interface gig 2/1 trunk
Port       Mode        Encapsulation  Status       Native vlan
Gi2/1      on          802.1q         trunking     1


Port       Vlans allowed on trunk
Gi2/1      1-4094


Port       Vlans allowed and active in management domain
Gi2/1      1-2,526,539,998,1002-1005


Port       Vlans in spanning tree forwarding state and not pruned
Gi2/1      1-2,526,539,998,1002-1005
```

Trunk Configuration Example

As an example of trunk configuration, consider two switches, Switch-D and Switch-A, which are distribution-layer and access-layer switches, respectively. The two switches are connected by a link between their GigabitEthernet 2/1 interfaces. This link should be configured to be a trunk carrying only VLAN numbers 100 through 105, although more VLANs exist and are used.

The trunk link should use 802.1Q encapsulation, with VLAN 100 as the native VLAN. First, configure Switch-D to actively negotiate a trunk with the far-end switch. You could use the following configuration commands on Switch-D:

```
Switch-D(config)# interface gig 2/1
Switch-D(config-if)# switchport trunk encapsulation dot1q
Switch-D(config-if)# switchport trunk native vlan 100
Switch-D(config-if)# switchport trunk allowed vlan 100-105
Switch-D(config-if)# switchport mode dynamic desirable
```

At this point, you assume that Switch-A is configured correctly, too. Now, you should try to verify that the trunk is working as expected. On Switch-D, you can view the trunk status with the following command:

```
Switch-D# show interface gig 2/1 trunk
Port          Mode          Encapsulation  Status        Native vlan
Gi1/1         desirable     802.1q         not-trunking  100
Port          Vlans allowed on trunk
Gi1/1         100
Port          Vlans allowed and active in management domain
Gi1/1         100
Port          Vlans in spanning tree forwarding state and not pruned
Gi1/1         none
```

To your surprise, the trunk's status is not-trunking. Next, you should verify that the physical link is up:

```
Switch-D# show interface status
Port          Name            Status      Vlan    Duplex  Speed Type
Gi1/1                         notconnect  1       auto    1000  1000BaseSX
Gi1/2                         notconnect  1       auto    1000  1000BaseSX
Gi2/1                         connected   100     full    1000  1000BaseSX
```

What could be preventing the trunk from being established? If Switch-D is in dynamic desirable negotiation mode, it is actively asking Switch-A to bring up a trunk. Obviously, Switch-A must not be in agreement. The desirable mode can negotiate a trunk with all other trunking modes, so Switch-A's interface must not be configured for trunking. Instead, it is most likely configured as an access port (**switchport mode access**).

Switch-A can be corrected by configuring its GigabitEthernet 2/1 interface to negotiate a trunk. Switch-D is in dynamic desirable mode, so Switch-A could use either trunk, dynamic desirable, or dynamic auto mode.

Now, suppose you realize that VLAN 103 should not be passed between these switches. You can use either of the following command sequences to manually prune VLAN 103 from the trunk:

```
Switch-D(config)# interface gig 2/1
Switch-D(config-if)# switchport trunk allowed vlan 100-102,104-105
```

or:

```
Switch-D(config-if)# switchport trunk allowed vlan remove 103
```

In the latter case, the previous range of 100 to 105 is kept in the configuration, and only 103 automatically is removed from the list.

When you manually prune VLANs from being allowed on a trunk, the same operation should be performed at both ends of the trunk link. Otherwise, one of the two switches still could flood broadcasts from that VLAN onto the trunk, using unnecessary bandwidth in only one direction.

For completeness, the configuration of Switch-A at this point would look like the following:

```
Switch-A(config)# interface gig 2/1
Switch-A(config-if)# switchport trunk encapsulation dot1q
Switch-A(config-if)# switchport trunk native vlan 100
Switch-A(config-if)# switchport trunk allowed vlan 100-105
Switch-A(config-if)# switchport trunk allowed vlan remove 103
Switch-A(config-if)# switchport mode dynamic desirable
```

Troubleshooting VLANs and Trunks

Remember that a VLAN is nothing more than a logical network segment that can be spread across many switches. If a PC in one location cannot communicate with a PC in another location, where both are assigned to the same IP subnet, make sure that both of their switch ports are configured for the same VLAN. If they are, examine the path between the two. Is the VLAN carried continuously along the path? If there are trunks along the way, is the VLAN being carried across the trunks?

To verify a VLAN's configuration on a switch, use the **show vlan id** *vlan-id* EXEC command, as demonstrated in Example 6-3. Make sure the VLAN is shown to have an active status and that it has been assigned to the correct switch ports.

Example 6-3   *Verifying Switch VLAN Configuration*

```
Switch# show vlan id 2

VLAN Name                             Status    Ports
---- -------------------------------- --------- ------------------------------
2    Engineering                      active    Gi2/1, Gi2/2, Gi2/3, Gi2/4
                                                Gi4/2, Gi4/3, Gi4/4, Gi4/5
                                                Gi4/6, Gi4/7, Gi4/8, Gi4/9
                                                Gi4/10, Gi4/11, Gi4/12


VLAN Type  SAID       MTU   Parent RingNo BridgeNo Stp  BrdgMode Trans1 Trans2
---- ----- ---------- ----- ------ ------ -------- ---- -------- ------ ------
2    enet  100002     1500  -      -      -        -    -        0      0


Primary Secondary Type              Ports
------- --------- ----------------- ----------------------------------------


Switch#
```

For a trunk, these parameters must be agreeable on both ends before the trunk can operate correctly:

■   Trunking mode (unconditional trunking, negotiated, or nonnegotiated).

■   Trunk encapsulation (ISL, IEEE 802.1Q, or negotiated through DTP).

- Native VLAN. You can bring up a trunk with different native VLANs on each end; however, both switches will log error messages about the mismatch, and the potential exists that traffic will not pass correctly between the two native VLANs.

  The native VLAN mismatch is discovered through the exchange of CDP messages, not through examination of the trunk itself. Also, the native VLAN is configured independently of the trunk encapsulation, so it is possible to have a native VLAN mismatch even if the ports use ISL encapsulation. In this case, the mismatch is only cosmetic and won't cause a trunking problem.

- Allowed VLANs. By default, a trunk allows all VLANs to be transported across it. If one end of the trunk is configured to disallow a VLAN, that VLAN will not be contiguous across the trunk.

To see a comparison of how a switch port is configured for trunking versus its active state, use the **show interface** *type mod/num* **switchport** command, as demonstrated in Example 6-4. Look for the administrative versus operational values, respectively, to see if the trunk is working the way you configured it.

Notice that the port has been configured to negotiate a trunk through DTP (dynamic auto), but the port is operating in the static access (nontrunking) mode. This should tell you that both ends of the link probably are configured for the auto mode so that neither actively will request a trunk.

Example 6-4 *Comparing Switch Port Trunking Configuration and Active State*

```
Switch# show interface fast 0/2 switchport
Name: Fa0/2
Switchport: Enabled
Administrative Mode: dynamic auto
Operational Mode: static access
Administrative Trunking Encapsulation: dot1q
Operational Trunking Encapsulation: native
Negotiation of Trunking: On
Access Mode VLAN: 1 (default)
Trunking Native Mode VLAN: 1 (default)
Administrative private-vlan host-association: none
Administrative private-vlan mapping: none
Operational private-vlan: none
Trunking VLANs Enabled: ALL
Pruning VLANs Enabled: 2-1001

Protected: false
Unknown unicast blocked: disabled
Unknown multicast blocked: disabled

Voice VLAN: none (Inactive)
Appliance trust: none
Switch#
```

For more concise information about a trunking port, you can use the **show interface** [*type mod/num*] **trunk** command, as demonstrated in Example 6-5.

Example 6-5   *Viewing Concise Information About a Trunking Port*

```
Switch# show interface fast 0/2 trunk

Port      Mode         Encapsulation  Status       Native vlan
Fa0/2     auto         802.1q         not-trunking  1

Port      Vlans allowed on trunk
Fa0/2     1

Port      Vlans allowed and active in management domain
Fa0/2     1

Port      Vlans in spanning tree forwarding state and not pruned
Fa0/2     1
Switch#
```

Again, notice that the port is in the auto negotiation mode, but it is currently not-trunking. Because the port is not trunking, only the access VLAN (VLAN 1 in this example) is listed as allowed and active on the trunk.

To see if and how DTP is being used on a switch, use the **show dtp** [**interface** *type mod/num*] command. Specifying an interface shows the DTP activity in greater detail.

Foundation Summary

The Foundation Summary is a collection of tables that provides a convenient review of many key concepts in this chapter. If you are already comfortable with the topics in this chapter, this summary could help you recall a few details. If you just read this chapter, this review should help solidify some key facts. If you are doing your final preparation before the exam, these tables and figures are a convenient way to review the day before the exam.

Table 6-2 *VLAN Trunk Encapsulations*

Encapsulation	Tagging Characteristics
ISL	Adds a 26-byte header and a 4-byte trailer to each frame, and includes a 15-bit VLAN ID
IEEE 802.1Q	Adds a 4-byte tag, includes a 12-bit VLAN ID

Table 6-3 *VLAN and Trunking Configuration Commands*

Task	Command Syntax
Create VLAN	`vlan` *vlan-num* `name` *vlan-name*
Assign port to VLAN	`interface` *type module/number* `switchport mode access` `switchport access vlan` *vlan-num*
Configure trunk	`interface` *type mod/port* `switchport trunk encapsulation {isl	dot1q	negotiate}` `switchport trunk native vlan` *vlan-id* `switchport trunk allowed vlan {`*vlan-list*`	all	{add	except	remove}` *vlan-list*`}` `switchport mode {trunk	dynamic {desirable	auto}}`

Table 6-4 *VLAN and Trunking Troubleshooting Commands*

Task	Command Syntax
Verify VLAN configuration	`show vlan id` *vlan-id*
Verify active trunk parameters	`show interface` *type mod/num* `trunk`
Compare trunk configuration and active parameters	`show interface` *type mod/num* `switchport`
Verify DTP operation	`show dtp [interface` *type mod/num*`]`

Q&A

The questions and scenarios in this book are more difficult than what you should experience on the actual exam. The questions do not attempt to cover more breadth or depth than the exam; however, they are designed to make sure that you know the answers. Instead of allowing you to derive the answers from clues hidden inside the questions themselves, the questions challenge your understanding and recall of the subject. Hopefully, these questions will help limit the number of exam questions on which you narrow your choices to two options and then guess.

The answers to these questions can be found in Appendix A.

1. What is a VLAN? When is it used?

2. When a VLAN is configured on a Catalyst switch port, in how much of the campus network will the VLAN number be unique and significant?

3. Name two types of VLANs in terms of spanning areas of the campus network.

4. What switch commands configure Fast Ethernet port 4/11 for VLAN 2?

5. Generally, what must be configured (both switch and end-user device) for a port-based VLAN?

6. What is the default VLAN on all ports of a Catalyst switch?

7. What is a trunk link?

8. What methods of Ethernet VLAN frame identification can be used on a Catalyst switch trunk?

9. What is the difference between the two trunking methods? How many bytes are added to trunked frames for VLAN identification in each method?

10. What is the purpose of the Dynamic Trunking Protocol (DTP)?

11. What commands are needed to configure a Catalyst switch trunk port Gigabit 3/1 to transport only VLANs 100, 200 through 205, and 300 using IEEE 802.1Q? (Assume that trunking is enabled and active on the port already. Also assume that the **interface gigabit 3/1** command already has been entered.)

12. Two neighboring switch trunk ports are set to the *auto* mode with *ISL* trunking encapsulation mode. What will the resulting trunk mode become?

13. Complete the following command to configure the switch port to use DTP to actively ask the other end to become a trunk:

```
switchport mode _____
```

14. Which command can set the native VLAN of a trunk port to VLAN 100 after the interface has been selected?

15. What command can configure a trunk port to stop sending and receiving DTP packets completely?

16. What command can be used on a Catalyst switch to verify exactly what VLANs will be transported over trunk link gigabitethernet 4/4?

17. Suppose that a switch port is configured with the following commands. A PC with a nontrunking NIC card then is connected to that port. What, if any, traffic will the PC successfully send and receive?

```
interface fastethernet 0/12
switchport trunk encapsulation dot1q
switchport trunk native vlan 10
switchport trunk allowed vlan 1-1005
switchport mode trunk
```

This chapter covers the following topics that you need to master for the CCNP BCMSN exam:

- **VLAN Trunking Protocol**—This section presents Cisco VLAN Trunking Protocol (VTP) for VLAN management in a campus network.

- **VTP Configuration**—This section covers the Catalyst switch commands used to configure VTP.

- **VTP Pruning**—This section details traffic management by pruning within VTP domains, along with the commands needed for configuration.

- **Troubleshooting VTP**—This section gives a brief summary of things to consider and commands to use when VTP is not operating properly.

VLAN Trunking Protocol

When VLANs are defined and used on switches throughout an enterprise or campus network, the administrative overhead easily can increase. Using the VLAN Trunking Protocol (VTP) makes VLAN administration more organized and manageable. This chapter covers VTP and its configuration.

A similar standards-based VLAN-management protocol for IEEE 802.1q trunks is called GARP VLAN Registration Protocol (GVRP). The GARP and GVRP protocols are defined in the IEEE 802.1D and 802.1q (clause 11) standards, respectively. At press time, GVRP was not supported in any of the Cisco IOS Software–based Catalyst switches. Therefore, it is not covered in this text or in the BCMSN course.

"Do I Know This Already?" Quiz

The purpose of the "Do I Know This Already?" quiz is to help you decide whether you need to read the entire chapter. If you already intend to read the entire chapter, you do not necessarily need to answer these questions now.

The 12-question quiz, derived from the major sections in the "Foundation Topics" portion of the chapter, helps you determine how to spend your limited study time.

Table 7-1 outlines the major topics discussed in this chapter and the "Do I Know This Already?" quiz questions that correspond to those topics.

Table 7-1 *"Do I Know This Already?" Foundation Topics Section-to-Question Mapping*

Foundation Topics Section	Questions Covered in This Section	Score
VTP	1–8	
VTP Configuration		
VTP Pruning	9–10	
Troubleshooting VTP	11–12	
Total Score		

> **CAUTION**   The goal of self-assessment is to gauge your mastery of the topics in this chapter. If you do not know the answer to a question or are only partially sure of the answer, you should mark this question wrong. Giving yourself credit for an answer you correctly guess skews your self-assessment results and might give you a false sense of security.

1. Which of the following is not a Catalyst switch VTP mode?

    a. Server

    b. Client

    c. Designated

    d. Transparent

2. A switch in VTP transparent mode can do which one of the following?

    a. Create a new VLAN

    b. Only listen to VTP advertisements

    c. Send its own VTP advertisements

    d. Cannot make VLAN configuration changes

3. Which one of the following is a valid VTP advertisement?

    a. Triggered update

    b. VLAN database

    c. Subset

    d. Domain

4. Which one of the following is needed for VTP communication?

    a. A management VLAN

    b. A trunk link

    c. An access VLAN

    d. An IP address

5. Which one of the following VTP modes does not allow any manual VLAN configuration changes?

    a. Server

    b. Client

    c. Designated

    d. Transparent

6.   Select all the parameters that decide whether to accept new VTP information:

    a. VTP priority

    b. VTP domain name

    c. Configuration revision number

    d. VTP server name

7.   How many VTP management domains can a Catalyst switch participate in?

    a. 1

    b. 2

    c. Unlimited

    d. 4096

8.   Which IOS command configures a Catalyst switch for VTP client mode?

    a. **set vtp mode client**

    b. **vtp client**

    c. **vtp mode client**

    d. **vtp client mode**

9.   What is the purpose of VTP pruning?

    a. Limit the number of VLANs in a domain

    b. Stop unnecessary VTP advertisements

    c. Limit the extent of broadcast traffic

    d. Limit the size of the virtual tree

10.   Which VLAN number is never eligible for VTP pruning?

    a. 0

    b. 1

    c. 1000

    d. 1001

11.   Which of the following might present a VTP problem?

    a. Two or more VTP servers in a domain

    b. Two servers with the same configuration revision number

    c. A server in two domains

    d. A new server with a higher configuration revision number

12. If a VTP server is configured for VTP version 2, what else must happen for successful VTP communication in a domain?

    a. A VTP version 2 password must be set.

    b. All other switches in the domain must be version 2 capable.

    c. All other switches must be configured for VTP version 2.

    d. The VTP configuration revision number must be reset.

The answers to the quiz are found in Appendix A, "Answers to the Chapter 'Do I Know This Already?' Quizzes and Q&A Sections." The suggested choices for your next step are as follows:

- **6 or less overall score**—Read the entire chapter, including the "Foundation Topics," "Foundation Summary," and "Q&A" sections.

- **7–9 overall score**—Begin with the "Foundation Summary" section and then follow with the "Q&A" section at the end of the chapter.

- **10 or more overall score**—If you want more review on these topics, skip to the "Foundation Summary" section and then go to the "Q&A" section at the end of the chapter. Otherwise, move on to Chapter 8, "Aggregating Switch Links."

Foundation Topics

VLAN Trunking Protocol

As the previous chapter demonstrated, VLAN configuration and trunking on a switch or a small group of switches is fairly intuitive. Campus network environments, however, usually consist of many interconnected switches. Configuring and managing a large number of switches, VLANs, and VLAN trunks quickly can get out of control.

Cisco has developed a method to manage VLANs across the campus network. The VLAN Trunking Protocol (VTP) uses Layer 2 trunk frames to communicate VLAN information among a group of switches. VTP manages the addition, deletion, and renaming of VLANs across the network from a central point of control. Any switch participating in a VTP exchange is aware of and can use any VLAN that VTP manages.

VTP Domains

VTP is organized into *management domains,* or areas with common VLAN requirements. A switch can belong to only one VTP domain, in addition to sharing VLAN information with other switches in the domain. Switches in different VTP domains, however, do not share VTP information.

Switches in a VTP domain advertise several attributes to their domain neighbors. Each advertisement contains information about the VTP management domain, VTP revision number, known VLANs, and specific VLAN parameters. When a VLAN is added to a switch in a management domain, other switches are notified of the new VLAN through *VTP advertisements*. In this way, all switches in a domain can prepare to receive traffic on their trunk ports using the new VLAN.

VTP Modes

To participate in a VTP management domain, each switch must be configured to operate in one of several modes. The VTP mode determines how the switch processes and advertises VTP information. You can use the following modes:

- **Server mode**—VTP servers have full control over VLAN creation and modification for their domains. All VTP information is advertised to other switches in the domain, while all received VTP information is synchronized with the other switches. By default, a switch is in VTP server mode. Note that each VTP domain must have at least one server so that VLANs can be created, modified, or deleted, and VLAN information can be propagated.

- **Client mode**—VTP clients do not allow the administrator to create, change, or delete any VLANs. Instead, they listen to VTP advertisements from other switches and modify their VLAN configurations accordingly. In effect, this is a passive listening mode. Received VTP information is forwarded out trunk links to neighboring switches in the domain, so the switch also acts as a VTP relay.

- **Transparent mode**—VTP transparent switches do not participate in VTP. While in transparent mode, a switch does not advertise its own VLAN configuration, and a switch does not synchronize its VLAN database with received advertisements. In VTP version 1, a transparent-mode switch does not even relay VTP information it receives to other switches unless its VTP domain names and VTP version numbers match those of the other switches. In VTP version 2, transparent switches do forward received VTP advertisements out of their trunk ports, acting as VTP relays. This occurs regardless of the VTP domain name setting.

TIP While a switch is in VTP transparent mode, it can create and delete VLANs that are local only to itself. These VLAN changes, however, are *not* propagated to any other switch.

VTP Advertisements

Each Cisco switch participating in VTP advertises VLANs (only VLANs 1 to 1005), revision numbers, and VLAN parameters on its trunk ports to notify other switches in the management domain. VTP advertisements are sent as multicast frames. The switch intercepts frames sent to the VTP multicast address and processes them with its supervisory processor. VTP frames are forwarded out trunk links as a special case.

Because all switches in a management domain learn of new VLAN configuration changes, a VLAN must be created and configured only on one VTP server switch in the domain.

By default, management domains are set to use nonsecure advertisements without a password. You can add a password to set the domain to secure mode. The same password must be configured on every switch in the domain so that all switches exchanging VTP information use identical encryption methods.

The VTP advertisement process starts with configuration revision number 0 (zero). When subsequent changes are made, the revision number is incremented before advertisements are sent. When listening switches (configured as members of the same VTP domain as the advertising switch) receive an advertisement with a greater revision number than is stored locally, the advertisement overwrites any stored VLAN information.

Because of this, it is very important to always force any newly added network switches to have revision number 0 before being attached to the network. The VTP revision number is stored in

NVRAM and is not altered by a power cycle of the switch. Therefore, the revision number can be initialized only to 0 using one of the following methods:

■ Change the switch's VTP mode to transparent and then change the mode back to server.

■ Change the switch's VTP domain to a bogus name (a nonexistent VTP domain), and then change the VTP domain back to the original name.

If the VTP revision number is not reset to 0, the switch might enter the network as a VTP server and have a pre-existing revision number (from a previous life) that is higher than in previous legitimate advertisements. The new switch's VTP information would be seen as more recent, so all other switches in the VTP domain gladly would accept its database of VLANs and overwrite their good VLAN database entries with null or deleted VLAN status information.

In other words, a new server switch inadvertently might cause every other working switch to flush all records of every VLAN in production. This is referred to as a *VTP synchronization problem.*

Advertisements can originate as requests from client-mode switches that want to learn about the VTP database at bootup. Advertisements also cam originate from server-mode switches as VLAN configuration changes occur.

VTP advertisements can occur in three forms:

■ **Summary advertisements**—VTP domain servers send summary advertisements every 300 seconds and every time a VLAN database change occurs. The summary advertisement lists information about the management domain, including VTP version, domain name, configuration revision number, time stamp, MD5 encryption hash code, and the number of subset advertisements to follow. For VLAN configuration changes, summary advertisements are followed by one or more subset advertisements with more specific VLAN configuration data. Figure 7-1 shows the summary advertisement format.

Figure 7-1 *VTP Summary Advertisement Format*

Version (1 byte)	Type (Summary Adv) (1 byte)	Number of subset advertisements to follow (1 byte)	Domain name length (1 byte)
Management Domain Name (zero-padded to 32 bytes)			
Configuration Revision Number (4 bytes)			
Updater Identity (orginating IP address: 4 bytes)			
Update Time Stamp (12 bytes)			
MD5 Digest hash code (16 bytes)			

- **Subset advertisements**—VTP domain servers send subset advertisements after a VLAN configuration change occurs. These advertisements list the specific changes that have been performed, such as creating or deleting a VLAN, suspending or activating a VLAN, changing the name of a VLAN, and changing a VLAN's Maximum Transmission Unit (MTU). Subset advertisements can list the following VLAN parameters: status of the VLAN, VLAN type (such as Ethernet or Token Ring), MTU, length of the VLAN name, VLAN number, Security Association Identifier (SAID) value, and VLAN name. VLANs are listed individually in sequential subset advertisements. Figure 7-2 shows the VTP subset advertisement format.

Figure 7-2 *VTP Subset Advertisement and VLAN Info Field Formats*

VTP Subset Advertisement

0	1	2	3
Version (1 byte)	Type (Subset Adv) (1 byte)	Subset sequence number (1 byte)	Domain name length (1 byte)
Management Domain Name (zero-padded to 32 bytes)			
Configuration Revision Number (4 bytes)			
VLAN Info Field 1 (see below)			
VLAN Info Field ...			
VLAN Info Field N			

VTP VLAN Info Field

0	1	2	3
Info Length	VLAN Status	VLAN Type	VLAN Name Length
VLAN ID		MTU Size	
802.10 SAID			
VLAN Name (padded with zeros to multiple of 4 bytes)			

- **Advertisement requests from clients**—A VTP client can request any VLAN information it lacks. For example, a client switch might be reset and have its VLAN database cleared, and its VTP domain membership might be changed, or it might hear a VTP summary advertisement with a higher revision number than it currently has. After a client advertisement request, the VTP domain servers respond with summary and subset advertisements to bring it up-to-date. Figure 7-3 shows the advertisement request format.

Figure 7-3   *VTP Advertisement Request Format*

0	1	2	3
Version (1 byte)	Type (Adv request) (1 byte)	Reserved (1 byte)	Domain name length (1 byte)
Management Domain Name (zero-padded to 32 bytes)			
Starting advertisement to request			

Catalyst switches in server mode store VTP information separately from the switch configuration in NVRAM. VLAN and VTP data are saved in the vlan.dat file on the switch's Flash memory file system. All VTP information, including the VTP configuration revision number, is retained even when the switch power is off. In this manner, a switch can recover the last known VLAN configuration from its VTP database after it reboots.

VTP Configuration

By default, every switch operates in VTP server mode for the management domain NULL (a blank string), with no password or secure mode. If the switch hears a VTP summary advertisement on a trunk port from any other switch, it automatically learns the VTP domain name, VLANs, and the configuration revision number it hears. This makes it easy to bring up a new switch in an existing VTP domain. However, be aware that the new switch stays in VTP server mode, something that might not be desirable.

> **TIP**   You should get into the habit of double-checking the VTP configuration of any switch before you add it into your network. Make sure the VTP configuration revision number is set to zero. You can do this by isolating the switch from the network, powering it up, and using the **show vtp status** command, as demonstrated in the following output:
>
> ```
> Switch# show vtp status
> VTP Version                    : 2
> Configuration Revision         : 0
> Maximum VLANs supported locally : 1005
> Number of existing VLANs       : 5
> VTP Operating Mode             : Server
> VTP Domain Name                :
> VTP Pruning Mode               : Disabled
> VTP V2 Mode                    : Disabled
> VTP Traps Generation           : Disabled
> MD5 digest                     : 0x57 0xCD 0x40 0x65 0x63 0x59 0x47 0xBD
> Configuration last modified by 0.0.0.0 at 0-0-00 00:00:00
> Local updater ID is 0.0.0.0 (no valid interface found)
> Switch#
> ```

The following sections discuss the commands and considerations that you should use to configure a switch for VTP operation.

You should be aware that there are two supported ways to configure VLAN and VTP information in Catalyst IOS switches:

- Global configuration mode commands (for example, **vlan**, **vtp mode**, and **vtp domain**)

- VLAN database mode commands

The **vlan database** EXEC command still is supported in Catalyst IOS Software only for backward-compatibility, but this is not covered in the BCMSN course or the exam.

Configuring a VTP Management Domain

Before a switch is added into a network, the VTP management domain should be identified. If this switch is the first one on the network, the management domain must be created. Otherwise, the switch might have to join an existing management domain with other existing switches.

You can use the following global configuration command to assign a switch to a management domain, where the *domain-name* is a text string up to 32 characters long:

```
Switch(config)# vtp domain domain-name
```

Configuring the VTP Mode

Next, you need to choose the VTP mode for the new switch. The three VTP modes of operation and their guidelines for use are as follows:

- **Server mode**—Server mode can be used on any switch in a management domain, even if other server and client switches are in use. This mode provides some redundancy in case of a server failure in the domain. Each VTP management domain should have at least one server. The first server defined in a network also defines the management domain that will be used by future VTP servers and clients. Server mode is the default VTP mode and allows VLANs to be created and deleted.

> **NOTE** Multiple VTP servers can coexist in a domain. This usually is recommended for redundancy. The servers do not elect a primary or secondary server; they all simply function as servers. If one server is configured with a new VLAN or VTP parameter, it advertises the changes to the rest of the domain. All other servers synchronize their VTP databases to this advertisement, just as any VTP client would.

■ **Client mode**—If other switches are in the management domain, you should configure a new switch for client mode operation. In this way, the switch is forced to learn any existing VTP information from a reliable existing server. After the switch has learned the current VTP information, you can reconfigure it for server mode if it will be used as a redundant server.

■ **Transparent mode**—This mode is used if a switch will not share VLAN information with any other switch in the network. VLANs still can be created, deleted, and modified on the transparent switch. However, they are not advertised to other neighboring switches. VTP advertisements received by a transparent switch, however, are forwarded to other switches on trunk links.

Keeping switches in transparent mode can eliminate the chance for duplicate, overlapping VLANs in a large network with many network administrators. For example, two administrators might configure VLANs on switches in their respective areas but use the same VLAN identification or VLAN number. Even though the two VLANs have different meanings and purposes, they could overlap if both administrators advertised them using VTP servers.

You can configure the VTP mode with the following sequence of global configuration commands:

```
Switch(config)# vtp mode {server | client | transparent}
Switch(config)# vtp password password
```

If the domain is operating in secure mode, a password also can be defined. The password can be configured only on VTP servers and clients. It builds an MD5 digest that is sent in VTP advertisements (servers) and is used to validate received advertisements (clients). The password is a string of 1 to 32 characters (case-sensitive).

If secure VTP is implemented using passwords, begin by configuring a password on the VTP servers. The client switches retain the last-known VTP information but cannot process received advertisements until the same password is configured on them, too.

Configuring the VTP Version

Two versions of VTP are available for use in a management domain. Catalyst switches are capable of running either VTP version 1 or VTP version 2. Within a management domain, the two versions are not interoperable. Therefore, the same VTP version must be configured on every switch in a domain. VTP version 1 is the default protocol on a switch.

If a switch is capable of running VTP version 2, however, a switch can coexist with other version 1 switches, as long as its VTP version 2 is not enabled. This situation becomes important if you want to use version 2 in a domain. Then only one server mode switch needs to have VTP version

2 enabled. The new version number is propagated to all other version 2–capable switches in the domain, causing them all to automatically enable version 2 for use.

> **TIP** A third version of VTP addresses some of the traditional shortcomings. For example, VTP version 3 supports extended VLAN numbers (1 to 4095) that are compatible with the IEEE 802.1Q trunking standard. At press time, VTPv3 is available only on Cisco Catalyst platforms running the CatOS (non-IOS) operating system. Therefore, only VTP versions 1 and 2 are covered on the BCMSN exam and in this text.

The two versions of VTP differ in the features they support. VTP version 2 offers the following additional features over version 1:

- **Version-dependent transparent mode**—In transparent mode, VTP version 1 matches the VTP version and domain name before forwarding the information to other switches using VTP. VTP version 2 in transparent mode forwards the VTP messages without checking the version number. Because only one domain is supported in a switch, the domain name doesn't have to be checked.

- **Consistency checks**—VTP version 2 performs consistency checks on the VTP and VLAN parameters entered from the command-line interface (CLI) or by the Simple Network Management Protocol (SNMP). This checking helps prevent errors in such things as VLAN names and numbers from being propagated to other switches in the domain. However, no consistency checks are performed on VTP messages that are received on trunk links or on configuration and database data that is read from NVRAM.

- **Token Ring support**—VTP version 2 supports the use of Token Ring switching and Token Ring VLANs. (If Token Ring switching is being used, VTP version 2 must be enabled.)

- **Unrecognized Type-Length-Value (TLV) support**—VTP version 2 switches propagate received configuration change messages out other trunk links, even if the switch supervisor cannot parse or understand the message. For example, a VTP advertisement contains a Type field to denote what type of VTP message is being sent. VTP message type 1 is a summary advertisement, and message type 2 is a subset advertisement. An extension to VTP that utilizes other message types and other message length values could be in use. Instead of dropping the unrecognized VTP message, version 2 still propagates the information and keeps a copy in NVRAM.

The VTP version number is configured using the following global configuration command:

```
Switch(config)# vtp version {1 | 2}
```

By default, a switch uses VTP version 1.

VTP Configuration Example

As an example, a switch is configured as the VTP server in a domain named MyCompany. The domain will use secure VTP with the password **bigsecret**. You can use the following configuration commands to accomplish this:

```
Switch(config)# vtp domain MyCompany
Switch(config)# vtp mode server
Switch(config)# vtp password bigsecret
```

VTP Status

The current VTP parameters for a management domain can be displayed using the **show vtp status** command. Example 7-1 demonstrates some sample output of this command from a switch acting as a VTP client in the VTP domain called CampusDomain.

Example 7-1   **show vtp status** *Reveals VTP Parameters for a Management Domain*

```
Switch# show vtp status
VTP Version                      : 2
Configuration Revision           : 89
Maximum VLANs supported locally  : 1005
Number of existing VLANs         : 74
VTP Operating Mode               : Client
VTP Domain Name                  : CampusDomain
VTP Pruning Mode                 : Enabled
VTP V2 Mode                      : Disabled
VTP Traps Generation             : Disabled
MD5 digest                       : 0x4B 0x07 0x75 0xEC 0xB1 0x3D 0x6F 0x1F
Configuration last modified by 192.168.199.1 at 11-19-02 09:29:56
Switch#
```

VTP message and error counters also can be displayed with the **show vtp counters** command. You can use this command for basic VTP troubleshooting to see if the switch is interacting with other VTP nodes in the domain. Example 7-2 demonstrates some sample output from the **show vtp counters** command.

Example 7-2   **show vtp counters** *Reveals VTP Message and Error Counters*

```
Switch# show vtp counters
VTP statistics:
Summary advertisements received   : 1
Subset advertisements received    : 2
Request advertisements received   : 1
Summary advertisements transmitted : 1630
Subset advertisements transmitted  : 0
Request advertisements transmitted : 4
Number of config revision errors   : 0
```

continues

Example 7-2   show vtp counters *Reveals VTP Message and Error Counters (Continued)*

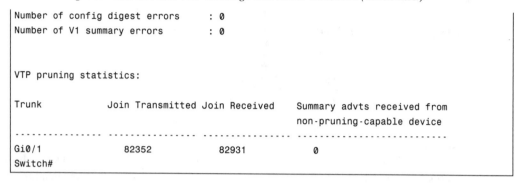

```
Number of config digest errors    : 0
Number of V1 summary errors        : 0


VTP pruning statistics:

Trunk             Join Transmitted  Join Received   Summary advts received from
                                                    non-pruning-capable device
----------------  ----------------  --------------- ---------------------------
Gi0/1                  82352             82931                   0
Switch#
```

VTP Pruning

Recall that, by definition, a switch must forward broadcast frames out all available ports in the broadcast domain because broadcasts are destined everywhere there is a listener. Unless forwarded by more intelligent means, multicast frames follow the same pattern.

In addition, frames destined for an address that the switch has not yet learned or has forgotten (the MAC address has aged out of the address table) must be forwarded out all ports in an attempt to find the destination. These frames are referred to as *unknown unicast.*

When forwarding frames out all ports in a broadcast domain or VLAN, trunk ports are included if they transport that VLAN. By default, a trunk link transports traffic from all VLANs, unless specific VLANs are removed from the trunk. Generally, in a network with several switches, trunk links are enabled between switches, and VTP is used to manage the propagation of VLAN information. This scenario causes the trunk links between switches to carry traffic from *all* VLANs, not just from the specific VLANs created.

Consider the network shown in Figure 7-4. When end user HostPC in VLAN 3 sends a broadcast, Catalyst switch C forwards the frame out all VLAN 3 ports, including the trunk link to Catalyst A. Catalyst A, in turn, forwards the broadcast on to Catalysts B and D over those trunk links. Catalysts B and D forward the broadcast out only their access links that have been configured for VLAN 3. If Catalysts B and D do not have any active users in VLAN 3, forwarding that broadcast frame to them would consume bandwidth on the trunk links and processor resources in both switches, only to have switches B and D discard the frames.

VTP pruning makes more efficient use of trunk bandwidth by reducing unnecessary flooded traffic. Broadcast and unknown unicast frames on a VLAN are forwarded over a trunk link only if the switch on the receiving end of the trunk has ports in that VLAN.

VTP pruning occurs as an extension to VTP version 1, using an additional VTP message type. When a Catalyst switch has a port associated with a VLAN, the switch sends an advertisement to its neighbor switches that it has active ports on that VLAN. The neighbors keep this information, enabling them to decide whether flooded traffic from a VLAN should use a trunk port.

Figure 7-4   *Flooding in a Catalyst Switch Network*

Figure 7-5 shows the network from Figure 7-4 with VTP pruning enabled. Because Catalyst B has not advertised its use of VLAN 3, Catalyst A will prune VLAN 3 from the trunk to B and will choose not to flood VLAN 3 traffic to B over the trunk link. Catalyst D has advertised the need for VLAN 3, so traffic will be flooded to it.

Figure 7-5   *Flooding in a Catalyst Switch Network Using VTP Pruning*

> **NOTE** Even when VTP pruning has determined that a VLAN is not needed on a trunk, an instance of the Spanning Tree Protocol (STP) will run for *every* VLAN that is allowed on the trunk link. To reduce the number of STP instances, you manually should "prune" unneeded VLANs from the trunk and allow only the needed ones. Use the **switchport trunk allowed vlan** command to identify the VLANs that should be added or removed from a trunk.

Enabling VTP Pruning

By default, VTP pruning is disabled on IOS-based switches. To enable pruning, use the following global configuration command:

```
Switch(config)# vtp pruning
```

If you use this command on a VTP server, it also advertises that pruning needs to be enabled for the entire management domain. All other switches listening to that advertisement also will enable pruning.

When pruning is enabled, all general-purpose VLANs become eligible for pruning on all trunk links, if needed. However, you can modify the default list of pruning eligibility with the following interface-configuration command:

```
Switch(config)# interface type mod/num
Switch(config-if)# switchport trunk pruning vlan {add | except | none | remove} vlan-list
```

By default, VLANs 2 through 1001 are eligible, or "enabled," for potential pruning on every trunk. Use the following keywords with the command to tailor the list:

- *vlan-list*—An explicit list of eligible VLAN numbers (anything from 2 to 1001), separated by commas or by dashes.

- **add** *vlan-list*—A list of VLAN numbers (anything from 2 to 1001) is added to the already configured list; this is a shortcut to keep from typing a long list of numbers.

- **except** *vlan-list*—All VLANs are eligible except for the VLAN numbers listed (anything from 2 to 1001); this is a shortcut to keep from typing a long list of numbers.

- **remove** *vlan-list*—A list of VLAN numbers (anything from 2 to 1001) is removed from the already configured list; this is a shortcut to keep from typing a long list of numbers.

> **TIP** Be aware that VTP pruning has no effect on switches in the VTP transparent mode. Instead, those switches must be configured manually to "prune" VLANs from trunk links. In this case, pruning always is configured on the upstream side of a trunk. (The downstream side switch doesn't have any ports that belong to the pruned VLAN, so there is no need to prune from that end.)
>
> By default, VLANs 2 to 1001 are eligible for pruning. VLAN 1 has a special meaning because it sometimes is used for control traffic and is the default access VLAN on switch ports. Because of these historical reasons, VLAN 1 is never eligible for pruning. In addition, VLANs 1002 through 1005 are reserved for Token Ring and FDDI VLANs and are never eligible for pruning.

Troubleshooting VTP

If a switch does not seem to be receiving updated information from a VTP server, consider these possible causes:

- The switch is configured for VTP transparent mode. In this mode, incoming VTP advertisements are not processed; they are relayed only to other switches in the domain.

- If the switch is configured as a VTP client, there might not be another switch functioning as a VTP server. In this case, configure the local switch to become a VTP server itself.

- The link toward the VTP server is not in trunking mode. VTP advertisements are sent only over trunks. Use the **show interface** *type mod/num* **switchport** to verify the operational mode as a trunk.

- Make sure the VTP domain name is configured correctly to match that of the VTP server.

- Make sure the VTP version is compatible with other switches in the VTP domain.

- Make sure the VTP password matches others in the VTP domain. If the server doesn't use a password, make sure the password is disabled or cleared on the local switch.

> **TIP** Above all else, verify a switch's VTP configuration *before* connecting it to a production network. If the switch has been configured previously or used elsewhere, it might already be in VTP server mode with a VTP configuration revision number that is higher than that of other switches in the production VTP domain. In that case, other switches will listen and learn from the new switch because it has a higher revision number and must know more recent information. This could cause the new switch to introduce bogus VLANs into the domain or, worse yet, to cause *all* other switches in the domain to delete all their active VLANs.
>
> To prevent this from happening, reset the configuration revision number of every new switch that is added to a production network.

Table 7-2 lists and describes the commands that are useful for verifying or troubleshooting VTP configuration.

Table 7-2 *VTP Configuration Troubleshooting Commands*

Function	Command syntax
Displays current VTP parameters, including the last advertising server	**show vtp status**
Displays VTP advertisement and pruning statistics	**show vtp counters**
Displays defined VLANs	**show vlan brief**
Displays trunk status, including pruning eligibility	**show interface** *type mod/num* **switchport**
Displays VTP pruning state	**show interface** *type mod/num* **pruning**

Foundation Summary

The Foundation Summary is a collection of information that provides a convenient review of many key concepts in this chapter. If you are already comfortable with the topics in this chapter, this summary can help you recall a few details. If you just read this chapter, this review should help solidify some key facts. If you are doing your final preparation before the exam, this information is a convenient way to review the day before the exam.

Table 7-3 *Catalyst VTP Modes*

VTP Mode	Characteristics
Server	All VLAN and VTP configuration changes occur here. The server advertises settings and changes to all other servers and clients in a VTP domain. (This is the default mode for Catalyst switches.)
Client	Listens to all VTP advertisements from servers in a VTP domain. Advertisements are relayed out other trunk links. No VLAN or VTP configuration changes can be made on a client.
Transparent	VLAN configuration changes are made locally, independent of any VTP domain. VTP advertisements are not received but merely are relayed out other trunk links, if possible.

Table 7-4 *Types of VTP Advertisements*

Advertisement Type	Function
Summary	Sent by server every 300 seconds and after a topology change. Contains a complete dump of all VTP domain information.
Subset	Sent by server only after a VLAN configuration change. Contains only information about the specific VLAN change.
Advertisement request	Sent by client when additional VTP information is needed. Servers sent summary or subset advertisements in response.
Pruning request	Sent by clients and servers to announce VLANs that are in active use on local switch ports. These VLANs should not be pruned by neighbors. (These messages are destined for nearest-neighbor switches and are not relayed throughout the domain.)

Table 7-5   *VTP Configuration Commands*

Task	Command Syntax
Defines the VTP domain	**vtp domain** *domain-name*
Sets the VTP mode	**vtp mode** {**server** | **client** | **transparent**}
Defines an optional VTP password	**vtp password** *password*
Configures VTP version	**vtp version** {**1** | **2**}
Enables VTP pruning	**vtp pruning**
Selects VLANs eligible for pruning on a trunk interface	**interface** *type* *mod/num* **switchport trunk pruning vlan** {**add** | **except** | **none** | **remove**} *vlan-list*

Q&A

The questions and scenarios in this book are more difficult than what you should experience on the actual exam. The questions do not attempt to cover more breadth or depth than the exam; however, they are designed to make sure that you know the answers. Rather than allowing you to derive the answers from clues hidden inside the questions themselves, the questions challenge your understanding and recall of the subject. Hopefully, these questions will help limit the number of exam questions on which you narrow your choices to two options and then guess.

The answers to these questions can be found in Appendix A.

1. True or false: You can use VTP domains to separate broadcast domains.

2. What VTP modes can a Catalyst switch be configured for? Can VLANs be created in each of the modes?

3. How many VTP management domains can a Catalyst switch participate in? How many VTP servers can a management domain have?

4. What conditions must exist for two Catalyst switches to be in the same VTP management domain?

5. On a VTP server switch, identify what you can do to reset the VTP configuration revision number to 0.

6. How can you clear the configuration revision number on a VTP client?

7. Complete this command to make all VLANs other than 30 and 100 eligible for pruning on the trunk interface:

        switchport trunk pruning vlan_____

8. Which VLAN numbers are never eligible for VTP pruning? Why?

9. What does the acronym VTP stand for?

10. What VTP domain name is defined on a new switch with no configuration?

11. In a network of switches, VTP domain Engineering has been configured with VLANs 1, 10 through 30, and 100. The VTP configuration revision number is currently at 23. Suppose a new switch is connected to the network, and it has the following configuration: VTP domain Engineering, VTP server mode, only VLANs 1 and 2 defined, and configuration revision number of 30.

What happens when the switch is connected to the network?

12. A VTP client switch has VLANs 1, 2, 3, 10, and 30 configured as part of a VTP domain; however, the switch has users connected only to access switch ports defined on VLANs 3 and 30. If VTP pruning is enabled and all VLANs are eligible, which VLANs will be pruned on the upstream switch?

13. The VTP domain Area3 consists of one server and several clients. The server's VTP configuration revision number is at 11. A new switch is added to the network. It has VTP domain name Area5 and a configuration revision number of 10. What happens when the new switch is added to the network? What happens when the VTP domain name is changed to Area3 on the new switch?

14. What command shows information about the VTP configuration on a Catalyst 3560?

This chapter covers the following topics that you need to master for the CCNP BCMSN exam:

- **Switch Port Aggregation with EtherChannel**—This section discusses the concept of aggregating, or "bundling," physical ports into a single logical link. Methods for load-balancing traffic across the physical links also are covered.

- **EtherChannel Negotiation Protocols**—This section discusses two protocols that dynamically negotiate and control EtherChannels: Port Aggregation Protocol (PAgP), a Cisco proprietary protocol, and Link Aggregation Control Protocol (LACP), a standards-based protocol.

- **EtherChannel Configuration**—This section discusses the Catalyst switch commands needed to configure EtherChannel.

- **Troubleshooting an EtherChannel**—This section gives a brief summary of things to consider and commands to use when an aggregated link is not operating properly.

CHAPTER **8**

Aggregating Switch Links

In previous chapters, you learned about campus network design and connecting and organizing switches into blocks and common workgroups. Using these principles, end users can be given effective access to resources both on and off the campus network. However, today's mission-critical applications and services demand networks that provide high availability and reliability.

This chapter presents technologies that you can use in a campus network to provide higher bandwidth and reliability between switches.

"Do I Know This Already?" Quiz

The purpose of the "Do I Know This Already?" quiz is to help you decide whether you need to read the entire chapter. If you already intend to read the entire chapter, you do not necessarily need to answer these questions now.

The 13-question quiz, derived from the major sections in the "Foundation Topics" portion of the chapter, helps you determine how to spend your limited study time.

Table 8-1 outlines the major topics discussed in this chapter and the "Do I Know This Already?" quiz questions that correspond to those topics.

Table 8-1 *"Do I Know This Already?" Foundation Topics Section-to-Question Mapping*

Foundation Topics Section	Questions Covered in This Section	Score
Switch Port Aggregation with EtherChannel	1–7	
EtherChannel Negotiation	8–11	
EtherChannel Configuration	11–12	
Troubleshooting an EtherChannel	13	
Total Score		

> **CAUTION**   The goal of self-assessment is to gauge your mastery of the topics in this chapter. If you do not know the answer to a question or are only partially sure of the answer, you should mark this question wrong. Giving yourself credit for an answer you correctly guess skews your self-assessment results and might give you a false sense of security.

1. If Fast Ethernet ports are bundled into an EtherChannel, what is the maximum throughput supported on a Catalyst switch?

    a. 100 Mbps

    b. 200 Mbps

    c. 400 Mbps

    d. 800 Mbps

    e. 1600 Mbps

2. Which of these methods distributes traffic over an EtherChannel?

    a. Round robin

    b. Least-used link

    c. A function of address

    d. A function of packet size

3. What type of interface represents an EtherChannel as a whole?

    a. Channel

    b. Port

    c. Port-channel

    d. Channel-port

4. Which of the following is not a valid method for EtherChannel load balancing?

    a. Source MAC address

    b. Source and destination MAC addresses

    c. Source IP address

    d. IP precedence

    e. UDP/TCP port

5. How can the EtherChannel load-balancing method be set?

    a. Per switch port

    b. Per EtherChannel

    c. Globally per switch

    d. Can't be configured

6. What logical operation is performed to calculate EtherChannel load balancing as a function of two addresses?

   a. OR

   b. AND

   c. XOR

   d. NOR

7. Which one of the following is a valid combination of ports for an EtherChannel?

   a. Two access links (one VLAN 5, one VLAN 5)

   b. Two access links (one VLAN 1, one VLAN 10)

   c. Two trunk links (one VLANs 1 to 10, one VLANs 1, 11 to 20)

   d. Two Fast Ethernet links (both full duplex, one 10 Mbps)

8. Which of these is a method for negotiating an EtherChannel?

   a. PAP

   b. CHAP

   c. LAPD

   d. LACP

9. Which of the following is a valid EtherChannel negotiation mode combination between two switches?

   a. PAgP auto, PAgP auto

   b. PAgP auto, PAgP desirable

   c. on, PAgP auto

   d. LACP passive, LACP passive

10. When is PagP's "desirable silent" mode useful?

    a. When the switch should not send PAgP frames

    b. When the switch should not form an EtherChannel

    c. When the switch should not expect to receive PAgP frames

    d. When the switch is using LACP mode

11. Which of the following EtherChannel modes does not send or receive any negotiation frames?

    a. **channel-group 1 mode passive**

    b. **channel-group 1 mode active**

    c. **channel-group 1 mode on**

    d. **channel-group 1 mode desirable**

    e. **channel-group 1 mode auto**

12. Two computers are the only hosts sending IP data across an EtherChannel between two switches. Several different applications are being used between them. Which of these load-balancing methods would be more likely to use the most links in the EtherChannel?

    a. Source and destination MAC addresses.

    b. Source and destination IP addresses.

    c. Source and destination TCP/UDP ports.

    d. None of the other answers is correct.

13. Which command can be used to see the status of an EtherChannel's links?

    a. **show channel link**

    b. **show etherchannel status**

    c. **show etherchannel summary**

    d. **show ether channel status**

The answers to the quiz are found in Appendix A, "Answers to Chapter 'Do I Know This Already?' Quizzes and Q&A Sections." The suggested choices for your next step are as follows:

■ **8 or less overall score**—Read the entire chapter. This includes the "Foundation Topics," "Foundation Summary," and "Q&A" sections.

■ **9–11 overall score**—Begin with the "Foundation Summary" section and then follow up with the "Q&A" section at the end of the chapter.

■ **12 or more overall score**—If you want more review on these topics, skip to the "Foundation Summary" section and then go to the "Q&A" section at the end of the chapter. Otherwise, move to Chapter 9, "Traditional Spanning Tree Protocol."

Foundation Topics

Switch Port Aggregation with EtherChannel

As discussed in Chapter 5, "Switch Port Configuration," switches can use Ethernet, Fast Ethernet, or Gigabit Ethernet ports to scale link speeds by a factor of ten. Cisco offers another method of scaling link bandwidth by aggregating, or bundling, parallel links, termed the *EtherChannel* technology. Two to eight links of either Fast Ethernet (FE) or Gigabit Ethernet (GE) are bundled as one logical link of *Fast EtherChannel (FEC)* or *Gigabit EtherChannel (GEC)*, respectively. This bundle provides a full-duplex bandwidth of up to 1600 Mbps (eight links of Fast Ethernet) or 16 Gbps (eight links of Gigabit Ethernet).

This also provides an easy means to "grow," or expand, a link's capacity between two switches, without having to continually purchase hardware for the next magnitude of throughput. For example, a single FastEthernet link (200 Mbps throughput) can be incrementally expanded up to eight Fast Ethernet links (1600 Mbps) as a single Fast EtherChannel. If the traffic load grows beyond that, the growth process can begin again with a single Gigabit Ethernet link (2 Gbps throughput), which can be expanded up to eight Gigabit Ethernet links as a Gigabit EtherChannel (16 Gbps). The process repeats again by moving to a single 10-Gigabit Ethernet link, and so on.

Ordinarily, having multiple or parallel links between switches creates the possibility of bridging loops, an undesirable condition. EtherChannel avoids this situation by bundling parallel links into a single, logical link, which can act as either an access or a trunk link. Switches or devices on each end of the EtherChannel link must understand and use the EtherChannel technology for proper operation.

Although an EtherChannel link is seen as a single logical link, the link doesn't necessarily have an inherent total bandwidth equal to the sum of its component physical links. For example, suppose an FEC link is made up of four full-duplex, 100-Mbps Fast Ethernet links. Although it is possible for the FEC link to carry a total throughput of 800 Mbps (if each link becomes fully loaded), the single resulting FEC bundle does not operate at this speed.

Instead, traffic is distributed across the individual links within the EtherChannel. Each of these links operates at its inherent speed (200 Mbps full duplex for FE) but carries only the frames placed on it by the EtherChannel hardware. If one link within the bundle is favored by the load-distribution algorithm, that link will carry a disproportionate amount of traffic. In other words, the load isn't always distributed equally among the individual links. The load-balancing process is explained further in the next section.

EtherChannel also provides redundancy with several bundled physical links. If one of the links within the bundle fails, traffic sent through that link automatically is moved to an adjacent link. Failover occurs in less than a few milliseconds and is transparent to the end user. As more links fail, more traffic is moved to further adjacent links. Likewise, as links are restored, the load automatically is redistributed among the active links.

Bundling Ports with EtherChannel

EtherChannel bundles can consist of up to eight physical ports of the same Ethernet media type and speed. Some configuration restrictions exist to ensure that only similarly configured links are bundled.

Generally, all bundled ports first must belong to the same VLAN. If used as a trunk, bundled ports must be in trunking mode, have the same native VLAN, and pass the same set of VLANs. Each of the ports should have the same speed and duplex settings before being bundled. Bundled ports also must be configured with identical spanning-tree settings.

Distributing Traffic in EtherChannel

Traffic in an EtherChannel is distributed across the individual bundled links in a deterministic fashion; however, the load is not necessarily balanced equally across all the links. Instead, frames are forwarded on a specific link as a result of a hashing algorithm. The algorithm can use source IP address, destination IP address, or a combination of source and destination IP addresses, source and destination MAC addresses, or TCP/UDP port numbers. The hash algorithm computes a binary pattern that selects a link number in the bundle to carry each frame.

If only one address or port number is hashed, a switch forwards each frame by using one or more low-order bits of the hash value as an index into the bundled links. If two addresses or port numbers are hashed, a switch performs an exclusive-OR (XOR) operation on one or more low-order bits of the addresses or TCP/UDP port numbers as an index into the bundled links.

For example, an EtherChannel consisting of two links bundled together requires a 1-bit index. If the index is 0, link 0 is selected; if the index is 1, link 1 is used. Either the lowest-order address bit or the XOR of the last bit of the addresses in the frame is used as the index. A four-link bundle uses a hash of the last 2 bits. Likewise, an eight-link bundle uses a hash of the last 3 bits. The hashing operation's outcome selects the EtherChannel's outbound link. Table 8-2 shows the results of an XOR on a two-link bundle, using the source and destination addresses.

The XOR operation is performed independently on each bit position in the address value. If the two address values have the same bit value, the XOR result is always 0. If the two address bits differ, the XOR result is always 1. In this way, frames can be distributed statistically among the links with the assumption that MAC or IP addresses themselves are distributed statistically throughout the network. In a four-link EtherChannel, the XOR is performed on the lower 2 bits of the address values, resulting in a 2-bit XOR value (each bit is computed separately) or a link number from 0 to 3.

Table 8-2 *Frame Distribution on a Two-Link EtherChannel*

Binary Addresses	Two-Link EtherChannel XOR and Link Number
Addr1: ... xxxxxxx0 Addr2: ... xxxxxxx0	... xxxxxxx0: Use link 0
Addr1: ... xxxxxxx0 Addr2: ... xxxxxxx1	... xxxxxxx1: Use link 1
Addr1: ... xxxxxxx1 Addr2: ... xxxxxxx0	... xxxxxxx1: Use link 1
Addr1: ... xxxxxxx1 Addr2: ... xxxxxxx1	... xxxxxxx0: Use link 0

As an example, consider a packet being sent from IP address 192.168.1.1 to 172.31.67.46. Because EtherChannels can be built from two to eight individual links, only the rightmost (least significant) 3 bits are needed as a link index. From the source and destination addresses, these bits are 001 (1) and 110 (6), respectively. For a two-link EtherChannel, a 1-bit XOR is performed on the rightmost address bit: 1 XOR 0 = 1, causing Link 1 in the bundle to be used. A four-link EtherChannel produces a 2-bit XOR: 01 XOR 10 = 11, causing Link 3 in the bundle to be used. Finally, an eight-link EtherChannel requires a 3-bit XOR: 001 XOR 110 = 111, where Link 7 in the bundle is selected.

A conversation between two devices always is sent through the same EtherChannel link because the two endpoint addresses stay the same. However, when a device talks to several other devices, chances are that the destination addresses are distributed equally with 0s and 1s in the last bit (even and odd address values). This causes the frames to be distributed across the EtherChannel links.

Note that the load distribution is still proportional to the volume of traffic passing between pairs of hosts or link indexes. For example, suppose that there are two pairs of hosts talking across a two-link channel, and each pair of addresses results in a unique link index. Frames from one pair of hosts always travel over one link in the channel, while frames from the other pair travel over the other link. The links both are being used as a result of the hash algorithm, so the load is being distributed across every link in the channel.

However, if one pair of hosts has a much greater volume of traffic than the other pair, one link in the channel will be used much more than the other. This still can create a load imbalance. To remedy this condition, you should consider other methods of hashing algorithms for the channel. For example, a method that uses the source and destination addresses along with UDP or TCP port numbers can distribute traffic much differently. Then, packets are placed on links within the bundle based on the applications used within conversations between two hosts.

Configuring EtherChannel Load Balancing

The hashing operation can be performed on either MAC or IP addresses and can be based solely on source or destination addresses, or both. Use the following command to configure frame distribution for all EtherChannel switch links:

```
Switch(config)# port-channel load-balance method
```

Notice that the load-balancing method is set with a global configuration command. You must set the method globally for the switch, not on a per-port basis. Table 8-3 lists the possible values for the *method* variable, along with the hashing operation and some example supporting switch models.

Table 8-3   *Types of EtherChannel Load-Balancing Methods*

method Value	Hash Input	Hash Operation	Switch Model
src-ip	Source IP address	bits	6500/4500/3750/3560/2970
dst-ip	Destination IP address	bits	6500/4500/3750/3560/2970
src-dst-ip	Source and destination IP address	XOR	6500/4500/3750/3560/2970
src-mac	Source MAC address	bits	6500/4500/3750/3560/2970
dst-mac	Destination MAC address	bits	6500/4500/3750/3560/2970
src-dst-mac	Source and destination MAC	XOR	6500/4500/3750/3560/2970
src-port	Source port number	bits	6500/4500
dst-port	Destination port number	bits	6500/4500
src-dst-port	Source and destination port	XOR	6500/4500

The default configuration is to use source XOR destination IP addresses, or the **src-dst-ip** method. The default for the Catalyst 2970 and 3560 is **src-mac** for Layer 2 switching. If Layer 3 switching is used on the EtherChannel, the **src-dst-ip** method always will be used, even though it is not configurable.

Normally, the default action should result in a statistical distribution of frames; however, you should determine whether the EtherChannel is imbalanced according to the traffic patterns present. For example, if a single server is receiving most of the traffic on an EtherChannel, the server's address (the destination IP address) always will remain constant in the many conversations. This can cause one link to be overused if the destination IP address is used as a component of a load-balancing method. In the case of a four-link EtherChannel, perhaps two of the four links are overused. Configuring the use of MAC addresses, or only the source IP addresses, might cause the distribution to be more balanced across all the bundled links.

> **TIP**   To verify how effectively a configured load-balancing method is performing, you can use the **show etherchannel port-channel** command. Each link in the channel is displayed, along with a hex "Load" value. Although this information is not intuitive, you can use the hex values to get an idea of each link's traffic loads relative to the others.

In some applications, EtherChannel traffic might consist of protocols other than IP. For example, IPX or SNA frames might be switched along with IP. Non-IP protocols need to be distributed according to MAC addresses because IP addresses are not applicable. Here, the switch should be configured to use MAC addresses instead of the IP default.

> **TIP**   A special case results when a router is connected to an EtherChannel. Recall that a router always uses its burned-in MAC address in Ethernet frames, even though it is forwarding packets to and from many different IP addresses. In other words, many end stations send frames to their local router address with the router's MAC address as the destination. This means that the destination MAC address is the same for all frames destined through the router.
>
> Usually, this will not present a problem because the source MAC addresses are all different. When two routers are forwarding frames to each other, however, both source and destination MAC addresses remains constant, and only one link of the EtherChannel is used. If the MAC addresses remain constant, choose IP addresses instead. Beyond that, if most of the traffic is between the same two IP addresses, as in the case of two servers talking, choose IP port numbers to disperse the frames across different links.

You should choose the load-balancing method that provides the greatest distribution or variety when the channel links are indexed. Also consider the type of addressing that is being used on the network. If most of the traffic is IP, it might make sense to load-balance according to IP addresses or TCP/UDP port numbers. But if IP load balancing is being used, what happens to non-IP frames? If a frame can't meet the load-balancing criteria, the switch automatically falls back to the "next lowest" method. With Ethernet, MAC addresses always must be present, so the switch distributes those frames according to their MAC addresses.

A switch also provides some inherent protection against bridging loops with EtherChannels. When ports are bundled into an EtherChannel, no inbound (received) broadcasts and multicasts are sent back out over any of the remaining ports in the channel. Outbound broadcast and multicast frames are load-balanced like any other: The broadcast or multicast address becomes part of the hashing calculation to choose an outbound channel link.

EtherChannel Negotiation Protocols

EtherChannels can be negotiated between two switches to provide some dynamic link configuration. Two protocols are available to negotiate bundled links in Catalyst switches. The Port Aggregation Protocol (PAgP) is a Cisco-proprietary solution, and the Link Aggregation Control Protocol (LACP) is standards based.

Port Aggregation Protocol

To provide automatic EtherChannel configuration and negotiation between switches, Cisco developed the *Port Aggregation Protocol (PAgP)*. PAgP packets are exchanged between switches over EtherChannel-capable ports. Neighbors are identified and port group capabilities are learned and compared with local switch capabilities. Ports that have the same neighbor device ID and port group capability are bundled together as a bidirectional, point-to-point EtherChannel link.

PAgP forms an EtherChannel only on ports that are configured for either identical static VLANs or trunking. PAgP also dynamically modifies parameters of the EtherChannel if one of the bundled ports is modified. For example, if the VLAN, speed, or duplex mode of a port in an established bundle is changed, PAgP changes that parameter for all ports in the bundle.

PAgP can be configured in active mode (desirable), in which a switch actively asks a far-end switch to negotiate an EtherChannel, or in passive mode (auto, the default), in which a switch negotiates an EtherChannel only if the far end initiates it.

Link Aggregation Control Protocol

LACP is a standards-based alternative to PAgP, defined in IEEE 802.3ad (also known as IEEE 802.3 Clause 43, "Link Aggregation"). LACP packets are exchanged between switches over EtherChannel-capable ports. As with PAgP, neighbors are identified and port group capabilities are learned and compared with local switch capabilities. However, LACP also assigns roles to the EtherChannel's endpoints.

The switch with the lowest *system priority* (a 2-byte priority value followed by a 6-byte switch MAC address) is allowed to make decisions about what ports actively are participating in the EtherChannel at a given time.

Ports are selected and become active according to their *port priority* value (a 2-byte priority followed by a 2-byte port number), where a low value indicates a higher priority. A set of up to 16 potential links can be defined for each EtherChannel. Through LACP, a switch selects up to eight of these having the lowest port priorities as active EtherChannel links at any given time. The other links are placed in a standby state and will be enabled in the EtherChannel if one of the active links goes down.

Like PAgP, LACP can be configured in active mode (active), in which a switch actively asks a far-end switch to negotiate an EtherChannel, or in passive mode (passive), in which a switch negotiates an EtherChannel only if the far end initiates it.

EtherChannel Configuration

For each EtherChannel on a switch, you must choose the EtherChannel negotiation protocol and assign individual switch ports to the EtherChannel. Both PAgP- and LACP-negotiated EtherChannels are described in the following sections. You also can configure an EtherChannel to use the on mode, which unconditionally bundles the links. In this case, neither PAgP nor LACP packets are sent or received.

As ports are configured to be members of an EtherChannel, the switch automatically creates a logical port-channel interface. This interface represents the channel as a whole.

Configuring a PAgP EtherChannel

To configure switch ports for PAgP negotiation (the default), use the following commands:

```
Switch(config)# interface type mod/num
Switch(config-if)# channel-protocol pagp
Switch(config-if)# channel-group number mode {on | {auto | desirable} [non-silent]}
```

On all Cisco IOS–based Catalyst models (2970, 3560, 4500, and 6500), you can select between PAgP and LACP as a channel-negotiation protocol. Older models such as the Catalyst 2950, however, offer only PAgP, so the **channel-protocol** command is not available. Each interface that will be included in a single EtherChannel bundle must be configured and assigned to the same unique channel group *number* (1 to 64). Channel negotiation must be set to on (unconditionally channel, no PAgP negotiation), auto (passively listen and wait to be asked), or desirable (actively ask).

> **TIP** IOS-based Catalyst switches do not assign interfaces to predetermined channel groups by default. In fact, the interfaces are not assigned to channel groups until you configure them manually.
>
> This is different from Catalyst OS (CatOS) switches, such as the Catalyst 4000 (Supervisors I and II), 5000, and 6500 (hybrid mode). On those platforms, Ethernet line cards are broken up into default channel groups.

By default, PAgP operates in silent submode with the desirable and auto modes, and allows ports to be added to an EtherChannel even if the other end of the link is silent and never transmits PAgP packets. This might seem to go against the idea of PAgP, in which two endpoints are supposed to negotiate a channel. After all, how can two switches negotiate anything if no PAgP packets are received?

The key is in the phrase "*if* the other end is silent." The silent submode listens for any PAgP packets from the far end, looking to negotiate a channel. If none is received, silent submode assumes that a channel should be built anyway, so no more PAgP packets are expected from the far end.

This allows a switch to form an EtherChannel with a device such as a file server or a network analyzer that doesn't participate in PAgP. In the case of a network analyzer connected to the far end, you also might want to see the PAgP packets generated by the switch, as if you were using a normal PAgP EtherChannel.

If you expect a PAgP-capable switch to be on the far end, you should add the **non-silent** keyword to the desirable or auto mode. This requires each port to receive PAgP packets before adding them to a channel. If PAgP isn't heard on an active port, the port remains in the up state, but PAgP reports to the Spanning Tree Protocol (STP) that the port is down.

> **TIP**   In practice, you might notice a delay from the time the links in a channel group are connected until the time the channel is formed and data can pass over it. You will encounter this if both switches are using the default PAgP auto mode and silent submode. Each interface waits to be asked to form a channel, and each interface waits and listens before accepting silent channel partners. The silent submode amounts to approximately a 15-second delay.
>
> Even if the two interfaces are using PAgP auto mode, the link will still eventually come up, although not as a channel. You might notice that the total delay before data can pass over the link is actually approximately 45 or 50 seconds. The first 15 seconds are the result of PAgP silent mode waiting to hear inbound PAgP messages, and the final 30 seconds are the result of the STP moving through the listening and learning stages.

As an example of PAgP configuration, suppose that you want a switch to use an EtherChannel load-balancing hash of both source and destination port numbers. A Gigabit EtherChannel (GEC) will be built from interfaces GigabitEthernet 3/1 through 3/4, with the switch actively negotiating a channel. The switch should not wait to listen for silent partners. You can use the following configuration commands to accomplish this:

```
Switch(config)# port-channel load-balance src-dst-port
Switch(config)# interface range gig 3/1 - 4
Switch(config-if)# channel-protocol pagp
Switch(config-if)# channel-group 1 mode desirable non-silent
```

Configuring a LACP EtherChannel

To configure switch ports for LACP negotiation, use the following commands:

```
Switch(config)# lacp system-priority priority
Switch(config)# interface type mod/num
Switch(config-if)# channel-protocol lacp
Switch(config-if)# channel-group number mode {on | passive | active}
Switch(config-if)# lacp port-priority priority
```

First, the switch should have its LACP system priority defined (1 to 65,535, default 32,768). If desired, one switch should be assigned a lower system priority than the other so that it can make decisions about the EtherChannel's makeup. Otherwise, both switches will have the same system priority (32,768), and the one with the lower MAC address will become the decision maker.

Each interface included in a single EtherChannel bundle must be assigned to the same unique channel group *number* (1 to 64). Channel negotiation must be set to on (unconditionally channel, no LACP negotiation), passive (passively listen and wait to be asked), or active (actively ask).

You can configure more interfaces in the channel group *number* than are allowed to be active in the channel. This prepares extra standby interfaces to replace failed active ones. Use the **lacp port-priority** command to configure a lower port priority (1 to 65,535, default 32,768) for any interfaces that must be active, and a higher priority for interfaces that might be held in the standby state. Otherwise, just use the default scenario, in which all ports default to 32,768 and the lower port numbers (in interface number order) are used to select the active ports.

As an example of LACP configuration, suppose that you want to configure a switch to negotiate a Gigabit EtherChannel (GEC) using interfaces GigabitEthernet 2/1 through 2/4 and 3/1 through 3/4. Interfaces GigabitEthernet 2/5 through 2/8 and 3/5 through 3/8 are also available, so these can be used as standby links to replace failed links in the channel. This switch actively should negotiate the channel and should be the decision maker about the channel operation.

You can use the following configuration commands to accomplish this:

```
Switch(config)# lacp system-priority 100
Switch(config)# interface range gig 2/1 - 4 , gig 3/1 - 4
Switch(config-if)# channel-protocol lacp
Switch(config-if)# channel-group 1 mode active
Switch(config-if)# lacp port-priority 100
Switch(config-if)# exit
Switch(config)# interface range gig 2/5 - 8 , gig 3/5 - 8
Switch(config-if)# channel-protocol lacp
Switch(config-if)# channel-group 1 mode active
```

Notice that interfaces GigabitEthernet 2/5-8 and 3/5-8 have been left to their default port priorities of 32768. This is higher than the others, which were configured for 100, so they will be held as standby interfaces.

Troubleshooting an EtherChannel

If you find that an EtherChannel is having problems, remember that the whole concept is based on consistent configurations on *both* ends of the channel. Here are some reminders about EtherChannel operation and interaction:

- EtherChannel on mode does not send or receive PAgP or LACP packets. Therefore, both ends should be set to on mode before the channel can form.

- EtherChannel desirable (PAgP) or active (LACP) mode attempts to ask the far end to bring up a channel. Therefore, the other end must be set to either desirable or auto mode.

- EtherChannel auto (PAgP) or passive (LACP) mode participates in the channel protocol, but only if the far end asks for participation. Therefore, two switches in the auto or passive mode will not form an EtherChannel.

- PAgP desirable and auto modes default to the silent submode, in which no PAgP packets are expected from the far end. If ports are set to nonsilent submode, PAgP packets must be received before a channel will form.

First, verify the EtherChannel state with the **show etherchannel summary** command. Each port in the channel is shown, along with flags indicating the port's state, as shown in Example 8-1.

Example 8-1 **show etherchannel summary** Command Output

```
Switch# show etherchannel summary
Flags:  D - down        P - in port-channel
        I - stand-alone s - suspended
        H - Hot-standby (LACP only)
        R - Layer3       S - Layer2
        u - unsuitable for bundling
        U - in use       f - failed to allocate aggregator
        d - default port
Number of channel-groups in use: 1
Number of aggregators:          1


Group  Port-channel  Protocol    Ports
------+------------+-----------+-----------------------------------------------
1      Po1(SU)       PAgP        Fa0/41(P)  Fa0/42(P)  Fa0/43  Fa0/44(P)
                                 Fa0/45(P)  Fa0/46(P)  Fa0/47(P)  Fa0/48(P)
```

The status of the port-channel shows the EtherChannel logical interface as a whole. This should show SU (Layer 2 channel, in use) if the channel is operational. You also can examine the status of each port within the channel. Notice that most of the channel ports have flags (P), indicating that they are active in the port-channel. One port shows because it is physically not connected or down. If a port is connected but not bundled in the channel, it will have an independent, or (I), flag.

You can verify the channel negotiation mode with the **show etherchannel port** command, as shown in Example 8-2. The local switch is shown using desirable mode with PAgP (Desirable-Sl is desirable silent mode). Notice that you also can see the far end's negotiation mode under the Partner Flags heading, as A, or auto mode.

Example 8-2 **show etherchannel port** *Command Output*

```
Switch# show etherchannel port
                Channel-group listing:
                ----------------------
```

Example 8-2 **show etherchannel port** *Command Output (Continued)*

```
Group: 1
----------
                    Ports in the group:
                    -------------------
Port: Fa0/41
------------

Port state    = Up Mstr In-Bndl
Channel group = 1            Mode = Desirable-Sl    Gcchange = 0
Port-channel  = Po1          GC   = 0x00010001          Pseudo port-channel = Po1
Port index    = 0            Load = 0x00        Protocol =  PAgP

Flags:  S - Device is sending Slow hello.  C - Device is in Consistent state.
        A - Device is in Auto mode.        P - Device learns on physical port.
        d - PAgP is down.
Timers: H - Hello timer is running.        Q - Quit timer is running.
        S - Switching timer is running.    I - Interface timer is running.

Local information:
                                Hello    Partner  PAgP     Learning  Group
Port       Flags State   Timers Interval Count    Priority Method    Ifindex
Fa0/41     SC    U6/S7   H      30s      1        128      Any       55

Partner's information:

           Partner            Partner         Partner         Partner Group
Port       Name               Device ID       Port       Age  Flags   Cap.
Fa0/41     FarEnd             00d0.5849.4100  3/1        19s  SAC     11

Age of the port in the current state: 00d:08h:05m:28s
```

Within a switch, an EtherChannel cannot form unless each of the component or member ports is configured consistently. Each must have the same switch mode (access or trunk), native VLAN, trunked VLANs, port speed, port duplex mode, and so on.

You can display a port's configuration by looking at the **show running-config interface** *type mod/ num* output. Also, the **show interface** *type mod/num* **etherchannel** shows all active EtherChannel parameters for a single port. If you configure a port inconsistently with others for an EtherChannel, you see error messages from the switch.

Some messages from the switch might look like errors but are part of the normal EtherChannel process. For example, as a new port is configured as a member of an existing EtherChannel, you might see this message:

```
4d00h: %EC-5-L3DONTBNDL2: FastEthernet0/2 suspended: incompatible partner port with
    FastEthernet0/1
```

When the port first is added to the EtherChannel, it is incompatible because the STP runs on the channel and the new port. After STP takes the new port through its progression of states, the port automatically is added into the EtherChannel.

Other messages do indicate a port-compatibility error. In these cases, the cause of the error is shown. For example, the following message tells that FastEthernet0/3 has a different duplex mode than the other ports in the EtherChannel:

```
4d00h: %EC-5-CANNOT_BUNDLE2: FastEthernet0/3 is not compatible with FastEthernet0/1
    and will be suspended (duplex of Fa0/3 is full, Fa0/1 is half)
```

Finally, you can verify the EtherChannel load-balancing or hashing algorithm with the **show etherchannel load-balance** command. Remember that the switches on either end of an EtherChannel can have different load-balancing methods. The only drawback to this is that the load balancing will be asymmetric in the two directions across the channel.

Table 8-4 lists the commands useful for verifying or troubleshooting EtherChannel operation.

Table 8-4 *EtherChannel Troubleshooting Commands*

Display Function	Command Syntax
Current EtherChannel status of each member port	**show etherchannel summary** **show etherchannel port**
Time stamps of EtherChannel changes	**show etherchannel port-channel**
Detailed status about each EtherChannel component	**show etherchannel detail**
Load-balancing hashing algorithm	**show etherchannel load-balance**
Load-balancing port index used by hashing algorithm	**show etherchannel port-channel**
EtherChannel neighbors on each port	**show {pagp I lacp} neighbor**
LACP system ID	**show lacp sys-id**

Foundation Summary

The Foundation Summary is a collection of information that provides a convenient review of many key concepts in this chapter. If you are already comfortable with the topics in this chapter, this summary can help you recall a few details. If you just read this chapter, this review should help solidify some key facts. If you are doing your final preparation before the exam, this information is a convenient way to review the day before the exam.

Table 8-5 *Frame Distribution on an EtherChannel*

Channel size	A1: ... xxxxx000 A2: ... xxxxx000 (address bits the same)	A1: ... xxxxx000 A2: ... xxxxx111 (address bits differ)
2-port	Link index: 0 (0) (lowest)	Link index: 1 (1) (highest)
4-port	Link index: 00 (0) (lowest)	Link index: 11 (3) (highest)
8-port	Link index: 000 (0) (lowest)	Link index: 111 (7) (highest)

Example address bits are shown. The XOR operation produces a 0 bit if the two input bits are the same (0,0 or 1,1) and a 1 bit if the two input bits are different (0,1 or 1,0).

Table 8-6 *EtherChannel Load-Balancing Methods*

method Value	Hash Input	Hash Operation	Switch Model
src-ip	Source IP address	bits	6500/4500/3750/3560/2970
dst-ip	Destination IP address	bits	6500/4500/3750/3560/2970
src-dst-ip	Source and destination IP address	XOR	6500/4500/3750/3560/2970
src-mac	Source MAC address	bits	6500/4500/3750/3560/2970
dst-mac	Destination MAC address	bits	6500/4500/3750/3560/2970
src-dst-mac	Source and destination MAC	XOR	6500/4500/3750/3560/2970
src-port	Source port number	bits	6500/4500
dst-port	Destination port number	bits	6500/4500
src-dst-port	Source and destination port	XOR	6500/4500

Table 8-7 *EtherChannel Negotiation Protocols*

Negotiation Mode	Negotiation Packets Sent?	Characteristics	
PAgP	LACP		
on	on	No	All ports channeling
auto	passive	Yes	Waits to channel until asked
desirable	active	Yes	Actively asks to form a channel

Table 8-8 *EtherChannel Configuration Commands*

Task	Command Syntax
Select a load-balancing method for the switch	**port-channel load-balance** *method*
Use a PAgP mode on an interface	**channel-protocol pagp** **channel-group** *number* **mode** {**on** | {**auto** | **desirable**} [**non-silent**]}
Assign the LACP system priority	**lacp system-priority** *priority*
Use an LACP mode on an interface	**channel-protocol lacp** **channel-group** *number* **mode** {**on** | **passive** | **active**} **lacp port-priority** *priority*

Q&A

The questions in this book are more difficult than what you should experience on the actual exam. The questions do not attempt to cover more breadth or depth than the exam; however, they are designed to make sure that you know the answers. Rather than allowing you to derive the answers from clues hidden inside the questions themselves, the questions challenge your understanding and recall of the subject. Hopefully, these questions will help limit the number of exam questions on which you narrow your choices to two options and then guess.

The answers to these questions can be found in Appendix A.

1. What are some benefits of an EtherChannel?

2. How many links can be aggregated into an EtherChannel?

3. Traffic between two hosts will be distributed across all links in an EtherChannel. True or false?

4. Which methods can you use to distribute traffic in an EtherChannel?

5. How does an EtherChannel distribute broadcasts and multicasts?

6. When load balancing, what hashing functions choose a link for a frame?

7. What protocols can negotiate an EtherChannel between two switches?

8. Suppose a switch at one end of an EtherChannel is configured to use source MAC addresses for load balancing. The switch on the other end is configured to use both source and destination IP addresses. What happens?

9. Two switches have a four-port EtherChannel between them. Both switches are load balancing using source and destination IP addresses. If a packet has the source address 192.168.15.10 and destination address 192.168.100.31, what is the EtherChannel link index?

10. What does the acronym PAgP stand for?

11. Two switches should be configured to negotiate an EtherChannel. If one switch is using PAgP auto mode, what should the other switch use?

12. What is the LACP system priority value used for?

13. Complete the following command to put an interface into EtherChannel group 3 and to use PAgP to ask the far-end switch to participate in the EtherChannel. This switch port also should require PAgP packets back from the far-end switch.

```
Switch(config-if)# channel-group _____
```

14. What interface configuration command is needed to select LACP as the EtherChannel negotiation protocol?

15. What command could you use to see the status of every port in an EtherChannel?

16. What command could you use to verify the hashing algorithm used for EtherChannel load balancing?

17. Suppose that a switch is used in a small data center where one server offers an IP-based application to many clients throughout the campus. An EtherChannel connects the data-center switch to a Layer 3 core switch, which routes traffic to all clients. What EtherChannel load-balancing method might be most appropriate at the data-center switch?

    a. Source MAC address

    b. Source IP address

    c. Destination MAC address

    d. Destination IP address

    e. Source and destination MAC address

    f. Source and destination IP address

18. Suppose that a mainframe is connected to a switch that has an EtherChannel uplink to a campus network. The EtherChannel has been configured with the **port-channel load-balance src-dst-ip** command. Most of the mainframe traffic is SNA (non-IP). What will happen to the SNA frames when they are switched? Would it be better to reconfigure the channel with **port-channel load-balance src-dst-mac**?

19. What attributes of a set of switch ports must match to form an EtherChannel?

20. What happens if one port of an EtherChannel is unplugged or goes dead? What happens when that port is reconnected?

This chapter covers the following topics that you need to master for the CCNP BCMSN exam:

- **IEEE 802.1D Overview**—This section discusses the original, or more traditional, Spanning Tree Protocol (STP). This protocol is the foundation for the default Catalyst STP and for all the enhancements that are described in Chapters 10, "Spanning Tree Configuration," through 12, "Advanced Spanning Tree Protocol."

- **Types of STP**—This section discusses other types of STP that might be running on a Catalyst switch—specifically, the Common Spanning Tree, Per-VLAN Spanning Tree (PVST), and PVST+.

CHAPTER 9

Traditional Spanning Tree Protocol

Previous chapters covered robust network designs where redundant links are used between switches. Although this increases the network availability, it also opens up the possibility for conditions that would impair the network. In a Layer 2 switched network, preventing bridging loops from forming over redundant paths is important. Spanning Tree Protocol (STP) was designed to monitor and control the Layer 2 network so that a loop-free topology is maintained.

This chapter discusses the theory and operation of the STP. More specifically, the original, or traditional, STP is covered, as defined in IEEE 802.1D. Several chapters explain STP topics in this book. Here is a brief roadmap so you can chart a course:

■ **Chapter 9, "Traditional Spanning Tree Protocol"**—Covers the theory of IEEE 802.1D

■ **Chapter 10, "Spanning Tree Configuration"**—Covers the configuration commands needed for IEEE 802.1D

■ **Chapter 11, "Protecting the Spanning Tree Protocol Topology"**—Covers the features and commands to filter and protect a converged STP topology from conditions that could destabilize it

■ **Chapter 12, "Advanced Spanning Tree Protocol"**—Covers the newer 802.1w and 802.1s enhancements to STP, allowing more scalability and faster convergence

"Do I Know This Already?" Quiz

The purpose of the "Do I Know This Already?" quiz is to help you decide whether you need to read the entire chapter. If you already intend to read the entire chapter, you do not necessarily need to answer these questions now.

The 12-question quiz, derived from the major sections in the "Foundation Topics" portion of the chapter, helps you determine how to spend your limited study time.

Table 9-1 outlines the major topics discussed in this chapter and the "Do I Know This Already?" quiz questions that correspond to those topics.

Table 9-1 *"Do I Know This Already?" Foundation Topics Section-to-Question Mapping*

Foundation Topics Section	Questions Covered in This Section	Score
IEEE 802.1D	1–10	
Types of STP	11–12	
Total Score		

CAUTION The goal of self-assessment is to gauge your mastery of the topics in this chapter. If you do not know the answer to a question or are only partially sure of the answer, you should mark this question wrong. Giving yourself credit for an answer you correctly guess skews your self- assessment results and might give you a false sense of security.

1. How is a bridging loop best described?

   a. A loop formed between switches for redundancy

   b. A loop formed by the Spanning Tree Protocol

   c. A loop formed between switches where frames circulate endlessly

   d. The round-trip path a frame takes from source to destination

2. Which of these is one of the parameters used to elect a Root Bridge?

   a. Root Path Cost

   b. Path Cost

   c. Bridge Priority

   d. BPDU revision number

3. If all switches in a network are left at their default STP values, which one of the following is not true?

   a. The Root Bridge will be the switch with the lowest MAC address.

   b. The Root Bridge will be the switch with the highest MAC address.

   c. One or more switches will have a Bridge Priority of 32,768.

   d. A secondary Root Bridge will be present on the network.

4. Configuration BPDUs are originated by which of the following?

    a. All switches in the STP domain

    b. Only the Root Bridge switch

    c. Only the switch that detects a topology change

    d. Only the secondary Root Bridge when it takes over

5. Which of these is the single most important design decision to be made in a network running STP?

    a. Removing any redundant links

    b. Making sure all switches run the same version of IEEE 802.1D

    c. Root Bridge placement

    d. Making sure all switches have redundant links

6. What happens to a port that is neither a Root Port nor a Designated Port?

    a. It is available for normal use.

    b. It can be used for load balancing.

    c. It is put into the Blocking state.

    d. It is disabled.

7. What is the maximum number of Root Ports that a Catalyst switch can have?

    a. 1

    b. 2

    c. Unlimited

    d. None

8. What mechanism is used to set STP timer values for all switches in a network?

    a. Configuring the timers on every switch in the network.

    b. Configuring the timers on the Root Bridge switch.

    c. Configuring the timers on both primary and secondary Root Bridge switches.

    d. The timers can't be adjusted.

9. MAC addresses can be placed into the CAM table, but no data can be sent or received if a switch port is in which of the following STP states?

    a. Blocking

    b. Forwarding

    c. Listening

    d. Learning

10. What is the default "hello" time for IEEE 802.1D?

   a. 1 second

   b. 2 seconds

   c. 30 seconds

   d. 60 seconds

11. Which of the following is the Spanning Tree Protocol defined in the IEEE 802.1Q standard?

   a. PVST

   b. CST

   c. EST

   d. MST

12. If a switch has 10 VLANs defined and active, how many instances of STP will run using PVST+ versus CST?

   a. 1 for PVST+, 1 for CST

   b. 1 for PVST+, 10 for CST

   c. 10 for PVST+, 1 for CST

   d. 10 for PVST+, 10 for CST

You can find the answers to the quiz in Appendix A, "Answers to Chapter 'Do I Know This Already?' Quizzes and Q&A Sections." The suggested choices for your next step are as follows:

■ **7 or less overall score**—Read the entire chapter. This includes the "Foundation Topics," "Foundation Summary," and "Q&A" sections.

■ **8–10 overall score**—Begin with the "Foundation Summary" section and then follow up with the "Q&A" section at the end of the chapter.

■ **11 or more overall score**—If you want more review on these topics, skip to the "Foundation Summary" section and then go to the "Q&A" section at the end of the chapter. Otherwise, move to Chapter 10.

Foundation Topics

IEEE 802.1D Overview

A robust network design not only includes efficient transfer of packets or frames, but also considers how to recover quickly from faults in the network. In a Layer 3 environment, the routing protocols in use keep track of redundant paths to a destination network so that a secondary path can be used quickly if the primary path fails. Layer 3 routing allows many paths to a destination to remain up and active, and allows load sharing across multiple paths.

In a Layer 2 environment (switching or bridging), however, no routing protocols are used, and active redundant paths are neither allowed nor desirable. Instead, some form of bridging provides data transport between networks or switch ports. The Spanning Tree Protocol (STP) provides network link redundancy so that a Layer 2 switched network can recover from failures without intervention in a timely manner. The STP is defined in the IEEE 802.1D standard.

STP is discussed in relation to the problems it solves in the sections that follow.

Bridging Loops

Recall that a Layer 2 switch mimics the function of a transparent bridge. A transparent bridge must offer segmentation between two networks while remaining transparent to all the end devices connected to it. For the purpose of this discussion, consider a two-port Ethernet switch and its similarities to a two-port transparent bridge.

A transparent bridge (and the Ethernet switch) must operate as follows:

■ The bridge has no initial knowledge of any end device's location; therefore, the bridge must "listen" to frames coming into each of its ports to figure out on which network each device resides. The bridge assumes that a device using the source MAC address is located behind the port that the frame arrives on. As the listening process continues, the bridge builds a table that correlates source MAC addresses with the Bridge Port numbers where they were detected.

The bridge constantly can update its bridging table upon detecting the presence of a new MAC address or upon detecting a MAC address that has changed location from one Bridge Port to another. The bridge then can forward frames by looking at the destination MAC address, looking up that address in the bridge table, and sending the frame out the port where the destination device is known to be located.

- If a frame arrives with the broadcast address as the destination address, the bridge must forward, or flood, the frame out all available ports. However, the frame is not forwarded out the port that initially received the frame. In this way, broadcasts can reach all available Layer 2 networks. A bridge segments only collision domains—it does not segment broadcast domains.

- If a frame arrives with a destination address that is not found in the bridge table, the bridge cannot determine which port to forward the frame to for transmission. This type of frame is known as an *unknown unicast*. In this case, the bridge treats the frame as if it were a broadcast and floods it out all remaining ports. When a reply to that frame is overheard, the bridge can learn the location of the unknown station and can add it to the bridge table for future use.

- Frames forwarded across the bridge cannot be modified by the bridge itself. Therefore, the bridging process is effectively *transparent*.

Bridging or switching in this fashion works well. Any frame forwarded, whether to a known or unknown destination, is forwarded out the appropriate port or ports so that it is likely to be received successfully at the end device. Figure 9-1 shows a simple two-port switch functioning as a bridge, forwarding frames between two end devices. However, this network design offers no additional links or paths for redundancy if the switch or one of its links fails. In that case, the networks on either side of the bridge would become isolated from each other.

Figure 9-1 *Transparent Bridging with a Switch*

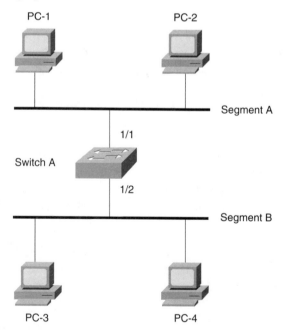

To add some redundancy, you can add a second switch between the two original network segments, as shown in Figure 9-2. Now, two switches offer the transparent bridging function in parallel. In theory, a single switch or a single link can fail without causing end-to-end connectivity to fail.

Figure 9-2 *Redundant Bridging with Two Switches*

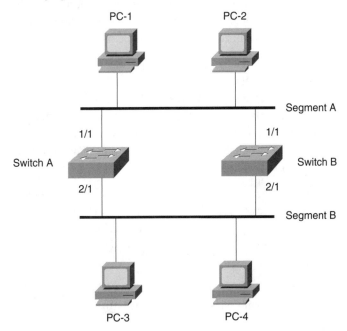

Consider what happens when PC-1 sends a frame to PC-4. For now, assume that both PC-1 and PC-4 are known to the switches and are in their address tables. PC-1 sends the frame onto network Segment A. Switch A and switch B both receive the frame on their 1/1 ports. Because PC-4 already is known to the switches, the frame is forwarded out ports 2/1 on each switch onto Segment B. The end result is that PC-4 receives two copies of the frame from PC-1. This is not ideal, but it is not disastrous, either.

Now, consider the same process of sending a frame from PC-1 to PC-4. This time, however, neither switch knows anything about the location of PC-1 or PC-4. PC-1 sends the frame to PC-4 by placing it on Segment A. The sequence of events is as follows:

Step 1   Both Switch A and switch B receive the frame on their 1/1 ports. Because the MAC address of PC-1 has not yet been seen or recorded, each switch records PC-1's MAC address in its address table along with the receiving port number, 1/1. From this information, both switches infer that PC-1 must reside on Segment A.

Step 2   Because the location of PC-4 is unknown, both switches correctly decide that they must flood the frame out all available ports. This is an unknown unicast condition and is their best effort to make sure that the frame eventually reaches its destination.

Step 3   Each switch floods or copies the frame to its 2/1 port on Segment B. PC-4, located on Segment B, receives the two frames destined for it. However, on Segment B, switch A now hears the new frame forwarded by switch B, and switch B hears the new frame forwarded by switch A.

Step 4   Switch A sees that the "new" frame is from PC-1 to PC-4. From the address table, the switch previously learned that PC-1 was on port 1/1, or Segment A. However, the source address of PC-1 has just been heard on port 2/1, or Segment B. By definition, the switch must relearn the location of PC-1 with the most recent information, which it now incorrectly assumes to be Segment B. (Switch B follows the same procedure, based on the "new" frame from switch A.)

Step 5   At this point, neither switch A nor switch B has learned the location of PC-4 because no frames have been received with PC-4 as the source address. Therefore, the new frame must be flooded out all available ports in an attempt to find PC-4. This frame then is sent out switch A's 1/1 port and onto Segment A, as well as switch B's 1/1 port and onto Segment A.

Step 6   Now both switches relearn the location of PC-1 as Segment A and forward the "new" frames back onto Segment B; then the entire process repeats.

This process of forwarding a single frame around and around between two switches is known as a *bridging loop*. Neither switch is aware of the other, so each happily forwards the same frame back and forth between its segments. Also note that because two switches are involved in the loop, the original frame has been duplicated and now is sent around in two counter-rotating loops. What stops the frame from being forwarded in this fashion forever? Nothing! PC-4 begins receiving frames addressed to it as fast as the switches can forward them.

Notice how the learned location of PC-1 keeps changing as frames get looped. Even a simple unicast frame has caused a bridging loop to form, and each switch's bridge table repeatedly is corrupted with incorrect data.

What would happen if PC-1 sent a broadcast frame instead? The bridging loops (remember that two of them are produced by the two parallel switches) form exactly as before. The broadcast frames continue to circulate forever. Now, however, every end-user device located on both Segments A and B receives and processes every broadcast frame. This type of broadcast storm easily can saturate the network segments and bring every host on the segments to a halt.

The only way to end the bridging loop condition is to physically break the loop by disconnecting switch ports or shutting down a switch. Obviously, it would be better to *prevent* bridging loops than to be faced with finding and breaking them after they form.

Preventing Loops with Spanning Tree Protocol

Bridging loops form because parallel switches (or bridges) are unaware of each other. STP was developed to overcome the possibility of bridging loops so that redundant switches and switch paths could be used for their benefits. Basically, the protocol enables switches to become aware of each other so they can negotiate a loop-free path through the network.

> **NOTE**   Because STP is involved in loop detection, many people refer to the catastrophic loops as "Spanning Tree loops." This is technically incorrect because the Spanning Tree Protocol's entire function is to *prevent* bridging loops. The correct terminology for this condition is a *bridging loop*.

Loops are discovered before they are made available for use, and redundant links effectively are shut down to prevent the loops from forming. In the case of redundant links, switches can be made aware that a link shut down for loop prevention should be brought up quickly in case of a link failure. The section "Redundant Link Convergence," in Chapter 10.

STP is communicated among all connected switches on a network. Each switch executes the Spanning Tree Algorithm based on information received from other neighboring switches. The algorithm chooses a reference point in the network and calculates all the redundant paths to that reference point. When redundant paths are found, the Spanning Tree Algorithm picks one path by which to forward frames and disables, or blocks, forwarding on the other redundant paths.

As its name implies, STP computes a tree structure that spans all switches in a subnet or network. Redundant paths are placed in a Blocking or Standby state to prevent frame forwarding. The switched network is then in a loop-free condition. However, if a forwarding port fails or becomes disconnected, the Spanning Tree Algorithm recomputes the spanning-tree topology so that the appropriate blocked links can be reactivated.

Spanning-Tree Communication: Bridge Protocol Data Units

STP operates as switches communicate with one another. Data messages are exchanged in the form of *Bridge Protocol Data Units (BPDU)*. A switch sends a BPDU frame out a port, using the unique MAC address of the port itself as a source address. The switch is unaware of the other switches around it, so BPDU frames are sent with a destination address of the well-known STP multicast address 01-80-c2-00-00-00.

Two types of BPDU exist:

■   *Configuration BPDU*, used for spanning-tree computation

■   *Topology Change Notification (TCN) BPDU*, used to announce changes in the network topology

The Configuration BPDU message contains the fields shown in Table 9-2. The TCN BPDU is discussed in the "Topology Changes" section later in this chapter.

Table 9-2   *Configuration BPDU Message Content*

Field Description	Number of Bytes
Protocol ID (always 0)	2
Version (always 0)	1
Message Type (Configuration or TCN BPDU)	1
Flags	1
Root Bridge ID	8
Root Path Cost	4
Sender Bridge ID	8
Port ID	2
Message Age (in 256ths of a second)	2
Maximum Age (in 256ths of a second)	2
Hello Time (in 256ths of a second)	2
Forward Delay (in 256ths of a second)	2

The exchange of BPDU messages works toward the goal of electing reference points as a foundation for a stable spanning-tree topology. Loops also can be identified and removed by placing specific redundant ports in a Blocking or Standby state. Notice that several key fields in the BPDU are related to bridge (or switch) identification, path costs, and timer values. These all work together so that the network of switches can converge upon a common spanning-tree topology and select the same reference points within the network. These reference points are defined in the sections that follow.

By default, BPDUs are sent out all switch ports every 2 seconds so that current topology information is exchanged and loops are identified quickly.

Electing a Root Bridge

For all switches in a network to agree on a loop-free topology, a common frame of reference must exist to use as a guide. This reference point is called the *Root Bridge*. (The term *bridge* continues to be used even in a switched environment because STP was developed for use in bridges. Therefore, when you see *bridge*, think *switch*.)

An election process among all connected switches chooses the Root Bridge. Each switch has a unique *Bridge ID* that identifies it to other switches. The Bridge ID is an 8-byte value consisting of the following fields:

■ **Bridge Priority (2 bytes)**—The priority or weight of a switch in relation to all other switches. The priority field can have a value of 0 to 65,535 and defaults to 32,768 (or 0x8000) on every Catalyst switch.

■ **MAC Address (6 bytes)**—The MAC address used by a switch can come from the Supervisor module, the backplane, or a pool of 1024 addresses that are assigned to every Supervisor or backplane, depending on the switch model. In any event, this address is hardcoded and unique, and the user cannot change it.

When a switch first powers up, it has a narrow view of its surroundings and assumes that it is the Root Bridge itself. (This notion probably will change as other switches check in and enter the election process.) The election process then proceeds as follows: Every switch begins by sending out BPDUs with a Root Bridge ID equal to its own Bridge ID and a Sender Bridge ID that is its own Bridge ID. The Sender Bridge ID simply tells other switches who is the actual sender of the BPDU message. (After a Root Bridge is decided upon, configuration BPDUs are sent only by the Root Bridge. All other bridges must forward or relay the BPDUs, adding their own Sender Bridge IDs to the message.)

Received BPDU messages are analyzed to see if a "better" Root Bridge is being announced. A Root Bridge is considered better if the Root Bridge ID value is *lower* than another. Again, think of the Root Bridge ID as being broken into Bridge Priority and MAC address fields. If two Bridge Priority values are equal, the lower MAC address makes the Bridge ID better. When a switch hears of a better Root Bridge, it replaces its own Root Bridge ID with the Root Bridge ID announced in the BPDU. The switch then is required to recommend or advertise the new Root Bridge ID in its own BPDU messages, although it still identifies itself as the Sender Bridge ID.

Sooner or later, the election converges and all switches agree on the notion that one of them is the Root Bridge. As might be expected, if a new switch with a lower Bridge Priority powers up, it begins advertising itself as the Root Bridge. Because the new switch does indeed have a lower Bridge ID, all the switches soon reconsider and record it as the new Root Bridge. This also can happen if the new switch has a Bridge Priority equal to that of the existing Root Bridge but has a lower MAC address. Root Bridge election is an ongoing process, triggered by Root Bridge ID changes in the BPDUs every 2 seconds.

As an example, consider the small network shown in Figure 9-3. For simplicity, assume that each Catalyst switch has a MAC address of all 0s, with the last hex digit equal to the switch label.

Figure 9-3 *Example of Root Bridge Election*

In this network, each switch has the default Bridge Priority of 32,768. The switches are interconnected with Fast Ethernet links. All three switches try to elect themselves as the Root, but all of them have equal Bridge Priority values. The election outcome produces the Root Bridge, determined by the lowest MAC address—that of Catalyst A.

Electing Root Ports

Now that a reference point has been nominated and elected for the entire switched network, each nonroot switch must figure out where it is in relation to the Root Bridge. This action can be performed by selecting only one *Root Port* on each nonroot switch. The Root Port always points toward the current Root Bridge.

STP uses the concept of cost to determine many things. Selecting a Root Port involves evaluating the *Root Path Cost*. This value is the cumulative cost of all the links leading to the Root Bridge. A particular switch link also has a cost associated with it, called the *Path Cost*. To understand the difference between these values, remember that only the Root Path Cost is carried inside the BPDU. (See Table 9-2 again.) As the Root Path Cost travels along, other switches can modify its value to make it cumulative. The Path Cost, however, is not contained in the BPDU. It is known only to the local switch where the port (or "path" to a neighboring switch) resides.

Path Costs are defined as a 1-byte value, with the default values shown in Table 9-3. Generally, the higher the bandwidth of a link, the lower the cost of transporting data across it. The original IEEE 802.1D standard defined Path Cost as 1000 Mbps divided by the link bandwidth in megabits per second. These values are shown in the center column of the table. Modern networks commonly use Gigabit Ethernet and OC-48 ATM, which are both either too close to or greater than the maximum scale of 1000 Mbps. The IEEE now uses a nonlinear scale for Path Cost, as shown in the right column of the table.

> **TIP** Be aware that there are two STP path cost scales, one that is little used with a linear scale and one commonly used that is nonlinear. If you decide to memorize some common Path Cost values, learn only the ones in the "new" right column of the table.

Table 9-3 *STP Path Cost*

Link Bandwidth	Old STP Cost	New STP Cost
4 Mbps	250	250
10 Mbps	100	100
16 Mbps	63	62
45 Mbps	22	39
100 Mbps	10	19
155 Mbps	6	14
622 Mbps	2	6
1 Gbps	1	4
10 Gbps	0	2

The Root Path Cost value is determined in the following manner:

1. The Root Bridge sends out a BPDU with a Root Path Cost value of 0 because its ports sit directly on the Root Bridge.

2. When the next-closest neighbor receives the BPDU, it adds the Path Cost of its own port where the BPDU arrived. (This is done as the BPDU is *received*.)

3. The neighbor sends out BPDUs with this new cumulative value as the Root Path Cost.

4. The Root Path Cost is incremented by the ingress port Path Cost as the BPDU is received at each switch down the line.

5. Notice the emphasis on incrementing the Root Path Cost as BPDUs are *received*. When computing the Spanning Tree Algorithm manually, remember to compute a new Root Path Cost as BPDUs *come in* to a switch port, not as they go out.

After incrementing the Root Path Cost, a switch also records the value in its memory. When a BPDU is received on another port and the new Root Path Cost is lower than the previously recorded value, this lower value becomes the new Root Path Cost. In addition, the lower cost tells the switch that the path to the Root Bridge must be better using this port than it was on other ports. The switch now has determined which of its ports has the best path to the Root: the Root Port.

Figure 9-4 shows the same network from Figure 9-3 in the process of Root Port selection.

Figure 9-4 *Example of Root Port Selection*

The Root Bridge, Catalyst A, already has been elected. Therefore, every other switch in the network must choose one port that has the best path to the Root Bridge. Catalyst B selects its port 1/1, with a Root Path Cost of 0 plus 19. Port 1/2 is not chosen because its Root Path Cost is 0 (BPDU from Catalyst A) plus 19 (Path Cost of A–C link), plus 19 (Path Cost of C–B link), or a total of 38. Catalyst C makes a similar choice of port 1/1.

Electing Designated Ports

By now, you should begin to see the process unfolding: A starting or reference point has been identified, and each switch "connects" itself toward the reference point with the single link that has the best path. A tree structure is beginning to emerge, but links have only been identified at this point. All links still are connected and could be active, leaving bridging loops.

To remove the possibility of bridging loops, STP makes a final computation to identify one *Designated Port* on each network segment. Suppose that two or more switches have ports connected to a single common network segment. If a frame appears on that segment, all the bridges attempt to forward it to its destination. Recall that this behavior was the basis of a bridging loop and should be avoided.

Instead, only one of the links on a segment should forward traffic to and from that segment—the one that is selected as the Designated Port. Switches choose a Designated Port based on the lowest cumulative Root Path Cost to the Root Bridge. For example, a switch always has an idea of its own Root Path Cost, which it announces in its own BPDUs. If a neighboring switch on a shared LAN segment sends a BPDU announcing a lower Root Path Cost, the neighbor must have the Designated Port. If a switch learns only of higher Root Path Costs from other BPDUs received on a port, however, it then correctly assumes that its own receiving port is the Designated Port for the segment.

Notice that the entire STP determination process has served only to identify bridges and ports. All ports are still active, and bridging loops still might lurk in the network. STP has a set of progressive states that each port must go through, regardless of the type or identification. These states actively prevent loops from forming and are described in the next section.

> **NOTE**   In each determination process discussed so far, two or more links might have identical Root Path Costs. This results in a tie condition, unless other factors are considered. All tie-breaking STP decisions are based on the following sequence of four conditions:
>
> **1.** Lowest Root Bridge ID
>
> **2.** Lowest Root Path Cost to Root Bridge
>
> **3.** Lowest Sender Bridge ID
>
> **4.** Lowest Sender Port ID

Figure 9-5 demonstrates an example of Designated Port selection. This figure is identical to Figure 9-3 and Figure 9-4, with further spanning-tree development shown. The only changes are the choices of Designated Ports, although seeing all STP decisions shown on one network diagram is handy.

Figure 9-5 *Example of Designated Port Selection*

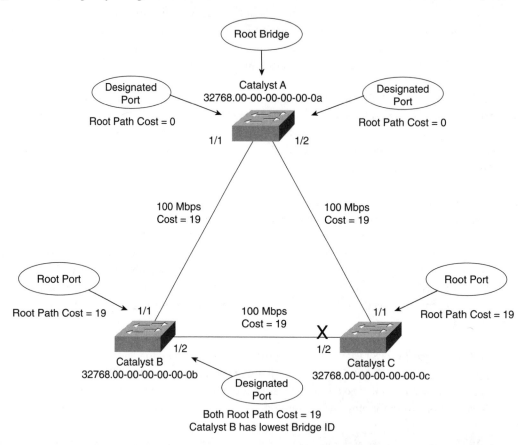

The three switches have chosen their Designated Ports (DP) for the following reasons:

- **Catalyst A**—Because this switch is the Root Bridge, all its active ports are Designated Ports, by definition. At the Root Bridge, the Root Path Cost of each port is 0.

- **Catalyst B**—Catalyst A port 1/1 is the DP for the Segment A–B because it has the lowest Root Path Cost (0). Catalyst B port 1/2 is the DP for segment B–C. The Root Path Cost for each end of this segment is 19, determined from the incoming BPDU on port 1/1. Because the Root Path Cost is equal on both ports of the segment, the DP must be chosen by the next criteria—the lowest Sender Bridge ID. When Catalyst B sends a BPDU to Catalyst C, it has the lowest MAC address in the Bridge ID. Catalyst C also sends a BPDU to Catalyst B, but its Sender Bridge ID is higher. Therefore, Catalyst B port 1/2 is selected as the segment's DP.

- **Catalyst C**—Catalyst A port 1/2 is the DP for Segment A–C because it has the lowest Root Path Cost (0). Catalyst B port 1/2 is the DP for Segment B–C. Therefore, Catalyst C port 1/2 will be neither a Root Port nor a Designated Port. As discussed in the next section, any port that is not elected to either position enters the Blocking state. Where blocking occurs, bridging loops are broken.

STP States

To participate in STP, each port of a switch must progress through several states. A port begins its life in a Disabled state, moving through several passive states and, finally, into an active state if allowed to forward traffic. The STP port states are as follows:

- **Disabled**—Ports that are administratively shut down by the network administrator, or by the system because of a fault condition, are in the Disabled state. This state is special and is not part of the normal STP progression for a port.

- **Blocking**—After a port initializes, it begins in the Blocking state so that no bridging loops can form. In the Blocking state, a port cannot receive or transmit data and cannot add MAC addresses to its address table. Instead, a port is allowed to receive only BPDUs so that the switch can hear from other neighboring switches. In addition, ports that are put into standby mode to remove a bridging loop enter the Blocking state.

- **Listening**—A port is moved from Blocking to Listening if the switch thinks that the port can be selected as a Root Port or Designated Port. In other words, the port is on its way to begin forwarding traffic.

  In the Listening state, the port still cannot send or receive data frames. However, the port is allowed to receive and send BPDUs so that it actively can participate in the Spanning Tree topology process. Here, the port finally is allowed to become a Root Port or Designated Port because the switch can advertise the port by sending BPDUs to other switches. If the port loses its Root Port or Designated Port status, it returns to the Blocking state.

- **Learning**—After a period of time called the Forward Delay in the Listening state, the port is allowed to move into the Learning state. The port still sends and receives BPDUs as before. In addition, the switch now can learn new MAC addresses to add to its address table. This gives the port an extra period of silent participation and allows the switch to assemble at least some address table information. The port cannot yet send any data frames, however.

- **Forwarding**—After another Forward Delay period of time in the Learning state, the port is allowed to move into the Forwarding state. The port now can send and receive data frames, collect MAC addresses in its address table, and send and receive BPDUs. The port is now a fully functioning switch port within the spanning-tree topology.

Remember that a switch port is allowed into the Forwarding state only if no redundant links (or loops) are detected and if the port has the best path to the Root Bridge as the Root Port or Designated Port.

Example 9-1 shows the output from a switch as one of its ports progresses through the STP port states.

Example 9-1 *Port Progressing Through the STP Port States*

```
*Mar 16 14:31:00 UTC: STP SW: Fa0/1 new disabled req for 1 vlans
Switch(config)# interface fast 0/1
Switch(config-if)#no shut
Switch(config-if)#^-Z
*Mar 16 14:31:00 UTC: STP SW: Fa0/1 new blocking req for 1 vlans


Switch#show spanning interface fast 0/1


Vlan              Port ID                    Designated               Port ID
Name              Prio.Nbr     Cost Sts      Cost Bridge ID           Prio.Nbr
---------------   --------   ---------  ---   ---------  -------------------  --------
VLAN0001          128.1          19 LIS         0 32769 000a.f40a.2980 128.1

*Mar 16 14:31:15 UTC: STP SW: Fa0/1 new learning req for 1 vlans

Switch#show spanning interface fast 0/1
Vlan              Port ID                    Designated               Port ID
Name              Prio.Nbr     Cost Sts      Cost Bridge ID           Prio.Nbr
---------------   --------   ---------  ---   ---------  -------------------  --------
VLAN0001          128.1          19 LRN         0 32768 00d0.5849.4100  32.129

*Mar 16 14:31:30 UTC: STP SW: Fa0/1 new forwarding req for 1 vlans

Switch#show spanning interface fast 0/1

Vlan              Port ID                    Designated               Port ID
Name              Prio.Nbr     Cost Sts      Cost Bridge ID           Prio.Nbr
---------------   --------   ---------  ---   ---------  -------------------  --------
VLAN0001          128.1          19 FWD         0 32768 00d0.5849.4100  32.129
```

The example begins as the port administratively is disabled from the command line. When the port is enabled, successive **show spanning-tree interface** *type mod/port* commands display the port state as Listening, Learning, and then Forwarding. These are shown in the shaded text of the example. Notice also the time stamps and port states provided by the **debug spanning-tree switch state** command, which give a sense of the timing between port states. Because this port was eligible as a Root Port, the **show** command never could execute fast enough to show the port in the Blocking state.

STP Timers

STP operates as switches send BPDUs to each other in an effort to form a loop-free topology. The BPDUs take a finite amount of time to travel from switch to switch. In addition, news of a topology change (such as a link or Root Bridge failure) can suffer from propagation delays as the announcement travels from one side of a network to the other. Because of the possibility of these delays, keeping the spanning-tree topology from settling out or converging until all switches have had time to receive accurate information is important.

STP uses three timers to make sure that a network converges properly before a bridging loop can form. The timers and their default values are as follows:

- **Hello Time**—The time interval between Configuration BPDUs sent by the Root Bridge. The Hello Time value configured in the Root Bridge switch determines the Hello Time for all nonroot switches because they just relay the Configuration BPDUs as they are received from the root. However, all switches have a locally configured Hello Time that is used to time TCN BPDUs when they are retransmitted. The IEEE 802.1D standard specifies a default Hello Time value of 2 seconds.

- **Forward Delay**—The time interval that a switch port spends in both the Listening and Learning states. The default value is 15 seconds.

- **Max (maximum) Age**—The time interval that a switch stores a BPDU before discarding it. While executing the STP, each switch port keeps a copy of the "best" BPDU that it has heard. If the switch port loses contact with the BPDU's source (no more BPDUs are received from it), the switch assumes that a topology change must have occurred after the Max Age time elapsed and so the BPDU is aged out. The default Max Age value is 20 seconds.

The STP timers can be configured or adjusted from the switch command line. However, the timer values never should be changed from the defaults without careful consideration. Then the values should be changed only on the Root Bridge switch. Recall that the timer values are advertised in fields within the BPDU. The Root Bridge ensures that the timer values propagate to all other switches.

TIP   The default STP timer values are based on some assumptions about the size of the network and the length of the Hello Time. A reference model of a network having a diameter of seven switches derives these values. The diameter is measured from the Root Bridge switch outward, including the Root Bridge.

In other words, if you drew the STP topology, the diameter would be the number of switches connected in series from the Root Bridge out to the end of any branch in the tree. The Hello Time is based on the time it takes for a BPDU to travel from the Root Bridge to a point seven switches away. This computation uses a Hello Time of 2 seconds.

The network diameter can be configured on the Root Bridge switch to more accurately reflect the true size of the physical network. Making that value more accurate reduces the total STP convergence time during a topology change. Cisco also recommends that if changes need to be made, only the network diameter value should be modified on the Root Bridge switch. When the diameter is changed, the switch calculates new values for all three timers automatically.

Topology Changes

To announce a change in the active network topology, switches send a TCN BPDU. Table 9-4 shows the format of these messages.

Table 9-4 *Topology Change Notification BPDU Message Content*

Field Description	# of Bytes
Protocol ID (always 0)	2
Version (always 0)	1
Message Type (Configuration or TCN BPDU)	1

A topology change occurs when a switch either moves a port into the Forwarding state or moves a port from the Forwarding or Learning states into the Blocking state. In other words, a port on an active switch comes up or goes down. The switch sends a TCN BPDU out its Root Port so that, ultimately, the Root Bridge receives news of the topology change. Notice that the TCN BPDU carries no data about the change but informs recipients only that a change has occurred. Also notice that the switch will not send TCN BPDUs if the port has been configured with PortFast enabled.

The switch continues sending TCN BPDUs every Hello Time interval until it gets an acknowledgment from its upstream neighbor. As the upstream neighbors receive the TCN BPDU, they propagate it on toward the Root Bridge and send their own acknowledgments. When the Root Bridge receives the TCN BPDU, it also sends out an acknowledgment. However, the Root Bridge sets the Topology Change flag in its Configuration BPDU, which is relayed to every other bridge in the network. This is done to signal the topology change and cause all other bridges to shorten their bridge table aging times from the default (300 seconds) to only the Forward Delay value (default 15 seconds).

This condition causes the learned locations of MAC addresses to be flushed out much sooner than they normally would, easing the bridge table corruption that might occur because of the change in topology. However, any stations that actively are communicating during this time are kept in the bridge table. This condition lasts for the sum of the Forward Delay and the Max Age (default 15 + 20 seconds).

The theory behind topology changes is fairly straightforward, but it's often difficult to grasp how a working network behaves during a change. For example, suppose you have a Layer 2 network (think of a single VLAN or a single instance of STP) that is stable and loop free. If a switch uplink suddenly failed or a new uplink was added, how would the various switches in the network react? Would users all over the network lose connectivity while the STP "recomputes" or reconverges?

Examples of different types of topology changes are presented in the following sections, along with the sequence of STP events. Each type has a different cause and a different effect. To provide continuity as the STP concepts are presented, the same network previously shown in Figures 9-3 through 9-5 is used in each of these examples.

Direct Topology Changes

A direct topology change is one that can be detected on a switch interface. For example, if a trunk link suddenly goes down, the switch on each end of the link immediately can detect a link failure. The absence of that link changes the bridging topology, so other switches should be notified.

Figure 9-6 shows a network that has converged into a stable STP topology. The VLAN is forwarding on all trunk links except port 1/2 on Catalyst C, where it is in the Blocking state.

Figure 9-6   *Effects of a Direct Topology Change*

This network has just suffered a link failure between Catalyst A and Catalyst C. The sequence of events unfolds as follows:

1. Catalyst C detects a link down on its port 1/1; Catalyst A detects a link down on its port 1/2.

2. Catalyst C removes the previous "best" BPDU it had received from the Root over port 1/1. Port 1/1 is now down so that BPDU is no longer valid.

   Normally, Catalyst C would try to send a TCN message out its Root Port, to reach the Root Bridge. Here, the Root Port is broken, so that isn't possible. Without an advanced feature such as STP UplinkFast, Catalyst C isn't yet aware that another path exists to the Root.

   Also, Catalyst A is aware of the link down condition on its own port 1/2. It normally would try to send a TCN message out its Root Port, to reach the Root Bridge. Here, Catalyst A *is* the Root, so that isn't really necessary.

3. The Root Bridge, Catalyst A, sends a Configuration BPDU with the TCN bit set out its port 1/1. This is received and relayed by each switch along the way, informing each one of the topology change.

4. Catalysts B and C receive the TCN message. The only reaction these switches take is to shorten their bridging table aging times to the Forward Delay time. At this point, they don't know how the topology has changed; they only know to force fairly recent bridging table entries to age out.

5. Catalyst C basically just sits and waits to hear from the Root Bridge again. The Config BPDU TCN message is received on port 1/2, which was previously in the Blocking state. This BPDU becomes the "best" one received from the Root, so port 1/2 becomes the new Root Port.

   Catalyst C now can progress port 1/2 from Blocking through the Listening, Learning, and Forwarding states.

As a result of a direct link failure, the topology has changed and STP has converged again. Notice that only Catalyst C has undergone any real effects from the failure. Switches A and B heard the news of the topology change but did not have to move any links through the STP states. In other words, the whole network did not go through a massive STP reconvergence.

The total time that users on Catalyst C lost connectivity was roughly the time that port 1/2 spent in the Listening and Learning states. With the default STP timers, this amounts to about two times the Forward Delay period (15 seconds), or 30 seconds total.

Indirect Topology Changes

Figure 9-7 shows the same network as Figure 9-6, but this time, the link failure indirectly involves Catalysts A and C. The link status at each switch stays up, but something between them has failed or is filtering traffic. This could be another device, such as a service provider's switch, a firewall, and so on. As a result, no data (including BPDUs) can pass between those switches.

Figure 9-7 *Effects of a Indirect Topology Change*

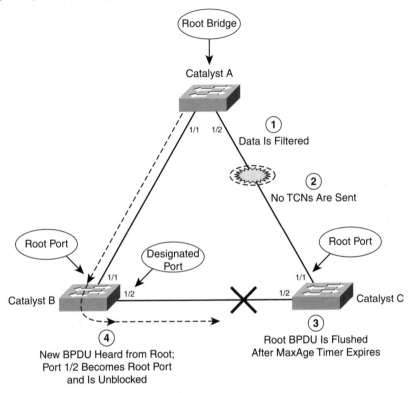

STP can detect and recover from indirect failures, thanks to timer mechanisms. The sequence of events unfolds as follows:

1. Catalysts A and C both show a link up condition; data begins to be filtered elsewhere on the link.

2. No link failure is detected, so no TCN messages are sent.

3. Catalyst C already has stored the "best" BPDU it had received from the Root over port 1/1. No further BPDUs are received from the Root over that port. After the MaxAge timer expires, no other BPDU is available to refresh the "best" entry, so it is flushed. Catalyst C now must wait to hear from the Root again on any of its ports.

4. The next Configuration BPDU from the Root is heard on Catalyst C port 1/2. This BPDU becomes the new "best" entry, and port 1/2 becomes the Root Port. Now the port is progressed from Blocking through the Listening, Learning, and finally Forwarding states.

As a result of the indirect link failure, the topology doesn't change immediately. The absence of BPDUs from the Root causes Catalyst C to take some action. Because this type of failure relies on STP timer activity, it generally takes longer to detect and mitigate.

In this example, the total time that users on Catalyst C lost connectivity was roughly the time until the MaxAge timer expired (20 seconds), plus the time until the next Configuration BPDU was received (2 seconds) on port 1/2, plus the time that port 1/2 spent in the Listening (15 seconds) and Learning (15 seconds) states. In other words, 52 seconds elapse if the default timer values are used.

Insignificant Topology Changes

Figure 9-8 shows the same network topology as Figure 9-6 and Figure 9-7, with the addition of a user PC on access-layer switch Catalyst C. The user's switch port, 2/12, is just another link as far as the switch is concerned. If the link status goes up or down, the switch must view that as a topology change and inform the Root Bridge.

Figure 9-8 *Effects of an Insignificant Topology Change*

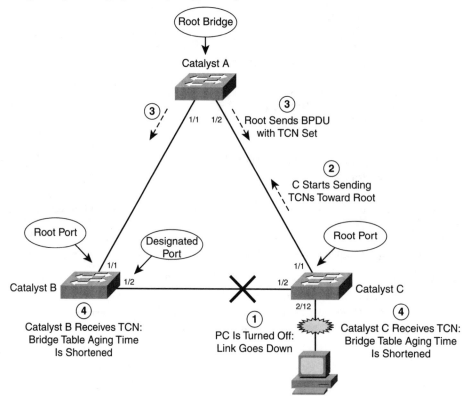

Obviously, user ports are expected to go up and down as the users reboot their machines, turn them on and off as they go to and from work, and so on. Regardless, TCN messages are sent by the switch, just as if a trunk link between switches had changed state.

To see what effect this has on the STP topology and the network, consider the following sequence of events:

1. The PC on Catalyst port 2/12 is turned off. The switch detects the link status going down.

2. Catalyst C begins sending TCN BPDUs toward the Root, over its Root Port (1/1).

3. The Root sends a TCN acknowledgment back to Catalyst C and then sends a Configuration BPDU with the TCN bit set to all downstream switches. This is done to inform every switch of a topology change somewhere in the network.

4. The TCN flag is received from the Root, and both Catalysts B and C shorten their bridge table aging times. This causes recently idle entries to be flushed, leaving only the actively transmitting stations in the table. The aging time stays short for the duration of the Forward Delay and Max Age timers.

Notice that this type of topology change is mostly cosmetic. No actual topology change occurred because none of the switches had to change port states to reach the Root Bridge. Instead, powering off the PC caused all the switches to age out entries from their bridge or CAM tables much sooner than normal.

At first, this doesn't seem like a major problem because the PC link state affects only the "newness" of the CAM table contents. If CAM table entries are flushed as a result, they probably will be learned again. This becomes a problem when every user PC is considered. Now every time *any* PC in the network powers up or down, *every* switch in the network must age out CAM table entries.

Given enough PCs, the switches could be in a constant state of flushing bridge tables. Also remember that when a switch doesn't have a CAM entry for a destination, the packet must be flooded out all its ports. Flushed tables mean more unknown unicasts, which mean more broadcasts or flooded packets throughout the network.

Fortunately, Catalyst switches have a feature that can designate a port as a special case. You can enable the STP PortFast feature on a port with a single attached PC. As a result, TCNs aren't sent when the port changes state, and the port is brought right into the Forwarding state when the link comes up. The section "Redundant Link Convergence," in Chapter 10, covers PortFast in more detail.

Types of STP

So far, this chapter has discussed STP in terms of its operation to prevent loops and to recover from topology changes in a timely manner. STP originally was developed to operate in a bridged environment, basically supporting a single LAN (or one VLAN). Implementing STP into a switched environment has required additional consideration and modification to support multiple VLANs. Because of this, the IEEE and Cisco have approached STP differently. This section reviews the three traditional types of STP that are encountered in switched networks and how they relate to one another. No specific configuration commands are associated with the various types of STP here. Instead, you need a basic understanding of how they interoperate in a network.

> **NOTE** The IEEE has produced additional standards for spanning-tree enhancements that greatly improve on its scalability and convergence aspects. These are covered in Chapter 12. When you have a firm understanding of the more traditional forms of STP presented in this chapter, you can grasp the enhanced versions much easier.

Common Spanning Tree

The IEEE 802.1Q standard specifies how VLANs are to be trunked between switches. It also specifies only a single instance of STP that encompasses all VLANs. This instance is referred to as the *Common Spanning Tree (CST)*. All CST BPDUs are transmitted over trunk links using the native VLAN with untagged frames.

Having a single STP for many VLANs simplifies switch configuration and reduces switch CPU load during STP calculations. However, having only one STP instance can cause limitations, too. Redundant links between switches will be blocked with no capability for load balancing. Conditions also can occur that would cause CST to mistakenly enable forwarding on a link that does not carry a specific VLAN, while other links would be blocked.

Per-VLAN Spanning Tree

Cisco has a proprietary version of STP that offers more flexibility than the CST version. *Per-VLAN Spanning Tree (PVST)* operates a separate instance of STP for each individual VLAN. This allows the STP on each VLAN to be configured independently, offering better performance and tuning for specific conditions. Multiple spanning-trees also make load balancing possible over redundant links when the links are assigned to different VLANs. One link might forward one set of VLANs, while another redundant link might forward a different set.

Because of its proprietary nature, PVST requires the use of Cisco Inter-Switch Link (ISL) trunking encapsulation between switches. In networks where PVST and CST coexist, interoperability problems occur. Each requires a different trunking method, so BPDUs are never exchanged between STP types.

Per-VLAN Spanning Tree Plus

Cisco has a second proprietary version of STP that allows devices to interoperate with both PVST and CST. *Per-VLAN Spanning Tree Plus (PVST+)* effectively supports three groups of STP operating in the same campus network:

- Catalyst switches running PVST

- Catalyst switches running PVST+

- Switches running CST over 802.1Q

To do this, PVST+ acts as a translator between groups of CST switches and groups of PVST switches. PVST+ can communicate directly with PVST by using ISL trunks. To communicate with CST, however, PVST+ exchanges BPDUs with CST as untagged frames over the native VLAN. BPDUs from other instances of STP (other VLANs) are propagated across the CST portions of the network by tunneling. PVST+ sends these BPDUs by using a unique multicast address so that the CST switches forward them on to downstream neighbors without interpreting them first. Eventually, the tunneled BPDUs reach other PVST+ switches where they are understood.

Foundation Summary

The Foundation Summary is a collection of information that provides a convenient review of many key concepts in this chapter. If you are already comfortable with the topics in this chapter, this summary can help you recall a few details. If you just read this chapter, this review should help solidify some key facts. If you are doing your final preparation before the exam, this information is a convenient way to review the day before the exam.

STP has a progression of states that each port moves through. Each state allows a port to do only certain functions, as shown in Table 9-5.

Table 9-5 *STP States and Port Activity*

STP State	The Port Can...	The Port Cannot...	Duration
Disabled		Send or receive data	
Blocking	Receive BPDUs	Send or receive data or learn MAC addresses	Indefinite if loop has been detected
Listening	Send and receive BPDUs	Send or receive data or learn MAC addresses	Forward Delay timer (15 seconds)
Learning	Send and receive BPDUs and learn MAC addresses	Send or receive data	Forward Delay timer (15 seconds)
Forwarding	Send and receive BPDUs, learn MAC addresses, and send and receive data		Indefinite as long as port is up and loop is not detected

Table 9-6 *Basic Spanning-Tree Operation*

Task	Procedure
1. Elect Root Bridge.	Lowest Bridge ID
2. Select Root Port (one per switch).	Lowest Root Path Cost; if equal, use tie-breakers
3. Select Designated Port (one per segment).	Lowest Root Path Cost; if equal, use tie-breakers
4. Block ports with loops.	Block ports that are non-Root and non–Designated Ports

To manually work out a spanning-tree topology using a network diagram, follow the basic steps in Table 9-7.

Table 9-7   *Manual STP Computation*

Task	Description
1. Identify Path Costs on links.	For each link between switches, write the Path Cost that each switch uses for the link.
2. Identify Root Bridge.	Find the switch with the lowest Bridge ID; mark it on the drawing.
3. Select Root Ports (one per switch).	For each switch, find the one port that has the best path to the Root Bridge. This is the one with the lowest Root Path Cost. Mark the port with an RP label.
4. Select Designated Ports (one per segment).	For each link between switches, identify which end of the link will be the Designated Port. This is the one with the lowest Root Path Cost; if equal on both ends, use STP tie-breakers. Mark the port with a DP label.
5. Identify the blocking ports.	Every switch port that is neither a Root nor a Designated Port will be put into the Blocking state. Mark these with an X.

Table 9-8   *Spanning-Tree Tie-Breaker Criteria*

Sequence	Criteria
1	Lowest Root Bridge ID
2	Lowest Root Path Cost
3	Lowest Sender Bridge ID
4	Lowest Sender Port ID

Table 9-9   *STP Path Cost*

Link Bandwidth	STP Cost (Nonlinear Scale)
4 Mbps	250
10 Mbps	100
16 Mbps	62
45 Mbps	39
100 Mbps	19
155 Mbps	14

continues

Table 9-9 *STP Path Cost (Continued)*

622 Mbps	6
1 Gbps	4
10 Gbps	2

Table 9-10 *STP Timers*

Timer	Function	DefaultValue
Hello	Interval between Configuration BPDUs.	2 seconds
Forward Delay	Time spent in Listening and Learning states before transitioning toward Forwarding state.	15 seconds
Max Age	Maximum length of time a BPDU can be stored without receiving an update. Timer expiration signals an indirect failure with Designated or Root Bridge.	20 seconds

Table 9-11 *Types of STP*

Type of STP	Function
CST	One instance of STP, over the native VLAN; 802.1Q based
PVST	One instance of STP per VLAN; Cisco ISL based
PVST+	Provides interoperability between CST and PVST; operates over both 802.1Q and ISL

Q&A

The questions and scenarios in this book are more difficult than what you should experience on the actual exam. The questions do not attempt to cover more breadth or depth than the exam; however, they are designed to make sure that you know the answers. Rather than allowing you to derive the answers from clues hidden inside the questions themselves, the questions challenge your understanding and recall of the subject. Hopefully, these questions will help limit the number of exam questions on which you narrow your choices to two options and then guess.

You can find the answers to these questions in Appendix A.

1. What is a bridging loop? Why is it bad?

2. Put the following STP port states in chronological order:

    a. Learning

    b. Forwarding

    c. Listening

    d. Blocking

3. Choose two types of STP messages used to communicate between bridges:

    a. Advertisement BPDU

    b. Configuration BPDU

    c. ACK BPDU

    d. TCN BPDU

4. What criteria are used to select the following?

    a. Root Bridge

    b. Root Port

    c. Designated Port

    d. Redundant (or secondary) Root Bridges

5. Which of the following switches becomes the Root Bridge, given the information in the following table? Which switch becomes the secondary Root Bridge if the Root Bridge fails?

Switch Name	Bridge Priority	MAC Address	Port Costs
Catalyst A	32,768	00-d0-10-34-26-a0	All are 19
Catalyst B	32,768	00-d0-10-34-24-a0	All are 4
Catalyst C	32,767	00-d0-10-34-27-a0	All are 19
Catalyst D	32,769	00-d0-10-34-24-a1	All are 19

6. What conditions cause an STP topology change? What effect does this have on STP and the network?

7. A Root Bridge has been elected in a switched network. Suppose that a new switch is installed with a lower Bridge ID than the existing Root Bridge. What will happen?

8. Suppose that a switch receives Configuration BPDUs on two of its ports. Both ports are assigned to the same VLAN. Each of the BPDUs announces Catalyst A as the Root Bridge. Can the switch use both of these ports as Root Ports? Why?

9. How is the Root Path Cost calculated for a switch port?

10. What conditions can cause ports on a network's Root Bridge to move into the Blocking state? (Assume that all switch connections are to other switches. No crossover cables are used to connect two ports on the same switch.)

11. What parameters can be tuned to influence the selection of a port as a Root or Designated Port?

12. After a bridging loop forms, how can you stop the endless flow of traffic?

13. In a BPDU, when can the Root Bridge ID have the same value as the Sender Bridge ID?

14. Which of these is true about the Root Path Cost?

    a. It is a value sent by the Root Bridge that cannot be changed along the way.

    b. It is incremented as a switch receives a BPDU.

    c. It is incremented as a switch sends a BPDU.

    d. It is incremented by the Path Cost of a port.

15. Suppose that two switches are connected by a common link. Each must decide which one will have the Designated Port on the link. Which switch takes on this role if these STP advertisements occur?

    a. The link is on switch A's port number 12 and on switch B's port number 5.

    b. Switch A has a Bridge ID of 32,768:0000.1111.2222, and switch B has 8192:0000.5555.6666.

    c. Switch A advertises a Root Path Cost of 8, while B advertises 12.

16. Using the default STP timers, how long does it take for a port to move from the Blocking state to the Forwarding state?

17. If the Root Bridge sets the Topology Change flag in the BPDU, what must the other switches in the network do?

18. Over what VLANs does the CST form of STP run?

   a. VLAN 1

   b. All active VLANs

   c. All VLANs (active or inactive)

   d. The native VLAN

19. What is the major difference between PVST and PVST+?

20. Two switches are connected by a common active link. When might neither switch have a Designated Port on the link?

   a. When neither has a better Root Path Cost.

   b. When the switches are actually the primary and secondary Root Bridges.

   c. When one switch has its port in the Blocking state.

   d. Never; this can't happen.

This chapter covers the following topics that you need to master for the CCNP BCMSN exam:

- **STP Root Bridge**—This section discusses the importance of identifying a Root Bridge, as well as suggestions for its placement in the network. This section also presents the Root Bridge configuration commands.

- **Spanning-Tree Customization**—This section covers the configuration commands that enable you to alter the spanning-tree topology.

- **Tuning Spanning-Tree Convergence**—This section discusses how to alter, or tune, the STP timers to achieve optimum convergence times in a network.

- **Redundant Link Convergence**—This section describes the methods that cause a network to converge more quickly after a topology change.

- **Troubleshooting STP**—This section offers a brief summary of the commands you can use to verify that an STP instance is working properly.

CHAPTER 10

Spanning Tree Configuration

This chapter presents the design and configuration considerations necessary to implement the IEEE 802.1D Spanning Tree Protocol (STP) in a campus network. This chapter also discusses the commands needed to configure the STP features, previously described in Chapter 9, "Traditional Spanning Tree Protocol."

You can also tune STP or make it converge more efficiently in a given network. This chapter presents the theory and commands needed to accomplish this.

"Do I Know This Already?" Quiz

The purpose of the "Do I Know This Already?" quiz is to help you decide what parts of this chapter to use. If you already intend to read the entire chapter, you do not necessarily need to answer these questions now.

The quiz, derived from the major sections in the "Foundation Topics" portion of the chapter, helps you determine how to spend your limited study time.

Table 10-1 outlines the major topics discussed in this chapter and the "Do I Know This Already?" quiz questions that correspond to those topics.

Table 10-1 *"Do I Know This Already?" Foundation Topics Section-to-Question Mapping*

Foundation Topics Section	Questions Covered in This Section	Score
STP Root Bridge	1–5	
Spanning-Tree Customization	6–7	
Tuning Spanning-Tree Convergence	8–9	
Redundant Link Convergence	10–12	
Total Score		

> **CAUTION** The goal of self-assessment is to gauge your mastery of the topics in this chapter. If you do not know the answer to a question or are only partially sure of the answer, you should mark this question wrong. Giving yourself credit for an answer you correctly guess skews your self-assessment results and might give you a false sense of security.

1. Where should the Root Bridge be placed on a network?

   a. On the fastest switch

   b. Closest to the most users

   c. Closest to the center of the network

   d. On the least-used switch

2. Which of the following is a result of a poorly placed Root Bridge in a network?

   a. Bridging loops form.

   b. STP topology can't be resolved.

   c. STP topology can take unexpected paths.

   d. Root Bridge election flapping occurs.

3. Which of these parameters should you change to make a switch become a Root Bridge?

   a. Switch MAC address

   b. Path cost

   c. Port priority

   d. Bridge priority

4. What is the default 802.1D STP bridge priority on a Catalyst switch?

   a. 0

   b. 1

   c. 32,768

   d. 65,535

5. Which of the following commands is most likely to make a switch become the Root Bridge for VLAN 5, assuming that all switches have the default STP parameters?

   a. **spanning-tree root**

   b. **spanning-tree root vlan 5**

   c. **spanning-tree vlan 5 priority 100**

   d. **spanning-tree vlan 5 root**

6. What is the default path cost of a Gigabit Ethernet switch port?

   a. 1

   b. 2

   c. 4

   d. 19

   e. 1000

7. What command can change the path cost of interface Gigabit Ethernet 3/1 to a value of 8?

   a. **spanning-tree path-cost 8**

   b. **spanning-tree cost 8**

   c. **spanning-tree port-cost 8**

   d. **spanning-tree gig 3/1 cost 8**

8. What happens if the Root Bridge switch and another switch are configured with different STP hello timer values?

   a. Nothing—each sends hellos at different times.

   b. A bridging loop could form because the two switches are out of sync.

   c. The switch with the lower Hello timer becomes the Root Bridge.

   d. The other switch changes its Hello timer to match the Root Bridge.

9. What network diameter value is the basis for the default STP timer calculations?

   a. 1

   b. 3

   c. 7

   d. 9

   e. 15

10. Where should the STP PortFast feature be used?

    a. An access-layer switch port connected to a PC

    b. An access-layer switch port connected to a hub

    c. A distribution-layer switch port connected to an access layer switch

    d. A core-layer switch port

11. Where should the STP UplinkFast feature be enabled?

    a. An access-layer switch

    b. A distribution-layer switch

    c. A core-layer switch

    d. All of the above

12. If used, the STP BackboneFast feature should be enabled on which of these?

    a. All backbone- or core-layer switches

    b. All backbone- and distribution-layer switches

    c. All access-layer switches

    d. All switches in the network

The answers to the "Do I Know This Already?" quiz are found in Appendix A, "Answers to Chapter 'Do I Know This Already?' Quizzes and Q&A Sections." The suggested choices for your next step are as follows:

- **10 or less overall score**—Read the entire chapter. This includes the "Foundation Topics," "Foundation Summary," and "Q&A" sections.

- **11 or 12 overall score**—If you want more review on these topics, skip to the "Foundation Summary" section and then go to the "Q&A" section at the end of the chapter. Otherwise, move to Chapter 11, "Protecting the Spanning Tree Protocol Topology."

Foundation Topics

STP Root Bridge

STP and its computations are predictable; however, other factors might subtly influence STP decisions, making the resulting tree structure neither expected nor ideal.

As the network administrator, you can make adjustments to the spanning-tree operation to control its behavior. The location of the Root Bridge should be determined as part of the design process. You can use redundant links for load balancing in parallel, if configured correctly. You can also configure Spanning Tree Protocol (STP) to converge quickly and predictably in the event of a major topology change.

> **TIP** By default, STP is enabled for all active VLANs and on all ports of a switch. STP should remain enabled in a network to prevent bridging loops from forming. However, you might find that STP has been disabled in some way.
>
> If an entire instance of STP has been disabled, you can re-enable it with the following global configuration command:
>
> ```
> Switch(config)# spanning-tree vlan vlan-id
> ```
>
> If STP has been disabled for a specific VLAN on a specific port, you can re-enable it with the following interface configuration command:
>
> ```
> Switch (config-if)# spanning-tree vlan vlan-id
> ```

Root Bridge Placement

Although STP is wonderfully automatic with its default values and election processes, the resulting tree structure might perform quite differently than expected. The Root Bridge election is based on the idea that one switch is chosen as a common reference point, and all other switches choose ports that have the best-cost path to the root. The Root BRIDGE election is also based on the idea that the Root Bridge can become a central hub that interconnects other legs of the network. Therefore, the Root Bridge can be faced with heavy switching loads in its central location.

If the Root Bridge election is left to its default state, several things can occur to result in a poor choice. For example, the *slowest* switch (or bridge) could be elected as the Root Bridge. If heavy traffic loads are expected to pass through the Root Bridge, the slowest switch is not the ideal candidate. Recall that the only criteria for Root Bridge election is that the switch must have the lowest Bridge ID (bridge priority and MAC address), which is not necessarily the best choice to ensure optimal performance. If the slowest switch has the same bridge priority as the others and has the lowest MAC address, the slowest switch will be chosen as the root.

A second factor to consider relates to redundancy. If all switches are left at their default states, only one Root Bridge is elected, with no clear choice for a backup. What happens if that switch fails? Another Root Bridge election occurs, but again, the choice might not be the ideal switch or the ideal location.

The final consideration is the location of the Root Bridge switch. As before, an election with default switch values could place the Root Bridge in an unexpected location in the network. More important, an inefficient spanning-tree structure could result, causing traffic from a large portion of the network to take a long and winding path just to pass through the Root Bridge.

Figure 10-1 shows a portion of a real-world hierarchical campus network.

Figure 10-1 *Campus Network with an Inefficient Root Bridge Election*

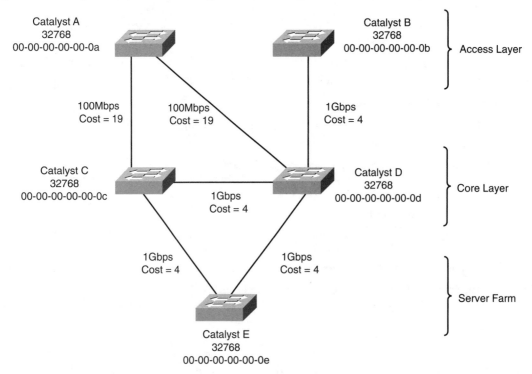

Catalyst switches A and B are two access-layer devices; Catalysts C and D form the core layer, and Catalyst E connects a server farm into the network core. Notice that most of the switches use redundant links to other layers of the hierarchy, as suggested in Chapter 2, "Modular Network

Design." At the time of this example, however, many switches, such as Catalyst B, still have only a single connection into the core. These switches are slated for an "upgrade," in which a redundant link will be added to the other half of the core.

As you will see, Catalyst A will become the Root Bridge because of its low MAC address. All switches have been left to their default STP states—the bridge priority of each is 32,768 (or 32,768 plus the VLAN ID, if the extended system ID is enabled). Figure 10-2 shows the converged state of STP. For the purposes of this discussion, the root ports and designated ports are simply shown on the network diagram. As an exercise, you should work through the spanning-tree process yourself, based on the information shown in the figure. The more examples you can work out by hand, the better you will understand the entire spanning-tree process.

Figure 10-2 *Campus Network with STP Converged*

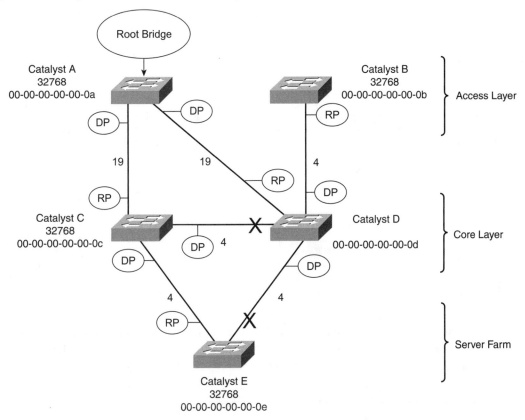

Notice that Catalyst A, one of the access-layer switches, has been elected the Root Bridge. Unfortunately, Catalyst A cannot take advantage of the 1-Gbps links, unlike the other switches.

Also note the location of the X symbols over the ports that are neither root ports nor designated ports. These ports will enter the Blocking state, and no data packets will pass through them.

Finally, Figure 10-3 shows the same network with the blocking links removed. Now you can see the true structure of the final spanning tree.

Figure 10-3   *Final Spanning-Tree Structure for the Campus Network*

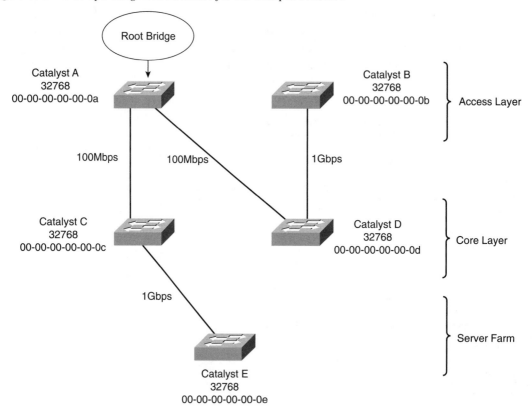

Catalyst A, an access-layer switch, is the Root Bridge. Workstations on Catalyst A can reach servers on Catalyst E by crossing through the core layer (Catalyst C), as expected. However, notice what has happened to the other access-layer switch, Catalyst B. Workstations on this switch must cross into the core layer (Catalyst D), back into the access layer (Catalyst A), back through the core (Catalyst C), and finally to the server farm (Catalyst E).

This action is obviously inefficient. For one thing, Catalyst A is probably not a high-end switch because it is used in the access layer. However, the biggest issue is that other access-layer areas are forced to thread through the relatively slow uplinks on Catalyst A. This winding path will become a major bottleneck to the users.

Root Bridge Configuration

To prevent the surprises outlined in the previous section, you should *always* do two things:

■ Configure one switch as a Root Bridge in a determined fashion.

■ Configure another switch as a secondary Root Bridge, in case of a primary Root Bridge failure.

As the common reference point, the Root Bridge (and the secondary) should be placed near the center of the Layer 2 network. For example, a switch in the distribution layer would make a better Root Bridge choice than one in the access layer because more traffic is expected to pass through the distribution-layer devices. In a flat switched network (no Layer 3 devices), a switch near a server farm would be a more efficient Root Bridge than switches elsewhere. Most traffic will be destined to and from the server farm and will benefit from a predetermined, direct path.

TIP   A Catalyst switch can be configured to use one of the following formats for its STP Bridge ID:

■ Traditional 802.1D bridge priority value (16 bits), followed by the unique switch MAC address for the VLAN

■ The 802.1t extended system ID (4-bit priority multiplier, plus a 12-bit VLAN ID), followed by a nonunique switch MAC address for the VLAN

If the switch can't support 1024 unique MAC addresses for its own use, the extended system ID is always enabled by default. Otherwise, the traditional method is enabled by default.

To begin using the extended system ID method, you can uses the following global configuration command:

```
Switch(config)# spanning-tree extend system-id
```

Otherwise, you can use the traditional method by beginning the command with the **no** keyword.

You can configure a Catalyst switch to become the Root Bridge using one of two methods, which are configured as follows:

■ Manually setting the bridge priority value so that a switch is given a lower-than-default Bridge ID value to win a Root Bridge election. You must know the bridge priorities of every other switch in a VLAN so that you can choose a value that is less than all the others. The command to accomplish this is as follows:

```
Switch(config)# spanning-tree vlan vlan-list priority bridge-priority
```

The *bridge-priority* value defaults to 32,768, but you can also assign a value of 0 to 65,535. If STP extended system ID is enabled, the default *bridge-priority* is 32,768 plus the VLAN number. In that case, the value can range from 0 to 61,440, but only as multiples of 4096. A lower bridge priority is preferable.

Remember that Catalyst switches run one instance of STP for each VLAN (PVST+), so the VLAN ID must always be given. You should designate an appropriate Root Bridge for each VLAN. For example, you could use the following command to set the bridge priority for VLAN 5 and VLANs 100 through 200 to 4096:

```
Switch(config)# spanning-tree vlan 5,100-200 priority 4096
```

- Causing the would-be Root Bridge switch to choose its own priority, based on some assumptions about other switches in the network. You can accomplish this with the following command:

```
Switch(config)# spanning-tree vlan vlan-id root {primary | secondary} [diameter
    diameter]
```

This command is actually a macro on the Catalyst that executes several other commands. The result is a more direct and automatic way to force one switch to become the Root Bridge. Notice that the actual bridge priorities are not given in the command. Instead, the switch modifies its STP values according to the current values in use within the active network. *These values are modified only once, when the macro command is issued.* Use the **primary** keyword to make the switch attempt to become the primary Root Bridge. This command modifies the switch's bridge priority value to become less than the bridge priority of the current Root Bridge. If the current root priority is more than 24,576, the local switch sets its priority to 24,576. If the current root priority is less than that, the local switch sets its priority to 4096 less than the current root.

For the **secondary** Root Bridge, the root priority is set to an artificially low value of 28,672. There is no way to query or listen to the network to find another potential secondary root simply because there are no advertisements or elections of secondary Root Bridges. Instead, the fixed secondary priority is used under the assumption that it will be less than the default priorities (32,768) that might be used on switches elsewhere. You can also modify the network diameter by adding the **diameter** keyword to this command. This modification is discussed further in the "Tuning Spanning-Tree Convergence" section later in the chapter.

As a final example, consider a switch that is currently using its default bridge priority for VLAN 100. In the extended system-id mode, the default priority is 32,768 plus 100 (the VLAN number). The output in Example 10-1 demonstrates this under the Bridge ID information. The default priority is greater than the current Root Bridge priority of 4200, so the local switch cannot become the root.

Example 10-1 *Displaying the STP Bridge Priority Values*

```
Switch# show spanning-tree vlan 100
VLAN0100
  Spanning tree enabled protocol ieee
  Root ID    Priority    4200
```

Example 10-1 *Displaying the STP Bridge Priority Values (Continued)*

```
            Address     000b.5f65.1f80
            Cost        4
            Port        1 (GigabitEthernet0/1)
            Hello Time  2 sec  Max Age 20 sec  Forward Delay 15 sec

  Bridge ID  Priority    32868  (priority 32768 sys-id-ext 100)
            Address     000c.8554.9a80
            Hello Time  2 sec  Max Age 20 sec  Forward Delay 15 sec
            Aging Time 300
[output omitted]
```

Now, the automatic method is used to attempt to make the switch become root for VLAN 100, using the command demonstrated in Example 10-2.

Example 10-2 *Using a Macro Command to Configure a Root Bridge*

```
Switch(config)# spanning-tree vlan 100 root primary
% Failed to make the bridge root for vlan 100
% It may be possible to make the bridge root by setting the priority
% for some (or all) of these instances to zero.
Switch(config)#
```

Why did this method fail? The current Root Bridge has a bridge priority of 4200. Because that priority is less than 24,576, the local switch will try to set its priority to 4096 less than the current root. Although the resulting priority would be 104, the local switch is using an extended system ID, which requires bridge priority values that are multiples of 4096. The only value that would work is 0, but the automatic method will not use it. Instead, the only other option is to manually configure the bridge priority to 0 with the following command:

```
Switch(config)# spanning-tree vlan 100 priority 0
```

Remember that on switches that use an extended system ID, the bridge priority is the configured priority (multiple of 4096) plus the VLAN number. Even though the priority was set to 0 with the previous command, the switch is actually using a value of 100—priority 0 plus VLAN number 100, as the output in Example 10-3 reveals.

Example 10-3 *Displaying Bridge Priorities with Extended System IDs*

```
Switch# show spanning-tree vlan 100
VLAN0100
  Spanning tree enabled protocol ieee
  Root ID     Priority    100
            Address     000c.8554.9a80
            This bridge is the root
            Hello Time  2 sec  Max Age 20 sec  Forward Delay 15 sec
```

continues

Example 10-3 *Displaying Bridge Priorities with Extended System IDs (Continued)*

```
  Bridge ID  Priority    100     (priority 0 sys-id-ext 100)
             Address     000c.8554.9a80
             Hello Time   2 sec  Max Age 20 sec  Forward Delay 15 sec
             Aging Time 300
[output omitted]
```

> **NOTE**   The **spanning-tree vlan** *vlan-id* **root** command will not be shown in a Catalyst switch
> configuration because the command is actually a macro executing other switch commands. The
> actual commands and values produced by the macro will be shown, however. For example, the
> macro can potentially adjust the four STP values as follows:
>
> ```
> Switch(config)# spanning-tree vlan 1 root primary
>   vlan 1 bridge priority set to 24576
>   vlan 1 bridge max aging time unchanged at 20
>   vlan 1 bridge hello time unchanged at 2
>   vlan 1 bridge forward delay unchanged at 15
> ```
>
> Be aware that this macro doesn't guarantee that the switch will become the root and maintain
> that status. After the macro is used, it is entirely possible for another switch in the network to
> have its bridge priority configured to a lower value. The other switch would become the new
> root, displacing the switch that ran the macro.
>
> On the root, it is usually good practice to directly modify the bridge priority to an artificially low
> value (even priority 1 or 0) with the **spanning-tree vlan** *vlan-id* **priority** *bridge-priority*
> command. This makes it more difficult for another switch in the network to win the Root Bridge
> election, unless it is manually configured with a priority that is even lower.

Spanning-Tree Customization

The most important decision you can make when designing your spanning-tree topology is the
placement of the Root Bridge. Other decisions, such as the exact loop-free path structure, will
occur automatically as a result of the Spanning Tree Algorithm (STA). Occasionally, the path
might need additional tuning, but only under special circumstances and after careful
consideration.

Recall the sequence of four criteria that STP uses to choose a path:

1. Lowest Bridge ID

2. Lowest root path cost

3. Lowest sender Bridge ID

4. Lowest sender port ID

The previous section discussed how to tune a switch's Bridge ID to force it to become the Root Bridge in a network. You can also change the bridge priority on a switch to influence the value it uses in the sender Bridge ID that it announced as it relays BPDUs to other neighboring switches.

Only the automatic STP computation has been discussed, using the default switch port costs to make specific path decisions. The following sections discuss ways you can influence the exact topology that results.

Tuning the Root Path Cost

The root path cost for each active port of a switch is determined by the cumulative cost as a BPDU travels along. As a switch *receives* a BPDU, the port cost of the receiving port is added to the root path cost in the BPDU. The port or port path cost is inversely proportional to the port's bandwidth. If desired, a port's cost can be modified from the default value.

> **NOTE**   Before modifying a switch port's path cost, you should always calculate the root path costs of other alternate paths through the network. Changing one port's cost might influence STP to choose that port as a root port, but other paths still could be preferred. You also should calculate a port's existing path cost to determine what the new cost value should be. Careful calculation will ensure that the desired path indeed will be chosen.

Use the following interface-configuration command to set a switch port's path cost:

```
Switch (config-if)# spanning-tree [vlan vlan-id] cost cost
```

If the **vlan** parameter is given, the port cost is modified only for the specified VLAN. Otherwise, the cost is modified for the port as a whole (all active VLANs). The *cost* value can range from 1 to 65,535. There are standard or default values that correspond to port bandwidth, as shown in Table 10-2.

Table 10-2 *STP Port Cost*

Link Bandwidth	STP Cost
4 Mbps	250
10 Mbps	100
16 Mbps	62
45 Mbps	39
100 Mbps	19
155 Mbps	14
622 Mbps	6
1 Gbps	4
10 Gbps	2

For example, a Gigabit Ethernet interface has a default port cost of 4. You can use the following command to change the cost to 2, but only for VLAN 10:

```
Switch(config)# spanning-tree vlan 10 cost 2
```

You can see the port cost of an interface by using the following command:

```
Switch# show spanning-tree interface type mod/num [cost]
```

As an example, GigabitEthernet 0/1 is configured as a trunk port, carrying VLANs 1, 10, and 20. Example 10-4 shows the port cost for each of the VLANs.

Example 10-4 *Displaying STP Port Cost Values on an Interface*

```
Switch# show spanning-tree interface gigabitEthernet 0/1
Vlan            Role Sts Cost      Prio.Nbr Type
---------------- ---- --- --------- -------- --------------------------------
VLAN0001        Root FWD 4         128.1    P2p
VLAN0010        Desg FWD 2         128.1    P2p
VLAN0020        Root FWD 4         128.1    P2p
```

Tuning the Port ID

The fourth criteria of an STP decision is the port ID. The port ID value that a switch uses is actually a 16-bit quantity: 8 bits for the port priority and 8 bits for the port number. The port priority is a value from 0 to 255 and defaults to 128 for all ports. The port number can range from 0 to 255 and represents the port's actual physical mapping. Port numbers begin with 1 at port 0/1 and increment across each module. (The numbers might not be consecutive because each module is assigned a particular range of numbers.)

TIP   Port numbers are usually intuitive on a fixed configuration switch, such as a 48-port Catalyst 3560. The STP port number is simply the interface number, from 1 to 48.

However, it is not easy to find the STP port number in a switch with many modules and many ports. Notice how GigabitEthernet 3/16 is also known as port number 144 in the following example:

```
Switch# show spanning-tree interface gigabitEthernet 3/16
Vlan            Role Sts Cost      Prio.Nbr Type
---------------- ---- --- --------- -------- --------------------------------
VLAN0010        Desg FWD 4         128.144  Edge P2p
VLAN0100        Desg FWD 4         128.144  Edge P2p
VLAN0200        Desg FWD 4         128.144  Edge P2p
Switch#
```

The entire port ID consists of the port priority followed by the port number. In the preceding example output, the port ID is 128.144. As a 16-bit quantity in hex, it is 8090. In addition, ports that are bundled into an EtherChannel or Port-channel interface always have a higher port ID than they would if they were not bundled.

Obviously, a switch port's port number is fixed because it is based only on its hardware location or index. The port ID, however, can be modified to influence an STP decision by using the port priority. You can configure the port priority with this interface-configuration command:

```
Switch(config-if)# spanning-tree [vlan vlan-list] port-priority port-priority
```

You can modify the port priority for one or more VLANs by using the **vlan** parameter. The VLAN numbers are given as *vlan-list*, a list of single values or ranges of values separated by commas. Otherwise, the port priority is set for the port as a whole (all active VLANs). The value of *port-priority* can range from 0 to 255 and defaults to 128. A lower port priority value indicates a more preferred path toward the Root Bridge.

As an example, you can use the following command sequence to change the port priority of GigabitEthernet 3/16 from 128 (the default) to 64 for VLANs 10 and 100:

```
Switch(config)# interface gigabitethernet 3/16
Switch(config-if)# spanning-tree vlan 10,100 port-priority 64
```

You can confirm the changes with the **show spanning-tree interface** command, as demonstrated in Example 10-5.

Example 10-5 *Confirming STP Port Priority Values After Configuration*

```
Switch# show spanning-tree interface gigabitEthernet 3/16
Vlan              Role Sts Cost      Prio.Nbr Type
----------------  ---- --- --------- -------- ----------------------------------
VLAN0010          Desg FWD 4         64.144   Edge P2p
VLAN0100          Desg FWD 4         64.144   Edge P2p
VLAN0200          Desg FWD 4         128.144  Edge P2p
Switch#
```

Tuning Spanning-Tree Convergence

STP uses several timers, a sequence of states that ports must move through, and specific topology change conditions to prevent bridging loops from forming in a complex network. Each of these parameters or requirements is based on certain default values for a typical network size and function. For the majority of cases, the default STP operation is sufficient to keep the network loop free and enable users to communicate.

However, in certain situations, the default STP can cause network access to be delayed while timers expire and while preventing loops on links where loops are not possible. For example, when a single PC is connected to a switch port, a bridging loop is simply not possible. Another situation relates to the size of a Layer 2 switched network: The default STP timers are based on a benchmark network size.

In a network that is smaller, waiting until the default timer values expire might not make sense when they could be safely set to shorter values. In situations like this, you can safely make adjustments to the STP convergence process for more efficiency.

Modifying STP Timers

Recall that STP uses three timers to keep track of various port operation states and communication between bridges. The three STP timers can be adjusted by using the commands documented in the sections that follow. Remember that the timers need to be modified only on the Root Bridge because the Root Bridge propagates all three timer values throughout the network as fields in the configuration BPDU.

Manually Configuring STP Timers

Use one or more of the following global configuration commands to modify STP timers:

```
Switch(config)# spanning-tree [vlan vlan-id] hello-time seconds
Switch(config)# spanning-tree [vlan vlan-id] forward-time seconds
Switch(config)# spanning-tree [vlan vlan-id] max-age seconds
```

Notice that the timers can be changed for a single instance (VLAN) of STP on the switch by using the **vlan** *vlan-id* parameters. If you omit the **vlan** keyword, the timer values are configured for *all* instances (all VLANs) of STP on the switch.

The *Hello timer* triggers periodic "hello" (actually, the configuration BPDU) messages that are sent from the root to other bridges in the network. This timer also sets the interval in which a bridge expects to hear a hello relayed from its neighboring bridges. Configuration BPDUs are sent every 2 seconds, by default. You can modify the Hello timer with the **hello-time** keyword, along with a value of 1 to 10 seconds, as in the following command:

```
Switch(config)# spanning-tree hello-time 1
```

The *Forward Delay timer* determines the amount of time a port stays in the Listening state before moving into the Learning state, and how long it stays in the Learning state before moving to the Forwarding state. You can modify the Forward Delay timer with the **forward-time** keyword. The default value is 15 seconds, but this can be set to a value of 4 to 30 seconds. This timer should be modified only under careful consideration because the value depends on the diameter of the network and the propagation of BPDUs across all switches. A value that is too low allows loops to form, possibly crippling a network.

The *Max Age timer* specifies a stored BPDU's lifetime that has been received from a neighboring switch with a designated port. Suppose that BPDUs are being received on a nondesignated switch port every 2 seconds, as expected. Then an *indirect failure*, or one that doesn't involve a physical link going down, occurs that prevents BPDUs from being sent. The receiving switch waits until the Max Age timer expires to listen for further BPDUs. If none is received, the nondesignated port moves into the Listening state, and the receiving switch generates configuration BPDUs. This port then becomes the designated port to restore connectivity on the segment.

To modify the Max Age timer, use the **max-age** keyword. The timer value defaults to 20 seconds but can be set from 6 to 40 seconds.

Automatically Configuring STP Timers

Modifying STP timers can be tricky, given the conservative nature of the default values and the calculations needed to derive proper STP operation. Timer values are basically dependent on the Hello Time and the switched network's diameter, in terms of switch hops. Catalyst switches offer a single command that can change the timer values in a more controlled fashion. Although described earlier, the **spanning-tree vlan** *vlan-list* **root** macro command is a better tool to use than setting the timers with the individual commands. This global configuration command has the following syntax:

```
Switch(config)# spanning-tree vlan vlan-list root {primary | secondary} [diameter
    diameter [hello-time hello-time]]
```

Here, STP timers will be adjusted according to the formulas specified in the 802.1D standard by giving only the network's diameter (the maximum number of switches that traffic will traverse across a Layer 2 network) and an optional *hello-time*. If you do not specify a Hello Time, the default value of 2 seconds is assumed.

This command can be used only on a per-VLAN basis, to modify the timers for a particular VLAN's spanning tree instance. The network diameter can be a value from one to seven switch hops. Because this command makes a switch become the Root Bridge, all the modified timer values resulting from this command will be propagated to other switches through the configuration BPDU.

As an example, suppose that a small network consists of three switches connected in a triangle fashion. The command output in Example 10-6 shows the current (default) STP timer values that are in use for VLAN 100.

Example 10-6 *Displaying the STP Timer Values in Use*

```
Switch# show spanning-tree vlan 100
VLAN0100
  Spanning tree enabled protocol ieee
  Root ID    Priority    100
             Address     000c.8554.9a80
             This bridge is the root
             Hello Time   2 sec  Max Age 20 sec  Forward Delay 15 sec

  Bridge ID  Priority    100    (priority 0 sys-id-ext 100)
             Address     000c.8554.9a80
             Hello Time   2 sec  Max Age 20 sec  Forward Delay 15 sec
             Aging Time 300
[output omitted]
```

The longest path that a packet can take through the example network is 3 switches. This is considerably less than the reference diameter of 7 that is used to calculate the default timer values. Therefore, you can safely assume that this network diameter is 3, provided that no additional switches will be added to lengthen the longest path. Suppose that a Hello Time of 1 second is also desired, to shorten the time needed to detect a dead neighbor. The following command attempts to make the local switch become the Root Bridge and automatically adjusts the STP timers:

```
Switch(config)# spanning-tree vlan 100 root primary diameter 3 hello-time 1
```

You can confirm the new timer values with the **show spanning-tree vlan** *vlan-id* command, as demonstrated in Example 10-7.

Example 10-7 *Confirming STP Timer Configuration Changes*

```
Switch# show spanning-tree vlan 100
VLAN0100
  Spanning tree enabled protocol ieee
  Root ID    Priority    100
             Address     000c.8554.9a80
             This bridge is the root
             Hello Time   1 sec  Max Age  7 sec  Forward Delay  5 sec

  Bridge ID  Priority    100    (priority 0 sys-id-ext 100)
             Address     000c.8554.9a80
             Hello Time   1 sec  Max Age  7 sec  Forward Delay  5 sec
             Aging Time 300
```

Redundant Link Convergence

Some additional methods allow faster STP convergence in the event of a link failure:

- **PortFast**—Enables fast connectivity to be established on access-layer switch ports to workstations that are booting up

- **UplinkFast**—Enables fast-uplink failover on an access-layer switch when dual uplinks are connected into the distribution layer

- **BackboneFast**—Enables fast convergence in the network backbone (core) after a spanning-tree topology change occurs

Instead of modifying timer values, these methods work by controlling convergence on specifically located ports within the network hierarchy.

> **NOTE** The STP has been enhanced to allow almost instantaneous topology changes instead of having to rely on these Cisco-proprietary extensions. This enhancement is known as the Rapid Spanning Tree Protocol, or IEEE 802.1w, and is covered in Chapter 12, "Advanced Spanning Tree Protocol." You should become familiar with the topics in this chapter first because they provide the basis for the concepts in Chapter 12.

PortFast: Access-Layer Nodes

An end-user workstation is usually connected to a switch port in the access layer. If the workstation is powered off and then turned on, the switch will sense that the port link status has gone down and back up. The port will not be in a usable state until STP cycles from the Blocking state to the Forwarding state. With the default STP timers, this transition takes at least 30 seconds (15 seconds for Listening to Learning, and 15 seconds for Learning to Forwarding). Therefore, the workstation cannot transmit or receive any useful data until the Forwarding state finally is reached on the port.

> **NOTE**   Port initialization delays of up to 50 seconds can be observed. As discussed, 30 of these seconds are due to the STP state transitions. If a switch port is running Port Aggregation Protocol (PAgP) to negotiate EtherChannel configuration, an additional 20-second delay can occur.

On switch ports that connect only to single workstations or specific devices, bridging loops never should be possible. The potential for a loop exists only if the workstation had additional connections back into the network and if it was bridging traffic itself. For example, this can happen on PCs that are running Windows XP when network bridging has been enabled. In most situations, this is not very likely to happen.

Catalyst switches offer the PortFast feature, which shortens the Listening and Learning states to a negligible amount of time. When a workstation link comes up, the switch immediately moves the PortFast port into the Forwarding state. Spanning-tree loop detection is still in operation, however, and the port moves into the Blocking state if a loop is ever detected on the port.

By default, PortFast is disabled on all switch ports. You can configure PortFast as a global default, affecting all switch ports with a single command. All ports that are configured for access mode (nontrunking) will have PortFast automatically enabled. You can use the following global configuration command to enable PortFast as the default:

```
Switch(config)# spanning-tree portfast default
```

You can also enable or disable the PortFast feature on specific switch ports by using the following interface-configuration command:

```
Switch(config-if)# [no] spanning-tree portfast
```

Obviously, you should not enable PortFast on a switch port that is connected to a hub or another switch because bridging loops could form. One other benefit of PortFast is that topology change notification (TCN) BPDUs are not sent when a switch port in PortFast mode goes up or down. This simplifies the TCN transmission on a large network when end-user workstations are coming up or shutting down.

> **TIP**   You can also use a macro configuration command to force a switch port to support a single host. The following command enables STP PortFast, sets the port to access (nontrunking) mode, and disables PAgP to prevent the port from participating in an EtherChannel:
>
> ```
> Switch(config)# interface type mod/num
>
> Switch(config-if)# switchport host
>
> switchport mode will be set to access
>
> spanning-tree portfast will be enabled
>
> channel group will be disabled
> ```

You can display the current PortFast status with the following command:

```
Switch# show spanning-tree interface type mod/num portfast
```

For example, the following output shows that port FastEthernet 0/1 supports only access VLAN 10 and has PortFast enabled:

```
Switch# show spanning-tree interface fastethernet 0/1 portfast
VLAN0010        enabled
Switch#
```

UplinkFast: Access-Layer Uplinks

Consider an access-layer switch that has redundant uplink connections to two distribution-layer switches. Normally, one uplink would be in the Forwarding state and the other would be in the Blocking state. If the primary uplink went down, up to 50 seconds could elapse before the redundant uplink could be used.

The *UplinkFast* feature on Catalyst switches enables leaf-node switches or switches at the ends of the spanning-tree branches to have a functioning root port while keeping *one or more* redundant or potential root ports in Blocking mode. When the primary root port uplink fails, another blocked uplink immediately can be brought up for use.

> **NOTE**   Many Catalyst switches have two built-in, high-speed uplink ports (Gigabit Ethernet, for example). You might get the idea that UplinkFast can only toggle between two leaf-node uplink ports. This is entirely untrue. UplinkFast keeps a record of *all* parallel paths to the Root Bridge. All uplink ports but one are kept in the Blocking state. If the root port fails, the uplink with the next-lowest root path cost is unblocked and used without delay.

To enable the UplinkFast feature, use the following global configuration command:

```
Switch(config)# spanning-tree uplinkfast [max-update-rate pkts-per-second]
```

When UplinkFast is enabled, it is enabled for the entire switch and all VLANs. UplinkFast works by keeping track of possible paths to the Root Bridge. Therefore, the command *is not allowed on the Root Bridge switch*. UplinkFast also makes some modifications to the local switch to ensure that it does not become the Root Bridge and that the switch is not used as a transit switch to get to the Root Bridge. In other words, the goal is to keep UplinkFast limited to leaf-node switches that are farthest from the root.

First, the switch's bridge priority is raised to 49,152, making it unlikely that the switch will be elected to Root Bridge status. The port cost of all local switch ports is incremented by 3000, making the ports undesirable as paths to the root for any downstream switches.

The command also includes a **max-update-rate** parameter. When an uplink on a switch goes down, UplinkFast makes it easy for the local switch to update its bridging table of MAC addresses to point to the new uplink. However, UplinkFast also provides a mechanism for the local switch to notify other upstream switches that stations downstream (or within the access layer) can be reached over the newly activated uplink.

The switch accomplishes this by sending dummy multicast frames to destination 0100.0ccd.cdcd on behalf of the stations contained in its Content-Addressable Memory (CAM) table. The MAC addresses are used as the source addresses in the dummy frames, as if the stations actually had sent them. The idea is to quickly send the multicast frames over the new uplink, giving upstream hosts a chance to receive the frames and learn of the new path to those source addresses.

These multicast frames are sent out at a rate specified by the **max-update-rate** parameter in packets per second. This limits the amount of bandwidth used for the dummy multicasts if the CAM table is quite large. The default is 150 packets per second (pps), but the rate can range from 0 to 65,535 pps. If the value is 0, no dummy multicasts are sent.

TIP   You can use the following command to display the current status of STP UplinkFast:

```
Switch# show spanning-tree uplinkfast
UplinkFast is enabled
Station update rate set to 150 packets/sec.
UplinkFast statistics
-----------------------
Number of transitions via uplinkFast (all VLANs)         : 2
Number of proxy multicast addresses transmitted (all VLANs) : 52
Name                   Interface List
-------------------    ------------------------------------------
VLAN0001               Gi0/1(fwd)
VLAN0010               Gi0/1(fwd)
VLAN0100               Gi0/1(fwd)
Switch#
```

BackboneFast: Redundant Backbone Paths

In the network backbone, or core layer, a different method is used to shorten STP convergence. *BackboneFast* works by having a switch actively determine whether alternate paths exist to the Root Bridge, in case the switch detects an *indirect link failure*. Indirect link failures occur when a link that is not directly connected to a switch fails.

A switch detects an indirect link failure when it receives inferior BPDUs from its designated bridge on either its root port or a blocked port. (Inferior BPDUs are sent from a designated bridge that has lost its connection to the Root Bridge, making it announce itself as the new root.)

Normally, a switch must wait for the Max Age timer to expire before responding to the inferior BPDUs. However, BackboneFast begins to determine whether other alternate paths to the Root Bridge exist according to the following port types that received the inferior BPDU:

- If the inferior BPDU arrives on a port in the Blocking state, the switch considers the root port and all other blocked ports to be alternate paths to the Root Bridge.

- If the inferior BPDU arrives on the root port itself, the switch considers all blocked ports to be alternate paths to the Root Bridge.

- If the inferior BPDU arrives on the root port and no ports are blocked, however, the switch assumes that it has lost connectivity with the Root Bridge. In this case, the switch assumes that it has become the Root Bridge, and BackboneFast allows it to do so before the Max Age timer expires.

Detecting alternate paths to the Root Bridge also involves an interactive process with other bridges. If the local switch has blocked ports, BackboneFast begins to use the *Root Link Query (RLQ)* protocol to see if upstream switches have stable connections to the Root Bridge.

First, RLQ Requests are sent out. If a switch receives an RLQ Request and either is the Root Bridge or has lost connection to the root, it sends an RLQ Reply. Otherwise, the RLQ Request is propagated on to other switches until an RLQ Reply can be generated. On the local switch, if an RLQ Reply is received on its current root port, the path to the Root Bridge is intact and stable. If it is received on a nonroot port, an alternate root path must be chosen. The Max Age timer immediately is expired so that a new root port can be found.

BackboneFast is simple to configure and operates by short-circuiting the Max Age timer when needed. Although this function shortens the time a switch waits to detect a root path failure, ports still must go through full-length Forward Delay timer intervals during the Listening and Learning states. Where PortFast and UplinkFast enable immediate transitions, BackboneFast can reduce the maximum convergence delay only from 50 to 30 seconds.

To configure BackboneFast, use the following global configuration command:

```
Switch(config)# spanning-tree backbonefast
```

When used, BackboneFast should be enabled on *all* switches in the network because BackboneFast requires the use of the RLQ Request and Reply mechanism to inform switches of root path stability. The RLQ protocol is active only when BackboneFast is enabled on a switch. By default, BackboneFast is disabled.

TIP   You can verify the current BackboneFast state with the following command:

```
Switch# show spanning-tree backbonefast
BackboneFast is enabled
Switch#
```

Troubleshooting STP

Because the STP running in a network uses several timers, costs, and dynamic calculations, predicting the current state is difficult. You can use a network diagram and work out the STP topology by hand, but any change on the network could produce an entirely different outcome. Then, figure in something like PVST+, in which you have one instance of STP running for each VLAN present. Obviously, simply viewing the STP status on the active network devices would be better.

You can display information about many aspects of the STP from a Catalyst switch command-line interface (CLI). Specifically, you need to find out the current Root Bridge and its location in the network. You also might want to see the Bridge ID of the switch where you are connected, to see how it participates in STP. Use the information in Table 10-3 to determine what command is useful for what situation.

Table 10-3   *Commands for Displaying Spanning Tree Information*

Task	Command Syntax
View all possible STP parameters for all VLANs. Port information is summarized.	Switch# **show spanning-tree**
View all possible STP information for all VLANs. Port information is very detailed.	Switch# **show spanning-tree detail**
View the total number of switch ports currently in each of the STP states.	Switch# **show spanning-tree** [**vlan** *vlan-id*] **summary**
Find the Root Bridge ID, the root port, and the root path cost.	Switch# **show spanning-tree** [**vlan** *vlan-id*] **root**
Show the Bridge ID and STP timers for the local switch.	Switch# **show spanning-tree** [**vlan** *vlan-id*] **bridge**
Show the STP UplinkFast status.	Switch# **show spanning-tree uplinkfast**
Show the STP BackboneFast status.	Switch# **show spanning-tree backbonefast**

Foundation Summary

The Foundation Summary is a collection of information that provides a convenient review of many key concepts in this chapter. If you are already comfortable with the topics in this chapter, this summary can help you recall a few details. If you just read this chapter, this review should help solidify some key facts. If you are doing your final preparation before the exam, these tables and figures are a convenient way to review the day before the exam.

Table 10-4 *STP Configuration Commands*

Task	Command Syntax
Enable STP	Switch(config)# **spanning-tree** *vlan-id*
Set bridge priority	Switch(config)# **spanning-tree vlan** *vlan-id* **priority** *bridge-priority*
Set Root Bridge (macro)	Switch(config)# **spanning-tree vlan** *vlan-id* **root** {**primary** I **secondary**} [**diameter** *diameter*]
Set port cost	Switch(config)# **spanning-tree** [**vlan** *vlan-id*] **cost** *cost*
Set port priority	Switch(config)# **spanning-tree** [**vlan** *vlan-id*] **port-priority** *port-priority*
Set STP timers	Switch(config)# **spanning-tree** [**vlan** *vlan-id*] **hello-time** *seconds*
	Switch(config)# **spanning-tree** [**vlan** *vlan-id*] **forward-time** *seconds*
	Switch(config)# **spanning-tree** [**vlan** *vlan-id*] **max-age** *seconds*
Set PortFast on an interface	Switch(config)# **spanning-tree portfast**
Set UplinkFast on a switch	Switch(config)# **spanning-tree uplinkfast** [**max-update-rate** *pkts-per-second*]
Set BackboneFast on a switch	Switch(config)# **spanning-tree backbonefast**

Q&A

The questions and scenarios in this book are more difficult than what you should experience on the actual exam. The questions do not attempt to cover more breadth or depth than the exam; however, they are designed to make sure that you know the answers. Rather than allowing you to derive the answers from clues hidden inside the questions themselves, the questions challenge your understanding and recall of the subject. Hopefully, these questions will help limit the number of exam questions on which you narrow your choices to two options and then guess.

You can find the answers to these questions in Appendix A.

1. What commands can configure a Catalyst 4500 switch as the Root Bridge on VLAN 10, assuming that the other switches are using the default STP values?

2. Using your Root Bridge answer from question 1, what commands can configure a Catalyst 3560 switch as a secondary or backup Root Bridge on VLAN 10?

3. Which of the following switches will become the Root Bridge, given the information in the following table? Which switch will become the secondary Root Bridge if the Root Bridge fails?

Switch Name	Bridge Priority	MAC Address	Port Costs
Catalyst A	32,768	00-d0-10-34-26-a0	All are 19.
Catalyst B	32,768	00-d0-10-34-24-a0	All are 4.
Catalyst C	32,767	00-d0-10-34-27-a0	All are 19.
Catalyst D	32,769	00-d0-10-34-24-a1	All are 19.

Questions 4 through 7 are based on a network that contains two switches, Catalyst A and B. Their bridge priorities and MAC addresses are 32,768:0000.aaaa.aaaa and 32,768:0000.bbbb.bbbb, respectively.

4. Which switch will become the Root Bridge?

5. If switch B's bridge priority is changed to 10,000, which one will be root?

6. If switch B's bridge priority is changed to 32,769, which one will be root?

7. If switch C is introduced with 40000:0000.0000.cccc, which will be the secondary root?

8. Suppose that a switch is configured with the **spanning-tree vlan 10 root primary** command. Then, another switch is connected to the network. The new switch has a bridge priority of 8192. Which one of the following happens?

   a. When the new switch advertises itself, the original Root Bridge detects it and lower its bridge priority to 4096 less than the new switch.

   b. The new switch becomes and stays the Root Bridge (bridge priority 8192).

   c. No change; both switches keep their current bridge priorities.

   d. The new switch detects that a Root Bridge already exists and raises its own bridge priority to 32,768.

9. Three switches in a network have the following bridge priorities: 32,768, 16,384, and 8192. If a fourth switch is configured with **spanning-tree vlan 1 root secondary**, what is the bridge priority of the switches that become the primary and secondary Root Bridges?

10. What STP timer values automatically can be modified by setting the network diameter?

11. Which STP timer determines how long a port stays in the Listening state? What is its default value?

12. What is the purpose of the Max Age timer?

13. Three switches are connected to each other, forming a triangle shape. STP prevents a loop from forming. What is the most accurate value that could be used for the network diameter?

14. Which of the following will not benefit from STP UplinkFast?

   a. An access-layer switch with one uplink port

   b. An access-layer switch with two uplink ports

   c. An access-layer switch with three uplink ports

   d. An access-layer switch with four uplink ports

15. What command can enable the STP PortFast feature on a switch? What configuration mode must you enter first?

16. What happens if the STP Hello Time is decreased to 1 second in an effort to speed up STP convergence? What happens if the Hello Time is increased to 10 seconds?

17. What switch command safely can adjust the STP timers on the Root Bridge in VLAN 7? Assume that the network consists of Catalysts A, B, and C, all connected to each other in a triangle fashion.

For questions 18 and 19, refer to the following output:

```
Switch# show spanning-tree vlan 50
VLAN50
  Spanning tree enabled protocol ieee
  Root ID    Priority    8000
             Address     00d0.0457.3831
             Cost        12
             Port        49 (GigabitEthernet0/1)
             Hello Time   2 sec  Max Age 20 sec  Forward Delay 15 sec

  Bridge ID  Priority    32818  (priority 32768 sys-id-ext 50)
             Address     0009.b7ee.9800
             Hello Time   2 sec  Max Age 20 sec  Forward Delay 15 sec
             Aging Time 300

Interface                                  Designated
Name             Port ID Prio  Cost Sts    Cost Bridge ID           Port ID
---------------- ------- ---  ------ ---    ---- -------------------- -------
FastEthernet0/1   128.1   128     19 FWD     12 32818 0009.b7ee.9800 128.1
FastEthernet0/2   128.2   128     19 FWD     12 32818 0009.b7ee.9800 128.2
FastEthernet0/4   128.4   128    100 FWD     12 32818 0009.b7ee.9800 128.4
FastEthernet0/7   128.7   128     19 FWD     12 32818 0009.b7ee.9800 128.7
FastEthernet0/8   128.8   128     19 FWD     12 32818 0009.b7ee.9800 128.8
FastEthernet0/9   128.9   128     19 FWD     12 32818 0009.b7ee.9800 128.9
FastEthernet0/10  128.10  128     19 FWD     12 32818 0009.b7ee.9800 128.10
FastEthernet0/11  128.11  128     19 FWD     12 32818 0009.b7ee.9800 128.11
FastEthernet0/12  128.12  128     19 FWD     12 32818 0009.b7ee.9800 128.12
FastEthernet0/17  128.13  128     19 FWD     12 32818 0009.b7ee.9800 128.13
FastEthernet0/20  128.16  128     19 FWD     12 32818 0009.b7ee.9800 128.16
FastEthernet0/21  128.17  128     19 FWD     12 32818 0009.b7ee.9800 128.17
FastEthernet0/23  128.19  128     19 FWD     12 32818 0009.b7ee.9800 128.19
FastEthernet0/24  128.20  128     19 FWD     12 32818 0009.b7ee.9800 128.20
```

18. What is the Bridge ID for the current Root Bridge? Is the switch that produced this output the actual Root Bridge?

19. What is the path cost of interface FastEthernet 0/4, and why is it different from the others?

20. Why does the column marked "Designated Bridge ID" have the same value for every switch port?

21. Suppose that you need to troubleshoot your spanning-tree topology and operation. What commands and information can you use on a switch to find information about the current STP topology in VLAN 39?

This chapter covers the following topics that you need to master for the CCNP BCMSN exam:

- **Root Guard**—This section discusses how to protect the STP topology against unexpected switches advertising to become the Root Bridge.

- **BPDU Guard**—This section covers unexpected STP advertisements on switch ports configured for PortFast, where single hosts connect.

- **Loop Guard**—This section discusses how to protect the STP topology against the loss of BPDUs from the Root Bridge on a switch port.

- **UDLD**—This section presents a feature to detect and protect against unidirectional, switch-to-switch links.

- **BPDU Filtering**—This section explains how to filter BPDUs on a switch port to prevent the port from participating in STP altogether. Bridging loops are neither detected nor prevented.

- **Troubleshooting STP Protection**—This section summarizes the commands that diagnose or verify actions to protect the topology.

CHAPTER 11

Protecting the Spanning Tree Protocol Topology

Achieving and maintaining a loop-free Spanning Tree Protocol (STP) topology revolves around the simple process of sending and receiving bridge protocol data units (BPDU). Under normal conditions, with all switches playing fairly and according to the rules, a loop-free topology dynamically is determined.

This chapter discusses two basic conditions that can occur to disrupt the loop-free topology (even while STP is running):

- On a port that has not been receiving BPDUs, BPDUs are not expected. When BPDUs suddenly appear for some reason, the STP topology can reconverge to give unexpected results.

- On a port that normally receives BPDUs, BPDUs always are expected. When BPDUs suddenly disappear for some reason, a switch can make incorrect assumptions about the topology and unintentionally create loops.

"Do I Know This Already?" Quiz

The purpose of the "Do I Know This Already?" quiz is to help you decide what parts of this chapter to use. If you intend to read the entire chapter, you do not necessarily need to answer these questions now.

The quiz, derived from the major sections in the "Foundation Topics" portion of the chapter, helps you determine how to spend your limited study time.

Table 11-1 outlines the major topics discussed in this chapter and the "Do I Know This Already?" quiz questions that correspond to those topics.

Table 11-1 *"Do I Know This Already?" Foundation Topics Section-to-Question Mapping*

Foundation Topics Section	Questions Covered in This Section	Score
Root Guard	1–4	
BPDU Guard	5	
Loop Guard	6–8	
UDLD	9–11	
BPDU Filtering	12	
Total Score		

CAUTION The goal of self-assessment is to gauge your mastery of the topics in this chapter. If you do not know the answer to a question or are only partially sure of the answer, you should mark this question wrong. Giving yourself credit for an answer you correctly guess skews your self-assessment results and might give you a false sense of security.

1. Why is it important to protect the placement of the Root Bridge?

   a. To keep two Root Bridges from becoming active

   b. To keep the STP topology stable

   c. So all hosts have the correct gateway

   d. So the Root Bridge can have complete knowledge of the STP topology

2. Which of the following features protects a switch port from accepting superior BPDUs?

   a. STP loop guard

   b. STP BPDU guard

   c. STP root guard

   d. UDLD

3. Which of the following commands can you use to enable STP root guard on a switch port?

   a. **spanning-tree root guard**

   b. **spanning-tree root-guard**

   c. **spanning-tree guard root**

   d. **spanning-tree rootguard enable**

4. Where should the STP root guard feature be enabled on a switch?

   a. All ports

   b. Only ports where the Root Bridge should never appear

   c. Only ports where the Root Bridge should be located

   d. Only ports with PortFast enabled

5. Which of the following features protects a switch port from accepting BPDUs when PortFast is enabled?

   a. STP loop guard

   b. STP BPDU guard

   c. STP root guard

   d. UDLD

6. To maintain a loop-free STP topology, which one of the following should a switch uplink be protected against?

   a. A sudden loss of BPDUs

   b. Too many BPDUs

   c. The wrong version of BPDUs

   d. BPDUs relayed from the Root Bridge

7. Which of the following commands can enable STP loop guard on a switch port?

   a. **spanning-tree loop guard**

   b. **spanning-tree guard loop**

   c. **spanning-tree loop-guard**

   d. **spanning-tree loopguard enable**

8. STP loop guard detects which of the following conditions?

   a. The sudden appearance of superior BPDUs

   b. The sudden lack of BPDUs

   c. The appearance of duplicate BPDUs

   d. The appearance of two Root Bridges

9. Which of the following features actively can test for the loss of the receive side of a link between switches?

  a. POST

  b. BPDU

  c. UDLD

  d. STP

10. UDLD must detect a unidirectional link before which of the following?

  a. The Max Age timer expires

  b. STP moves the link to the blocking state

  c. STP moves the link to the forwarding state

  d. STP moves the link to the listening state

11. What must a switch do when it receives a UDLD message on a link?

  a. Relay the message on to other switches

  b. Send a UDLD acknowledgment

  c. Echo the message back across the link

  d. Drop the message

12. Which of the following features effectively disables spanning-tree operation on a switch port?

  a. STP PortFast

  b. STP BPDU filtering

  c. STP BPDU guard

  d. STP root guard

You can find the answers to the "Do I Know This Already?" quiz in Appendix A, "Answers to Chapter 'Do I Know This Already?' Quizzes and Q&A Sections." The suggested choices for your next step are as follows:

- **10 or less overall score**—Read the entire chapter. This includes the "Foundation Topics," "Foundation Summary," and "Q&A" sections.

- **11 or 12 overall score**—If you want more review on these topics, skip to the "Foundation Summary" section, and then go to the "Q&A" section at the end of the chapter. Otherwise, move to Chapter 12, "Advanced Spanning Tree Protocol."

Foundation Topics

Protecting Against Unexpected BPDUs

A network running STP uses BPDUs to communicate between switches (bridges). Switches become aware of each other and of the topology that interconnects them. After a Root Bridge is elected, BPDUs are generated by the root and are relayed down through the spanning-tree topology. Eventually, all switches in the STP domain receive the root's BPDUs so that the network converges and a stable loop-free topology forms.

To maintain an efficient topology, the placement of the Root Bridge must be predictable. Hopefully, you configured one switch to become the Root Bridge and a second one to be the secondary root. What happens when a "foreign" or rogue switch is connected to the network, and that switch suddenly is capable of becoming the Root Bridge? Cisco added two STP features that help prevent the unexpected: root guard and BPDU guard.

Root Guard

After an STP topology has converged and becomes loop free, switch ports are assigned the following roles:

- **Root port**—The one port on a switch that is closest (with the lowest root path cost) to the Root Bridge.

- **Designated port**—The port on a LAN segment that is closest to the root. This port relays, or transmits, BPDUs down the tree.

- **Blocking port**—Ports that are neither root nor designated ports.

- **Alternate port**—Ports that are candidate root ports (they are also close to the Root Bridge) but are in the Blocking state. These ports are identified for quick use by the STP UplinkFast feature.

- **Forwarding port**—Ports where no other STP activity is detected or expected. These are ports with normal end-user connections.

The Root Bridge always is expected to be seen on the root port and the alternate ports because these are "closest" (have the best-cost path) to it.

Suppose that another switch is introduced into the network with a bridge priority that is more desirable (lower) than that of the current Root Bridge. The new switch then would become the Root Bridge, and the STP topology might reconverge to a new shape. This is entirely permissible by the STP because the switch with the lowest Bridge ID always wins the root election.

However, this is not always desirable for you, the network administrator, because the new STP topology might be something totally unacceptable. In addition, while the topology is reconverging, your production network might become unavailable.

The *root guard* feature was developed as a means to control where candidate Root Bridges can be connected and found on a network. Basically, a switch learns the current Root Bridge's Bridge ID. If another switch advertises a *superior BPDU*, or one with a better Bridge ID, on a port where root guard is enabled, the local switch will not allow the new switch to become the root. As long as the superior BPDUs are being received on the port, the port will be kept in the *root-inconsistent* STP state. No data can be sent or received in that state, but the switch can listen to BPDUs received on the port to detect a new root advertising itself.

In essence, root guard designates that a port can only forward or relay BPDUs; the port can't be used to receive BPDUs. Root guard prevents the port from ever becoming a root port where BPDUs normally would be received from the Root Bridge.

You can enable root guard only on a per-port basis. By default, it is disabled on all switch ports. To enable it, use the following interface-configuration command:

```
Switch(config-if)# spanning-tree guard root
```

When the superior BPDUs no longer are received, the port is cycled through the normal STP states to return to normal use.

Use root guard on switch ports where you never expect to find the Root Bridge for a VLAN. In fact, root guard affects the entire port so that a Root Bridge never can be allowed on *any* VLAN on the port. When a superior BPDU is heard on the port, the entire port, in effect, becomes blocked.

> **TIP** You can display switch ports that root guard has put into the *root-inconsistent* state with the following command:
>
> ```
> Switch# show spanning-tree inconsistentports
> ```

BPDU Guard

Recall that the traditional STP offers the PortFast feature, in which switch ports are allowed to immediately enter the Forwarding state as soon as the link comes up. Normally, PortFast provides quick network access to end-user devices, where bridging loops never are expected to form. Even while PortFast is enabled on a port, STP still is running and can detect a bridging loop. However, a loop can be detected only in a finite amount of time—the length of time required to move the port through the normal STP states.

> **NOTE** Remember that enabling PortFast on a port is not the same as disabling the STP on it.

By definition, if you enable PortFast, you do not expect to find anything that can cause a bridging loop—especially another switch or device that produces BPDUs. Suppose that a switch is connected by mistake to a port where PortFast is enabled. Now there is a potential for a bridging loop to form. An even greater consequence is that the potential now exists for the newly connected device to advertise itself and become the new Root Bridge.

The BPDU guard feature was developed to further protect the integrity of switch ports that have PortFast enabled. If any BPDU (whether superior to the current root or not) is received on a port where BPDU guard is enabled, that port immediately is put into the *errdisable* state. The port is shut down in an error condition and must be either manually re-enabled or automatically recovered through the errdisable timeout function.

By default, BPDU guard is disabled on all switch ports. You can configure BPDU guard as a global default, affecting all switch ports with a single command. All ports that have PortFast enabled also have BPDU guard automatically enabled. You can use the following global configuration command to enable BPDU guard as the default:

```
Switch(config)# spanning-tree portfast bpduguard default
```

You also can enable or disable BPDU guard on a per-port basis, using the following interface-configuration command:

```
Switch(config-if)# [no] spanning-tree bpduguard enable
```

When the BPDUs no longer are received, the port still remains in the errdisable state. See Chapter 5, "Switch Port Configuration," for more information about recovering from the errdisable state.

You should use BPDU guard on all switch ports where STP PortFast is enabled. This prevents any possibility that a switch will be added to the port, either intentionally or by mistake. An obvious application for BPDU guard is on access-layer switch ports where users and end devices connect. BPDUs normally would not be expected there and would be detected if a switch or hub inadvertently was connected.

Naturally, BPDU guard does not prevent a bridging loop from forming if an Ethernet hub is connected to the PortFast port. This is because a hub doesn't transmit BPDUs itself; it merely repeats Ethernet frames from its other ports. A loop could form if the hub became connected to two locations in the network, providing a path for frames to be looped without any STP activity.

You never should enable BPDU guard on any switch uplink where the Root Bridge is located. If a switch has multiple uplinks, any of those ports could receive legitimate BPDUs from the root—even if they are in the Blocking state as a result of the UplinkFast feature. If BPDU guard is enabled on an uplink port, BPDUs will be detected and the uplink will be put into the errdisable state. This will preclude that uplink port from being used as an uplink into the network.

Protecting Against Sudden Loss of BPDUs

STP BPDUs are used as probes to learn about a network topology. When the switches participating in STP converge on a common and consistent loop-free topology, BPDUs still must be sent by the Root Bridge and must be relayed by every other switch in the STP domain. The STP topology's integrity then depends on a continuous and regular flow of BPDUs from the root.

What happens if a switch doesn't receive BPDUs in a timely manner or when it doesn't receive any? The switch can view that condition as acceptable—perhaps an upstream switch or an upstream link is dead. In that case, the topology must have changed, so blocked ports eventually can be unblocked again.

However, if the absence of BPDUs is actually a mistake and BPDUs are not being received even though there is no topology change, bridging loops easily can form.

Cisco has added two STP features that help detect or prevent the unexpected loss of BPDUs:

■   Loop guard

■   Unidirectional Link Detection (UDLD)

Loop Guard

Suppose that a switch port is receiving BPDUs and the switch port is in the Blocking state. The port makes up a redundant path; it is blocking because it is neither a root port nor a designated port. It will remain in the Blocking state as long as a steady flow of BPDUs is received.

If BPDUs are being sent over a link but the flow of BPDUs stops for some reason, the last-known BPDU is kept until the Max Age timer expires. Then that BPDU is flushed, and the switch thinks there is no longer a need to block the port. After all, if no BPDUs are received, there must not be another STP device connected there.

The switch then moves the port through the STP states until it begins to forward traffic—and forms a bridging loop. In its final state, the port becomes a designated port where it begins to relay or send BPDUs downstream, when it actually should be receiving BPDUs from upstream.

To prevent this situation, you can use the loop guard STP feature. When enabled, loop guard keeps track of the BPDU activity on nondesignated ports. While BPDUs are received, the port is allowed to behave normally. When BPDUs go missing, loop guard moves the port into the *loop-inconsistent* state. The port is effectively blocking at this point to prevent a loop from forming and to keep it in the nondesignated role.

When BPDUs are received on the port again, loop guard allows the port to move through the normal STP states and become active. In this fashion, loop guard automatically governs ports without the need for manual intervention.

By default, loop guard is disabled on all switch ports. You can enable loop guard as a global default, affecting all switch ports, with the following global configuration command:

```
Switch(config)# spanning-tree loopguard default
```

You also can enable or disable loop guard on a specific switch port by using the following interface-configuration command:

```
Switch(config-if)# [no] spanning-tree guard loop
```

Although loop guard is configured on a switch port, its corrective blocking action is taken on a per-VLAN basis. In other words, loop guard doesn't block the entire port; only the offending VLANs are blocked.

You can enable loop guard on all switch ports, regardless of their functions. The switch figures out which ports are nondesignated and monitors the BPDU activity to keep them nondesignated. Nondesignated ports are generally the root port, alternate root ports, and ports that normally are blocking.

UDLD

In a campus network, switches are connected by bidirectional links, where traffic can flow in two directions. Clearly, if a link has a physical layer problem, the two switches it connects detect a problem and the link is shown as not connected.

What would happen if just one side of the link (receive or transmit) had an odd failure, such as malfunctioning transmit circuitry in a gigabit interface converter (GBIC)? In some cases, the two switches still might see a functional bidirectional link, although traffic actually would be delivered in only one direction. This is known as a *unidirectional link*.

A unidirectional link poses a potential danger to STP topologies because BPDUs will not be received on one end of the link. If that end of the link normally would be in the Blocking state, it will not be that way for long. A switch interprets the absence of BPDUs to mean that the port safely can be moved through the STP states so that traffic can be forwarded. However, if that is done on a unidirectional link, a bridging loop forms and the switch never realizes the mistake.

To prevent this situation, you can use the Cisco-proprietary UniDirectional Link Detection (UDLD) STP feature. When enabled, UDLD interactively monitors a port to see if the link is truly bidirectional. A switch sends special Layer 2 UDLD frames identifying its switch port at regular intervals. UDLD expects the far-end switch to echo those frames back across the same link, with the far-end switch port's identification added.

If a UDLD frame is received in return and both neighboring ports are identified in the frame, the link must be bidirectional. However, if the echoed frames are not seen, the link must be unidirectional for some reason.

Naturally, an echo process such as this requires *both ends* of the link to be configured for UDLD. Otherwise, one end of the link will not echo the frames back to the originator. In addition, each switch at the end of a link sends its own UDLD messages independently, expecting echoes from the far end. This means that two echo processes are occurring on any given link.

UDLD messages are sent at regular intervals, as long as the link is active. You can configure the message interval UDLD uses (the default is 15 seconds). The objective behind UDLD is to detect a unidirectional link condition before STP has time to move a blocked port into the Forwarding state. To do this, the target time must be less than the Max Age timer plus two intervals of the Forward Delay timer, or 50 seconds. UDLD can detect a unidirectional link after about three times the UDLD message interval (45 seconds total, using the default).

UDLD has two modes of operation:

■ **Normal mode**—When a unidirectional link condition is detected, the port is allowed to continue its operation. UDLD merely marks the port as having an *undetermined* state and generates a syslog message.

■ **Aggressive mode**—When a unidirectional link condition is detected, the switch takes action to re-establish the link. UDLD messages are sent out once a second for 8 seconds. If none of those messages is echoed back, the port is placed in the *errdisable* state so that it cannot be used.

You configure UDLD on a per-port basis, although you globally can enable it for all fiber-optic switch ports (either native fiber or fiber-based GBIC or SFP modules). By default, UDLD is disabled on all switch ports. To enable it globally, use the following global configuration command:

```
Switch(config)# udld {enable | aggressive | message time seconds}
```

For normal mode, use the **enable** keyword; for aggressive mode, use the **aggressive** keyword. You can use the **message time** keywords to set the message interval to *seconds*, ranging from 7 to 90 seconds. (The default interval varies according to switch platform. For example, the Catalyst 3550 default is 7 seconds; the Catalyst 4500 and 6500 default is 15 seconds.)

You also can enable or disable UDLD on individual switch ports, if needed, using the following interface-configuration command:

```
Switch(config-if)# udld {enable | aggressive | disable}
```

Here, you can use the **disable** keyword to completely disable UDLD on a fiber-optic interface.

> **NOTE**   The default UDLD message interval times differ among Catalyst switch platforms. Although two neighbors might have mismatched message time values, UDLD still works correctly. This is because each of the two neighbors simply echoes UDLD messages back as they are received, without knowledge of their neighbor's own time interval. The time interval is used only to decide when to send UDLD messages and as a basis for detecting a unidirectional link from the absence of echoed messages.
>
> If you decide to change the default message time, make sure that UDLD still can detect a fault *before* STP decides to move a link to the Forwarding state.

You safely can enable UDLD on all switch ports. The switch globally enables UDLD only on ports that use fiber-optic media. Twisted-pair or copper media does not suffer from the physical layer conditions that allow a unidirectional link to form. However, you can enable UDLD on nonfiber links individually, if you want.

At this point, you might be wondering how UDLD can be enabled gracefully on the two end switches. Recall that in aggressive mode, UDLD disables the link if the neighbor does not reflect the messages back within a certain time period. If you are enabling UDLD on a production network, is there a chance that UDLD will disable working links before you can get the far end configured?

The answer is no. UDLD makes some intelligent assumptions when it is enabled on a link for the first time. First, UDLD has no record of any neighbor on the link. It starts sending out messages, hoping that a neighboring switch will hear them and echo them back. Obviously, the device at the far end also must support UDLD so that the messages will be echoed back.

If the neighboring switch does not yet have UDLD enabled, no messages will be echoed. UDLD will keep trying (indefinitely) to detect a neighbor and will not disable the link. After the neighbor has UDLD configured also, both switches become aware of each other and the bidirectional state of the link through their UDLD message exchanges. From then on, if messages are not echoed, the link accurately can be labeled as unidirectional.

Finally, be aware that if UDLD detects a unidirectional condition on a link, it takes action on only that link. This becomes important in an EtherChannel: If one link within the channel becomes unidirectional, UDLD flags or disables only the offending link in the bundle, not the entire EtherChannel. UDLD sends and echoes its messages on each link within an EtherChannel channel independently.

Using BPDU Filtering to Disable STP on a Port

Ordinarily, STP operates on all switch ports in an effort to eliminate bridging loops before they can form. BPDUs are sent on all switch ports—even ports where PortFast has been enabled. BPDUs also can be received and processed if any are sent by neighboring switches.

You always should allow STP to run on a switch to prevent loops. However, in special cases when you need to prevent BPDUs from being sent or processed on one or more switch ports, you can use BPDU filtering to effectively disable STP on those ports.

By default, BPDU filtering is disabled on all switch ports. You can configure BPDU filtering as a global default, affecting all switch ports with the following global configuration command:

```
Switch(config)# spanning-tree portfast bpdufilter default
```

All ports that have PortFast enabled also have BPDU filtering automatically enabled.

You also can enable or disable BPDU filtering on specific switch ports by using the following interface-configuration command:

```
Switch(config-if)# spanning-tree bpdufilter {enable | disable}
```

Be very careful to enable BPDU filtering only under controlled circumstances in which you are absolutely sure that a switch port will have a single host connected and that a loop will be impossible. Enable BPDU filtering only if the connected device cannot allow BPDUs to be accepted or sent. Otherwise, you should permit STP to operate on the switch ports as a precaution.

Troubleshooting STP Protection

With several different types of STP protection features available, you might need to know which (if any) has been configured on a switch port. Table 11-2 lists and describes the EXEC commands useful for verifying the features presented in this chapter.

Table 11-2   *Commands for Verifying and Troubleshooting STP Protection Features*

Display Function	Command Syntax
List the ports that have been labeled in an inconsistent state	Switch# **show spanning-tree inconsistentports**
Look for detailed reasons for inconsistencies	Switch# **show spanning-tree interface** *type mod/num* [**detail**]
Display the global BPDU guard, BPDU filter, and loop guard states	Switch# **show spanning-tree summary**
Display the UDLD status on one or all ports	Switch# **show udld** [*type mod/num*]
Re-enable ports that UDLD aggressive mode has errdisabled	Switch# **udld reset**

Foundation Summary

The Foundation Summary is a collection of information that provides a convenient review of many key concepts in this chapter. If you are already comfortable with the topics in this chapter, this summary could help you recall a few details. If you just read this chapter, this review can help solidify some key facts. If you are doing your final preparation before the exam, these tables and figures are a convenient way to review the day before the exam.

With so many similar and mutually exclusive STP protection features available, you might have a hard time remembering which ones to use where. Use Figure 11-1 as a quick reference.

Figure 11-1 *Guidelines for Applying STP Protection Features in a Network*

Root guard: Apply to ports where root is never expected.

BPDU guard: Apply to all user ports where PortFast is enabled.

Loop guard: Apply to nondesignated ports but okay to apply to all ports.

UDLD: Apply to all fiber-optic links between switches (must be enabled on both ends).

Permissible combinations on a switch port:
    Loop guard and UDLD
    Root guard and UDLD

Not permissible on a switch port:
    Root guard and Loop guard
    Root guard and BPDU guard

Figure 11-1 shows two backbone switches (Catalyst A and B), along with an access-layer switch (Catalyst C), with redundant uplinks. Users are connected to the access switch, where PortFast is in use. An additional access switch (Catalyst D) has an uplink to access-layer switch C. All switch-to-switch links are fiber-based Gigabit Ethernet. Obviously, a Root Bridge never should appear out of Catalyst D.

Table 11-3 *STP Protection Configuration Commands*

Task	Global Command Syntax	Interface Command Syntax
Enable root guard	—	`Switch(config-if)# `**`spanning-tree guard root`**
Enable BPDU guard	`Switch(config)# `**`spanning-tree portfast bpduguard default`**	`Switch(config-if)# `**`spanning-tree bpduguard enable`**
Enable loop guard	`Switch(config)# `**`spanning-tree loopguard default`**	`Switch(config-if)# `**`spanning-tree guard loop`**
Enable UDLD	`Switch(config)# `**`udld {enable ǀ aggressive ǀ message time `***`seconds`***`}`**	`Switch(config-if)# `**`udld {enable ǀ aggressive ǀ disable}`**
Enable BPDU filtering	`Switch(config)# `**`spanning-tree bpdufilter default`**	`Switch(config-if)# `**`spanning-tree bpdufilter enable`**

Table 11-4 *STP Protection Activity Commands*

Task	Command Syntax
Look for ports that have been put in an inconsistent state	`Switch# `**`show spanning-tree inconsistentports`**
Display the global BPDU guard, BPDU filter, and loop guard states	`Switch# `**`show spanning-tree summary`**
Show UDLD status	`Switch# `**`show udld`** `[`*`type mod/num`*`]`
Re-enable all ports that UDLD has errdisabled	`Switch# `**`udld reset`**

Q&A

The questions and scenarios in this book are more difficult than what you should experience on the actual exam. The questions do not attempt to cover more breadth or depth than the exam; however, they are designed to make sure that you know the answers. Rather than allowing you to derive the answers from clues hidden inside the questions themselves, the questions challenge your understanding and recall of the subject. Hopefully, these questions will help limit the number of exam questions on which you narrow your choices to two options and then guess.

The answers to these questions can be found in Appendix A.

1. Why would a unidirectional link be bad?

2. What condition must be met to keep a switch port in the Blocking state?

3. If a switch port is shown to be in the root-inconsistent state, what has happened on it?

4. When root guard has been triggered on a switch port, what must be done to enable the port for use again?

5. When BPDU guard is enabled on a switch port, what state will the port be put in if a BPDU is received on it?

6. When BPDU guard has been triggered on a switch port, what must be done to enable the port for use again?

7. When loop guard is enabled on a switch port, what state will the port be put in if BPDUs are noted to be missing?

8. Can STP loop guard be enabled on all switch ports?

9. When UDLD is enabled on a switch port, what else must be done to detect a unidirectional link on the port?

10. What is the difference between the UDLD normal and aggressive modes?

11. What command enables UDLD aggressive mode on a switch interface?

12. If two switches enable UDLD on the ports that have a common link, do their UDLD message times have to agree?

13. UDLD should be used on switch ports with what type of media?

14. Can UDLD be used on all switch ports without causing problems?

15. Is it possible to disable STP on a single switch port without disabling the whole STP instance? If so, how can you do that?

16. Complete the following command to display all ports that are disabled because of STP protection features:

```
show spanning-tree _____
```

This chapter covers the following topics that you need to master for the CCNP BCMSN exam:

- **Rapid Spanning Tree Protocol (RSTP)**—This section discusses the enhancements that allow switches to run STP efficiently, offering fast convergence.

- **Multiple Spanning Tree (MST) Protocol**—This section discusses the latest IEEE standard that supports a reduced number of STP instances for a campus network, while using RSTP for efficient operation.

CHAPTER 12

Advanced Spanning Tree Protocol

Familiarity with the IEEE 802.1D STP standard is essential because that protocol is used universally to maintain loop-free bridged and switched networks. However, it now is considered a legacy protocol, offering topology change and convergence times that are not as acceptable as they once were.

This chapter discusses the many STP enhancements that are available in new standards. Rapid STP (RSTP) is presented first because it provides the foundation for efficient STP activity. RSTP can be coupled with either per-VLAN STP (PVST+) or Multiple STP modes. This allows a Layer 2 campus network to undergo change quickly and efficiently, with little downtime for today's applications.

This chapter also covers Multiple STP (MST or MSTP). MST allows VLANs to be individually mapped into arbitrary STP instances while RSTP operates in the background. You can use MST to greatly simplify the Layer 2 topologies and STP operations when many VLANs (and many instances of STP) are present in a network.

"Do I Know This Already?" Quiz

The purpose of the "Do I Know This Already?" quiz is to help you decide whether you need to read the entire chapter. If you already intend to read the entire chapter, you do not necessarily need to answer these questions now.

The quiz, derived from the major sections in the "Foundation Topics" portion of the chapter, helps you determine how to spend your limited study time.

Table 12-1 outlines the major topics discussed in this chapter and the "Do I Know This Already?" quiz questions that correspond to those topics.

Table 12-1 *"Do I Know This Already?" Foundation Topics Section-to-Question Mapping*

Foundation Topics Section	Questions Covered in This Section	Score
Rapid STP	1–8	
Multiple STP (MST)	9–12	
Total Score		

> **CAUTION** The goal of self-assessment is to gauge your mastery of the topics in this chapter. If you do not know the answer to a question or are only partially sure of the answer, you should mark this question wrong. Giving yourself credit for an answer you correctly guess skews your self- assessment results and might give you a false sense of security.

1. Which one of the following enables the use of RSTP?

    a. PVST+

    b. RPVST+

    c. 802.1D

    d. CST

    e. MST

2. Upon which standard is RSTP based?

    a. 802.1Q

    b. 802.1D

    c. 802.1w

    d. 802.1s

3. Which of the following is not a port state in RSTP?

    a. Listening

    b. Learning

    c. Discarding

    d. Forwarding

4. When a switch running RSTP receives an 802.1D BPDU, what happens?

    a. The BPDU is discarded or dropped.

    b. An ICMP message is returned.

    c. The switch begins to use 802.1D rules on that port.

    d. The switch disables RSTP.

5. When does an RSTP switch consider a neighbor to be down?

   a. After three BPDUs are missed

   b. After six BPDUs are missed

   c. After the Max Age timer expires

   d. After the Forward timer expires

6. Which process is used during RSTP convergence?

   a. BPDU propagation

   b. Synchronization

   c. Forward timer expiration

   d. BPDU acknowledgments

7. What causes RSTP to view a port as a point-to-point port?

   a. Port speed

   b. Port media

   c. Port duplex

   d. Port priority

8. Which of the following events triggers a topology change with RSTP on a nonedge port?

   a. A port comes up or goes down.

   b. A port comes up.

   c. A port goes down.

   d. A port moves to the Forwarding state.

9. Which of the following is *not* a characteristic of MST?

   a. A reduced number of STP instances

   b. Fast STP convergence

   c. Eliminated need for CST

   d. Interoperability with PVST+

10. Which of the following standards defines the MST protocol?

    a. 802.1Q

    b. 802.1D

    c. 802.1w

    d. 802.1s

11. How many instances of STP are supported in the Cisco implementation of MST?

    a. 1

    b. 16

    c. 256

    d. 4096

12. What switch command can be used to change from PVST+ to MST?

    a. **spanning-tree mst enable**

    b. **no spanning-tree pvst+**

    c. **spanning-tree mode mst**

    d. **spanning-tree mst**

You can find the answers to the "Do I Know This Already?" quiz in Appendix A, "Answers to Chapter 'Do I Know This Already?' Quizzes and Q&A Sections." The suggested choices for your next step are as follows:

- **10 or less overall score**—Read the entire chapter. This includes the "Foundation Topics," "Foundation Summary," and "Q&A" sections.

- **11 or 12 overall score**—If you want more review on these topics, skip to the "Foundation Summary" section and then go to the "Q&A" section at the end of the chapter. Otherwise, move to Chapter 13, "Multilayer Switching."

Foundation Topics

Rapid Spanning Tree Protocol

The IEEE 802.1D Spanning Tree Protocol was designed to keep a switched or bridged network loop free, with adjustments made to the network topology dynamically. A topology change typically takes 30 seconds, with a port moving from the Blocking state to the Forwarding state after two intervals of the Forward Delay timer. As technology has improved, 30 seconds has become an unbearable length of time to wait for a production network to fail over or "heal" itself during a problem.

The IEEE 802.1w standard was developed to use 802.1D's principle concepts and make the resulting convergence much faster. This is also known as the Rapid Spanning Tree Protocol (RSTP), which defines how switches must interact with each other to keep the network topology loop free, in a very efficient manner.

As with 802.1D, RSTP's basic functionality can be applied as a single instance or multiple instances. This can be done by using RSTP as the underlying mechanism for the Cisco-proprietary Per-VLAN Spanning Tree Protocol (PVST+). The resulting combination is called *Rapid PVST+* (RPVST+). RSTP also is used as part of the IEEE 802.1s Multiple Spanning Tree (MST) operation. RSTP operates consistently in each, but replicating RSTP as multiple instances requires different approaches.

RSTP Port Behavior

In 802.1D, each switch port is assigned a role and a state at any given time. Depending on the port's proximity to the Root Bridge, it takes on one of the following roles:

- Root port

- Designated port

- Blocking port (neither root nor designated)

The Cisco-proprietary UplinkFast feature also reserved a hidden alternate port role for ports that offered parallel paths to the root but were in the Blocking state.

Recall that each switch port also is assigned one of five possible states:

- Disabled

- Blocking

■ Listening

■ Learning

■ Forwarding

Only the Forwarding state allows data to be sent and received. A port's state is somewhat tied to its role. For example, a blocking port cannot be a root port or a designated port.

RSTP achieves its rapid nature by letting each switch interact with its neighbors through each port. This interaction is performed based on a port's role, not strictly on the BPDUs that are relayed from the Root Bridge. After the role is determined, each port can be given a state that determines what it does with incoming data.

The Root Bridge in a network using RSTP is elected just as with 802.1D—by the lowest Bridge ID. After all switches agree on the identity of the root, the following port roles are determined:

■ **Root port**—The one switch port on each switch that has the best root path cost to the root. This is identical to 802.1D. (By definition, the Root Bridge has no root ports.)

■ **Designated port**—The switch port on a network segment that has the best root path cost to the root.

■ **Alternate port**—A port that has an alternate path to the root, different than the path the root port takes. This path is less desirable than that of the root port. (An example of this is an access-layer switch with two uplink ports; one becomes the root port, and the other is an alternate port.)

■ **Backup port**—A port that provides a redundant (but less desirable) connection to a segment where another switch port already connects. If that common segment is lost, the switch might or might not have a path back to the root.

RSTP defines port states only according to what the port does with incoming frames. (Naturally, if incoming frames are ignored or dropped, so are outgoing frames.) Any port role can have any of these port states:

■ **Discarding**—Incoming frames simply are dropped; no MAC addresses are learned. (This state combines the 802.1D Disabled, Blocking, and Listening states because all three did not effectively forward anything. The Listening state is not needed because RSTP quickly can negotiate a state change without listening for BPDUs first.)

■ **Learning**—Incoming frames are dropped, but MAC addresses are learned.

■ **Forwarding**—Incoming frames are forwarded according to MAC addresses that have been (and are being) learned.

BPDUs in RSTP

In 802.1D, BPDUs basically originate from the Root Bridge and are relayed by all switches down through the tree. Because of this propagation of BPDUs, 802.1D convergence must wait for steady-state conditions before proceeding.

RSTP uses the 802.1D BPDU format for backward-compatibility. However, some previously unused bits in the Message Type field are used. The sending switch port identifies itself by its RSTP role and state. The BPDU version also is set to 2, to distinguish RSTP BPDUs from 802.1D BPDUs. In addition, RSTP uses an interactive process so that two neighboring switches can negotiate state changes. Some BPDU bits are used to flag messages during this negotiation.

BPDUs are sent out every switch port at Hello Time intervals, regardless of whether BPDUs are received from the root. In this way, any switch anywhere in the network can play an active role in maintaining the topology. Switches also can expect to receive regular BPDUs from their neighbors. When three BPDUs are missed in a row, that neighbor is presumed to be down, and all information related to the port leading to the neighbor immediately is aged out. This means that a switch can detect a neighbor failure in three Hello intervals (default 6 seconds), versus the Max Age timer interval (default 20 seconds) for 802.1D.

Because RSTP distinguishes its BPDUs from 802.1D BPDUs, it can coexist with switches still using 802.1D. Each port attempts to operate according to the STP BPDU that is received. For example, when an 802.1D BPDU (version 0) is received on a port, that port begins to operate according to the 802.1D rules.

However, each port has a measure that locks the protocol in use, in case BPDUs from both 802.1D and RSTP are received within a short time frame. This can occur if the switches in a network are being migrated from one STP type to another. Instead of flapping or toggling the STP type during a migration, the switch holds the protocol type for the duration of a migration delay timer. After this timer expires, the port is free to change protocols if needed.

RSTP Convergence

The convergence of STP in a network is the process that takes all switches from a state of independence (each thinks it must be the STP root) to one of uniformity, in which each switch has a place in a loop-free tree topology. You can think of convergence as a two-stage process:

1.   One common Root Bridge must be "elected," and all switches must know about it.

2.   The state of every switch port in the STP domain must be brought from a Blocking state to the appropriate state to prevent loops.

Convergence generally takes time because messages are propagated from switch to switch. The traditional 802.1D STP also requires the expiration of several timers before switch ports safely can be allowed to forward data.

RSTP takes a different approach when a switch needs to decide how to participate in the tree topology. When a switch first joins the topology (perhaps it was just powered up) or has detected a failure in the existing topology, RSTP requires it to base its forwarding decisions on the type of port.

Port Types

Every switch port can be considered one of the following types:

- **Edge port**—A port at the "edge" of the network, where only a single host connects. Traditionally, this has been identified by enabling the STP PortFast feature. RSTP keeps the PortFast concept for familiarity. By definition, the port cannot form a loop as it connects to one host, so it can be placed immediately in the Forwarding state. However, if a BPDU ever is received on an edge port, the port immediately loses its edge port status.

- **Root port**—The port that has the best cost to the root of the STP instance. Only one root port can be selected and active at any time, although alternate paths to the root can exist through other ports. If alternate paths are detected, those ports are identified as alternate root ports and immediately can be placed in the Forwarding state when the existing root port fails.

- **Point-to-point port**—Any port that connects to another switch and becomes a designated port. A quick handshake with the neighboring switch, rather than a timer expiration, decides the port state. BPDUs are exchanged back and forth in the form of a proposal and an agreement. One switch proposes that its port becomes a designated port; if the other switch agrees, it replies with an agreement message.

  Point-to-point ports automatically are determined by the duplex mode in use. Full-duplex ports are considered point to point because only two switches can be present on the link. STP convergence can occur quickly over a point-to-point link through RSTP handshake messages.

  Half-duplex ports, on the other hand, are considered to be on a shared medium with possibly more than two switches present. They are not point-to-point ports. STP convergence on a half-duplex port must occur between several directly connected switches. Therefore, the traditional 802.1D style convergence must be used. This results in a slower response because the shared-medium ports must go through the fixed Listening and Learning state time periods.

It's easy to see how two switches quickly can converge to a common idea of which one is the root and which one will have the designated port after just a single exchange of BPDUs. What about a larger network, where 802.1D BPDUs normally would have to be relayed from switch to switch?

RSTP handles the complete STP convergence of the network as a propagation of handshakes over point-to-point links. When a switch needs to make an STP decision, a handshake is made with the nearest neighbor. When that is successful, the handshake sequence is moved to the next switch and the next, as an ever-expanding wave moving toward the network's edges.

During each handshake sequence, a switch must take measures to completely ensure that it will not introduce a bridging loop before moving the handshake outward. This is done through a synchronization process.

Synchronization

To participate in RSTP convergence, a switch must decide the state of each of its ports. Nonedge ports begin in the Discarding state. After BPDUs are exchanged between the switch and its neighbor, the Root Bridge can be identified. If a port receives a superior BPDU from a neighbor, that port becomes the root port.

For each nonedge port, the switch exchanges a proposal-agreement handshake to decide the state of each end of the link. Each switch assumes that its port should become the designated port for the segment, and a proposal message (a configuration BPDU) is sent to the neighbor suggesting this.

When a switch receives a proposal message on a port, the following sequence of events occurs Figure 12-1 shows the sequence, based on the center Catalyst switch:

1. If the proposal's sender has a superior BPDU, the local switch realizes that the sender should be the designated switch (having the designated port) and that its own port must become the new root port.

2. Before the switch agrees to anything, it must synchronize itself with the topology.

3. All nonedge ports immediately are moved into the Discarding (blocking) state so that no bridging loops can form.

4. An agreement message (a configuration BPDU) is sent back to the sender, indicating that the switch is in agreement with the new designated port choice. This also tells the sender that the switch is in the process of synchronizing itself.

5. The root port immediately is moved to the Forwarding state. The sender's port also immediately can begin forwarding.

6. For each nonedge port that is currently in the Discarding state, a proposal message is sent to the respective neighbor.

7. An agreement message is expected and received from a neighbor on a nonedge port.

8. The nonedge port immediately is moved to the Forwarding state.

Figure 12-1   *Sequence of Events During RSTP Convergence*

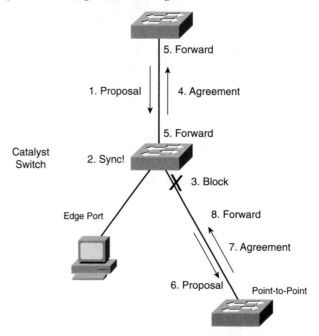

Notice that the RSTP convergence begins with a switch sending a proposal message. The recipient of the proposal must synchronize itself by effectively isolating itself from the rest of the topology. All nonedge ports are blocked until a proposal message can be sent, causing the nearest neighbors to synchronize themselves. This creates a moving "wave" of synchronizing switches, which quickly can decide to start forwarding on their links only if their neighbors agree. Figure 12-2 shows how the synchronization wave travels through a network at three successive time intervals. Isolating the switches along the traveling wave inherently prevents bridging loops.

The entire convergence process happens quickly, at the speed of BPDU transmission, without the use of any timers. However, a designated port that sends a proposal message might not receive an agreement message reply. Suppose that the neighboring switch does not understand RSTP or has a problem replying. The sending switch then must become overly cautious and must begin playing by the 802.1D rules—the port must be moved through the legacy Listening and Learning states (using the Forward Delay timer) before moving to the Forwarding state.

Figure 12-2   *RSTP Synchronization Traveling Through a Network*

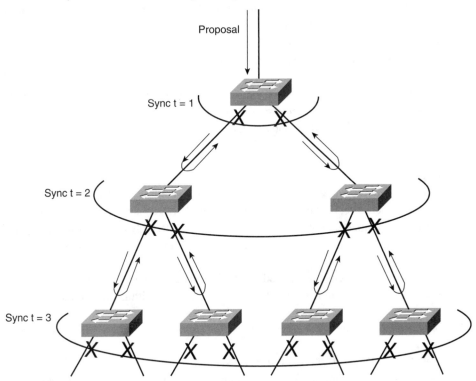

Topology Changes and RSTP

Recall that when an 802.1D switch detects a port state change (either up or down), it signals the Root Bridge by sending topology change notification (TCN) BPDUs. The Root Bridge, in turn, must signal the topology change by sending out a TCN message that is relayed to all switches in the STP domain.

RSTP detects a topology change only when a nonedge port transitions to the Forwarding state. This might seem odd because a link failure is not used as a trigger. RSTP uses all of its rapid convergence mechanisms to prevent bridging loops from forming. Therefore, topology changes are detected only so that bridging tables can be updated and corrected as hosts appear first on a failed port and then on a different functioning port.

When a topology change is detected, a switch must propagate news of the change to other switches in the network so that they can correct their bridging tables, too. This process is similar to the convergence and synchronization mechanism; topology change (TC) messages propagate through the network in an ever-expanding wave.

BPDUs, with their TC bit set, are sent out all of the nonedge designated ports. This is done until the TC While timer expires, after two intervals of the Hello time. This notifies neighboring switches of the new link and the topology change. In addition, all MAC addresses associated with the nonedge designated ports are flushed from the content-addressable memory (CAM) table. This forces the addresses to be relearned after the change, in case hosts now appear on a different link.

All neighboring switches that receive the TC messages also must flush the MAC addresses learned on all ports except the one that received the TC message. Those switches then must send TC messages out their nonedge designated ports, and so on.

RSTP Configuration

By default, a switch operates in Per-VLAN Spanning Tree Plus (PVST+) mode using traditional 802.1D STP. Therefore, RSTP cannot be used until a different spanning-tree mode (MST or RPVST+) is enabled. Remember that RSTP is just the underlying mechanism that a spanning-tree mode can use to detect topology changes and converge a network into a loop-free topology.

The only configuration changes related to RSTP affect the port or link type. The link type is used to determine how a switch negotiates topology information with its neighbors.

To configure a port as an RSTP edge port, use the following interface-configuration command:

```
Switch(config-if)# spanning-tree portfast
```

You already should be familiar with this command from the 802.1D STP configuration. After PortFast is enabled, the port is considered to have only one host and is positioned at the edge of the network.

By default, RSTP automatically decides that a port is a point-to-point link if it is operating in full-duplex mode. Ports connecting to other switches are usually full duplex because there are only two switches on the link. However, you can override the automatic determination, if needed. For example, a port connecting to one other switch might be operating at half duplex, for some reason. To force the port to act as a point-to-point link, use the following interface-configuration command:

```
Switch(config-if)# spanning-tree link-type point-to-point
```

Rapid Per-VLAN Spanning Tree Protocol

Chapter 9, "Traditional Spanning Tree Protocol," described PVST+ as the default STP mode on Catalyst switches. In PVST+, one spanning tree instance is created and used for each active VLAN that is defined on the switch. Each STP instance behaves according to the traditional 802.1D STP rules.

You can improve the efficiency of each STP instance by configuring a switch to begin using RSTP instead. This means that each VLAN will have its own independent instance of RSTP running on the switch. This mode is known as *Rapid PVST+ (RPVST+)*.

You need only one configuration step to change the STP mode and begin using RPVST+. You can use the following global configuration command to accomplish this:

```
Switch(config)# spanning-tree mode rapid-pvst
```

Be careful when you use this command on a production network because any STP process that currently is running must be restarted. This can cause functioning links to move through the traditional STP states, preventing data from flowing for a short time.

> **TIP** To revert back to the default PVST+ mode, using traditional 802.1D STP, you can use the following command:
>
> ```
> Switch(config)# spanning-tree mode pvst
> ```

After you enable the RPVST+ mode, the switch must support both RSTP and 802.1D STP neighbors. The switch can detect the neighbor's STP type by the BPDU version that is received. You can see the neighbor type in the output of the **show spanning-tree vlan** *vlan-id* command, as demonstrated in Example 12-1.

Example 12-1 *Detecting a Neighboring Switch's STP Type*

```
Switch# show spanning-tree vlan 171
VLAN0171
  Spanning tree enabled protocol rstp
  Root ID    Priority    4267
             Address     00d0.0457.38aa
             Cost        3
             Port        833 (Port-channel1)
             Hello Time   2 sec  Max Age 20 sec  Forward Delay 15 sec

  Bridge ID  Priority    32939  (priority 32768 sys-id-ext 171)
             Address     0007.0d55.a800
             Hello Time   2 sec  Max Age 20 sec  Forward Delay 15 sec
             Aging Time 300


Interface        Role Sts Cost      Prio.Nbr Type
---------------- ---- --- --------- -------- --------------------------------
Gi7/8            Desg FWD 4         128.392  P2p
Gi9/6            Altn BLK 4         128.518  P2p Peer(STP)
Po1              Root FWD 3         128.833  P2p
Po2              Desg FWD 3         128.834  P2p
Po3              Desg FWD 3         128.835  P2p
Switch#
```

The output in Example 12-1 shows information about the RSTP instance for VLAN 171. The first shaded line confirms that the local switch indeed is running RSTP. (The only other way to confirm the STP mode is to locate the **spanning-tree mode** command in the running configuration.)

In addition, this output displays all of the active ports participating in the VLAN 171 instance of RSTP, along with their port types. The string **P2p** denotes a point-to-point RSTP port type in which a full-duplex link connects two neighboring switches that both are running RSTP. If you see **P2p Peer(STP)**, the port is a point-to-point type but the neighboring device is running traditional 802.1D STP.

Multiple Spanning Tree Protocol

Chapter 9 covered two "flavors" of spanning-tree implementations—IEEE 802.1Q and PVST+— both based on the 802.1D STP. These also represent the two extremes of STP operation in a network:

- **802.1Q**—Only a single instance of STP is used for all VLANs. If there are 500 VLANs, only one instance of STP will be running. This is called the Common Spanning Tree (CST) and operates over the trunk's native VLAN.

- **PVST+**—One instance of STP is used for each active VLAN in the network. If there are 500 VLANs, 500 independent instances of STP will be running.

In most networks, each switch has a redundant path to another switch. For example, an access-layer switch usually has two uplinks, each connecting to a different distribution- or core-layer switch. If 802.1Q's CST is used, only one STP instance will run. This means that there is only one loop-free topology at any given time and that only one of the two uplinks in the access-layer switch will be forwarding. The other uplink always will be blocking.

Obviously, arranging the network so that both uplinks can be used simultaneously would be best. One uplink should carry one set of VLANs, while the other carries a different set as a type of load balancing.

PVST+ seems more attractive to meet that goal because it allows different VLANs to have different topologies so that each uplink can be forwarding. But think of the consequences: As the number of VLANs increases, so does the number of independent STP instances. Each instance uses some amount of the switch CPU and memory resources. The more instances that are in use, the fewer CPU resources will be available for switching.

Beyond that, what is the real benefit of having 500 STP topologies for 500 VLANs, when only a small number of possible topologies exist for a switch with two uplinks? Figure 12-3 shows a typical network with an access-layer switch connecting to a pair of core switches. Two VLANs are in use, with the Root Bridges configured to support load balancing across the two uplinks. The right portion of the figure shows every possible topology for VLANs A and B. Notice that because the access-layer switch has only two uplinks, only two topologies actually matter—one in which the left uplink forwards, and one in which the right uplink forwards.

Figure 12-3 *Possible STP Topologies for Two VLANs*

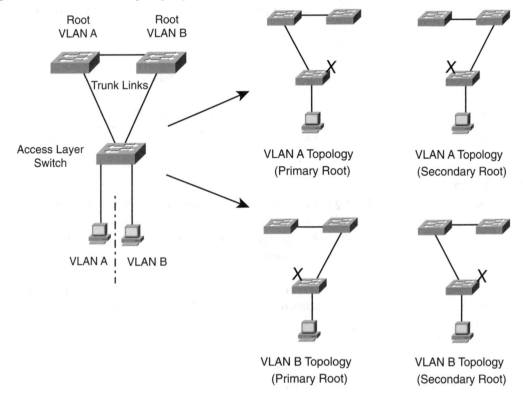

Notice also that the number of useful topologies is independent of the number of VLANs. If 10 or 100 VLANs were used in the figure, there would still be only two possible outcomes at the access-layer switch. Therefore, running 10 or 100 instances of STP when only a couple would suffice is rather wasteful.

The Multiple Spanning Tree Protocol (MST or MSTP) was developed to address the lack of and surplus of STP instances. As a result, the network administrator can configure exactly the number of STP instances that make sense for the enterprise network, no matter how many VLANs are in use. MST is defined in the IEEE 802.1s standard.

MST Overview

MST is built on the concept of mapping one or more VLANs to a single STP instance. Multiple instances of STP can be used (hence the name MST), with each instance supporting a different group of VLANs.

For the network shown in Figure 12-3, only two MST instances would be needed. Each could be tuned to result in a different topology so that Instance 1 would forward on the left uplink, while Instance 2 would forward on the right uplink. Therefore, VLAN A would be mapped to Instance 1, and VLAN B would be mapped to Instance 2.

To implement MST in a network, you need to determine the following:

- The number of STP instances needed to support the desired topologies

- Whether to map a set of VLANs to each instance

MST Regions

MST is different than 802.1Q and PVST+, although it can interoperate with them. If a switch is configured to use MST, it somehow must figure out which of its neighbors are using which type of STP. This is done by configuring switches into common MST regions, where every switch in a region runs MST with compatible parameters.

In most networks, a single MST region is sufficient, although you can configure more than one region. Within the region, all switches must run the instance of MST that is defined by the following attributes:

- MST configuration name (32 characters)

- MST configuration revision number (0 to 65535)

- MST instance-to-VLAN mapping table (4096 entries)

If two switches have the same set of attributes, they belong to the same MST region. If not, they belong to two independent regions.

MST BPDUs contain configuration attributes so that switches receiving BPDUs can compare them against their local MST configurations. If the attributes match, the STP instances within MST can be shared as part of the same region. If not, a switch is seen to be at the MST region boundary, where one region meets another or one region meets traditional 802.1D STP.

NOTE   The entire MST instance-to-VLAN mapping table is not sent in the BPDUs because the instance mappings must be configured on each switch. Instead, a digest, or a hash code computed from the table contents, is sent. As the contents of the table change, the digest value will be different. Therefore, a switch quickly can compare a received digest to its own to see if the advertised table is the same.

Spanning Tree Instances Within MST

MST was designed to interoperate with all other forms of STP. Therefore, it also must support STP instances from each. This is where MST can get confusing. Think of the entire enterprise network as having a single CST topology so that one instance of STP represents any and all VLANs and MST regions present. The CST maintains a common loop-free topology while integrating all forms of STP that might be in use.

To do this, CST must regard each MST region as a single "black box" bridge because it has no idea what is inside the region, nor does it care. CST maintains a loop-free topology only with the links that connect the regions to each other and to standalone switches running 802.1Q CST.

IST Instances

Something other than CST must work out a loop-free topology inside each MST region. Within a single MST region, an Internal Spanning Tree (IST) instance runs to work out a loop-free topology between the links where CST meets the region boundary and all switches inside the region. Think of the IST instance as a locally significant CST, bounded by the edges of the region.

The IST presents the entire region as a single virtual bridge to the CST outside. BPDUs are exchanged at the region boundary only over the native VLAN of trunks, as if a single CST were in operation. And, indeed, it is.

Figure 12-4 shows the basic concept behind the IST instance. The network at the left has an MST region, where several switches are running compatible MST configurations. Another switch is outside the region because it is running only the CST from 802.1Q.

The same network is shown at the right, where the IST has produced a loop-free topology for the network inside the region. The IST makes the internal network look like a single bridge (the "big switch" in the cloud) that can interface with the CST running outside the region.

Figure 12-4 *Concepts Behind the IST Instance*

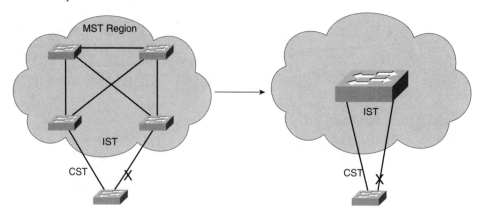

MST Instances

Recall that the whole idea behind MST is the capability to map multiple VLANs to a smaller number of STP instances. Inside a region, the actual MST instances (MSTIs) exist alongside the IST. Cisco supports a maximum of 16 MSTIs in each region. IST always exists as MSTI number 0, leaving MSTIs 1 through 15 available for use.

Figure 12-5 shows how different MSTIs can exist within a single MST region. The left portion of the figure is identical to that of Figure 12-4. In this network, two MST instances, MSTI 1 and MSTI 2, are configured with different VLANs mapped to each. Their topologies follow the same structure as the network on the left side of the figure, but each has converged differently.

Figure 12-5 *Concepts Behind MST Instances*

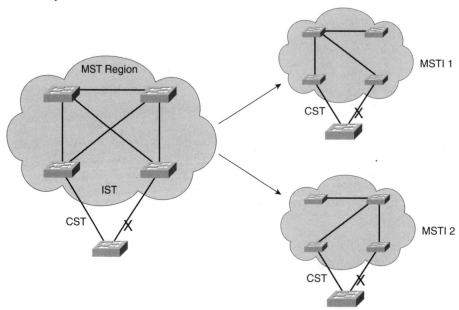

Notice that within the MST cloud, there are now three independent STP instances coexisting—MSTI1, MSTI 2, and the IST.

Only the IST (MSTI 0) is allowed to send and receive MST BPDUs. Information about each of the other MSTIs is appended to the MST BPDU as an M-record. Therefore, even if a region has all 16 instances active, only one BPDU is needed to convey STP information about them all.

Each of the MSTIs is significant only within a region, even if an adjacent region has the same MSTIs in use. In other words, the MSTIs combine with the IST only at the region boundary to form a subtree of the CST. That means only IST BPDUs are sent into and out of a region.

What if an MST region connects with a switch running traditional PVST+? MST can detect this situation by listening to the received BPDUs. If BPDUs are heard from more than one VLAN (the CST), PVST+ must be in use. When the MST region sends a BPDU toward the PVST+ switch, the IST BPDUs are replicated into all of the VLANs on the PVST+ switch trunk.

> **NOTE**   Keep in mind that the IST instance is active on *every* port on a switch. Even if a port does not carry VLANs that have been mapped to the IST, IST must be running on the port. Also, by default, all VLANs are mapped to the IST instance. You must explicitly map them to other instances, if needed.

MST Configuration

You must manually configure the MST configuration attributes on each switch in a region. There is currently no method to propagate this information from one switch to another, as is done with a protocol such as VLAN Trunking Protocol (VTP). To define the MST region, use the following configuration commands in the order shown:

Step 1   Enable MST on the switch:

```
Switch(config)# spanning-tree mode mst
```

Step 2   Enter the MST configuration mode:

```
Switch(config)# spanning-tree mst configuration
```

Step 3   Assign a region configuration name (up to 32 characters):

```
Switch(config-mst)# name name
```

Step 4   Assign a region configuration revision number (0 to 65,535):

```
Switch(config-mst)# revision version
```

The configuration revision number gives you a means of tracking changes to the MST region configuration. Each time you make changes to the configuration, you should increase the number by one. Remember that the region configuration (including the revision number) must match on all switches in the region. Therefore, you also need to update the revision numbers on the other switches to match.

Step 5   Map VLANs to an MST instance:

```
Switch(config-mst)# instance instance-id vlan vlan-list
```

The *instance-id* (0 to 15) carries topology information for the VLANs listed in *vlan-list*. The list can contain one or more VLANs separated by commas. You also can add a range of VLANs to the list by separating numbers with a hyphen. VLAN numbers can range from 1 to 4094. (Remember that, by default, all VLANs are mapped to instance 0, the IST.)

Step 6   Show the pending changes you have made:

```
Switch(config-mst)# show pending
```

Step 7   Exit the MST configuration mode; commit the changes to the active MST region configuration:

```
Switch(config-mst)# exit
```

After MST is enabled and configured, PVST+ operation stops and the switch changes to RSTP operation. A switch cannot run both MST and PVST+ at the same time.

You also can tune the parameters that MST uses when it interacts with CST or traditional 802.1D. The parameters and timers are identical to those discussed in Chapter 10, "Spanning Tree Configuration." In fact, the commands are very similar except for the addition of the **mst** keyword and the *instance-id*. Instead of tuning STP for a VLAN instance, you use an MST instance.

Table 12-2 summarizes the commands as a quick reference. Notice that the timer configurations are applied to MST as a whole, not to a specific MST instance. This is because all instance timers are defined through the IST instance and BPDUs.

Table 12-2 *MST Configuration Commands*

Task	Command Syntax
Set Root Bridge (macro)	Switch(config)# **spanning-tree mst** *instance-id* **root** {**primary** | **secondary**} [**diameter** *diameter*]
Set bridge priority	Switch(config)# **spanning-tree mst** *instance-id* **priority** *bridge-priority*
Set port cost	Switch(config)# **spanning-tree mst** *instance-id* **cost** *cost*
Set port priority	Switch(config)# **spanning-tree mst** *instance-id* **port-priority** *port-priority*
Set STP timers	Switch(config)# **spanning-tree mst hello-time** *seconds* Switch(config)# **spanning-tree mst forward-time** *seconds* Switch(config)# **spanning-tree mst max-age** *seconds*

Foundation Summary

The Foundation Summary is a collection of information that provides a convenient review of many key concepts in this chapter. If you are already comfortable with the topics in this chapter, this summary can help you recall a few details. If you just read this chapter, this review should help solidify some key facts. If you are doing your final preparation before the exam, this information is a convenient way to review the day before the exam.

RSTP port roles:

- Root port

- Designated port

- Alternate port

- Backup port

RSTP port states:

- Discarding

- Learning

- Forwarding

Table 12-3   *RSTP Configuration Commands*

Task	Command Syntax
Define an edge port	Switch(config-if)# **spanning-tree portfast**
Override a port type	Switch(config-if)# **spanning-tree link-type point-to-point**

STP instances involved with MST:

- **Common Spanning Tree (CST)**—Used to maintain a single loop-free topology for the entire network

- **Internal Spanning Tree (IST)**—Used like CST, to maintain a single, loop-free topology *inside* an MST region

- **MST instances (MSTIs)**—Used inside an MST region to maintain loop-free topologies for sets of mapped VLANs

Table 12-4 *MST Region Configuration Commands*

Task	Command Syntax
Enable MST on a switch	Switch(config)# **spanning-tree mode mst**
Enter MST configuration mode	Switch(config)# **spanning-tree mst configuration**
Name the MST region	Switch(config-mst)# **name** *name*
Set the configuration revision number	Switch(config-mst)# **revision** *version*
Map VLANs to an MST instance	Switch(config-mst)# **instance** *instance-id* **vlan** *vlan-list*
Confirm new MST configuration changes	Switch(config-mst)# **show pending**
Commit new MST changes	Switch(config-mst)# **exit**

Table 12-5 *MST Tuning Configuration Commands*

Task	Command Syntax
Set the Root Bridge	Switch(config)# **spanning-tree mst** *instance-id* **root {primary	secondary}** [**diameter** *diameter*]
Set bridge priority	Switch(config)# **spanning-tree mst** *instance-id* **priority** *bridge-priority*
Set port cost	Switch(config)# **spanning-tree mst** *instance-id* **cost** *cost*
Set port priority	Switch(config)# **spanning-tree mst** *instance-id* **port-priority** *port-priority*
Set STP timers	Switch(config)# **spanning-tree mst hello-time** *seconds*
	Switch(config)# **spanning-tree mst forward-time** *seconds*
	Switch(config)# **spanning-tree mst max-age** *seconds*

Q&A

The questions and scenarios in this book are more difficult than what you should experience on the actual exam. The questions do not attempt to cover more breadth or depth than the exam; however, they are designed to make sure that you know the answers. Rather than allowing you to derive the answers from clues hidden inside the questions themselves, the questions challenge your understanding and recall of the subject. Hopefully, these questions will help limit the number of exam questions on which you narrow your choices to two options and then guess.

You can find the answers to these questions in Appendix A.

1.   What is synchronization in RSTP?

2.   What is an alternate port?

3.   What is the difference between an alternate port and a backup port?

4.   Can a switch port be a designated port and be in the Discarding state?

5.   Which port type *cannot* participate in RSTP synchronization?

6.   What two messages must be exchanged during RSTP synchronization?

7.   After an agreement message is received from a neighboring switch, how much time elapses before the port can begin forwarding? (Consider any timers that must expire or other conditions that must be met.)

8.   After a switch receives news of a topology change, how long does it wait to flush entries from its CAM table?

9.   What command configures a port as an RSTP edge port?

10. Suppose interface FastEthernet 0/1 is in half-duplex mode, but you want it to be considered a point-to-point link for RSTP. What command can accomplish this?

11. Put the following in order of the number of supported STP instances, from lowest to highest:

   a. MST

   b. PVST+

   c. CST

   d. 802.1D

12. What three parameters must be configured to uniquely define an MST region?

13. What parameter does a switch examine to see if its neighbors have the same VLAN-to-MST instance mappings? How is that information passed among switches?

14. Which MST instance in a region corresponds to the CST of 802.1Q?

15. Which MST instance is the IST?

16. When an MST region meets a PVST+ domain, how is each MST instance propagated into PVST+?

17. Is it wise to assign VLANs to MST instance 0? Why or why not?

18. The commands have just been entered to define an MST region on a switch. You are still at the MST configuration prompt. What command must you enter to commit the MST changes on the switch?

19. How can MST configuration information be propagated to other Cisco switches?

20. A switch can interact with both 802.1D and RSTP. Can it run both PVST+ and MST simultaneously?

Layer 3 Switching

This part of the book covers the following BCMSN exam topics:

Technology

- Identify the specific types of Cisco route switch processors, and provide implementation details

- List and describe the operation of the key components required to implement interVLAN routing

- Explain the types of redundancy in a multilayer switched network, including hardware and software redundancy

- Explain how IP multicast operates on a multilayer switched network, including PIM, CGMP, and IGMP

Implementation and Operation

- Configure and verify router redundancy using HSRP, VRRP, GLBP and SRM

Planning and Design

- Select multilayer switching architectures, given specific multilayer switching needs

Troubleshooting

- Identify interVLAN routing performance and scalability issues, and propose solutions

- Verify and troubleshoot interVLAN routing on a switched network

This chapter covers the following topics that you need to master for the CCNP BCMSN exam:

- **InterVLAN Routing**—This section discusses how you can use a routing function with a switch to forward packets between VLANs.

- **Multilayer Switching with CEF**—This section discusses Cisco Express Forwarding (CEF) and how it is implemented on Catalyst switches. CEF forwards or routes packets in hardware at a high throughput.

- **Troubleshooting Multilayer Switching**—This section provides a brief summary of the commands that can verify the configuration and operation of InterVLAN routing, CEF, and fallback bridging.

CHAPTER 13

Multilayer Switching

Chapter 3, "Switch Operation," presents a functional overview of how multilayer switching (MLS) is performed at Layers 3 and 4. The actual MLS process can take two forms— InterVLAN routing and Cisco Express Forwarding (CEF). This chapter expands on multilayer switch operation by discussing both of these topics in greater detail.

"Do I Know This Already?" Quiz

The purpose of the "Do I Know This Already?" quiz is to help you decide what parts of this chapter to use. If you already intend to read the entire chapter, you do not necessarily need to answer these questions now.

The quiz, derived from the major sections in the "Foundation Topics" portion of the chapter, helps you determine how to spend your limited study time.

Table 13-1 outlines the major topics discussed in this chapter and the "Do I Know This Already?" quiz questions that correspond to those topics.

Table 13-1   *"Do I Know This Already?" Foundation Topics Section-to-Question Mapping*

Foundation Topics Section	Questions Covered in This Section	Score
InterVLAN Routing	1–5	
Multilayer Switching with CEF	6–11	
Troubleshooting Multilayer Switching	12	
Total Score		

CAUTION   The goal of self-assessment is to gauge your mastery of the topics in this chapter. If you do not know the answer to a question or are only partially sure of the answer, you should mark this question wrong. Giving yourself credit for an answer you correctly guess skews your self-assessment results and might give you a false sense of security.

1. Which of the following arrangements can be considered InterVLAN routing?

    a. One switch, two VLANs, one connection to a router

    b. One switch, two VLANs, two connections to a router

    c. Two switches, two VLANs, two connections to a router

    d. All of the above

2. How many interfaces are needed in a "router on a stick" implementation for InterVLAN routing among four VLANs?

    a. 1

    b. 2

    c. 4

    d. Cannot be determined

3. Which of the following commands configures a switch port for Layer 2 operation?

    a. **switchport**

    b. **no switchport**

    c. **ip address 192.168.199.1 255.255.255.0**

    d. **no ip address**

4. Which of the following commands configures a switch port for Layer 3 operation?

    a. **switchport**

    b. **no switchport**

    c. **ip address 192.168.199.1 255.255.255.0**

    d. **no ip address**

5. Which one of the following interfaces is an SVI?

    a. **interface fastethernet 0/1**

    b. **interface gigabit 0/1**

    c. **interface vlan 1**

    d. **interface svi 1**

6. What information must be learned before CEF can forward packets?

    a. The source and destination of the first packet in a traffic flow

    b. The MAC addresses of both the source and destination

    c. The contents of the routing table

    d. The outbound port of the first packet in a flow

7. Which of the following best defines an adjacency?

   a. Two switches connected by a common link

   b. Two contiguous routes in the FIB

   c. Two multilayer switches connected by a common link

   d. The MAC address of a host is known

8. Assume that CEF is active on a switch. What happens to a packet that arrives needing fragmentation?

   a. The packet is switched by CEF and kept intact.

   b. The packet is fragmented by CEF.

   c. The packet is dropped.

   d. The packet is sent to the Layer 3 engine.

9. Suppose that a host sends a packet to a destination IP address and that the CEF-based switch does not yet have a valid MAC address for the destination. How is the ARP entry (MAC address) of the next-hop destination in the FIB obtained?

   a. The sending host must send an ARP request for it.

   b. The Layer 3 forwarding engine (CEF hardware) must send an ARP request for it.

   c. CEF must wait until the Layer 3 engine sends an ARP request for it.

   d. All packets to the destination are dropped.

10. During a packet rewrite, what happens to the source MAC address?

   a. There is no change.

   b. It is changed to the destination MAC address.

   c. It is changed to the MAC address of the outbound Layer 3 switch interface.

   d. It is changed to the MAC address of the next-hop destination.

11. What Spanning Tree Protocol is used for fallback bridging?

   a. 802.1D

   b. IBM STP

   c. PVST+

   d. VLAN-bridge

12. What command can you use to view the CEF FIB table contents?

   a. **show fib**

   b. **show ip cef fib**

   c. **show ip cef**

   d. **show fib-table**

You can find the answers to the "Do I Know This Already?" quiz in Appendix A, "Answers to Chapter 'Do I Know This Already?' Quizzes and Q&A Sections." The suggested choices for your next step are as follows:

- **10 or less overall score**—Read the entire chapter. This includes the "Foundation Topics," "Foundation Summary," and "Q&A" sections.

- **11 or 12 overall score**—If you want more review on these topics, skip to the "Foundation Summary" section and then go to the "Q&A" section at the end of the chapter. Otherwise, move to Chapter 14, "Router Redundancy and Load Balancing."

Foundation Topics

InterVLAN Routing

Recall that a Layer 2 network is defined as a broadcast domain. A Layer 2 network also can exist as a VLAN inside one or more switches. VLANs essentially are isolated from each other so that packets in one VLAN cannot cross into another VLAN.

To transport packets between VLANs, you must use a Layer 3 device. Traditionally, this has been a router's function. The router must have a physical or logical connection to each VLAN so that it can forward packets between them. This is known as *interVLAN routing*.

InterVLAN routing can be performed by an external router that connects to each of the VLANs on a switch. Separate physical connections can be used, or the router can access each of the VLANs through a single trunk link. Part A of Figure 13-1 illustrates this concept. The external router also can connect to the switch through a single trunk link, carrying all the necessary VLANs, as illustrated in Part B of Figure 13-1. Part B illustrates what commonly is referred to as a "router on a stick" or a "one-armed router" because the router needs only a single interface to do its job.

Finally, Part C of Figure 13-1 shows how the routing and switching functions can be combined into one device: a multilayer switch. No external router is needed.

Figure 13-1   *Examples of InterVLAN Routing Connections*

Types of Interfaces

Multilayer switches can perform both Layer 2 switching and interVLAN routing, as appropriate. Layer 2 switching occurs between interfaces that are assigned to Layer 2 VLANs or Layer 2 trunks. Layer 3 switching can occur between any type of interface, as long as the interface can have a Layer 3 address assigned to it.

As with a router, a multilayer switch can assign a Layer 3 address to a physical interface. It also can assign a Layer 3 address to a logical interface that represents an entire VLAN. This is known as a *switched virtual interface (SVI)*.

Configuring InterVLAN Routing

InterVLAN routing first requires that routing be enabled for the Layer 3 protocol. In addition, you must configure static routes or a dynamic routing protocol. These topics are covered fully in the BSCI course.

Because a multilayer switch supports many different types of interfaces for Layer 2 or Layer 3 switching, you must define each interface on a switch that will be used. By default, every switch port on platforms such as the Catalyst 2950, 3560, or 4500 is a Layer 2 interface, whereas every switch port on a Catalyst 6500 (native IOS) is a Layer 3 interface. If another type or mode is needed, you must explicitly configure it.

A port is either in Layer 2 or Layer 3 mode, depending on the use of the **switchport** configuration command. You can display a port's current mode with the following command:

```
Switch# show interface type mod/num switchport
```

If the **Switchport:** line is shown as enabled, the port is in Layer 2 mode. If this line is shown as disabled, as in the following example, the port is in Layer 3 mode:

```
Switch# show interface gigabitethernet 0/1 switchport
Name: Gi0/1
Switchport: Disabled
Switch#
```

Figure 13-2 shows how the different types of interface modes can be used within a single switch.

Layer 2 Port Configuration

By default, all switch ports on Catalyst 2950, 3560, and 4500 platforms operate in Layer 2 mode. If you need to reconfigure a port for Layer 2 functionality, use the following command sequence:

```
Switch(config)# interface type mod/num
Switch(config-if)# switchport
```

Figure 13-2 *Catalyst Switch with Various Types of Ports*

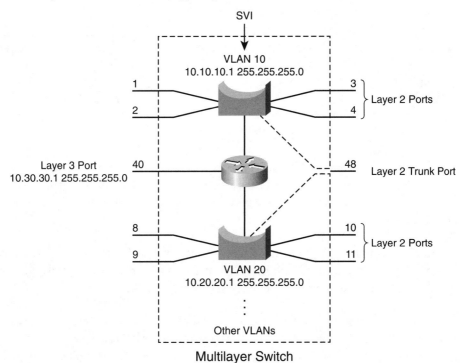

The **switchport** command puts the port in Layer 2 mode. Then you can use other **switchport** command keywords to configure trunking, access VLANs, and so on. Figure 13-2 shows several Layer 2 ports, each assigned to a specific VLAN. A Layer 2 port also can act as a trunk, transporting multiple VLANs.

Layer 3 Port Configuration

Physical switch ports also can operate as Layer 3 interfaces, where a Layer 3 network address is assigned and routing can occur. Figure 13-2 shows an example of this. By default, all switch ports on the Catalyst 6500 (native IOS) platform operate in the Layer 3 mode. For Layer 3 functionality, you must explicitly configure switch ports with the following command sequence:

```
Switch(config)# interface type mod/num
Switch(config-if)# no switchport
Switch(config-if)# ip address ip-address mask [secondary]
```

The **no switchport** command takes the port out of Layer 2 operation. You then can assign a network address to the port, as you would to a router interface.

> **NOTE** Keep in mind that a Layer 3 port assigns a network address to one specific physical interface. If using EtherChannel, it, too, can become a Layer 3 port. In that case, the network address is assigned to the **port-channel** interface, not to the individual physical links within the channel.

SVI Port Configuration

On a multilayer switch, you also can enable Layer 3 functionality for an entire VLAN on the switch. This allows a network address to be assigned to a logical interface: that of the VLAN itself. This is useful when the switch has many ports assigned to a common VLAN, and routing is needed in and out of that VLAN.

Figure 13-2 shows how an IP address is applied to the switched virtual interface (SVI) called VLAN 10. Notice that the SVI itself has no physical connection to the outside world; to reach the outside, VLAN 10 must extend through a Layer 2 port or trunk.

The logical Layer 3 interface is known as an *SVI*. However, when it is configured, it uses the much more intuitive interface name **vlan** *vlan-id*, as if the VLAN itself is a physical interface. First, define or identify the VLAN interface; then assign any Layer 3 functionality to it with the following configuration commands:

```
Switch(config)# interface vlan vlan-id
Switch(config-if)# ip address ip-address mask [secondary]
```

The VLAN must be defined and active on the switch before the SVI can be used. Make sure the new VLAN interface also is enabled with the **no shutdown** interface-configuration command.

> **NOTE** The VLAN and the SVI are configured separately, even though they interoperate. Creating or configuring the SVI doesn't create or configure the VLAN; you still must define each one independently.
>
> As an example, the following commands show how VLAN 100 is created and then defined as a Layer 3 SVI:
>
> ```
> Switch(config)# vlan 100
> Switch(config-vlan)# name Example_VLAN
> Switch(config-vlan)# exit
> Switch(config)# interface vlan 100
> Switch(config-if)# ip address 192.168.100.1 255.255.255.0
> Switch(config-if)# no shutdown
> ```

Multilayer Switching with CEF

Catalyst switches can use several methods to forward packets based on Layer 3 and Layer 4 information. The current generation of Catalyst multilayer switches uses the efficient Cisco Express Forwarding (CEF) method. This section describes the evolution of multilayer switching and discusses CEF in detail. Although CEF is easy to configure and use, the underlying switching mechanisms are more involved and should be understood.

Traditional MLS Overview

Multilayer switching began as a dual effort between a route processor (RP) and a switching engine (SE). The basic idea is to "route once and switch many." The RP receives the first packet of a new traffic flow between two hosts, as usual. A routing decision is made, and the packet is forwarded toward the destination.

To participate in multilayer switching, the SE must know the identity of each RP. The SE then can listen in to the first packet going to the router and also going away from the router. If the SE can switch the packet in both directions, it can learn a "shortcut path" so that subsequent packets of the same flow can be switched directly to the destination port without passing through the RP.

This technique also is known as *NetFlow switching* or *route cache switching*. Traditionally, NetFlow switching was performed on Cisco hardware, such as the Catalyst 6000 Supervisor 1/1a and Multilayer Switch Feature Card (MSFC), Catalyst 5500 with a Route Switch Module (RSM), Route Switch Feature Card (RSFC), or external router. Basically, the hardware consisted of an independent RP component and a NetFlow-capable SE component.

CEF Overview

NetFlow switching has given way to a more efficient form of multilayer switching: Cisco Express Forwarding (CEF). Cisco developed CEF for its line of routers, offering high-performance packet forwarding through the use of dynamic lookup tables.

CEF also has been carried over to the Catalyst switching platforms. The following platforms all perform CEF in hardware:

- Catalyst 6500 Supervisor 720 (with an integrated MSFC3)

- Catalyst 6500 Supervisor 2/MSFC2 combination

- Catalyst 4500 Supervisor III, IV, and V

- Fixed-configuration switches, such as the Catalyst 3750, 3560, 3550, and 2950

CEF runs by default, taking advantage of the specialized hardware.

A CEF-based multilayer switch consists of two basic functional blocks, as shown in Figure 13-3: The *Layer 3 Engine* is involved in building routing information that the *Layer 3 Forwarding Engine* can use to switch packets in hardware.

Figure 13-3   *Packet Flow Through a CEF-Based Multilayer Switch*

Forwarding Information Base

The Layer 3 engine (essentially a router) maintains routing information, whether from static routes or dynamic routing protocols. Basically, the routing table is reformatted into an ordered list with the most specific route first, for each IP destination subnet in the table. The new format is called a Forwarding Information Base (FIB) and contains routing or forwarding information that the network prefix can reference.

In other words, a route to 10.1.0.0/16 might be contained in the FIB along with routes to 10.1.1.0/24 and 10.1.1.128/25, if those exist. Notice that these examples are increasingly more specific subnets, as designated by the longer subnet masks. In the FIB, these would be ordered with the most specific, or *longest match,* first, followed by less specific subnets. When the switch receives a packet, it easily can examine the destination address and find the longest-match destination route entry in the FIB.

The FIB also contains the next-hop address for each entry. When a longest-match entry is found in the FIB, the Layer 3 next-hop address is found, too.

You might be surprised to know that the FIB also contains host route (subnet mask 255.255.255.255) entries. These normally are not found in the routing table unless they are advertised or manually configured. Host routes are maintained in the FIB for the most efficient routing lookup to directly connected or *adjacent* hosts.

As with a routing table, the FIB is dynamic in nature. When the Layer 3 engine sees a change in the routing topology, it sends an update to the FIB. Any time the routing table receives a change to a route prefix or the next-hop address, the FIB receives the same change. Also, if a next-hop address is changed or aged out of the Address Resolution Protocol (ARP) table, the FIB must reflect the same change.

You can display FIB table entries related to a specific interface or VLAN with the following form of the **show ip cef** command:

```
Switch# show ip cef [type mod/num | vlan vlan-id] [detail]
```

The FIB entries corresponding to the VLAN 101 switched virtual interface might be shown as demonstrated in Example 13-1.

Example 13-1 *Displaying FIB Table Entries for a Specified VLAN*

```
Switch# show ip cef vlan 101
Prefix              Next Hop           Interface
10.1.1.0/24         attached           Vlan101
10.1.1.2/32         10.1.1.2           Vlan101
10.1.1.3/32         10.1.1.3           Vlan101
Switch#
```

You also can view FIB entries by specifying an IP prefix address and mask, using the following form of the **show ip cef** command:

```
Switch# show ip cef [prefix-ip prefix-mask] [longer-prefixes] [detail]
```

The output in Example 13-2 displays any subnet within 10.1.0.0/16 that is known by the switch, regardless of the prefix or mask length. Normally, only an exact match of the IP prefix and mask will be displayed if it exists in the CEF table. To see other longer match entries, you can add the **longer-prefixes** keyword.

Example 13-2 *Displaying FIB Table Entries for a Specified IP Prefix Address/Mask*

```
Switch# show ip cef 10.1.0.0 255.255.0.0 longer-prefixes
Prefix              Next Hop           Interface
10.1.1.0/24         attached           Vlan101
10.1.1.2/32         10.1.1.2           Vlan101
10.1.1.3/32         10.1.1.3           Vlan101
10.1.2.0/24         attached           Vlan102
10.1.3.0/26         192.168.1.2        Vlan99
```

Example 13-2 *Displaying FIB Table Entries for a Specified IP Prefix Address/Mask (Continued)*

```
                     192.168.1.3        Vlan99
10.1.3.64/26         192.168.1.2        Vlan99
                     192.168.1.3        Vlan99
10.1.3.128/26        192.168.1.4        Vlan99
                     192.168.1.3        Vlan99
[output omitted]
Switch#
```

Notice that the first three entries are the same ones listed in Example 13-1. Other subnets also are displayed, along with their next-hop router addresses and switch interfaces.

You can add the **detail** keyword to see more information about each FIB table entry for CEF, as demonstrated in Example 13-3.

Example 13-3 *Displaying Detailed CEF Entry Information*

```
Switch# show ip cef 10.1.3.0 255.255.255.192 detail
10.1.3.0/26, version 270, epoch 0, per-destination sharing
0 packets, 0 bytes
  via 192.168.1.2, Vlan99, 0 dependencies
    traffic share 1
    next hop 192.168.1.2, Vlan99
    valid adjacency
  via 192.168.1.3, Vlan99, 0 dependencies
    traffic share 1
    next hop 192.168.1.3, Vlan99
    valid adjacency
  0 packets, 0 bytes switched through the prefix
  tmstats: external 0 packets, 0 bytes
           internal 0 packets, 0 bytes
Switch#
```

The version number describes the number of times the CEF entry has been updated since the table was generated. The epoch number denotes the number of times the CEF table has been flushed and regenerated as a whole. The 10.1.3.0/26 subnet has two next-hop router addresses, so the local switch is using per-destination load sharing between the two routers.

After the FIB is built, packets can be forwarded along the bottom dashed path in Figure 13-3. This follows the hardware switching process, in which no "expensive" or time-consuming operations are needed. At times, however, a packet cannot be switched in hardware, according to the FIB. Packets then are marked as "CEF punt" and immediately are sent to the Layer 3 engine for further processing, as shown in the top dashed path in Figure 13-3. Here are some of the conditions that cause this:

■ An entry cannot be located in the FIB.

■ The FIB table is full.

- The IP Time To Live (TTL) has expired.

- The maximum transmission unit (MTU) is exceeded, and the packet must be fragmented.

- An Internet Control Message Protocol (ICMP) redirect is involved.

- The encapsulation type is not supported.

- Packets are tunneled, requiring a compression or encryption operation.

- An access list with the **log** option is triggered.

- A Network Address Translation (NAT) operation must be performed (except on the Catalyst 6500 Supervisor 720, which can handle NAT in hardware).

CEF operations can be handled on a single hardware platform, such as the Catalyst 3560 switch. The FIB is generated and contained centrally in the switch. CEF also can be optimized through the use of specialized forwarding hardware, using the following techniques:

- **Accelerated CEF (aCEF)**—CEF is distributed across multiple Layer 3 forwarding engines, typically located on Catalyst 6500 line cards. These engines do not have the capability to store and use the entire FIB, so only a portion of the FIB is downloaded to them at any time. This functions as an FIB "cache," containing entries that are likely to be used again. If FIB entries are not found in the cache, requests are sent to the Layer 3 engine for more FIB information. The net result is that CEF is accelerated on the line cards, but not necessarily at a sustained wire-speed rate.

- **Distributed CEF (dCEF)**—CEF can be distributed completely among multiple Layer 3 forwarding engines for even greater performance. Because the FIB is self-contained for complete Layer 3 forwarding, it can be replicated across any number of independent Layer 3 forwarding engines. The Catalyst 6500 has line cards that support dCEF, each with its own FIB table and forwarding engine. A central Layer 3 engine (the MSFC3, for example) maintains the routing table and generates the FIB, which then dynamically is downloaded in full to each of the line cards.

Adjacency Table

A router normally maintains a routing table containing Layer 3 network and next-hop information, and an ARP table containing Layer 3 to Layer 2 address mapping. These tables are kept independently.

Recall that the FIB keeps the Layer 3 next-hop address for each entry. To streamline packet forwarding even more, the FIB has corresponding Layer 2 information for every next-hop entry. This portion of the FIB is called the *adjacency table*, consisting of the MAC addresses of nodes that can be reached in a single Layer 2 hop.

You can display the adjacency table's contents with the following command:

```
Switch# show adjacency [type mod/num | vlan vlan-id] [summary | detail]
```

As an example, the total number of adjacencies known on each physical or VLAN interface can be displayed with the **show adjacency summary** command, as demonstrated in Example 13-4.

Example 13-4   *Displaying the Total Number of Known Adjacencies*

```
Switch# show adjacency summary
Adjacency Table has 106 adjacencies
  Table epoch: 0 (106 entries at this epoch)
  Interface               Adjacency Count
  Vlan99                  21
  Vlan101                 3
  Vlan102                 1
  Vlan103                 47
  Vlan104                 7
  Vlan105                 27
Switch#
```

Adjacencies are kept for each next-hop router and each host that is connected directly to the local switch. You can see more detailed information about the adjacencies by using the **detail** keyword, as demonstrated in Example 13-5.

Example 13-5   *Displaying Detailed Information About Adjacencies*

```
Switch# show adjacency vlan 99 detail
Protocol Interface            Address
IP      Vlan99               192.168.1.2(5)
                             0 packets, 0 bytes
                             000A5E45B145000E387D51000800
                             ARP        01:52:50
                             Epoch: 0
IP      Vlan99               192.168.1.3(5)
                             1 packets, 104 bytes
                             000CF1C909A0000E387D51000800
                             ARP        04:02:11
                             Epoch: 0
```

Notice that the adjacency entries include both the IP address (Layer 3) and the MAC address (Layer 2) of the directly attached host. The MAC address could be shown as the first six octets of the long string of hex digits (as shaded in the previous output) or on a line by itself. The remainder of the string of hex digits contains the MAC address of the Layer 3 engine's interface (six octets, corresponding to the Vlan99 interface in the example) and the EtherType value (two octets, where 0800 denotes IP).

The adjacency table information is built from the ARP table. Example 13-5 shows adjacency with the age of its ARP entry. As a next-hop address receives a valid ARP entry, the adjacency table is updated. If an ARP entry does not exist, the FIB entry is marked as "CEF glean." This means that the Layer 3 forwarding engine can't forward the packet in hardware because of the missing Layer 2 next-hop address. The packet is sent to the Layer 3 engine so that it can generate an ARP request and receive an ARP reply. This is known as the "CEF glean" state, in which the Layer 3 engine must glean the next-hop destination's MAC address.

The glean state can be demonstrated in several ways, as demonstrated in Example 13-6.

Example 13-6 *Displaying Adjacencies in the CEF Glean State*

```
Switch# show ip cef adjacency glean
Prefix              Next Hop             Interface
10.1.1.2/32         attached             Vlan101
127.0.0.0/8         attached             EOBC0/0
[output omitted]
Switch# show ip arp 10.1.1.2

Switch# show ip cef 10.1.1.2 255.255.255.255 detail
10.1.1.2/32, version 688, epoch 0, attached, connected
0 packets, 0 bytes
  via Vlan101, 0 dependencies
    valid glean adjacency
Switch#
```

Notice that the FIB entry for directly connected host 10.1.1.2/32 is present but listed in the glean state. The **show ip arp** command shows that there is no valid ARP entry for the IP address.

During the time that an FIB entry is in the CEF glean state waiting for the ARP resolution, subsequent packets to that host immediately are dropped so that the input queues do not fill and the Layer 3 engine does not become too busy worrying about the need for duplicate ARP requests. This is called *ARP throttling* or *throttling adjacency*. If an ARP reply is not received in 2 seconds, the throttling is released so that another ARP request can be triggered. Otherwise, after an ARP reply is received, the throttling is released, the FIB entry can be completed, and packets can be forwarded completely in hardware.

The adjacency table also can contain other types of entries so that packets can be handled efficiently. For example, you might see the following adjacency types listed:

■ **Null adjacency**—Used to switch packets destined for the null interface. The null interface always is defined on a router or switch; it represents a logical interface that silently absorbs packets without actually forwarding them.

■ **Drop adjacency**—Used to switch packets that can't be forwarded normally. In effect, these packets are dropped without being forwarded. Packets can be dropped because of an encapsulation failure, an unresolved address, an unsupported protocol, no valid route present, no valid adjacency, or a checksum error. You can gauge drop adjacency activity with the following command:

```
Switch# show cef drop
CEF Drop Statistics
Slot  Encap_fail  Unresolved Unsupported   No_route    No_adj  ChkSum_Err
RP     8799327          1        45827      5089667        32           0
Switch#
```

■ **Discard adjacency**—Used when packets must be discarded because of an access list or other policy action.

■ **Punt adjacency**—Used when packets must be sent to the Layer 3 engine for further processing. You can gauge the CEF punt activity by looking at the various punt adjacency reasons listed by the **show cef not-cef-switched** command:

```
Switch# show cef not-cef-switched
CEF Packets passed on to next switching layer
Slot  No_adj No_encap Unsupp'ted Redirect  Receive  Options  Access    Frag
RP   3579706     0         0        0 41258564      0        0       0
Switch#
```

The reasons shown are as follows:

— An incomplete adjacency (No_adj)

— An incomplete ARP resolution (No_encap)

— Unsupported packet features (Unsupp'ted)

— ICMP redirect (Redirect)

— Layer 3 engine interfaces (Receive)

— IP options present (Options)

— Access list evaluation failure (Access)

— Fragmentation failure (Frag)

The Receive reason includes packets destined for IP addresses that are assigned to interfaces on the Layer 3 engine, IP network addresses, and IP broadcast addresses.

Packet Rewrite

When a multilayer switch finds valid entries in the FIB and adjacency tables, a packet is almost ready to be forwarded. One step remains: The packet header information must be rewritten. Keep in mind that multilayer switching occurs as quick table lookups, to find the next-hop address and the outbound switch port. The packet is untouched and still has the original destination MAC address of the switch itself. The IP header also must be adjusted, as if a traditional router had done the forwarding.

The switch has an additional functional block that performs a packet rewrite in real time. The packet rewrite engine (shown in Figure 13-3) makes the following changes to the packet just before forwarding:

- **Layer 2 destination address**—Changed to the next-hop device's MAC address

- **Layer 2 source address**—Changed to the outbound Layer 3 switch interface's MAC address

- **Layer 3 IP Time To Live (TTL)**—Decremented by one because one router hop has just occurred

- **Layer 3 IP checksum**—Recalculated to include changes to the IP header

- **Layer 2 frame checksum**—Recalculated to include changes to the Layer 2 and Layer 3 headers

A traditional router normally would make the same changes to each packet. The multilayer switch must act as if a traditional router were being used, making identical changes. However, the multilayer switch can do this very efficiently with dedicated packet-rewrite hardware and address information obtained from table lookups.

Configuring CEF

CEF is enabled on all CEF-capable Catalyst switches by default. In fact, the Catalyst 6500 (with a Supervisor 720 and its integrated MSFC3, or a Supervisor 2 and MSFC2 combination) runs CEF inherently, so CEF never can be disabled.

> **TIP**   Switches such as the Catalyst 3750 and 4500 run CEF by default, but you can disable CEF on a per-interface basis. You can use the **no ip route-cache cef** and **no ip cef** interface configuration commands to disable CEF on the Catalyst 3750 and 4500, respectively.
>
> You always should keep CEF enabled whenever possible, except when you need to disable it for debugging purposes.

Fallback Bridging

For protocols that CEF can't route or switch, a technique known as *fallback bridging* is used. Example protocols are IPX and AppleTalk, which are routable but not supported by CEF, as well as SNA and LAT, which are not routable. To summarize fallback bridging operation, each SVI associated with a VLAN in which nonroutable protocols are being used is assigned to a bridge group. Packets that cannot be routed from one VLAN to another are bridged transparently instead, as long as the two VLANs belong to the same bridge group.

> **NOTE** Only the Catalyst 3560 and 3750 offer fallback bridging; it can CEF switch IP packets but no others. The Catalyst 4500 and 6500 (all Supervisor models running Cisco IOS Software) also can CEF-switch IP but can handle other routable protocols more slowly with their Layer 3 engines. Those two platforms have no need for fallback bridging.

Bridge groups used in fallback bridging do not interact with normal Layer 2 switching (also using bridging). They do use a special Spanning Tree Protocol to maintain loop-free fallback bridging, but these bridge protocol data units (BPDU) are not exchanged with other 802.1D, Rapid Spanning Tree Protocol (RSTP), or Multiple Spanning Tree (MST) BPDUs on VLANs. Instead, the *VLAN-bridge* STP is used, with one instance per fallback bridge group.

To configure fallback bridging, first decide which VLANs have traffic that CEF cannot route. Begin by enabling a fallback bridge group and its instance of the VLAN-bridge STP:

```
Switch(config)# bridge-group bridge-group protocol vlan-bridge
```

Next, for each VLAN SVI in which nonroutable traffic will be bridged, assign it to the appropriate bridge group:

```
Switch(config)# interface vlan vlan-id
Switch(config-if)# bridge-group bridge-group
```

You can configure up to 31 different fallback bridge groups on a switch. Although the VLAN bridge STP instance running on each bridge group does not interact with normal 802.1D STP, it does behave similarly. For example, you can configure the bridge priority, port priority and cost, Hello timer, Forward Delay timer, and Max Age timer. These parameters all should look familiar because they are used in the 802.1D STP. Instead of using the **spanning-tree** command to adjust the parameter values, you must adjust them according to the bridge group number with the **bridge-group** *bridge-group* command keywords.

Verifying Multilayer Switching

The multilayer switching topics presented in this chapter are not difficult to configure; however, you might need to verify how a switch is forwarding packets. In particular, the following sections discuss the commands that you can use to verify the operation of InterVLAN routing, CEF, and fallback bridging.

Verifying InterVLAN Routing

To verify the configuration of a Layer 2 port, you can use the following EXEC command:

```
Switch# show interface type mod/num switchport
```

The output from this command displays the access VLAN or the trunking mode and native VLAN. The *administrative* modes reflect what has been configured for the port, while the *operational* modes show the port's active status.

You can use this same command to verify the configuration of a Layer 3 or routed port. In this case, you should see the switchport (Layer 2) mode disabled, as in Example 13-7.

Example 13-7 *Verifying Configuration of a Layer 3 Switch Port*

```
Switch# show interface fastethernet 0/16 switchport
Name: Fa0/16
Switchport: Disabled
```

To see the physical interface's status and counters, use the command without the **switchport** keyword. To see a summary listing of all interfaces, you can use the **show interface status** command.

To verify the configuration of an SVI, you can use the following EXEC command:

```
Switch# show interface vlan vlan-id
```

The VLAN interface should be up, with the line protocol also up. If this is not true, either the interface is disabled with the **shutdown** command or the VLAN itself has not been defined on the switch. Use the **show vlan** command to see a list of configured VLANs.

Example 13-8 shows the output produced from the **show vlan** command. Notice that each defined VLAN is shown, along with the switch ports that are assigned to it.

Example 13-8 *Displaying a List of Configured VLANs*

```
Switch# show vlan

VLAN Name                             Status    Ports
---- -------------------------------- --------- -------------------------------
1    default                          active    Fa0/5, Fa0/6, Fa0/7, Fa0/8
                                                Fa0/9, Fa0/10, Fa0/11, Fa0/12
                                                Fa0/13, Fa0/14, Fa0/15, Fa0/17
                                                Fa0/18, Fa0/19, Fa0/20, Fa0/21
                                                Fa0/22, Fa0/23, Fa0/24, Fa0/25
                                                Fa0/26, Fa0/27, Fa0/28, Fa0/29
                                                Fa0/30, Fa0/32, Fa0/33, Fa0/34
                                                Fa0/36, Fa0/37, Fa0/38, Fa0/39
                                                Fa0/41, Fa0/42, Fa0/43, Fa0/44
                                                Fa0/45, Fa0/46, Fa0/47, Gi0/1
                                                Gi0/2
2    VLAN0002                         active    Fa0/40
5    VLAN0005                         active
```

continues

Example 13-8 *Displaying a List of Configured VLANs (Continued)*

```
10   VLAN0010                    active
11   VLAN0011                    active    Fa0/31
12   VLAN0012                    active
99   VLAN0099                    active    Fa0/35
```

You also can display the IP-related information about a switch interface with the **show ip interface** command, as demonstrated in Example 13-9.

Example 13-9 *Displaying IP-Related Information About a Switch Interface*

```
Switch# show ip interface vlan 101
Vlan101 is up, line protocol is up
  Internet address is 10.1.1.1/24
  Broadcast address is 255.255.255.255
  Address determined by setup command
  MTU is 1500 bytes
  Helper address is not set
  Directed broadcast forwarding is disabled
  Outgoing access list is not set
  Inbound  access list is not set
  Proxy ARP is enabled
  Local Proxy ARP is disabled
  Security level is default
  Split horizon is enabled
  ICMP redirects are always sent
  ICMP unreachables are always sent
  ICMP mask replies are never sent
  IP fast switching is enabled
  IP fast switching on the same interface is disabled
  IP Flow switching is disabled
  IP CEF switching is enabled
  IP Feature Fast switching turbo vector
  IP Feature CEF switching turbo vector
  IP multicast fast switching is enabled
  IP multicast distributed fast switching is disabled
  IP route-cache flags are Fast, Distributed, CEF
  Router Discovery is disabled
  IP output packet accounting is disabled
  IP access violation accounting is disabled
  TCP/IP header compression is disabled
  RTP/IP header compression is disabled
  Probe proxy name replies are disabled
  Policy routing is disabled
  Network address translation is disabled
  WCCP Redirect outbound is disabled
  WCCP Redirect inbound is disabled
```

Example 13-9   *Displaying IP-Related Information About a Switch Interface (Continued)*

```
WCCP Redirect exclude is disabled
BGP Policy Mapping is disabled
Sampled Netflow is disabled
IP multicast multilayer switching is disabled
```

You can use the **show ip interface brief** command to see a summary listing of the interfaces involved in routing IP traffic, as demonstrated in Example 13-10.

Example 13-10   *Displaying a Summary Listing of Interfaces Routing IP Traffic*

```
Switch# show ip interface brief
Interface           IP-Address      OK? Method Status              Protocol
Vlan1               unassigned      YES NVRAM  administratively down down
Vlan54              10.3.1.6        YES manual up                  up
Vlan101             10.1.1.1        YES manual up                  up
GigabitEthernet1/1  10.1.5.1        YES manual up                  up
[output omitted]
```

Verifying CEF

CEF operation depends on the correct routing information being generated and downloaded to the Layer 3 forwarding engine hardware. This information is contained in the FIB and is maintained dynamically. To view the entire FIB, use the following EXEC command:

```
Switch# show ip cef
```

Example 13-11 shows sample output from this command.

Example 13-11   *Displaying the FIB Contents for a Switch*

```
Switch# show ip cef
Prefix              Next Hop          Interface
0.0.0.0/32          receive
192.168.199.0/24    attached          Vlan1
192.168.199.0/32    receive
192.168.199.1/32    receive
192.168.199.2/32    192.168.199.2     Vlan1
192.168.199.255/32  receive
```

On this switch, only VLAN 1 has been configured with the IP address 192.168.199.1 255.255.255.0. Notice several things about the FIB for such a small configuration:

- **0.0.0.0/32**—An FIB entry has been reserved for the default route. No next hop is defined, so the entry is marked "receive" so that packets will be sent to the Layer 3 engine for further processing.

- **192.168.199.0/24**—The subnet assigned to the VLAN 1 interface is given its own entry. This is marked "attached" because it is connected directly to an SVI, VLAN 1.

- **192.168.199.0/32**—An FIB entry has been reserved for the exact network address. This is used to contain an adjacency for packets sent to the network address, if the network is not directly connected. In this case, there is no adjacency, and the entry is marked "receive."

- **192.168.199.1/32**—An entry has been reserved for the VLAN 1 SVI's IP address. Notice that this is a host route (/32). Packets destined for the VLAN 1 interface must be dealt with internally, so the entry is marked "receive."

- **192.168.199.2/32**—This is an entry for a neighboring multilayer switch, found on the VLAN 1 interface. The next-hop field has been filled in with the same IP address, denoting that an adjacency is available.

- **192.168.199.255/32**—An FIB entry has been reserved for the 192.168.199.0 subnet's broadcast address. The route processor (Layer 3 engine) handles all directed broadcasts, so the entry is marked "receive."

To see complete FIB table information for a specific interface, use the following EXEC command:

```
Switch# show ip cef type mod/num [detail]
```

Verifying Fallback Bridging

To verify the operation of fallback bridging, you can use the following EXEC commands:

```
Switch# show bridge group
Switch# show bridge bridge-group [verbose]
```

The first command shows a summary of all active fallback bridge groups, along with their STP states. The second command displays the bridging table contents for a specific fallback bridge group.

Foundation Summary

The Foundation Summary is a collection of information that provides a convenient review of many key concepts in this chapter. If you are already comfortable with the topics in this chapter, this summary can help you recall a few details. If you just read this chapter, this review should help solidify some key facts. If you are doing your final preparation before the exam, this information is a convenient way to review the day before the exam.

Table 13-2 *InterVLAN Routing Configuration Commands*

Task	Command Syntax
Put a port into Layer 2 mode	Switch(config-if)# **switchport**
Put a port into Layer 3 mode	Switch(config-if)# **no switchport**
Define an SVI	Switch(config)# **interface vlan** *vlan-id*

Components of CEF:

- **Forwarding Information Base (FIB)**—Contains routing and next-hop information. Lookups are performed according to longest-match IP prefix.

- **Adjacency table**—Contains Layer 2 address information for next-hop FIB entries that are one hop away.

- **Packet rewrite**—Hardware dedicated to rewriting the Layer 2 and Layer 3 header information of outbound packets after the forwarding decisions have been made.

Table 13-3 *Fallback Bridging Configuration Commands*

Task	Command Syntax
Define a fallback bridge group	Switch(config)# **bridge-group** *bridge-group* **protocol vlan-bridge**
Assign an interface to a bridge group	Switch(config)# **interface vlan** *vlan-id* Switch(config-if)# **bridge-group** *bridge-group*

Table 13-4 *Multilayer Switching Verification Commands*

Task	Command Syntax
Show a Layer 2 port status	Switch# **show interface** *type mod/num* **switchport**
Show a Layer 3 port status	Switch# **show interface** *type mod/num*
Show an SVI status	Switch# **show interface vlan** *vlan-id*
View the FIB contents	Switch# **show ip cef**
View FIB information for an interface	Switch# **show ip cef** [*type mod/num* | **vlan** *vlan-id*] [**detail**]
View FIB information for an IP prefix	Switch# **show ip cef** [*prefix-ip prefix-mask*] [**longer-prefixes**] [**detail**]
View FIB adjacency information	Switch# **show adjacency** [*type mod/num* | **vlan** *vlan-id*] [**summary** | **detail**]
View counters for packets not switched by CEF	Switch# **show cef not-cef-switched**
Show fallback bridge group status	Switch# **show bridge group**
Show fallback bridging table contents	Switch# **show bridge** *bridge-group*

Q&A

The questions and scenarios in this book are more difficult than what you should experience on the actual exam. The questions do not attempt to cover more breadth or depth than the exam; however, they are designed to make sure that you know the answers. Rather than allowing you to derive the answers from clues hidden inside the questions themselves, the questions challenge your understanding and recall of the subject. Hopefully, these questions will help limit the number of exam questions on which you narrow your choices to two options and then guess.

You can find the answers to these questions in Appendix A.

1. What might you need to implement interVLAN routing?

2. Can interVLAN routing be performed over a single trunk link?

3. To configure an SVI, what commands are needed?

4. What command can verify the VLAN assignments on a Layer 2 port?

5. A switch has the following interface configurations in its running configuration:

```
interface fastethernet 0/1
 switchport access vlan 5
!
interface vlan 5
 ip address 192.168.10.1 255.255.255.0
 no shutdown
```

What is necessary for packets to get from the FastEthernet interface to the VLAN 5 SVI?

6. What is the source of FIB information?

7. How often is the FIB updated?

8. What is meant by the term "CEF punt"?

9. What happens to the FIB when distributed CEF (dCEF) is used?

10. What happens during a "CEF glean" process?

11. What does a multilayer switch do to the IP TTL value just before a packet is forwarded?

12. What is fallback bridging?

13. Is it possible for an SVI to go down? If so, for what reasons?

This chapter covers the following topics that you need to master for the CCNP BCMSN exam:

- **Router Redundancy**—This section discusses three protocols that are available on Catalyst switches to provide redundant router or gateway addresses. The protocols include Hot Standby Routing Protocol (HSRP), Virtual Router Redundancy Protocol (VRRP), and Gateway Load Balancing Protocol (GLBP).

- **Supervisor and Route Processor Redundancy**—This section covers the methods that can be used on some Catalyst switch platforms to operate an active-standby pair of hardware modules in one chassis. The redundancy modes include Route Processor Redundancy (RPR), RPR+, Stateful Switchover (SSO), and Non-Stop Forwarding (NSF).

- **Power Supply Redundancy**—This section explains how two power supplies can be used in a Catalyst 4500R or 6500 chassis. Both power supplies can be active; you can configure whether one supply provides the total chassis load or whether both supplies share the total load.

CHAPTER 14

Router, Supervisor, and Power Redundancy

A multilayer switch can provide routing functions for devices on a network, as described in Chapter 13, "Multilayer Switching." If that switch happens to fail, clients have no way of having their traffic forwarded; their gateway has gone away.

Other multilayer switches can be added into the network to provide redundancy in the form of redundant router or gateway addresses. This chapter describes the protocols that can be used for redundant router addresses, load balancing across multiple routers, and load balancing into a server farm.

This chapter also describes the features that support redundancy in hardware. Within a single multilayer switch chassis, two supervisor modules with integrated route processors can be used to provide hardware redundancy. If an entire supervisor module fails, the other module can pick up the pieces and continue operating the switch. The same is true for redundant power supplies within a single chassis.

"Do I Know This Already?" Quiz

The purpose of the "Do I Know This Already?" quiz is to help you decide what parts of this chapter to use. If you already intend to read the entire chapter, you do not necessarily need to answer these questions now.

The quiz, derived from the major sections in the "Foundation Topics" portion of the chapter, helps you determine how to spend your limited study time.

Table 14-1 outlines the major topics discussed in this chapter and the "Do I Know This Already?" quiz questions that correspond to those topics.

Table 14-1 *"Do I Know This Already?" Foundation Topics Section-to-Question Mapping*

Foundation Topics Section	Questions Covered in This Section	Score
Router Redundancy: HSRP	1–5	
Router Redundancy: VRRP	6–7	
Router Redundancy: GLBP	8–10	
Hardware Redundancy	11–12	
Total Score		

CAUTION The goal of self-assessment is to gauge your mastery of the topics in this chapter. If you do not know the answer to a question or are only partially sure of the answer, you should mark this question wrong. Giving yourself credit for an answer you correctly guess skews your self-assessment results and might give you a false sense of security.

---

1. Which one of the following do multilayer switches share when running HSRP?

   a. Routing tables

   b. ARP cache

   c. CAM table

   d. IP address

2. What HSRP group uses the MAC address 0000.0c07.ac11?

   a. Group 0

   b. Group 7

   c. Group 11

   d. Group 17

3. Two routers are configured for an HSRP group. One router uses the default HSRP priority. What priority should be assigned to the other router to make it more likely to be the active router?

   a. 1

   b. 100

   c. 200

   d. 500

4. How many routers are in the Standby state in an HSRP group?

   a. 0

   b. 1

   c. 2

   d. All but the active router

5. A multilayer switch is configured as follows:

```
interface fastethernet 1/1
no switchport
ip address 192.168.199.3 255.255.255.0
standby 1 ip 192.168.199.2
```

Which IP address should a client PC use as its default gateway?

a. 192.168.199.1

b. 192.168.199.2

c. 192.168.199.3

d. Any of the above

6. Which one of the following is based on an IETF RFC standard?

a. HSRP

b. VRRP

c. GLBP

d. STP

7. What VRRP group uses the virtual MAC address 0000.5e00.01ff?

a. Group 0

b. Group 1

c. Group 255

d. Group 94

8. Which one of the following protocols is the best choice for load-balancing redundant gateways?

a. HSRP

b. VRRP

c. GLBP

d. GVRP

9. Which one of the following GLBP functions answers ARP requests?

a. AVF

b. VARP

c. AVG

d. MVR

10. By default, which of the following virtual MAC addresses will be sent to the next client that looks for the virtual gateway?

a. The GLBP interface's MAC address

b. The next virtual MAC address in the sequence

c. The virtual MAC address of the least-used router

d. 0000.0c07.ac00

11. Which one of these features is used to reduce the amount of time needed to rebuild the routing information after a supervisor module failure?

    a. NFS

    b. NSF

    c. RPR+

    d. SSO

12. Which one of the following features provides the fastest failover for supervisor or route processor redundancy?

    a. SSL

    b. SSO

    c. RPR+

    d. RPR

The answers to the "Do I Know This Already?" quiz are found in Appendix A, "Answers to Chapter 'Do I Know This Already?' Quizzes and Q&A Sections." The suggested choices for your next step are as follows:

■ **10 or less overall score**—Read the entire chapter. This includes the "Foundation Topics," "Foundation Summary," and "Q&A" sections.

■ **11 or 12 overall score**—If you want more review on these topics, skip to the "Foundation Summary" section and then go to the "Q&A" section at the end of the chapter. Otherwise, move to Chapter 15, "IP Multicast."

Foundation Topics

Router Redundancy in Multilayer Switching

Multilayer switches can act as IP gateways for connected hosts by providing gateway addresses at VLAN SVIs and Layer 3 physical interfaces. These switches can also participate in routing protocols, just as traditional routers do.

For high availability, multilayer switches should offer a means of preventing one switch (gateway) failure from isolating an entire VLAN. This chapter discusses several approaches to providing router redundancy, including the following:

- Hot Standby Router Protocol (HSRP)

- Virtual Router Redundancy Protocol (VRRP)

- Gateway Load Balancing Protocol (GLBP)

Packet Forwarding Review

When a host must communicate with a device on its local subnet, it can generate an Address Resolution Protocol (ARP) request, wait for the ARP reply, and exchange packets directly. However, if the far end is located on a different subnet, the host must rely on an intermediate system (a router, for example) to relay packets to and from that subnet.

A host identifies its nearest router, also known as the default gateway or next hop, by its IP address. If the host understands something about routing, it recognizes that all packets destined off-net must be sent to the gateway's MAC address rather than the far end's MAC address. Therefore, the host first sends an ARP request to find the gateway's MAC address. Then packets can be relayed to the gateway directly without having to look for ARP entries for individual destinations.

If the host is not so savvy about routing, it might still generate ARP requests for every off-net destination, hoping that someone will answer. Obviously, the off-net destinations cannot answer because they never receive the ARP request broadcasts; these requests are not forwarded across subnets. Instead, you can configure the gateway to provide a proxy ARP function so that it will reply to ARP requests with its own MAC address, as if the destination itself had responded.

Now the issue of gateway availability becomes important. If the gateway router for a subnet or VLAN goes down, packets have no way of being forwarded off the local subnet. Several protocols are available that allow multiple routing devices to share a common gateway address so that if one goes down, another automatically can pick up the active gateway role. The sections that follow describe these protocols.

Hot Standby Router Protocol

HSRP is a Cisco-proprietary protocol developed to allow several routers (or multilayer switches) to appear as a single gateway IP address. RFC 2281 describes this protocol in more detail.

Basically, each of the routers that provides redundancy for a given gateway address is assigned to a common HSRP group. One router is elected as the primary, or *active,* HSRP router; another is elected as the *standby* HSRP router; and all the others remain in the *listen* HSRP state. The routers exchange HSRP hello messages at regular intervals so they can remain aware of each other's existence and that of the active router.

> **NOTE**   HSRP sends its hello messages to the multicast destination 224.0.0.2 ("all routers") using UDP port 1985.

An HSRP group can be assigned an arbitrary group number, from 0 to 255. If you configure HSRP groups on several VLAN interfaces, it can be handy to make the group number the same as the VLAN number. However, most Catalyst switches support only up to 16 unique HSRP group numbers. If you have more than 16 VLANs, you will quickly run out of group numbers. An alternative is to make the group number the same (that is, 1) for every VLAN interface. This is perfectly valid because the HSRP groups are only locally significant on an interface. In other words, HSRP Group 1 on interface VLAN 10 is unique and independent from HSRP Group 1 on interface VLAN 11.

HSRP Router Election

HSRP election is based on a priority value (0 to 255) that is configured on each router in the group. By default, the priority is 100. The router with the highest priority value (255 is highest) becomes the active router for the group. If all router priorities are equal or set to the default value, the router with the highest IP address on the HSRP interface becomes the active router. To set the priority, use the following interface-configuration command:

```
Switch(config-if)# standby group priority priority
```

For example, suppose that one switch is left at its default priority of 100, while the local switch is intended to win the active role election. You can use the following command to set the HSRP priority to 200:

```
Switch(config-if)# standby 1 priority 200
```

When HSRP is configured on an interface, the router progresses through a series of states before becoming active. This forces a router to listen for others in a group and see where it fits into the pecking order. Devices participating in HSRP must progress their interfaces through the following state sequence:

1. Disabled

2. Init

3. Listen

4. Speak

5. Standby

6. Active

Only the standby (the one with the second-highest priority) router monitors the hello messages from the active router. By default, hellos are sent every 3 seconds. If hellos are missed for the duration of the *holdtime* timer (default 10 seconds, or three times the hello timer), the active router is presumed to be down. The standby router is then clear to assume the active role.

At that point, if other routers are sitting in the Listen state, the next-highest priority router is allowed to become the new standby router.

If you need to change the timer values, use the following interface-configuration command. If you decide to change the timers on a router, you should change them identically on all routers in the HSRP group.

```
Switch(config-if)# standby group timers [msec] hello [msec] holdtime
```
The hello and holdtime values can be given in seconds or in milliseconds, if the **msec** keyword precedes a value. The hello time can range from 1 to 254 seconds or from 15 to 999 milliseconds. The holdtime always should be at least three times the hello timer, and can range from 1 to 255 seconds or 50 to 3000 milliseconds.

As an example, the following command can be used to set the hello time at 100 milliseconds and the holdtime to 300 milliseconds:

```
Switch(config-if)# standby 1 timers msec 100 msec 300
```

NOTE   Be aware that decreasing the HSRP hello time allows a router failure to be detected more quickly. At the same time, HSRP hellos will be sent more often, increasing the amount of traffic on the interface.

Normally, after the active router fails and the standby becomes active, the original active router cannot immediately become active when it is restored. In other words, if a router is not already active, it cannot become active again until the current active router fails—even if its priority is higher than that of the active router. An interesting case arises when routers are just being powered up or added to a network. The first router to bring up its interface becomes the HSRP active router, even if it has the lowest priority of all.

You can configure a router to pre-empt or immediately take over the active role if its priority is the highest *at any time*. Use the following interface-configuration command to allow pre-emption:

```
Switch(config-if)# standby group preempt [delay [minimum seconds] [reload seconds]]
```

By default, the local router immediately can pre-empt another router that has the active role. To delay the pre-emption, use the **delay** keyword followed by one or both of the following parameters:

■ Add the **minimum** keyword to force the router to wait for *seconds* (0 to 3600 seconds) before attempting to overthrow an active router with a lower priority. This delay time begins as soon as the router is capable of assuming the active role, such as after an interface comes up or after HSRP is configured.

■ Add the **reload** keyword to force the router to wait for *seconds* (0 to 3600 seconds) after it has been reloaded or restarted. This is handy if there are routing protocols that need time to converge. The local router should not become the active gateway before its routing table is fully populated; otherwise, it might not be capable of routing traffic properly.

HSRP also can use an authentication method to prevent unexpected devices from spoofing or participating in HSRP. All routers in the same standby group must have an identical authentication method and key. You can use either plain-text or MD5 authentication, as described in the following sections.

Plain-Text HSRP Authentication

HSRP messages are sent with a plain-text key string (up to 8 characters), as a simple method to authenticate HSRP peers. If the key string in a message matches the key configured on an HSRP peer, the message is accepted.

When keys are sent in the clear, they can be easily intercepted and used to impersonate legitimate peers. Plain-text authentication is intended only to prevent peers with a default configuration from participating in HSRP. Cisco devices use "cisco" as the default key string.

You can configure a plain-text authentication key for an HSRP group with the following interface-configuration command:

```
Switch(config-if)# standby group authentication string
```

MD5 Authentication

A Message Digest 5 (MD5) hash is computed on a portion of each HSRP message and a secret key known only to legitimate HSRP group peers. The MD5 hash value is sent along with HSRP messages. As a message is received, the peer recomputes the hash of the expected message contents and its own secret key; if the hash values are identical, the message is accepted.

MD5 authentication is more secure than plain-text authentication because the hash value contained in the HSRP messages is extremely difficult (if not impossible) to reverse. The hash value itself is not used as a key; instead, the hash is used to validate the message contents.

You can configure MD5 authentication by associating a key string with an interface, using the following interface-configuration command:

```
Switch(config-if)# standby group authentication md5 key-string [0 | 7] string
```

By default, the key *string* (up to 64 characters) is given as plain text. This is the same as specifying the **0** keyword. After the key string is entered, it is shown as an encrypted value in the switch configuration. You also can copy and paste an encrypted key string value into this command by preceding the string with the **7** keyword.

Alternatively, you can define an MD5 key string as a key on a key chain. This method is more flexible, enabling you to define more than one key on the switch. Any of the keys then can be associated with HSRP on any interface. If a key needs to be changed, you simply add a new key to the key chain and retire (delete) an old key.

First define the key chain globally with the **key chain** command; then add one key at a time with the **key** and **key-string** commands. The *key-number* index is arbitrary, but keys are tried in sequential order. Finally, associate the key chain with HSRP on an interface by referencing its *chain-name*. You can use the following commands to configure HSRP MD5 authentication:

```
Switch(config)# key chain chain-name
Switch(config-keychain)# key key-number
Switch(config-keychain-key)# key-string [0 | 7] string
Switch(config)# interface type mod/num
Switch(config-if)# standby group authentication md5 key-chain chain-name
```

TIP   HSRP MD5 authentication was introduced into some Catalyst switch platforms with Cisco IOS Software Release 12.2(25)S. At press time, this feature was available only on the Catalyst 3560 and 3750.

Conceding the Election

Consider an active router in an HSRP group: A group of clients sends packets to it for forwarding, and it has one or more links to the rest of the world. If one of those links fails, the router remains active. If all of those links fail, the router still remains active. But sooner or later, the path to the rest of the world is either crippled or removed, and packets from the clients no longer can be forwarded.

HSRP has a mechanism for detecting link failures and swaying the election, giving another router an opportunity to take over the active role. When a specific interface is tracked, HSRP reduces the router's priority by a configurable amount as soon as the interface goes down. If more than one interface is tracked, the priority is reduced even more with each failed interface. The priority is incremented by the same amount as interfaces come back up.

This is particularly useful when a switch has several paths out of a VLAN or subnet; as more interfaces fail and remove the possible paths, other HSRP peers should appear to be more desirable and take over the active role. To configure interface tracking, use the following interface-configuration command:

```
Switch(config-if)# standby group track type mod/num [decrementvalue]
```

By default, the *decrementvalue* for an interface is 10. Keep in mind that interface tracking doesn't involve the state of the HSRP interface itself. Instead, the state of other specific interfaces affects the usefulness of the local router as a gateway. You also should be aware that the only way another router can take over the active role after interface tracking reduces the priority is if the following two conditions are met:

■ Another router now has a higher HSRP priority.

■ That same router is using **preempt** in its HSRP configuration.

Without pre-emption, the active role cannot be given to any other router.

HSRP Gateway Addressing

Each router in an HSRP group has its own unique IP address assigned to an interface. This address is used for all routing protocol and management traffic initiated by or destined to the router. In addition, each router has a common gateway IP address, the *virtual router* address, that is kept alive by HSRP. This address also is referred to as the *HSRP address* or the *standby address*. Clients can point to that virtual router address as their default gateway, knowing that a router always keeps that address active. Keep in mind that the actual interface address and the virtual (standby) address must be configured to be in the same IP subnet.

You can assign the HSRP address with the following interface command:

```
Switch(config-if)# standby group ip ip-address [secondary]
```

When HSRP is used on an interface that has secondary IP addresses, you can add the **secondary** keyword so that HSRP can provide a redundant secondary gateway address.

Naturally, each router keeps a unique MAC address for its interface. This MAC address always is associated with the unique IP address configured on the interface. For the virtual router address, HSRP defines a special MAC address of the form 0000.0c07.ac*xx*, where *xx* represents the HSRP group number as a two-digit hex value. For example, HSRP Group 1 appears as 0000.0c07.ac01, HSRP Group 16 appears as 0000.0c07.ac10, and so on.

Figure 14-1 shows a simple network in which two multilayer switches use HSRP Group 1 to provide the redundant gateway address 192.168.1.1. CatalystA is the active router, with priority 200, and answers the ARP request for the gateway address. Because CatalystB is in the standby state, it never is used for traffic sent to 192.168.1.1. Instead, only CatalystA performs the gateway routing function, and only its uplink to the access layer is utilized.

Figure 14-1 *Typical HSRP Scenario with One HSRP Group*

Example 14-1 shows the configuration commands you can use on CatalystA. CatalystB would be configured similarly, except that its HSRP priority would use the default value of 100.

Example 14-1 *Configuring an HSRP Group on a Switch*

```
CatalystA(config)# interface vlan 50
CatalystA(config-if)# ip address 192.168.1.10 255.255.255.0
CatalystA(config-if)# standby 1 priority 200
CatalystA(config-if)# standby 1 preempt
CatalystA(config-if)# standby 1 ip 192.168.1.1
```

Load Balancing with HSRP

Consider a network in which HSRP is used on two distribution switches to provide a redundant gateway address for access-layer users. Only one of the two becomes the active HSRP router; the other remains in standby. All the users send their traffic to the active router, over the uplink to the active router. The standby router and its uplink essentially sit idle until a router failure occurs.

Load balancing traffic across two uplinks to two HSRP routers with a single HSRP group is not possible. Then how is it possible to load-balance with HSRP? The trick is to use two HSRP groups:

■ One group assigns an active router to one switch.

■ The other group assigns another active router to the other switch.

In this way, two different virtual router or gateway addresses can be used simultaneously. The rest of the trick is to make each switch function as the standby router for its partner's HSRP group. In other words, each router is active for one group and standby for the other group. The clients or end users also must have their default gateway addresses configured as one of the two virtual HSRP group addresses.

Figure 14-2 presents this scenario. Now, CatalystA is not only the active router for HSRP Group 1 (192.168.1.1), but it is also the standby router for HSRP Group 2 (192.168.1.2). CatalystB is configured similarly, but with its roles reversed. The remaining step is to configure half of the client PCs with the HSRP Group 1 virtual router address and the other half with the Group 2 address. This makes load balancing possible and effective. Each half of the hosts uses one switch as its gateway over one uplink.

Figure 14-2 *Load Balancing with Two HSRP Groups*

Example 14-2 shows the configuration commands you can use for the scenario shown in Figure 14-2.

Example 14-2 *Configuring Load Balancing Between HSRP Groups*

```
CatalystA(config)# interface vlan 50
CatalystA(config-if)# ip address 192.168.1.10 255.255.255.0
CatalystA(config-if)# standby 1 priority 200
CatalystA(config-if)# standby 1 preempt
CatalystA(config-if)# standby 1 ip 192.168.1.1
CatalystA(config-if)# standby 1 authentication MyKey
CatalystA(config-if)# standby 2 priority 100
CatalystA(config-if)# standby 2 ip 192.168.1.2
CatalystA(config-if)# standby 2 authentication MyKey

CatalystB(config)# interface vlan 50
CatalystB(config-if)# ip address 192.168.1.11 255.255.255.0
CatalystB(config-if)# standby 1 priority 100
CatalystB(config-if)# standby 1 ip 192.168.1.1
CatalystB(config-if)# standby 1 authentication MyKey
CatalystB(config-if)# standby 2 priority 200
CatalystB(config-if)# standby 2 preempt
CatalystB(config-if)# standby 2 ip 192.168.1.2
CatalystB(config-if)# standby 2 authentication MyKey
```

You can use the following command to display information about the status of one or more HSRP groups and interfaces:

```
Router# show standby [brief] [vlan vlan-id | type mod/num]
```

Based on the configuration in Example 14-2, the output in Example 14-3 shows that the CatalystA switch is the active router for HSRP group 1 and the standby router for HSRP group 2 on interface VLAN 50.

Example 14-3 *Displaying the HSRP Router Role of a Switch: CatalystA*

```
CatalystA# show standby vlan 50 brief
                     P indicates configured to preempt.
                     |
Interface  Grp Prio P State   Active addr   Standby addr   Group addr
Vl50        1   200 P Active  local         192.168.1.11   192.168.1.1
Vl50        2   100   Standby 192.168.1.11  local          192.168.1.2
CatalystA#
CatalystA# show standby vlan 50
Vlan50 - Group 1
  Local state is Active, priority 200, may preempt
  Hellotime 3 sec, holdtime 10 sec
  Next hello sent in 2.248
```

continues

Example 14-3 *Displaying the HSRP Router Role of a Switch: CatalystA (Continued)*

```
    Virtual IP address is 192.168.1.1 configured
    Active router is local
    Standby router is 192.168.1.11 expires in 9.860
    Virtual mac address is 0000.0c07.ac01
    Authentication text "MyKey"
    2 state changes, last state change 00:11:58
    IP redundancy name is "hsrp-Vl50-1" (default)
Vlan50 - Group 2
    Local state is Standby, priority 100
    Hellotime 3 sec, holdtime 10 sec
    Next hello sent in 1.302
    Virtual IP address is 192.168.1.2 configured
    Active router is 192.168.1.11, priority 200 expires in 7.812
    Standby router is local
    Authentication text "MyKey"
    4 state changes, last state change 00:10:04
    IP redundancy name is "hsrp-Vl50-2" (default)
CatalystA#
```

The output from CatalystB in Example 14-4 shows that it has inverted roles from CatalystA for HSRP groups 1 and 2.

Example 14-4 *Displaying the HSRP Router Role of a Switch: CatalystB*

```
CatalystB#show standby vlan 50 brief
                     P indicates configured to preempt.
                     |
Interface  Grp Prio P State   Active addr    Standby addr   Group addr
Vl50        1   100   Standby 192.168.1.10   local          192.168.1.1
Vl50        2   200 P Active  local          192.168.1.10   192.168.1.2
CatalystB#
CatalystB#show standby vlan 50
Vlan50 - Group 1
    Local state is Standby, priority 100
    Hellotime 3 sec, holdtime 10 sec
    Next hello sent in 0.980
    Virtual IP address is 192.168.1.1 configured
    Active router is 192.168.1.10, priority 200 expires in 8.128
    Standby router is local
    Authentication text "MyKey"
    1 state changes, last state change 00:01:12
    IP redundancy name is "hsrp-Vl50-1" (default)
Vlan50 - Group 2
    Local state is Active, priority 200, may preempt
    Hellotime 3 sec, holdtime 10 sec
    Next hello sent in 2.888
```

Example 14-4   *Displaying the HSRP Router Role of a Switch: CatalystB (Continued)*

```
     Virtual IP address is 192.168.1.2 configured
     Active router is local
     Standby router is 192.168.1.10 expires in 8.500
     Virtual mac address is 0000.0c07.ac02
     Authentication text "MyKey"
     1 state changes, last state change 00:01:16
CatalystB#
```

Virtual Router Redundancy Protocol

The Virtual Router Redundancy Protocol (VRRP) is a standards-based alternative to HSRP, defined in IETF standard RFC 2338. VRRP is so similar to HSRP that you need to learn only slightly different terminology and a couple of slight functional differences. When you understand HSRP operation and configuration, you also will understand VRRP. This section is brief, highlighting only the differences between HSRP and VRRP.

- VRRP provides one redundant gateway address from a group of routers. The active router is called the *master router*, while all others are in the *backup state*. The master router is the one with the highest router priority in the VRRP group.

- VRRP group numbers range from 0 to 255; router priorities range from 1 to 254 (254 is the highest, 100 is the default).

- The virtual router MAC address is of the form 0000.5e00.01*xx*, where *xx* is a two-digit hex VRRP group number.

- VRRP advertisements are sent at 1-second intervals. Backup routers optionally can learn the advertisement interval from the master router.

- By default, all VRRP routers are configured to pre-empt the current master router if their priorities are greater.

- VRRP has no mechanism for tracking interfaces to allow more capable routers to take over the master role.

> **NOTE**   VRRP sends its advertisements to the multicast destination address 224.0.0.18 (VRRP), using IP protocol 112. VRRP was introduced in Cisco IOS Software Release 12.0(18)ST for routers. At press time, VRRP is available only for the Catalyst 6500 Supervisor 2 (Cisco IOS Software Release 12.2[9]ZA or later) and Supervisor 720 (Cisco IOS Software Release 12.2[17a]SX4 or later).

To configure VRRP, use the interface-configuration commands documented in Table 14-2.

Table 14-2 *VRRP Configuration Commands*

Task	Command Syntax
Assign a VRRP router priority (default 100)	**vrrp** *group* **priority** *level*
Alter the advertisement timer (default 1 second)	**vrrp** *group* **timers advertise** [*msec*] *interval*
Learn the advertisement interval from the master router	**vrrp** *group* **timers learn**
Disable pre-empting (default is to preempt)	**no vrrp** *group* **preempt**
Change the pre-empt delay (default 0 seconds)	**vrrp** *group* **preempt** [**delay** *seconds*]
Use authentication for advertisements	**vrrp** *group* **authentication** *string*
Assign a virtual IP address	**vrrp** *group* **ip** *ip-address* [**secondary**]

As an example, the load-balancing scenario shown in Figure 14-2 is implemented using VRRP. You would use the configuration commands in Example 14-5 on the two Catalyst switches.

Example 14-5 *Configuring Load Balancing with VRRP*

```
CatalystA(config)# interface vlan 50
CatalystA(config-if)# ip address 192.168.1.10 255.255.255.0
CatalystA(config-if)# vrrp 1 priority 200
CatalystA(config-if)# vrrp 1 ip 192.168.1.1
CatalystA(config-if)# vrrp 2 priority 100
CatalystA(config-if)# no vrrp 2 preempt
CatalystA(config-if)# vrrp 2 ip 192.168.1.2
CatalystB(config)# interface vlan 50
CatalystB(config-if)# ip address 192.168.1.11 255.255.255.0
CatalystB(config-if)# vrrp 1 priority 100
CatalystA(config-if)# no vrrp 1 preempt
CatalystB(config-if)# vrrp 1 ip 192.168.1.1
CatalystB(config-if)# vrrp 2 priority 200
CatalystB(config-if)# vrrp 2 ip 192.168.1.2
```

You can use the following command to display information about VRRP status on one or more interfaces:

```
Switch# show vrrp [brief]
```

Example 14-6 shows this command executed on both CatalystA and CatalystB, with the output showing the alternating roles for the two VRRP groups configured in Example 14-5.

Example 14-6 *Displaying Switch Roles for VRRP Load Balancing*

```
CatalystA# show vrrp brief
Interface        Grp Pri Time  Own Pre State   Master addr     Group addr
Vlan50            1  200 3218    Y   Master  192.168.1.10    192.168.1.1
Vlan50            2  100 3609        Backup  192.168.1.11    192.168.1.2
CatalystA#
```
```
CatalystB# show vrrp brief
Interface        Grp Pri Time  Own Pre State   Master addr     Group addr
Vlan50            1  100 3609        Backup  192.168.1.10    192.168.1.1
Vlan50            2  200 3218    Y   Master  192.168.1.11    192.168.1.2
CatalystB#
```

Table 14-3 compares the detailed VRRP status between the CatalystA and CatalystB switches.

Table 14-3 *Verifying VRRP Status for Multiple VRRP Groups*

CatalystA	CatalystB

CatalystA# **show vrrp**
Vlan50 - Group 1
  State is Master
  Virtual IP address is 192.168.1.1
  Virtual MAC address is 0000.5e00.0101
  Advertisement interval is 1.000 sec
  Preemption is enabled
    min delay is 0.000 sec
  Priority is 200
  Authentication is enabled
  Master Router is 192.168.1.10
(local), priority is 200
  Master Advertisement interval is
1.000 sec
  Master Down interval is 3.218 sec
 	
Vlan50 - Group 2
  State is Backup
  Virtual IP address is 192.168.1.2
  Virtual MAC address is 0000.5e00.0102
  Advertisement interval is 1.000 sec
  Preemption is disabled
  Priority is 100
  Authentication is enabled
  Master Router is 192.168.1.11,
priority is 200
  Master Advertisement interval is
1.000 sec
  Master Down interval is 3.609 sec
(expires in 2.977 sec)
CatalystA#
	CatalystB# **show vrrp**
	Vlan50 - Group 1
	  State is Backup
	  Virtual IP address is 192.168.1.1
	  Virtual MAC address is 0000.5e00.0101
	  Advertisement interval is 1.000 sec
	  Preemption is disabled
	  Priority is 100
	  Authentication is enabled
	  Master Router is 192.168.1.10,
	priority is 200
	  Master Advertisement interval is
	1.000 sec
	  Master Down interval is 3.609 sec
	(expires in 2.833 sec)
	
	Vlan50 - Group 2
	  State is Master
	  Virtual IP address is 192.168.1.2
	  Virtual MAC address is 0000.5e00.0102
	  Advertisement interval is 1.000 sec
	  Preemption is enabled
	    min delay is 0.000 sec
	  Priority is 200
	  Authentication is enabled
	  Master Router is 192.168.1.11
	(local), priority is 200
	  Master Advertisement interval is
	1.000 sec
	  Master Down interval is 3.218 sec
	CatalystB#

Gateway Load Balancing Protocol

You should now know how both HSRP and VRRP can effectively provide a redundant gateway (virtual router) address. You can accomplish load balancing by configuring only multiple HSRP/VRRP groups to have multiple virtual router addresses. More manual configuration is needed so that the client machines are divided among the virtual routers. Each group of clients must point to the appropriate virtual router. This makes load balancing somewhat labor-intensive, having a more or less fixed, or static, behavior.

The Gateway Load Balancing Protocol (GLBP) is a Cisco-proprietary protocol designed to overcome the limitations of existing redundant router protocols. Some of the concepts are the same as with HSRP/VRRP, but the terminology is different and the behavior is much more dynamic and robust.

> **NOTE**   GLBP was introduced in Cisco IOS Software Release 12.2(14)S for routers. At press time, GLBP is available only for the Catalyst 6500 Supervisor 2 with IOS Release 12.2(14)SY4 or later, and Supervisor 720 with IOS Release 12.2(17a)SX4 switch platforms.

To provide a virtual router, multiple switches (routers) are assigned to a common GLBP group. Instead of having just one active router performing forwarding for the virtual router address, *all* routers in the group can participate and offer load balancing by forwarding a portion of the overall traffic.

The advantage is that none of the clients has to be pointed toward a specific gateway address; they can all have the same default gateway set to the virtual router IP address. The load balancing is provided completely through the use of virtual router MAC addresses in ARP replies returned to the clients. As a client sends an ARP request looking for the virtual router address, GLBP sends back an ARP reply with the virtual MAC address of a selected router in the group. The result is that all clients use the same gateway address but have differing MAC addresses for it.

Active Virtual Gateway

The trick behind this load balancing lies in the GLBP group. One router is elected the *active virtual gateway (AVG)*. This router has the highest priority value, or the highest IP address in the group, if there is no highest priority. The AVG answers all ARP requests for the virtual router address. Which MAC address it returns depends upon which load-balancing algorithm it is configured to use. In any event, the virtual MAC address supported by one of the routers in the group is returned.

The AVG also assigns the necessary virtual MAC addresses to each of the routers participating in the GLBP group. Up to four virtual MAC addresses can be used in any group. Each of these routers is referred to as an *active virtual forwarder (AVF)*, forwarding traffic received on its virtual MAC address. Other routers in the group serve as backup or secondary virtual forwarders, in case the AVF fails. The AVG also assigns secondary roles.

Assign the GLBP priority to a router with the following interface-configuration command:

```
Switch(config-if)# glbp group priority level
```

GLBP group numbers range from 0 to 1023. The router priority can be 1 to 255 (255 is the highest priority), defaulting to 100.

As with HSRP, another router cannot take over an active role until the current active router fails. GLBP does allow a router to pre-empt and become the AVG if it has a higher priority than the current AVG. Use the following command to enable pre-empting and to set a time delay before pre-empting begins:

```
Switch(config-if)# glbp group preempt [delay minimum seconds]
```

Routers participating in GLBP must monitor each other's presence so that another router can assume the role of a failed router. To do this, the AVG sends periodic hello messages to each of the other GLBP peers. In addition, it expects to receive hello messages from each of them.

Hello messages are sent at *hellotime* intervals, with a default of 3 seconds. If hellos aren't received from a peer within a *holdtime*, defaulting to 10 seconds, that peer is presumed to have failed. You can adjust the GLBP timers with the following interface-configuration command:

```
Switch(config-if)# glbp group timers [msec] hellotime [msec] holdtime
```

The timer values normally are given in seconds, unless they are preceded by the **msec** keyword, to indicate milliseconds. The *hellotime* can range from 1 to 60 seconds or from 50 to 60,000 milliseconds. The *holdtime* must be greater than the *hellotime* and can go up to 180 seconds or 180,000 milliseconds. You always should make the *holdtime* at least three times greater than the *hellotime*, to give some tolerance to missed or delayed hellos from a functional peer.

TIP   Although you can use the previous command to configure the GLBP timers on each peer router, it isn't necessary. Instead, just configure the timers on the router you have identified as the AVG. The AVG will advertise the timer values it is using, and every other peer will learn those values if they have not already been explicitly set.

Active Virtual Forwarder

By default, GLBP uses the periodic hello messages to detect AVF failures, too. Each router within a GLBP group must send hellos to every other GLBP peer. Hellos also are expected from every other peer. For example, if hellos from the AVF are not received by the AVG before its holdtime timer expires, the AVG assumes that the current AVF has failed. The AVG then assigns the AVF role to another router.

Naturally, the router that is given the new AVF role might already be an AVF for a different virtual MAC address. Although a router can masquerade as two different virtual MAC addresses to support the two AVF functions, it doesn't make much sense to continue doing that for a long period of time. The AVG maintains two timers that help resolve this condition.

The *redirect* timer is used to determine when the AVG will stop using the old virtual MAC address in ARP replies. The AVF corresponding to the old address continues to act as a gateway for any clients that try to use it.

When the *timeout* timer expires, the old MAC address and the virtual forwarder using it are flushed from all the GLBP peers. The AVG assumes that the previously failed AVF will not return to service, so the resources assigned to it must be reclaimed. At this point, clients still using the old MAC address in their ARP caches must refresh the entry to obtain the new virtual MAC address.

The *redirect* timer defaults to 600 seconds (10 minutes) and can range from 0 to 3600 seconds (1 hour). The *timeout* timer defaults to 14,400 seconds (4 hours) and can range from 700 to 64,800 seconds (18 hours). You can adjust these timers with the following interface-configuration command:

```
Switch(config-if)# glbp group timers redirect redirect timeout
```

GLBP also can use a weighting function to determine which router becomes the AVF for a virtual MAC address in a group. Each router begins with a maximum weight value (1 to 254). As specific interfaces go down, the weight is decreased by a configured amount. GLBP uses thresholds to determine when a router can and cannot be the AVF. If the weight falls below the lower threshold, the router must give up its AVF role. When the weight rises above the upper threshold, the router can resume its AVF role.

By default, a router receives a maximum weight of 100. If you want to make a dynamic weighting adjustment, GLBP must know which interfaces to track and how to adjust the weight. You first must define an interface as a tracked object with the following global configuration command:

```
Switch(config)# track object-number interface type mod/num {line-protocol | ip routing}
```

The *object-number* is an arbitrary index (1 to 500) that is used for weight adjustment. The condition that triggers an adjustment can be **line-protocol** (the interface line protocol is up) or **ip routing** (IP routing is enabled, the interface has an IP address, and the interface is up).

Next, you must define the weighting thresholds for the interface with the following interface-configuration command:

```
Switch(config-if)# glbp group weighting maximum [lower lower] [upper upper]
```

The maximum weight can range from 1 to 254 (default 100). The upper (default *maximum*) and lower (default 1) thresholds define when the router can and cannot be the AVF, respectively.

Finally, you must configure GLBP to know which objects to track so that the weighting can be adjusted with the following interface-configuration command:

```
Switch(config-if)# glbp group weighting track object-number [decrement value]
```

When the tracked object fails, the weighting is decremented by *value* (1 to 254, default 10).

Likewise, a router that might serve as an AVF cannot pre-empt another when it has a higher weight value.

GLBP Load Balancing

The AVG establishes load balancing by handing out virtual router MAC addresses to clients in a deterministic fashion. Naturally, the AVG first must inform the AVFs in the group of the virtual MAC address that each should use. Up to four virtual MAC addresses, assigned in sequential order, can be used in a group.

You can use one of the following load-balancing methods in a GLBP group:

- **Round robin**—Each new ARP request for the virtual router address receives the next available virtual MAC address in reply. Traffic load is distributed evenly across all routers participating as AVFs in the group, assuming that each of the clients sends and receives the same amount of traffic. This is the default method used by GLBP.

- **Weighted**—The GLBP group interface's weighting value determines the proportion of traffic that should be sent to that AVF. A higher weighting results in more frequent ARP replies containing the virtual MAC address of that router. If interface tracking is not configured, the maximum weighting value configured is used to set the relative proportions among AVFs.

- **Host-dependent**—Each client that generates an ARP request for the virtual router address always receives the same virtual MAC address in reply. This method is used if the clients have a need for a consistent gateway MAC address. (Otherwise, a client could receive replies with different MAC addresses for the router over time, depending on the load-balancing method in use.)

On the AVG router (or its successors), use the following interface-configuration command to define the method:

```
Switch(config-if)# glbp group load-balancing [round-robin | weighted | host-dependent]
```

Enabling GLBP

To enable GLBP, you must assign a virtual IP address to the group by using the following interface-configuration command:

```
Switch(config-if)# glbp group ip [ip-address [secondary]]
```

If the *ip-address* is not given in the command, it is learned from another router in the group. However, if this router is to be the AVG, you must explicitly configure the IP address; otherwise, no other router knows what the value should be.

Figure 14-3 shows a typical network in which three multilayer switches are participating in a common GLBP group. CatalystA is elected the AVG, so it coordinates the entire GLBP process. The AVG answers all ARP requests for the virtual router 192.168.1.1. It has identified itself, CatalystB, and CatalystC as AVFs for the group.

Figure 14-3 *Multilayer Switches in a GLBP Group*

In this figure, round-robin load balancing is being used. Each of the client PCs looks for the virtual router address in turn, from left to right. Each time the AVG replies, the next sequential virtual MAC address is sent back to a client. After the fourth PC sends a request, all three virtual MAC addresses (and AVF routers) have been used, so the AVG cycles back to the first virtual MAC address.

Notice that only one GLBP group has been configured, and all clients know of only one gateway IP address: 192.168.1.1. However, all uplinks are being utilized, and all routers are proportionately forwarding traffic.

Figure 14-4 *How GLBP Reacts to a Component Failure*

Redundancy is also inherent in the GLBP group: CatalystA is the AVG, but the next-highest priority router can take over if the AVG fails. All routers have been given an AVF role for a unique virtual MAC address in the group. If one AVF fails, some clients remember the last-known virtual MAC address that was handed out. Therefore, another of the routers also takes over the AVF role for the failed router, causing the virtual MAC address to remain alive at all times.

Figure 14-4 shows how these redundancy features react when the current active AVG fails. Before its failure, CatalystA was the AVG because of its higher GLBP priority. After it failed, CatalystB became the AVG, answering ARP requests with the appropriate virtual MAC address for gateway 192.168.1.1. CatalystA also had been acting as an AVF, participating in the gateway load balancing. CatalystB also picks up this responsibility, using its virtual MAC address 0000.0000.0002 along with the one CatalystA had been using, 000.0000.0001. Therefore, any hosts that know the gateway by any of its virtual MAC addresses still can reach a live gateway or AVF.

You can implement the scenario shown in Figures 14-3 and 14-4 with the configuration commands in Example 14-7 for CatalystA, CatalystB, and CatalystC, respectively.

Example 14-7 *Configuring GLBP Load Balancing*

```
CatalystA(config)# interface vlan 50
CatalystA(config-if)# ip address 192.168.1.10 255.255.255.0
CatalystA(config-if)# glbp 1 priority 200
CatalystA(config-if)# glbp 1 preempt
CatalystA(config-if)# glbp 1 ip 192.168.1.1
CatalystB(config)# interface vlan 50
CatalystB(config-if)# ip address 192.168.1.11 255.255.255.0
CatalystB(config-if)# glbp 1 priority 150
CatalystB(config-if)# glbp 1 preempt
CatalystB(config-if)# glbp 1 ip 192.168.1.1
CatalystC(config)# interface vlan 50
CatalystC(config-if)# ip address 192.168.1.12 255.255.255.0
CatalystC(config-if)# glbp 1 priority 100
CatalystC(config-if)# glbp 1 ip 192.168.1.1
```

You can verify GLBP operation with the **show glbp [brief]** command, as demonstrated in Example 14-8. With the **brief** keyword, the GLBP roles are summarized showing the interface, GLBP group number (Grp), virtual forwarder number (Fwd), GLBP priority (Pri), state, and addresses.

Example 14-8 *Verifying GLBP Operation*

```
CatalystA# show glbp brief
Interface   Grp  Fwd Pri State    Address         Active router   Standby router
Vl50        1    -   200 Active   192.168.1.1     local           192.168.1.11
Vl50        1    1   7   Active   0007.b400.0101  local           -
Vl50        1    2   7   Listen   0007.b400.0102  192.168.1.11    -
Vl50        1    3   7   Listen   0007.b400.0103  192.168.1.13    -
CatalystA#
CatalystB# show glbp brief
Interface   Grp  Fwd Pri State    Address         Active router   Standby router
Vl50        1    -   150 Standby  192.168.1.1     192.168.1.10    local
```

Example 14-8   *Verifying GLBP Operation (Continued)*

```
V150        1    1    7    Listen    0007.b400.0101    192.168.1.10    -
V150        1    2    7    Active    0007.b400.0102    local           -
V150        1    3    7    Listen    0007.b400.0103    192.168.1.13    -
CatalystB#
CatalystC# show glbp brief
Interface   Grp  Fwd  Pri  State     Address           Active router    Standby router
V150        1    -    100  Listen    192.168.1.1       192.168.1.10     192.168.1.11
V150        1    1    7    Listen    0007.b400.0101    192.168.1.10     -
V150        1    2    7    Listen    0007.b400.0102    192.168.1.11     -
V150        1    3    7    Active    0007.b400.0103    local            -
CatalystC#
```

Notice that CatalystA is shown to be the AVG because it has a dash in the Fwd column and is in the Active state. It also is acting as AVF for virtual forwarder number 1. Because the GLBP group has three routers, there are three virtual forwarders and virtual MAC addresses. CatalystA is in the Listen state for forwarders number 2 and 3, waiting to be given an active role in case one of those AVFs fails.

CatalystB is shown to have the Standby role, waiting to take over in case the AVG fails. It is the AVF for virtual forwarder number 2.

Finally, CatalystC has the lowest GLBP priority, so it stays in the Listen state waiting for the active or standby AVG to fail. It is also the AVF for virtual forwarder number 3.

You also can display more detailed information about the GLBP configuration and status by omitting the **brief** keyword. Example 14-9 shows this output on the AVG router. Because this is the AVG, the virtual forwarder roles it has assigned to each of the routers in the GLBP group also are shown.

Example 14-9   *Displaying Detailed GLBP Configuration and Status Information*

```
CatalystA# show glbp
Vlan50 - Group 1
  State is Active
    7 state changes, last state change 03:28:05
  Virtual IP address is 192.168.1.1
  Hello time 3 sec, hold time 10 sec
    Next hello sent in 1.672 secs
  Redirect time 600 sec, forwarder time-out 14400 sec
  Preemption enabled, min delay 0 sec
  Active is local
  Standby is 192.168.1.11, priority 150 (expires in 9.632 sec)
  Priority 200 (configured)
  Weighting 100 (default 100), thresholds: lower 1, upper 100
```

continues

Example 14-9 *Displaying Detailed GLBP Configuration and Status Information (Continued)*

```
 Load balancing: round-robin
 There are 3 forwarders (1 active)
 Forwarder 1
   State is Active
     3 state changes, last state change 03:27:37
   MAC address is 0007.b400.0101 (default)
   Owner ID is 00d0.0229.b80a
   Redirection enabled
   Preemption enabled, min delay 30 sec
   Active is local, weighting 100
 Forwarder 2
   State is Listen
   MAC address is 0007.b400.0102 (learnt)
   Owner ID is 0007.b372.dc4a
   Redirection enabled, 598.308 sec remaining (maximum 600 sec)
   Time to live: 14398.308 sec (maximum 14400 sec)
   Preemption enabled, min delay 30 sec
   Active is 192.168.1.11 (primary), weighting 100 (expires in 8.308 sec)
 Forwarder 3
   State is Listen
   MAC address is 0007.b400.0103 (learnt)
   Owner ID is 00d0.ff8a.2c0a
   Redirection enabled, 599.892 sec remaining (maximum 600 sec)
   Time to live: 14399.892 sec (maximum 14400 sec)
   Preemption enabled, min delay 30 sec
   Active is 192.168.1.13 (primary), weighting 100 (expires in 9.892 sec)
 CatalystA#
```

Verifying Gateway Redundancy

To verify the operation of the features discussed in this chapter, you can use the commands listed in Table 14-4. In particular, look for the active, standby, or backup routers in use.

Table 14-4 *Gateway Redundancy Verification Commands*

Task	Command Syntax
HSRP and VRRP	
Display HSRP status	**show standby brief**
Display HSRP on an interface	**show standby** *type mod/num*
Display VRRP status	**show vrrp brief all**
Display VRRP on an interface	**show vrrp interface** *type mod/num*
GLBP	
Display status of a GLBP group	**show glbp** [*group*] [**brief**]

Redundancy Within a Switch Chassis

The router or gateway redundancy protocols, such as HSRP, VRRP, and GLBP, can provide high availability only for the default gateway addresses. If one of the redundant gateway routers fails, another can pick up the pieces and appear to be the same gateway address.

But what happens to the devices that are connected directly to the router that fails? If the switching or routing engine fails, packets probably will not get routed and interfaces will go down. Some Cisco switches have the capability to provide redundancy for the supervisor engine itself. This is accomplished by having redundant hardware in place within a switch chassis, ready to take over during a failure.

You also should consider switch power as a vital part of achieving high availability. For example, if a switch has a single power supply and a single power cord, the whole switch will fail if the power supply fails or if the power cord accidentally is unplugged. Some switch platforms can have multiple power supplies; if one power supply fails, another immediately takes over the load.

Redundant Switch Supervisors

Modular switch platforms such as the Catalyst 4500R and 6500 can accept two supervisor modules installed in a single chassis. The first supervisor module to successfully boot up becomes the active supervisor for the chassis. The other supervisor remains in a standby role, waiting for the active supervisor to fail.

The active supervisor always is allowed to boot up and become fully initialized and operational. All switching functions are provided by the active supervisor. The standby supervisor, however, is allowed to boot up and initialize only to a certain level. When the active module fails, the standby module can proceed to initialize any remaining functions and take over the active role.

Redundant supervisor modules can be configured in several modes. The redundancy mode affects how the two supervisors handshake and synchronize information. In addition, the mode limits the standby supervisor's state of readiness. The more ready the standby module is allowed to become, the less initialization and failover time will be required.

You can use the following redundancy modes on Catalyst switches:

- **Route Processor Redundancy (RPR)**—The redundant supervisor is only partially booted and initialized. When the active module fails, the standby module must reload every other module in the switch and then initialize all the supervisor functions.

■ **Route Processor Redundancy Plus (RPR+)**—The redundant supervisor is booted, allowing the supervisor and route engine to initialize. No Layer 2 or Layer 3 functions are started, however. When the active module fails, the standby module finishes initializing without reloading other switch modules. This allows switch ports to retain their state.

■ **Stateful Switchover (SSO)**—The redundant supervisor is fully booted and initialized. Both the startup and running configuration contents are synchronized between the supervisor modules. Layer 2 information is maintained on both supervisors so that hardware switching can continue during a failover. The state of the switch interfaces also is maintained on both supervisors so that links don't flap during a failover.

TIP Sometimes the redundancy mode terminology can be confusing. In addition to the RPR, RPR+, and SSO terms, you might see Single Router Mode (SRM) and Dual Router Mode (DRM).

SRM simply means that two route processors (integrated into the supervisors) are being used, but only one of them is active at any time. In DRM, two route processors are active at all times. HSRP usually is used to provide redundancy in DRM.

Although RPR and RPR+ have only one active supervisor, the route processor portion is not initialized on the standby unit. Therefore, SRM is not compatible with RPR or RPR+.

SRM is inherent with SSO, which brings up the standby route processor. You usually will find the two redundancy terms together, as "SRM with SSO."

Configuring the Redundancy Mode

Table 14-5 details the redundancy modes you can configure on supported switch platforms.

Table 14-5 *Redundancy Modes, Platform Support, and Failover Time*

Redundancy Mode	Supported Platforms	Failover Time
RPR	Catalyst 6500 Supervisors 2 and 720, Catalyst 4500R Supervisors IV and V	Good (> 2 minutes)
Route Processor Redundancy Plus (RPR+)	Catalyst 6500 Supervisors 2 and 720	Better (> 30 seconds)
Stateful Switchover (SSO)	Catalyst 6500 Supervisor 720, Catalyst 4500R Supervisors IV and V	Best (> 1 second)

Figure 14-5 shows how the supervisor redundancy modes compare with respect to the functions they perform. The shaded functions are performed as the standby supervisor initializes and then waits for the active supervisor to fail. When a failure is detected, the remaining functions must be performed in sequence before the standby supervisor can become fully active. Notice how the redundancy modes get progressively more initialized and ready to become active.

Figure 14-5 *Standby Supervisor Readiness as a Function of Redundancy Mode*

You can configure the supervisor redundancy mode by entering the redundancy-configuration mode with the following command:

```
Router(config)# redundancy
```

Next, select the redundancy mode with one of the following commands:

```
Router(config-red)# mode {rpr | rpr-plus | sso}
```

If you are configuring redundancy for the first time on the switch, you must enter the previous commands on both supervisor modules. When the redundancy mode is enabled, you will make all configuration changes on the active supervisor only. The running configuration is synchronized automatically from the active to the standby module.

TIP   If you configure RPR+ with the **rpr-plus** keyword, the supervisor attempts to bring up RPR+ with its peer module. The IOS images must be of exactly the same release before RPR+ will work. If the images differ, the supervisor automatically falls back to RPR mode instead.

You can verify the redundancy mode and state of the supervisor modules by using the following command:

```
Router# show redundancy states
```

The output in Example 14-10 shows that the switch is using RPR+ and that the second supervisor module (denoted by unit ID 2 and "my state") holds the active role. The other supervisor module is in the standby state and is "HOT", meaning that it has initialized as far as the redundancy mode will allow.

Example 14-10   *Verifying Supervisor Module Redundancy Mode and State*

```
Router# show redundancy states
       my state = 13 -ACTIVE
     peer state = 8   -STANDBY HOT
           Mode = Duplex
           Unit = Secondary
        Unit ID = 2

Redundancy Mode (Operational) = Route Processor Redundancy Plus
Redundancy Mode (Configured)  = Route Processor Redundancy Plus
     Split Mode = Disabled
   Manual Swact = Enabled
 Communications = Up

   client count = 11
 client_notification_TMR = 30000 milliseconds
         keep_alive TMR = 9000 milliseconds
       keep_alive count = 1
   keep_alive threshold = 18
           RF debug mask = 0x0
Router#
```

Configuring Supervisor Synchronization

By default, the active supervisor synchronizes its startup configuration and configuration register values with the standby supervisor. You also can specify other information that should be synchronized.

First, use the following commands to enter the main-cpu configuration mode:

```
Router(config)# redundancy
Router(config-red)# main-cpu
```

Then use the following command to specify the information that will be synchronized:

```
Router(config-r-mc)# auto-sync {startup-config | config-register | bootvar}
```

You can repeat the command if you need to use more than one of the keywords. To return to the default, use the **auto-sync standard** command.

Non-Stop Forwarding

You can enable another redundancy feature along with SSO on the Catalyst 4500R and 6500 (Supervisor 720 only). Non-Stop Forwarding (NSF) is an interactive method that focuses on quickly rebuilding the routing information base (RIB) table after a supervisor switchover. The RIB is used to generate the FIB table for CEF, which is downloaded to any switch modules or hardware that can perform CEF.

Instead of waiting on any configured Layer 3 routing protocols to converge and rebuild the FIB, a router can use NSF to get assistance from other NSF-aware neighbors. The neighbors then can provide routing information to the standby supervisor, allowing the routing tables to be assembled quickly. In a nutshell, the Cisco-proprietary NSF functions must be built into the routing protocols on both the router that will need assistance and the router that will provide assistance.

NSF is supported by the BGP, EIGRP, OSPF, and IS-IS routing protocols. NSF is available on the Catalyst 6500 Supervisor 720 (with the integrated MSFC3) and on the Catalyst 4500R Supervisor III, IV, and V running IOS Software Release 12.2(20)EWA or later.

To configure NSF, you must add the commands in Table 14-6 to any routing protocol configuration on the switch.

Table 14-6 *Configuring NSF (by Routing Protocol)*

Routing Protocol	Configuration Commands
BGP	`Router(config)# router bgp `*`as-number`* `Router(config-router)# bgp graceful-restart`
EIGRP	`Router(config)# router eigrp `*`as-number`* `Router(config-router)# nsf`
OSPF	`Router(config)# router ospf `*`process-id`* `Router(config-router)# nsf`
IS-IS	`Router(config)# router isis [`*`tag`*`]` `Router(config-router)# nsf [cisco	ietf]`   `Router(config-router)# nsf interval [`*`minutes`*`]`   `Router(config-router)# nsf t3 {manual [`*`seconds`*`]	adjacency}`   `Router(config-router)# nsf interface wait `*`seconds`*

Redundant Power Supplies

The Cisco Catalyst 6500 and 4500R platforms can accept two power supply modules in a single chassis. The power supplies must be identical, having the same power input and maximum power output ratings. The switch can be configured to operate in one of two possible power modes:

- **Combined mode**—Both power supplies work together to share the total power load for all modules that are installed in the switch chassis. The total load required can exceed the maximum power output rating of one power supply but must not exceed the sum of both supplies.

  Combined mode is useful for meeting large power requirements if many switch modules are installed or if Power over Ethernet (PoE) is being used to supply power to end devices such as IP Telephones. However, combined mode *does not* provide power redundancy. If one power supply fails, the switch powers down some of its modules until the required power load can be met by the one functioning power supply.

- **Redundant mode**—Each of the installed power supplies can supply the total power load that is required by the whole switch chassis. If one power supply fails, the other immediately can carry the total power load of the switch without powering down any modules.

By default, a switch is configured for redundant mode. If two power supplies are installed and functioning, they are managed as redundant replacements for each other. Both supplies are enabled and active, as if they were both supplying power. In fact, you probably won't be able to tell which supply is actually powering the switch until one of them is turned off or fails.

You can display the current power configuration and status of a switch with the following command:

Switch# **show power** [**redundancy-mode** | **status** | **available** | **used** | **total**]

If you don't use any of the optional keywords, the resulting output yields all information about the system power. For instance, notice that the switch in Example 14-11 is in redundant mode and that both power supplies are operational.

Example 14-11 *Verifying Switch Redundant Mode and Power Supply Operational Status*

```
Switch# show power
system power redundancy mode = redundant
system power total =     1153.32 Watts (27.46 Amps @ 42V)
system power used =       693.42 Watts (16.51 Amps @ 42V)
system power available =  459.90 Watts (10.95 Amps @ 42V)
                      Power-Capacity PS-Fan Output Oper
PS    Type            Watts    A @42V Status Status State
----  ----------------  -------  ------ ------- ------- -----
1     WS-CAC-1300W    1153.32 27.46  OK      OK      on
2     WS-CAC-1300W    1153.32 27.46  OK      OK      on
                      Pwr-Requested  Pwr-Allocated  Admin Oper
Slot  Card-Type       Watts    A @42V Watts    A @42V State State
----  ----------------  -------  ------ -------  ------ ----- -----
1     WS-X6K-SUP2-2GE  145.32  3.46   145.32  3.46   on    on
2                        -       -     145.32  3.46   -     -
3     WS-X6348-RJ45    100.38  2.39   100.38  2.39   on    on
4     WS-X6516-GBIC    142.80  3.40   142.80  3.40   on    on
5     WS-C6500-SFM     117.18  2.79   117.18  2.79   on    on
Switch#
```

The **show power** command also displays information about the status of each switch module, the amount of power it has requested to receive, and the amount of power it is actually being budgeted. Most switch modules have a fixed power requirement, so the power requested and allocated values are equal.

One important exception is any switch module that supplies inline power or PoE to end devices. These end devices can request a power budget when they initialize and can request a different budget at any later time. Cisco IP Telephones and wireless access points are good examples of this. Power requests are handled through Cisco Discovery Protocol (CDP) exchanges between the device and the switch. You can display the current power status of inline power switch ports with the **show power inline** command, as demonstrated in Example 14-12.

Example 14-12 *Verifying Inline Power Switch Port Status*

```
Switch# show power inline
Interface  Admin    Oper       Power       Device
                               (Watts)
---------- -----  ----------  -------  ------------------
Fa3/1      auto   off              0   n/a
Fa3/2      auto   on             6.2   cisco AIR-AP1230B-A
Fa3/3      auto   on             6.2   cisco AIR-AP1230B-A
Fa3/4      auto   on             5.6   Cisco IP Phone 7905
Fa3/5      auto   on             5.6   Cisco IP Phone 7905
Fa3/6      auto   on             6.3   Cisco IP Phone 7940
Fa3/7      auto   on             6.3   Cisco IP Phone 7940
Fa3/8      auto   on             6.3   Cisco IP Phone 7940
Fa3/9      auto   off              0   n/a
Fa3/10     auto   on             6.3   Cisco IP Phone 7912
Fa3/11     auto   off              0   n/a
Fa3/12     auto   on             6.3   Cisco IP Phone 7940
Fa3/13     auto   on             6.3   Cisco IP Phone 7940
Fa3/14     auto   on             6.3   Cisco IP Phone 7940
[output omitted]
```

You can change the power supply mode by using the following command:

```
Switch(config)# power redundancy-mode {redundant | combined}
```

You also can control the power that is being supplied to a switch module. For example, if you want to remove a module for repair or relocation, you can disable its power before it is pulled out of the chassis. Use the following command to control the power to the module in chassis slot number *slot*:

```
Switch(config)# [no] power enable module slot
```

Without the **no** keyword, the module is powered on; include the **no** keyword to remove power from the module.

Foundation Summary

The Foundation Summary is a collection of information that provides a convenient review of many key concepts in this chapter. If you are already comfortable with the topics in this chapter, this summary can help you recall a few details. If you just read this chapter, this review should help solidify some key facts. If you are doing your final preparation before the exam, this information is a convenient way to review the day before the exam.

Table 14-7 *Comparison of Router Redundancy Protocols*

	HSRP	VRRP	GLBP
Standardized	No; Cisco-proprietary, RFC 2281	Yes; RFC 2338	No; Cisco-proprietary
Router roles	Active router, standby router	Master router, backup router	AVG, AVF
Load balancing	Only through multiple HSRP groups, different client gateways	Only through multiple VRRP groups, different client gateways	Inherent with one GLBP group; all clients use same gateway; several methods available
Interface tracking	Yes	No	Yes
Virtual router MAC address	0000.0c07.acxx	0000.5e00.01xx	Assigned by AVG

Table 14-8 *HSRP Configuration Commands*

Task	Command Syntax
Set the HSRP priority	**standby** *group* **priority** *priority*
Set the HSRP timers	**standby** *group* **timer**s *hello holdtime*
Allow router pre-emption	**standby** *group* **preempt** [**delay** *seconds*]
Use group authentication	**standby** *group* **authentication** *string*
Adjust priority by tracking an interface	**standby** *group* **track** *type mod/num decrementvalue*
Assign the virtual router address	**standby** *group* **ip** *ip-address* [**secondary**]

Table 14-9 *VRRP Configuration Commands*

Task	Command Syntax
Assign a VRRP router priority (default 100)	**vrrp** *group* **priority** *level*
Alter the advertisement timer (default 1 second)	**vrrp** *group* **timers advertise** [**msec**] *interval*
Learn the advertisement interval from the master router	**vrrp** *group* **timers learn**
Disable pre-empting (default is to pre-empt)	**no vrrp** *group* **preempt**
Change the pre-empt delay (default 0 seconds)	**vrrp** *group* **preempt** [**delay** *seconds*]
Use authentication for advertisements	**vrrp** *group* **authentication** *string*
Assign a virtual IP address	**vrrp** *group* **ip** *ip-address* [**secondary**]

Table 14-10 *GLBP Configuration Commands*

Task	Command Syntax
Assign a GLBP priority	**glbp** *group* **priority** *level*
Allow GLBP pre-emption	**glbp** *group* **preempt** [**delay minimum** *seconds*]
Define an object to be tracked	**track** *object-number* **interface** *type mod/num* {**line-protocol** ı **ip routing**}
Define the weighting thresholds	**glbp** *group* **weighting** *maximum* [**lower** *lower*] [**upper** *upper*]
Track an object	**glbp** *group* **weighting track** *object-number* [**decrement** *value*]
Choose the load-balancing method	**glbp** *group* **load-balancing** [**round-robin** ı **weighted** ı **host-dependent**]
Assign a virtual router address	**glbp** *group* **ip** [*ip-address* [**secondary**]]

Q&A

The questions and scenarios in this book are more difficult than what you should experience on the actual exam. The questions do not attempt to cover more breadth or depth than the exam; however, they are designed to make sure that you know the answer. Rather than allowing you to derive the answers from clues hidden inside the questions themselves, the questions challenge your understanding and recall of the subject. Hopefully, these questions will help limit the number of exam questions on which you narrow your choices to two options and then guess.

You can find the answers to these questions in Appendix A.

1. A multilayer switch has been configured with the command **standby 5 priority 120**. What router-redundancy protocol is being used?

2. What feature can you use to prevent other routers from accidentally participating in an HSRP group?

3. What command can configure an HSRP group to use a virtual router address of 192.168.222.100?

4. The **show standby vlan 271** command produces the following output:

```
Vlan271 - Group 1
  Local state is Active, priority 210, may preempt
  Hellotime 3 holdtime 40 configured hellotime 3 sec holdtime 40 sec
  Next hello sent in 00:00:00.594
  Virtual IP address is 192.168.111.1 configured
    Secondary virtual IP address 10.1.111.1
    Secondary virtual IP address 172.21.111.1
  Active router is local
  Standby router is unknown expires in 00:00:37
  Standby virtual mac address is 0000.0c07.ac01
  2 state changes, last state change 5d17h
```

If the local router fails, which router takes over the active role for the virtual router address 192.168.111.1?

5. What is meant by pre-empting in HSRP?

6. What protocols discussed in this chapter support interface tracking?

7. The **show standby brief** command has been used to check the status of all HSRP groups on the local router. The output from this command is as follows:

```
Switch# show standby brief
                     P indicates configured to preempt.
                     |
Interface Grp Prio P  State   Active addr  Standby addr   Group addr
V1100      1   210  P  Active  local        192.168.75.2   192.168.75.1
V1101      1   210  P  Active  local        192.168.107.2  192.168.107.1
V1102      1   210  P  Active  local        192.168.71.2   192.168.71.1
```

   Each interface is shown to have Group 1. Is this a problem?

8. How many HSRP groups are needed to load-balance traffic over two routers?

9. What load-balancing methods can GLBP use?

10. What command can you use to see the status of the active and standby routers on the VLAN 171 interface?

11. How many GLBP groups are needed to load-balance traffic over four routers?

12. To use NSF on a multilayer switch with redundant supervisor modules, what must be configured in addition to the redundancy mode? What else must be present in the network?

13. How is SSO different from SRM with SSO redundancy mode?

14. If two Catalyst 6500 power supplies are configured with the **power redundancy-mode combined**, what will happen if one of them fails?

This chapter covers the following topics that you need to master for the CCNP BCMSN exam:

- **Multicast Overview**—This section discusses multicast addressing and general multicast traffic forwarding.

- **Routing Multicast Traffic**—This section covers the protocols used by Layer 3 devices to maintain multicast groups and their members, and to constrain multicast forwarding.

- **Switching Multicast Traffic**—This section explains techniques that you can use to intelligently forward multicast traffic at Layer 2.

- **Verifying Multicast**—This section provides a brief summary of the commands that can verify the configuration and operation of multicast routing and switching.

CHAPTER 15

IP Multicast

Multicast traffic is typically sent by one source and received by a group of recipients that might be spread throughout a network. In addition, the recipients within the group might change over time. Examples of multicast traffic include video streams for instruction or entertainment, certain audio conference calls, and one-to-many PC file-imaging applications.

Because not everyone on a network wants to receive the traffic from a multicast source, switches and routers must have some means of forwarding traffic to exactly the destinations that want to receive it. This chapter covers IP multicast and the various protocols used to forward multicast packets.

"Do I Know This Already?" Quiz

The purpose of the "Do I Know This Already?" quiz is to help you decide what parts of this chapter to use. If you already intend to read the entire chapter, you do not necessarily need to answer these questions now.

The quiz, derived from the major sections in the "Foundation Topics" portion of the chapter, helps you determine how to spend your limited study time.

Table 15-1 outlines the major topics discussed in this chapter and the "Do I Know This Already?" quiz questions that correspond to those topics.

Table 15-1 *"Do I Know This Already?" Foundation Topics Section-to-Question Mapping*

Foundation Topics Section	Questions Covered in This Section	Score
Multicast Overview	1–7	
Routing Multicast Traffic	8–11	
Switching Multicast Traffic	12	
Total Score		

CAUTION The goal of self-assessment is to gauge your mastery of the topics in this chapter. If you do not know the answer to a question or are only partially sure of the answer, you should mark this question wrong. Giving yourself credit for an answer you correctly guess skews your self-assessment results and might give you a false sense of security.

1. How many sources are typically present in a multicast group?

   a. 1

   b. 2

   c. As many as are registered with the router

   d. Cannot be determined

2. Which one of the following is a multicast address?

   a. 128.224.1.1

   b. 172.17.224.1

   c. 225.17.1.1

   d. 242.17.1.1

3. 224.1.2.3 corresponds to which of the following MAC addresses?

   a. 0102.0300.0000

   b. 0100.5e01.0203

   c. e000.0001.0203

   d. 1000.5e01.0203

4. How many unique multicast IP addresses can correspond to one multicast MAC address?

   a. 1

   b. 2

   c. 8

   d. 32

5. Which of the following is the test that is performed before a multicast packet can be forwarded?

   a. Shortest path first

   b. Cyclic redundancy check

   c. Reverse Path Forwarding

   d. Multicast route verification

6. Which protocol registers hosts for multicast group membership?

   a. CGMP

   b. IGRP

   c. IGMP

   d. PIM

7. A host sends Internet Group Management Protocol (IGMP) packets to which of the following?

   a. The local switch

   b. The local router

   c. The multicast source

   d. The root of the multicast tree

8. If a multicast group has recipients on every subnet, which of the PIM modes should be used?

   a. Dense mode

   b. Sparse mode

   c. Sparse-compress mode

   d. Flood mode

9. Which type of tree structure is built for sparse-mode multicast routing?

   a. Spanning tree

   b. Shared tree

   c. Sparse tree

   d. Simple tree

10. What router maintains the RP-to-group correlation for Auto-RP in PIMv1?

   a. RP agent

   b. PIM root

   c. Mapping agent

   d. RP discovery server

11. What router advertises candidate RP routers in PIMv2?

   a. Auto-RP

   b. Mapping agent

   c. Bootstrap router

   d. PIM root

12. Which of the following methods requires a router to assist a Layer 2 switch in constraining multicast traffic?

   a. PIM

   b. IGMP

   c. CGMP

   d. IGMP snooping

You can find the answers to the "Do I Know This Already?" quiz in Appendix A, "Answers to Chapter 'Do I Know This Already?' Quizzes and Q&A Sections." The suggested choices for your next step are as follows:

■ **10 or less overall score**—Read the entire chapter. This includes the "Foundation Topics," "Foundation Summary," and "Q&A" sections.

■ **11 or 12 overall score**—If you want more review on these topics, skip to the "Foundation Summary" section and then go to the "Q&A" section at the end of the chapter. Otherwise, move to Chapter 16, "IP Telephony."

Foundation Topics

Multicast Overview

In a network, three basic types of IP traffic traverse the routers and switches:

- **Unicast**—Packets that are sent from one source host address to a single destination host address. A router or Layer 3 switch forwards them by finding the destination IP address in its routing table. A Layer 2 switch relies on the destination's MAC address only.

- **Broadcast**—Packets that are sent from one source host address to a broadcast destination address. The destination can be all hosts (255.255.255.255), a directed broadcast to a subnet (that is, 192.168.10.255), or some portion of a subnet. A router or Layer 3 switch will not forward these by default unless some method of relaying has been configured. A Layer 2 switch floods the packet out all ports on the destination VLAN.

- **Multicast**—Packets that are sent from one source host address to a special group-based destination address. The destination represents only the hosts that are interested in receiving the packets, and no others. A router or Layer 3 switch does not forward these packets by default unless some form of multicast routing is enabled. A Layer 2 switch cannot learn the location of the destination multicast address, so the packets are flooded to all ports on the destination VLAN by default.

Two extremes are covered here:

- A unicast, which travels from host to host

- A broadcast, which travels from one host to everyone on a segment

Multicast falls somewhere in the middle. The intention is to send packets from one host to only the users who want to receive them—namely, those known to belong in the designated *multicast group*. Ideally, the recipients of multicast packets could be located anywhere, not just on the local segment.

Multicast traffic is generally unidirectional. Because many hosts are receiving the same data, it makes little sense to allow one of the hosts to send packets back toward the source over the multicast mechanism. Instead, a receiving host can send return traffic to the source as a unicast. Multicast traffic also is sent in a best-effort connectionless format. UDP (connectionless) commonly is used, whereas TCP (connection-oriented) is not.

Hosts that want to receive data from a multicast source can join or leave a multicast group dynamically. In addition, a host can decide to become a member of more than one multicast group at any time. The principal network task is then to figure out how to deliver multicast traffic to the group members without disturbing other uninterested hosts.

Multicast Addressing

Routers and switches must have a way to distinguish multicast traffic from unicasts or broadcasts. This is done through IP addressing by reserving the Class D IP address range, 224.0.0.0 through 239.255.255.255, strictly for multicasting. Network devices quickly can pick out multicast IP addresses by looking at the four most significant bits, which are always 1110. For example, the first octet of 224.0.0.0 is 224, which also can be written as **1110** 0000. The upper end of the address range begins with 239, or **1110** 1111.

How does a router or switch relate a multicast IP address with a MAC address? There is no Address Resolution Protocol (ARP) equivalent for multicast address mapping. Instead, a reserved organizationally unique identifier (OUI) value is set aside so that multicast MAC addresses always begin with **0100.5e** (plus the next lower bit, which is 0). The lower 28 bits of the multicast IP address also must be mapped into the lower 23 bits of the MAC address by a simple algorithm.

Figure 15-1 shows the address mapping concept. Only the lower 23 bits of the address are copied from IP to MAC (or vice versa). The high-order prefixes of both IP and MAC addresses are fixed, predictable values.

Figure 15-1 *Multicast IP-to-MAC Address Translation*

Notice, however, that 5 bits of the IP address are not transferred into the MAC address at all. This gives the possibility that the multicast MAC addresses are not entirely unique. There are 32 (5 bits' worth) different multicast IP addresses that all could correspond to a single multicast MAC address.

Because of this ambiguity, a multicast host has a small problem when it receives an Ethernet frame destined for a multicast MAC address. That one MAC address actually could correspond to 32 different multicast IP addresses. Therefore, the host must receive and examine every frame that has the MAC address it is interested in—regardless of which of the 32 IP addresses the frame was originally destined for. The host then must examine the IP header inside each frame to verify that the more specific IP multicast address is a desired multicast group. If not, the frame is discarded.

Some of the IP multicast address space has been reserved for a particular use:

- **Complete multicast space: 224.0.0.0 through 239.255.255.255**—This entire range of IP addresses can be used for multicast purposes.

- **Link-local addresses (224.0.0.0 through 224.0.0.255)**—This space can be used by network protocols only on the local network segment. Routers do not forward these packets.

   This space includes the *all-hosts* address 224.0.0.1, *all-routers* 224.0.0.2, *OSPF-routers* 224.0.0.5, and so on. These are also known as *fixed-group addresses* because they are well-known and predefined.

- **Administratively scoped addresses (239.0.0.0 through 239.255.255.255)**—This space can be used in private multicast domains, much like the private IP address ranges from RFC 1918. These addresses are not routed between domains, so they can be reused.

- **Globally scoped addresses (224.0.1.0 through 238.255.255.255)**—This space can be used by any entity; these addresses can be routed across an organization or the Internet, so they must be unique and globally significant. (Think of this range as neither local nor private; it is the rest of the multicast range.)

Routing Multicast Traffic

IP multicast traffic must be routed, just like any other Layer 3 packets. The difference is in knowing where to forward the packets. Unicast IP packets have only one destination interface (even if multiple paths exist), whereas multicast IP packets can have many destination interfaces, depending upon where the recipients are located.

Several multicast routing protocols are available. This text focuses only on Protocol Independent Multicast (PIM), as does the BCMSN course and exam. Multicast routing as a whole is better covered in IP routing courses and textbooks. This section provides an overview of the PIM operation to provide a good understanding of the routing concepts. This is a necessary foundation for understanding multicast switching (Layer 2).

Regardless of the multicast routing protocol used, you first must enable multicast routing on the router or switch with the following global configuration command:

```
Switch(config)# ip multicast-routing
```

Multicast Trees

The routers (or multilayer switches) in a network must determine a forwarding path to get multicast packets from the source (sender) to each of the recipients (receivers). Think of the network as a tree structure. At the root of the tree is the source, blindly sending IP packets to a specific multicast address. The source is never aware of list of hosts or recipients that are members of a multicast group. Instead, it depends upon multicast routers and switches to handle the actual multicast packet delivery.

Each router along the way sits at a branch or fork in the tree. If a router knows which branches of the tree have interested the multicast group recipients located on them, it also knows which of its interfaces to replicate the multicast packets onto. Some routers have no downstream recipients, so they do not need to forward the multicast traffic. Other routers have many downstream recipients.

This tree structure is somewhat similar to a spanning-tree topology because it has a root at one end and leaf nodes (the recipients) at the other end. Although a spanning tree must connect the root to all end nodes, the multicast tree does not necessarily have to. The tree is also loop free so that none of the multicast traffic gets fed back into the tree.

Reverse Path Forwarding

Routers usually have one test to perform on every multicast packet they receive. *Reverse Path Forwarding (RPF)* is a means to make sure packets are not being injected back into the tree at an unexpected location. In other words, all multicast traffic always should flow away from the root of the tree, from the source toward the recipients.

As a packet is received on a router interface, the source IP address is inspected. The idea is to look backward and verify that the packet arrived on the same interface where the source can be found. If this is true, the packet actually is proceeding out the branches of the tree, away from the source. If it is not true, someone else has injected the packet on an unexpected interface, headed back down the branches of the tree toward the source.

To perform the RPF test, the PIM router looks up the source address in its unicast routing table. Notice that this is the *reverse* of normal packet forwarding, which uses the destination address. If the next-hop interface used to reach the source address also matches the interface where the packet was received, the packet can be forwarded or replicated toward the multicast recipients. If not, the packet quietly is discarded.

IGMP

How does a router know of the recipients in a multicast group, much less their locations? To receive multicast traffic from a source, every recipient first must join a common multicast group. This group also is known by its multicast IP address. The source doesn't necessarily have to join the group, though; it only needs to know the multicast address used by the recipients so it can send traffic to them. A host can join a multicast group by sending a request to its local router. This is done through the Internet Group Management Protocol (IGMP). IGMPv1 is defined in RFC 1112 and its successor, IGMPv2, in RFC 2236. When several hosts join a group by contacting their local routers, the multicast routing protocol (such as PIM) "connects the dots" and forms the multicast tree between routers.

IGMPv1

To join a multicast group, a host can dynamically send a *Membership Report* IGMP message to its local router. This message tells the router what multicast address (group) the host is joining. The multicast address is used as the destination IP address and the group address listed in the message. Therefore, the multicast router must intercept all packets that are destined to multicast addresses to receive the membership reports and add hosts to the appropriate groups.

Every 60 seconds, one router on each network segment queries all hosts to see if they are interested in receiving multicast traffic. This router is known as the *IGMPv1 querier* and functions simply to invite hosts to join a group. Queries are sent to the 224.0.0.1 all-hosts multicast address for quick distribution. If a host is interested in joining a group, or if it wants to continue receiving a group that it already has joined, it must respond with a membership report.

> **TIP**   Notice that the querier sends its invitations to a multicast group address, 224.0.0.1. Does this mean that every host on a network first must join the 224.0.0.1 group? Actually, every host is inherently a member of this group, without a formal IGMP exchange. The IP protocol stack that runs on a host already knows to accept and examine any message that is sent to 224.0.0.1.
>
> The same is true of other protocols, such as OSPF, which use other multicast link-local addresses. In the OSPF case, every participating router automatically knows to listen to the 224.0.0.5 "all-OSPF-routers" address.

Hosts can join multicast groups at any time. However, IGMPv1 does not have a mechanism to allow a host to leave a group if it is no longer interested in the group's content. Instead, routers age a multicast group out of an interface (network segment) if no membership reports are received for three consecutive query intervals. This means that, by default, multicast traffic still is sent onto a segment for up to 3 minutes after all the group members have stopped listening.

Notice that a router does not need to keep a complete host membership list for each multicast group that is active. Instead, it needs to only record which multicast groups are active on which interfaces. Whether 1 host or 100 hosts on a network segment are members of a group, the router still needs to send only one copy of a multicast packet onto that segment.

IGMPv2

IGMP version 2 introduced several differences from the first version. Queries can be sent as *general queries* to the all-hosts address (as in IGMPv1) or *group-specific queries*, which are sent only to members of a specific group.

In addition, hosts are allowed to leave a group dynamically. When a host decides to leave a group it has joined, it sends a *Leave Group* message to the all-routers address (224.0.0.2). All routers on the local segment take note, and the querier router decides to investigate further. It responds with a group-specific query message, asking if anyone is still interested in receiving traffic for that group. Any other interested hosts must reply with a membership report. Otherwise, the querier safely assumes that there is no need to continue forwarding the group traffic on that segment.

> **NOTE**   If any IGMPv1 routers are on a segment, *all* routers on the segment must run IGMPv1. Otherwise, the IGMPv1 routers cannot understand the IGMPv2 messages.
>
> On interfaces where PIM is configured, IGMPv2 is enabled by default. PIM is covered in the next section. To change the IGMP version, you can use the following interface-configuration command:
>
> ```
> Switch(config-if)# ip igmp version {1 | 2 | 3}
> ```

IGMPv3

The third version of IGMP is documented in RFC 3376. Basically, IGMPv3 offers the functionality of IGMPv2 and adds support for multicast source filtering. With source filtering, a recipient host can request membership in a multicast group and also supply a list of IP addresses representing multicast sources to include or exclude. In other words, a recipient can specify which sources it is or isn't interested in receiving multicast content from.

A router running IGMPv3 can coexist with other hosts running an older version. To do this, the router must keep itself compatible with the lowest IGMP version learned in each multicast group.

> **TIP**   IGMPv3 primarily is used for source-specific multicast (SSM). SSM is based on PIM sparse mode, with a separate source-distribution tree for each source that is used within each group. IGMPv3 is discussed briefly in comparison to the previous versions, although SSM is beyond the scope of the BCMSN course and exam.

PIM

Protocol Independent Multicast (PIM) is a routing protocol that can be used for forwarding multicast traffic between IP subnets or network segments. PIM operates independently of any particular IP routing protocol. Therefore, PIM makes use of the IP unicast routing table and does not keep a separate multicast routing table. (The unicast routing table is itself routing protocol–independent because one or more routing protocols can be used to populate a single table.)

PIM can operate in two modes, depending on the density of the recipients in a multicast group. Cisco has developed a third hybrid mode as well. The PIM modes are as follows:

- PIM dense mode

- PIM sparse mode

- PIM sparse-dense mode

In addition, two versions of the PIM protocol can be used in a network: PIM version 1 and PIM version 2. By default, PIM version 2 is used on a router interface. To change the version, you can use the following interface-configuration command:

```
Switch(config-if)# ip pim version {1 | 2}
```

PIM Dense Mode

PIM routers can be configured for *dense mode* (also called *PIM-DM*) if it is safe to assume that a multicast group's recipients are located on every subnet. In other words, the multicast group is densely populated across the network.

The multicast traffic's source becomes the root of the tree, and the multicast tree is formed from the source to each of the recipients. This is also termed *(S,G)* multicast traffic, where the path between the source and group members is unique and well defined.

The multicast tree is built by first allowing a flood of traffic from the source to every dense-mode router in the network. The tree is grown from the root toward the leaves. For a brief time, unnecessary traffic is allowed, much as a broadcast would do. However, as each router receives traffic for the group, it must decide whether it already has active recipients wanting to receive the data. If so, the router can remain quiet and let the flow continue.

If no hosts have registered for the multicast group with the router (via IGMP), the router sends a *Prune* message to its neighbor, toward the source. That branch of the tree then is pruned off so that the unnecessary traffic does not continue. The resulting tree is called a *source tree* or a *source distribution tree* because it is unique from the source to the receivers.

Figure 15-2 shows dense mode's flood-then-prune operation. The tree is built by a wave of join requests moving through all dense-mode multilayer switches. Then the switches that have no interested hosts request to be pruned from the tree. The resulting tree and multicast flow are shown in Figure 15-4 in the section on PIM sparse mode.

Figure 15-2 *PIM Dense Mode Constructs a Multicast Tree*

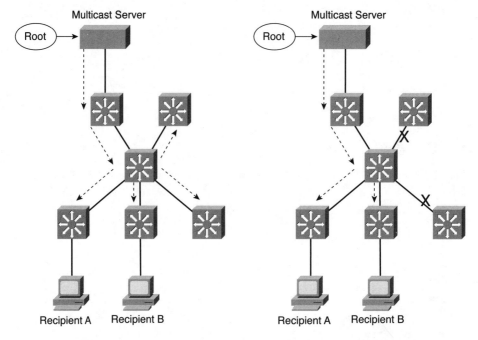

PIM-DM routers become aware of their neighbors by exchanging hello messages. This neighbor information is used first to build the tree to all neighbors and then to prune branches.

If a multicast flow has begun and the tree has been built and then pruned, the tree exists only where active group members are located. After that, if a new host registers for the group, the branch of the network where it is located can be added or *grafted* back onto the tree.

To configure PIM dense mode on an interface, use the following interface-configuration command:

```
Switch(config-if)# ip pim dense-mode
```

PIM Sparse Mode

PIM *sparse mode* (also called *PIM-SM*) takes a different approach: The multicast tree isn't extended to a router unless a host there already has joined the group. The multicast tree is built by beginning with the group members at the end leaf nodes and extending back toward a central root point. The tree is grown in reverse, from the leaves toward the root.

Sparse mode also works on the idea of a shared tree structure, where the root is not necessarily the multicast source. Instead, the root is a PIM-SM router that is centrally located in the network. This root router is called the *rendezvous point (RP)*.

The tree from the RP to the group members is actually a subset of the tree that could be drawn from the source to the group members. Subsequently, if a multicast source anywhere in the network can register for group membership with the RP, the tree can be completed. Because of this, the sparse-mode tree is called a *shared tree*. Sparse mode multicast flows are described as *(*,G)* because the tree allows any source to send to a group.

As a recipient joins a multicast group via IGMP, the local router forwards the membership report toward the RP at the root of the tree. Each router along the way adds that branch to the shared tree. Pruning is performed only when a group member is removed from the group. This process is shown in Figure 15-3. Notice that it consists of only one step: Only routers with active group members join the tree. The routers that did not join the group are not pruned because they never became a part of the tree in the first place.

Figure 15-3   *PIM Sparse Mode Constructs a Multicast Tree*

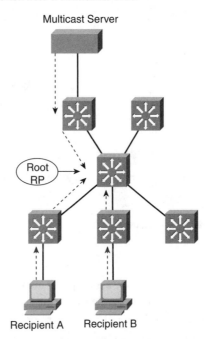

Step 1: Members join the group
to build a tree.

Figure 15-4 illustrates the resulting tree structures for both PIM dense mode and PIM sparse mode, along with the multicast data flow. Notice that both PIM modes have constructed identical tree structures, yielding the same multicast traffic flow patterns.

Figure 15-4   *Identical Results from PIM Dense and Sparse Modes*

To configure PIM sparse mode on an interface, use the following interface-configuration command:

```
Switch(config-if)# ip pim sparse-mode
```

PIM Sparse-Dense Mode

PIM has the potential to support both dense and sparse modes because they can exist on different multicast groups in a network and even on the same router interface. Cisco offers the hybrid *sparse-dense* mode, allowing a PIM router to use sparse or dense mode on a per-group basis. If a group has an RP defined, sparse mode is used; otherwise, dense mode is used.

To configure PIM sparse-dense mode on an interface, use the following interface-configuration command:

```
Switch(config-if)# ip pim sparse-dense-mode
```

PIM Version 1

For routers using the first version of PIM, RPs can be configured manually or by the more dynamic *auto-RP* process. To manually identify an RP, use the following global configuration command:

```
Switch(config)# ip pim rp-address ip-address [access-list] [override]
```

You can limit the range of multicast groups supported by the RP by using an access list. The **override** keyword causes this RP to be preferred over any that is automatically determined. Because the RP doesn't advertise itself, its address and function must be defined on *every* router in the PIM domain, including the RP itself. This makes future changes in the RP location difficult to carry out because every router must be reconfigured with the new RP address.

Cisco also provides a proprietary means of automatically informing PIM-SM routers of the appropriate RP for a group. This is known as *Auto-RP*. This is done by identifying a centrally located and well-connected router to function as the *mapping agent*. The mapping agent learns of all candidate RPs that are announced over the *Cisco-RP-Announce* multicast address 224.0.1.39. (By definition, all PIM-SM routers automatically must join 224.0.1.39.)

To define a router as a mapping agent, use the following global configuration command:

```
Switch(config)# ip pim send-rp-discovery scope ttl
```

The mapping agent sends RP-to-group mapping information to all PIM routers over the *Cisco-RP-Discovery* multicast address 224.0.1.40. The Time To Live (TTL) value is sent in these messages to limit the scope of the mapping. This limits how many router hops away the information will reach and still be valid.

You then explicitly must define each candidate RP router. When a router knows it can be an RP, it begins sending announcements to the mapping agent. Configure a router as a candidate RP with the following global configuration command:

```
Switch(config)# ip pim send-rp-announce type mod/num scope ttl [group-list access-
list] [interval seconds]
```

The interface must be given because it corresponds to the advertised RP address and identifies where the mapping agent can be found. The announcement's scope is limited by the number of router hops (TTL). The router also can advertise itself as a candidate RP for the multicast groups permitted in the **group-list** access list. By adding the **interval** keyword, the announcements will be sent at an interval of *seconds*.

PIM Version 2

The second version of PIM also includes a dynamic RP-to-group mapping advertisement mechanism. This is known as the *bootstrap router method* and is standards based.

PIMv2 is similar to the Cisco auto-RP method. First, a *bootstrap router (BSR)* is identified; this router learns about RP candidates for a group and advertises them to PIM routers. You need to configure only the BSR and candidate RPs; all other PIM routers learn of the appropriate RP from the BSR. Define a BSR using the following global configuration command:

```
Switch(config)# ip pim bsr-candidate type mod/num hash-mask-length [priority]
```

The interface specified determines the BSR address. RP selection for a group is based on a hashing function. The length of the hash mask controls the number of consecutive multicast groups that hash to the same RP.

Next, you must identify each of the candidate RP routers. Configure each RP with the following global configuration command:

```
Switch(config)# ip pim rp-candidate type mod/num ttl [group-list access-list]
```

Finally, by default, the bootstrap messages permeate the entire PIM domain. You can limit the scope of the advertisements by defining PIMv2 border routers, which will not forward the bootstrap messages any further. Use the following global configuration command:

```
Switch(config)# ip pim border
```

Switching Multicast Traffic

Routers or multilayer switches can build multicast trees and set up forwarding in an efficient, intelligent manner. At Layer 2, however, a switch can examine only the Ethernet frame header to find the source and destination MAC addresses. These switches cannot enjoy the luxury of on-demand multicast forwarding; the best information they have is the destination multicast address, and that signifies only that the frame needs to be flooded out all ports on the VLAN.

Two methods have been developed to help switches make intelligent forwarding decisions for multicast traffic: IGMP snooping and CGMP. One method requires more sophisticated switching hardware, whereas the other method leans on a nearby router for assistance.

IGMP Snooping

In normal operation, a host that desires multicast group membership must contact a local router so that it is added into the multicast tree. IGMP snooping allows a switch to eavesdrop on these IGMP membership reports so that it can find out who is requesting which group.

Recall that to join a group, a host must send its IGMP membership report to the multicast address of the group itself. To eavesdrop, a Layer 2–only switch must listen to *every multicast frame* to find the IGMP information. Clearly, this becomes a burden to the switch CPU.

A multilayer or Layer 3 switch has a clear advantage: It inherently can pick out Layer 3 information within frames. This type of switch must listen only to *every IGMP packet*. When a membership report is overheard, the switch adds the multicast group's MAC address to its Content Addressable Memory (CAM) table (if it doesn't already exist), along with the source switch port where the IGMP packet was received. This links the group address with the host that requested membership.

As other hosts request membership to the group, the respective switch ports are added to the CAM table list for the group address. Now, when a frame destined for the multicast group arrives, it can be replicated out exactly the right ports to reach the recipients.

With IGMP snooping, there are two special cases of group membership in the CAM table:

- All multicast routers known by the switch (dynamically learned) also are recorded for a group in the CAM table. Multicast frames also must be replicated toward any routers so that they can be routed elsewhere, if needed.

- The switch CPU itself is also a member of every multicast group so that it can watch IGMP messages come and go. Only IGMP traffic is processed; the CPU does not inspect other multicast frames.

IGMP snooping is not supported on all Cisco switch platforms. It is supported on the Catalyst 2950, 3560, 3750, 4500, and 6500 families because each has additional hardware to support Layer 3 functionality. On those platforms, IGMP snooping is enabled on all switch ports and VLAN interfaces, by default. To enable or disable IGMP snooping, use the following global configuration command:

```
Switch(config)# [no] ip igmp snooping
```

CGMP

When a Layer 2 switch cannot perform IGMP snooping itself, a nearby multicast router can assist. Cisco developed the proprietary Cisco Group Membership Protocol (CGMP) for this purpose.

A router or multilayer switch configured for multicast routing also can be configured for CGMP. As hosts send IGMP membership reports to join or leave multicast groups, the CGMP router relays this message to all interested switches. The CGMP messages are multicast over the well-known address 0100.0cdd.dddd; by definition, this multicast group is flooded everywhere as a special case so that CGMP messages can be transported across non-CGMP switches.

The CGMP messages include the requesting host's MAC address, along with the MAC address of the multicast group it wants to join or leave. When a Layer 2 switch receives this CGMP information, it becomes a simple task to add the multicast group and associated hosts to its CAM table. In effect, the router has become a "hearing aid" for a switch that is IGMP snooping "hearing impaired."

By default, CGMP is disabled on all interfaces on multicast routers. To enable it, use the following interface-configuration command:

```
Switch(config-if)# ip cgmp
```

Only the multicast router must be configured for CGMP. All IOS-based Layer 2 switches have CGMP enabled by default, so they automatically process CGMP messages from routers.

> **NOTE**   As a rule, IGMP snooping and CGMP are mutually exclusive; they cannot be used simultaneously on a switch. For switches that have IGMP snooping capability, IGMP snooping is enabled by default. For switches that cannot do IGMP snooping, CGMP is enabled by default.
>
> If you are configuring IP multicast support in your network, be sure to identify any legacy Layer 2 switches that are capable only of flooding multicast traffic. Enable CGMP on these switches, and then enable CGMP on an upstream multicast router or multilayer switch. This way, your entire network will be capable of intelligently constraining the flooding of multicast traffic.

Verifying Multicast Routing and Switching

To verify the operation of the features discussed in this chapter, you can use the commands listed in the sections that follow.

Multicast Routing with PIM

Remember that PIM is based on the unicast routing table; no separate multicast routing table is kept. Table 15-2 lists those commands that you need to verify that the multicast routing with PIM operations is working as intended.

Table 15-2   *Commands for Verifying Multicast Routing with PIM*

Command	Task
show ip route	Displays valid routes
show ip pim neighbor	Displays neighboring PIM routers
show ip rpf *ip-address*	Verifies RPF information for a host address
show ip pim rp	Displays PIM RPs
show ip pim autorp	Displays PIMv1 Auto-RP
show ip pim bsr-router	Displays PIM v2 BSRs

Multicast Switching

Table 15-3 lists those commands that you need to verify that IGMP snooping is configured and working as intended.

Table 15-3   *Commands for Verifying IGMP Operation*

Command	Task
show ip igmp groups	Displays active IGMP groups and members
show ip igmp interface *type mod/num*	Displays IGMP activity on an interface
show ip igmp snooping	Displays IGMP snooping activity

You also can perform some multicast testing with multilayer switches. Choose a multicast group address that several switches can join. Configure a specific interface to join the group with the following interface-configuration command:

```
Switch(config-if)# ip igmp join-group multicast-address
```

Then you can use **show** commands to see information about the group and the IGMP membership. After several switches have joined the group, you can issue a **ping** to the multicast group IP address. Every switch that has joined the group should answer with a reply.

What Would Happen Without a Multicast Router?

Suppose that a network is so small that a multicast router is not available. Instead, only one or more Layer 2 or Layer 3 switches are used. Can a multicast group be supported for users who want to view a streaming video from a server?

Multicast always can be supported, with or without a router. When a host sends an IGMP membership report to join a group, it does so blindly. After all, a host does not know about multicast routers at all—it just sends out a request to join and hopes that it will start receiving traffic destined for the multicast group address. Even if a multicast router is present, it doesn't send a reply to a host that has joined a group. A router only periodically sends out membership queries asking if hosts still want to remain a member of the group.

In this small network, Layer 2 switches simply flood the server's multicast traffic out all ports on the VLAN. No CGMP router is available to lend its intelligence. Layer 3 switches can use IGMP snooping, however, to constrain the multicast flooding. Although a router isn't present, the switch can still listen to the membership reports being sent to the nonexistent router.

Foundation Summary

The Foundation Summary is a collection of information that provides a convenient review of many key concepts in this chapter. If you are already comfortable with the topics in this chapter, this summary can help you recall a few details. If you just read this chapter, this review should help solidify some key facts. If you are doing your final preparation before the exam, this information is a convenient way to review the day before the exam.

- IP multicast addresses range from 224.0.0.0 to 239.255.255.255 (highest 4 bits are always 1110).

- Multicast MAC addresses always start with *0100.5e* (next bit is always 0). The lower 28 bits of the IP address are mapped over into the lower 23 bits of the MAC address.

- RPF decides whether a multicast packet can be forwarded: If it arrived on an interface where the source can be found, it is forwarded; if not, it is dropped.

- IGMP is the protocol used to join and leave (as well as to maintain) multicast groups.

- PIM is a multicast routing protocol used to build multicast tree topologies.

Table 15-4 *A Comparison of PIM Modes*

	Multicast Flows	**Tree Construction**	**Tree Refinements**
Dense Mode	(S,G)	Root to leaves; source is the root, recipients are leaf nodes	First flood, then prune
Sparse Mode	(*,G)	Leaves to root; RP is the root, source can be anywhere, recipients are leaf nodes	Group extended from recipients toward RP; pruning only when member leaves group
Sparse-Dense Mode	(S,G) or (*,G)	Hybrid on a per-group basis	Not applicable

Table 15-5 *IP PIM Multicast Configuration Commands*

Command Syntax	Task
ip multicast-routing	Enables multicast routing
ip pim dense-mode	Enables PIM dense mode on an interface
ip pim sparse-mode	Enables PIM sparse mode on an interface
ip pim sparse-dense-mode	Enables PIM sparse-dense mode
ip pim rp-address *ip-address* [*access-list*] [**override**]	Defines a PIMv1 RP
ip pim send-rp-discovery scope *ttl*	Defines a PIMv1 Auto-RP mapping agent
ip pim send-rp-announce *type mod/num* scope *ttl* **group-list** *access-list*	Identifies the PIMv1 Auto-RP RP routers
ip pim bsr-candidate *type mod/num hash-mask-length* [*priority*]	Defines a PIMv2 BSR
ip pim rp-candidate *type mod/num ttl* **group-list** *access-list*	Identifies the PIMv2 candidate RP routers
ip pim border	Defines a PIMv2 border router

■ IGMP snooping allows a switch to intercept IGMP messages to learn of group members and their port locations.

■ CGMP allows a router to relay IGMP join and leave requests to Layer 2 switches. The switches then learn of group members and their port locations.

Q&A

The questions and scenarios in this book are more difficult than what you should experience on the actual exam. The questions do not attempt to cover more breadth or depth than the exam; however, they are designed to make sure that you know the answers. Rather than allowing you to derive the answers from clues hidden inside the questions themselves, the questions challenge your understanding and recall of the subject. Hopefully, these questions will help limit the number of exam questions on which you narrow your choices to two options and then guess.

The answers to these questions can be found in Appendix A.

1. By default, what does a router or Layer 3 switch do with multicast packets?

2. By default, what does a Layer 2 switch do with a multicast packet?

3. What high-order bit combination signals that an IP address is used for multicast?

4. If the IP-to-MAC multicast address mapping is somewhat ambiguous, how can a frame be forwarded to the correct destination group?

5. What IP multicast address range is set aside for use only on the local network segment?

6. For the RPF check, the source IP address is looked up in the unicast routing table. To forward the packet, what should the result of the test be?

7. What important difference exists between IGMPv1 and IGMPv2?

8. To join a multicast group, what type of message is sent? Where is this message sent?

9. What is the purpose of the IGMP querier?

10. For PIM dense mode, how is the multicast tree built?

11. Where is the root of the PIM sparse-mode tree located?

12. With PIM sparse-dense mode, is the PIM mode determined per interface or per group?

13. What routing table is used for PIM?

14. What command is used to configure an interface for the hybrid PIM mode?

15. When a switch performs IGMP snooping, what is it snooping for?

16. What else does a Layer 2 switch need when it is configured for CGMP?

17. When should IGMP snooping and CGMP be used together on a switch?

18. At a trade show, several PCs and servers are connected to a single Layer 2 switch. The switch has CGMP enabled. When a server begins to send video data to a multicast address, what happens to that traffic?

PART IV

Campus Network Services

Chapter 16 IP Telephony

Chapter 17 Securing Switch Access

Chapter 18 Securing with VLANs

This part of the book covers the following BCMSN exam topics:

Technology

- Describe the quality issues with voice traffic on a switched data network, including jitter and delay

- Describe the QoS solutions that address voice quality issues

Implementation and Operation

- Implement IP technology on a switched network with auxiliary VLANs

- Configure QoS features on multilayer switched networks to provide optimal quality and bandwidth utilization for applications and data

Planning and Design

- Describe the general design models when implementing IP telephony in a switched network environment

Troubleshooting

- Identify voice VLAN issues at the network access layer

This chapter covers the following topics that you need to master for the CCNP BCMSN exam:

- **Power over Ethernet**—This section discusses how a Catalyst switch can provide power to operate devices such as Cisco IP Phones.

- **Voice VLANs**—This section explains how voice traffic can be carried over the links between an IP Phone and a Catalyst switch.

- **Voice QoS**—This section provides an overview of the mechanisms that provide premium quality of service (QoS) for voice traffic.

CHAPTER 16

IP Telephony

In addition to carrying regular data, switched campus networks can carry packets that are related to telephone calls. Voice over IP (VoIP), otherwise known as IP Telephony (IPT), uses IP Phones that are connected to switched Ethernet ports.

To properly and effectively carry the traffic for a successful phone call, a combination of many switching features must be used. For example, the Catalyst switches can provide power to IP Phones, form trunk links with IP Phones, and provide the proper level of QoS for voice packet delivery. This chapter covers all these topics as related to the Cisco IP Phone.

"Do I Know This Already?" Quiz

The purpose of the "Do I Know This Already?" quiz is to help you decide what parts of this chapter to use. If you already intend to read the entire chapter, you do not necessarily need to answer these questions now.

The quiz, derived from the major sections in the "Foundation Topics" portion of the chapter, helps you determine how to spend your limited study time.

Table 16-1 outlines the major topics discussed in this chapter and the "Do I Know This Already?" quiz questions that correspond to those topics.

Table 16-1 *"Do I Know This Already?" Foundation Topics Section-to-Question Mapping*

Foundation Topics Section	Questions Covered in This Section	Score
Power over Ethernet	1–2	
Voice VLANs	3–7	
Voice QoS	8–10	
Verifying IP Telephony	11–12	
Total Score		

CAUTION   The goal of self-assessment is to gauge your mastery of the topics in this chapter. If you do not know the answer to a question or are only partially sure of the answer, you should mark this question wrong. Giving yourself credit for an answer you correctly guess skews your self-assessment results and might give you a false sense of security.

---

1. For a Catalyst switch to offer Power over Ethernet to a device, what must occur?

    a. Nothing; power always is enabled on a port.

    b. The switch must detect that the device needs inline power.

    c. The device must send a CDP message asking for power.

    d. The switch is configured to turn on power to the port.

2. Which one of these commands can enable Power over Ethernet to a switch interface?

    a. **inline power enable**

    b. **inline power on**

    c. **power inline on**

    d. **power inline auto**

3. What does a Cisco IP Phone contain to allow it to pass both voice and data packets?

    a. An internal Ethernet hub

    b. An internal two-port switch

    c. An internal three-port switch

    d. An internal four-port switch

4. How can voice traffic be kept separate from any other data traffic through an IP Phone?

    a. Voice and data travel over separate links.

    b. A special-case 802.1Q trunk is used to connect to the switch.

    c. Voice and data can't be separated; they must intermingle on the link.

    d. Voice and data packets both are encapsulated over an ISL trunk.

5. What command configures an IP Phone to use VLAN 9 for voice traffic?

    a. **switchport voice vlan 9**

    b. **switchport voice-vlan 9**

    c. **switchport voice 9**

    d. **switchport voip 9**

6. What is the default voice VLAN condition for a switch port?

   a. **switchport voice vlan 1**

   b. **switchport voice vlan dot1p**

   c. **switchport voice vlan untagged**

   d. **switchport voice vlan none**

7. If the **switchport voice vlan 50** command has been used, what VLAN numbers will the voice and PC data be carried over, respectively?

   a. VLAN 50, native VLAN

   b. VLAN 50, VLAN 1

   c. VLAN 1, VLAN 50

   d. native VLAN, VLAN 50

8. When a PC is connected to the PC switch port on an IP Phone, how is QoS trust handled?

   a. The IP Phone always trusts the class of service (CoS) information coming from the PC.

   b. The IP Phone never trusts the PC and always overwrites the CoS bits.

   c. QoS trust for the PC data is handled at the Catalyst switch port, not the IP Phone.

   d. The Catalyst switch instructs the IP Phone how to trust the PC QoS information.

9. An IP Phone should mark all incoming traffic from an attached PC to have CoS 1. Complete the following switch command to make that happen:

```
switchport priority extend _____
```

   a. **untrusted**

   b. **1**

   c. **cos 1**

   d. **overwrite 1**

10. What command can verify the Power over Ethernet status of each switch port?

   a. **show inline power**

   b. **show power inline**

   c. **show interface**

   d. **show running-config**

11. What command can verify the voice VLAN used by a Cisco IP Phone?

   a. **show cdp neighbor**

   b. **show interface switchport**

   c. **show vlan**

   d. **show trunk**

12. Which DSCP codepoint name usually is used for time-critical packets containing voice data?

    a. 7

    b. Critical

    c. AF

    d. EF

The answers to the "Do I Know This Already?" quiz are found in Appendix A, "Answers to Chapter 'Do I Know This Already?' Quizzes and Q&A Sections." The suggested choices for your next step are as follows:

- **10 or less overall score**—Read the entire chapter. This includes the "Foundation Topics," "Foundation Summary," and "Q&A" sections.

- **11 or 12 overall score**—If you want more review on these topics, skip to the "Foundation Summary" section and then go to the "Q&A" section at the end of the chapter. Otherwise, move to Chapter 17, "Securing Switch Access."

Foundation Topics

Power over Ethernet (PoE)

A Cisco IP Phone is like any other node on the network—it must have power to operate. Power can come from two sources:

■ An external AC adapter

■ Power over Ethernet (DC) over the network data cable

The external AC adapter plugs into a normal AC wall outlet and provides 48V DC to the phone. These adapters, commonly called "wall warts," are handy if no other power source is available. However, if a power failure occurs to the room or outlet where the adapter is located, the IP Phone will fail.

A more elegant solution is available as *inline power* or *Power over Ethernet (PoE)*. Here, the same 48V DC supply is provided to an IP Phone over the same unshielded twisted-pair cable that is used for Ethernet connectivity. The DC power's source is the Catalyst switch itself. No other power source is needed, unless an AC adapter is required as a redundant source.

PoE has the benefit that it can be managed, monitored, and offered only to an IP Phone. In fact, this capability isn't limited to Cisco IP Phones—any device that can request and use inline power in a compatible manner can be used. Otherwise, if a nonpowered device such as a normal PC is plugged into the same switch port, the switch will not offer power to it.

The Catalyst switch also can be connected to an uninterruptible power supply (UPS) so that it continues to receive and offer power even if the regular AC source fails. This allows an IP Phone or other powered device to be available for use even across a power failure.

How Power over Ethernet Works

A Catalyst switch can offer power over its Ethernet ports only if it is designed to do so. It must have one or more power supplies that are rated for the additional load that will be offered to the connected devices. PoE is available on many platforms, including the Catalyst 3750-PWR, Catalyst 4500, and Catalyst 6500.

Two methods provide PoE to connected devices:

■ **Cisco Inline Power (ILP)**—A Cisco-proprietary method developed before the IEEE 802.3af standard

■ **IEEE 802.3af**—A standards-based method that offers vendor interoperability (see http://standards.ieee.org/getieee802/download/802.3af-2003.pdf)

Detecting a Powered Device

The switch always keeps the power disabled when a switch port is down. However, the switch must continually try to detect whether a powered device is connected to a port. If it is, the switch must begin providing power so that the device can initialize and become operational. Only then will the Ethernet link be established.

Because there are two PoE methods, a Catalyst switch tries both to detect a powered device. For IEEE 802.3af, the switch begins by supplying a small voltage across the transmit and receive pairs of the copper twisted-pair connection. It then can measure the resistance across the pairs to detect whether current is being drawn by the device. If 25K Ohm resistance is measured, a powered device is indeed present.

The switch also can apply several predetermined voltages to test for corresponding resistance values. These values are applied by the powered device to indicate which of the five IEEE 802.3af power classes it belongs to. Knowing this, the switch can begin allocating the appropriate maximum power needed by the device. Table 16-2 defines the power classes.

Table 16-2   *IEEE 802.3af Power Classes*

Power Class	Maximum Power Offered at 48V DC	Notes
0	15.4W	Default class
1	4.0W	Optional class
2	7.0W	Optional class
3	15.4W	Optional class
4	—	Reserved for future use

The default class is used if either the switch or the powered device doesn't support or doesn't attempt the optional power class discovery. At press time, class 4 is not used; it holds a place for future devices that will require a greater power budget than the current Catalyst switches can supply.

Cisco inline power device discovery takes a totally different approach than IEEE 802.3af. Instead of offering voltage and checking resistance, the switch sends out a 340-kHz test tone on the transmit pair of the twisted-pair Ethernet cable. A tone is transmitted instead of DC power because the switch first must detect an inline power-capable device before offering it power. Otherwise, other types of devices (normal PCs, for example) could be damaged.

A powered device such as a Cisco IP Phone loops the transmit and receive pairs of its Ethernet connection while it is powered off. When it is connected to an inline power switch port, the switch can "hear" its test tone looped back. Then it safely assumes that a known powered device is present, and power can be applied to it.

Supplying Power to a Device

A switch first offers a default power allocation to the powered device. On a Catalyst 3750-24-PWR, for example, an IP Phone first receives 15.4W (0.32 amps at 48V DC).

Power can be supplied in two ways:

- For Cisco ILP, inline power is provided over data pairs 2 and 3 (RJ-45 pins 1,2 and 3,6) at 48V DC.

- For IEEE 802.3af, power can be supplied in the same fashion (pins 1,2 and 3,6) or over pairs 1 and 4 (RJ-45 pins 4,5 and 7,8).

Now the device has a chance to power up and bring up its Ethernet link, too. The power budget offered to the device can be changed from the default to a more appropriate value. This can help prevent the switch from wasting its total power budget on devices that use far less power than the per-port default. With IEEE 802.3af, the power budget can be changed by detecting the device's power class.

For Cisco ILP, the switch can attempt a Cisco Discovery Protocol (CDP) message exchange with the device. If CDP information is returned, the switch can discover the device type (Cisco IP Phone, for example) and the device's actual power requirements. The switch then can reduce the inline power to the amount requested by the device.

To see this in operation, look at Example 16-1. Here, the power was reduced from 15,000 mW to 6300 mW. This output was produced by the **debug ilpower controller** and **debug cdp packets** commands.

Example 16-1 *Displaying Inline Power Adjustment*

```
00:58:46: ILP uses AC Disconnect(Fa1/0/47): state= ILP_DETECTING_S, event=
PHY_CSCO_DETECTED_EV
00:58:46: %ILPOWER-7-DETECT: Interface Fa1/0/47: Power Device detected: Cisco PD
00:58:46: Ilpower PD device 1 class 2 from interface (Fa1/0/47)
00:58:46: ilpower new power from pd discovery Fa1/0/47, power_status ok
00:58:46: Ilpower interface (Fa1/0/47) power status change, allocated power 15400
00:58:46: ILP Power apply to ( Fa1/0/47 ) Okay
00:58:46: ILP Start PHY Cisco IP phone detection ( Fa1/0/47 ) Okay
00:58:46: %ILPOWER-5-POWER_GRANTED: Interface Fa1/0/47: Power granted
00:58:46: ILP uses AC Disconnect(Fa1/0/47): state= ILP_CSCO_PD_DETECTED_S, event=
IEEE_PWR_GOOD_EV
00:58:48: ILP State_Machine ( Fa1/0/47 ): State= ILP_PWR_GOOD_USE_IEEE_DISC_S, Event=
PHY_LINK_UP_EV
00:58:48: ILP uses AC Disconnect(Fa1/0/47): state= ILP_PWR_GOOD_USE_IEEE_DISC_S, event=
PHY_LINK_UP_EV
00:58:50: %LINK-3-UPDOWN: Interface FastEthernet1/0/47, changed state to up
00:58:50: CDP-AD: Interface FastEthernet1/0/47 coming up
00:58:50: ilpower_powerman_power_available_tlv: about sending patlv on Fa1/0/47
00:58:50:    req id 0, man id 1, pwr avail 15400, pwr man -1
00:58:50: CDP-PA: version 2 packet sent out on FastEthernet1/0/47
00:58:51: %LINEPROTO-5-UPDOWN: Line protocol on Interface FastEthernet1/0/47, changed state
to up
00:58:54: CDP-PA: Packet received from SIP0012435D594D on interface FastEthernet1/0/47
00:58:54: **Entry NOT found in cache**
00:58:54: Interface(Fa1/0/47) - processing old tlv from cdp, request 6300, current
allocated 15400
00:58:54: Interface (Fa1/0/47) efficiency is 100
00:58:54: ilpower_powerman_power_available_tlv: about sending patlv on Fa1/0/47
00:58:54:    req id 0, man id 1, pwr avail 6300, pwr man -1
00:58:54: CDP-PA: version 2 packet sent out on FastEthernet1/0/47
```

Configuring Power over Ethernet

PoE or inline power configuration is simple. Each switch port automatically can detect the presence of an inline power-capable device before applying power, or the feature can be disabled to ensure that the port never can detect or offer inline power. By default, every switch port attempts to discover an inline-powered device. To change this behavior, use the following interface-configuration commands:

```
Switch(config)# interface type mod/num
Switch(config-if)# power inline {auto [max milli-watts] | static [max milli-watts] |
never}
```

By default, every switch interface is configured for **auto** mode, where the device and power budget automatically is discovered. In addition, the default power budget is 15.4W. You can change the maximum power offered as **max** *milli-watts* (4000 to 15400).

You can configure a **static** power budget for a switch port if you have a device that can't interact with either of the powered device-discovery methods. Again, you can set the maximum power offered to the device with **max** *milli-watts*. Otherwise, the default value of 15.4W is used.

If you want to disable PoE on a switch port, use the **never** keyword. Power never will be offered and powered devices never will be detected on that port.

Verifying Power over Ethernet

You can verify the power status for a switch port with the following EXEC command:

```
Switch# show power inline [type mod/num]
```

Example 16-2 provides some sample output from this command. If the class is shown as **n/a**, Cisco ILP has been used to supply power. Otherwise, the IEEE 802.3af power class (0 through 4) is shown.

Example 16-2 *Displaying PoE Status for Switch Ports*

```
Switch# show power inline
Module    Available    Used    Remaining
          (Watts)      (Watts)  (Watts)
------    ----------   --------  ----------
1            370.0      39.0      331.0
Interface Admin  Oper       Power   Device                Class Max
                            (Watts)
--------- ------ ---------- ------- -------------------- ----- ----
Fa1/0/1   auto   on         6.5     AIR-AP1231G-A-K9      n/a   15.4
Fa1/0/2   auto   on         6.3     IP Phone 7940         n/a   15.4
Fa1/0/3   auto   on         6.3     IP Phone 7960         n/a   15.4
Fa1/0/4   auto   on         15.4    Ieee PD               0     15.4
Fa1/0/5   auto   on         4.5     Ieee PD               1     15.4
Fa1/0/6   static on         15.4    n/a                   n/a   15.4
Fa1/0/7   auto   off        0.0     n/a                   n/a   15.4
[output omitted]
```

CAUTION A Catalyst switch waits for 4 seconds after inline power is applied to a port to see if an IP Phone comes alive. If not, the power is removed from the port.

Be careful if you plug an IP phone into a switch port, and then remove it and plug in a normal Ethernet device. The inline power still could be applied during the 4-second interval, damaging a nonpowered device. Wait 10 seconds after unplugging an IP Phone before plugging anything back into the same port.

Voice VLANs

A Cisco IP Phone provides a data connection for a user's PC, in addition to its own voice data stream. This allows a single Ethernet drop to be installed per user. The IP Phone also can control some aspects of how the packets (both voice and user data) are presented to the switch.

Most Cisco IP Phone models contain a three-port switch, connecting to the upstream switch, the user's PC, and the internal VoIP data stream, as illustrated in Figure 16-1. The voice and user PC ports always function as access-mode switch ports. The port that connects to the upstream switch, however, can operate as an 802.1Q trunk or as an access-mode (single VLAN) port.

Figure 16-1   *Basic Connections to a Cisco IP Phone*

The link mode between the IP Phone and the switch is negotiated; you can configure the switch to instruct the phone to use a special-case 802.1Q trunk or a single VLAN access link. With a trunk, the voice traffic can be isolated from other user data, providing security and QoS capabilities.

As an access link, both voice and data must be combined over the single VLAN. This simplifies other aspects of the switch configuration because a separate voice VLAN is not needed, but it could compromise the voice quality, depending on the PC application mix and traffic load.

Voice VLAN Configuration

Although you can configure the IP Phone uplink as a trunk or nontrunk, the real consideration pertains to how the voice traffic will be encapsulated. The voice packets must be carried over a unique voice VLAN (known as the voice VLAN ID or *VVID*) or over the regular data VLAN (known as the native VLAN or the port VLAN ID, *PVID*). The QoS information from the voice packets also must be carried.

To configure the IP Phone uplink, just configure the switch port where it connects. The switch instructs the phone to follow the mode that is selected. In addition, the switch port does not need any special trunking configuration commands if a trunk is wanted. If an 802.1Q trunk is needed, a special-case trunk automatically is negotiated by the Dynamic Trunking Protocol (DTP) and CDP.

Use the following interface-configuration command to select the voice VLAN mode that will be used:

```
Switch(config-if)# switchport voice vlan {vlan-id | dot1p | untagged | none}
```

Figure 16-2 shows the four different voice VLAN configurations. Pay particular attention to the link between the IP Phone and the switch.

Table 16-3 documents the four different voice VLAN configurations.

Table 16-3 *Trunking Modes with a Cisco IP Phone*

Keyword	Representation in Figure 16-2	Native VLAN (Untagged)	Voice VLAN	Voice QoS (CoS bits)
vlan-id	A	PC data	VLAN *vlan-id*	802.1p
dot1p	B	PC data	VLAN 0	802.1p
untagged	C	PC data/voice	—	—
none (default)	D	PC data/voice	—	—

The default condition for every switch port is **none**, where a trunk is not used. All modes except for **none** use the special-case 802.1Q trunk. The only difference between the **dot1p** and **untagged** modes is the encapsulation of voice traffic. The **dot1p** mode puts the voice packets on VLAN 0, which requires a VLAN ID (not the native VLAN) but doesn't require a unique voice VLAN to be created. The **untagged** mode puts voice packets in the native VLAN, requiring neither a VLAN ID nor a unique voice VLAN.

The most versatile mode uses the *vlan-id*, as shown in case A in Figure 16-2. Here, voice and user data are carried over separate VLANs. VoIP packets in the voice VLAN also carry the CoS bits in the 802.1p trunk encapsulation field.

Figure 16-2 *Trunking Modes for Voice VLANs with a Cisco IP Phone*

Be aware that the special-case 802.1Q trunk automatically is enabled through a CDP information exchange between the switch and the IP Phone. The trunk contains only two VLANs—a voice VLAN (tagged VVID) and the data VLAN. The switch port's access VLAN is used as the data VLAN that carries packets to and from a PC that is connected to the phone's PC port.

If an IP Phone is removed and a PC is connected to the same switch port, the PC still will be capable of operating because the data VLAN still will appear as the access VLAN—even though the special trunk no longer is enabled.

Verifying Voice VLAN Operation

You can verify the switch port mode (access or trunk) and the voice VLAN by using the **show interface switchport** command. As demonstrated in Example 16-3, the port is in access mode and uses access VLAN 10 and voice VLAN 110.

Example 16-3 *Verifying Switch Port Mode and Voice VLAN*

```
Switch# show interfaces fastEthernet 1/0/1 switchport
Name: Fa1/0/1
Switchport: Enabled
Administrative Mode: dynamic auto
Operational Mode: static access
Administrative Trunking Encapsulation: negotiate
Operational Trunking Encapsulation: native
Negotiation of Trunking: On
Access Mode VLAN: 10 (VLAN0010)
Trunking Native Mode VLAN: 1 (default)
Administrative Native VLAN tagging: enabled
Voice VLAN: 110 (VoIP)
Administrative private-vlan host-association: none
Administrative private-vlan mapping: none
Administrative private-vlan trunk native VLAN: none
Administrative private-vlan trunk Native VLAN tagging: enabled
Administrative private-vlan trunk encapsulation: dot1q
Administrative private-vlan trunk normal VLANs: none
Administrative private-vlan trunk private VLANs: none
Operational private-vlan: none
Trunking VLANs Enabled: ALL
Pruning VLANs Enabled: 2-1001
Capture Mode Disabled
Capture VLANs Allowed: ALL
Protected: false
Unknown unicast blocked: disabled
Unknown multicast blocked: disabled
Appliance trust: none
Switch#
```

When the IP Phone trunk is active, it is not shown in the trunking mode from any Cisco IOS Software **show** command. However, you can verify the VLANs being carried over the trunk link by looking at the Spanning Tree Protocol (STP) activity. STP runs with two instances—one for the voice VLAN and one for the data VLAN, which can be seen with the **show spanning-tree interface** command.

For example, suppose a switch port is configured with access VLAN 10, voice VLAN 110, and native VLAN 99. Example 16-4 shows the switch port configuration and STP information when the switch port is in access mode.

Example 16-4   *IP Phone Trunk Configuration and STP Information*

```
Switch# show running-config interface fastethernet 1/0/1
interface FastEthernet1/0/1
 switchport trunk native vlan 99
 switchport access vlan 63
 switchport voice vlan 306
Switch# show spanning-tree interface fastethernet 1/0/1
Vlan              Role Sts Cost      Prio.Nbr Type
---------------- ---- --- --------- -------- --------------------------------
VLAN0010          Desg FWD 19        128.51   P2p
VLAN0110          Desg FWD 19        128.51   P2p
Switch#
```

The access VLAN (10) is being used as the data VLAN from the IP Phone.

Voice QoS

On a quiet, underutilized network, a switch generally can forward packets as soon as they are received. However, if a network is congested, packets can't always be delivered in a timely manner. Traditionally, network congestion has been handled by increasing link bandwidths and switching hardware performance. This does little to address how one type of traffic can be preferred or delivered ahead of another.

Quality of service (QoS) is the overall method used in a network to protect and prioritize time-critical or important traffic. The most important aspect of transporting voice traffic across a switched campus network is maintaining the proper QoS level. Voice packets must be delivered in the most timely fashion possible, with little jitter, little loss, and little delay.

Remember, a user expects to receive a dial tone, a call to go through, and a good-quality audio connection with the far end when an IP Phone is used. Above that, any call that is made could be an emergency 911 call. It is then very important that QoS be implemented properly.

QoS Overview

The majority of this book has discussed how Layer 2 and Layer 3 Catalyst switches forward packets from one switch port to another. On the surface, it might seem that there is only one way to forward packets—just look up the next packet's destination in a Content Addressable Memory (CAM) or Cisco Express Forwarding (CEF) table and send it on its way. But that addresses only *if* the packet can be forwarded, not *how* it can be forwarded.

Different types of applications have different requirements for how their data should be sent end to end. For example, it might be acceptable to wait a short time for a web page to be displayed after a user requests it. That same user probably cannot tolerate the same delays in receiving packets that belong to a streaming video presentation or an audio telephone call. Any loss or delay in packet delivery could ruin the purpose of the application.

Three basic things can happen to packets as they are sent from one host to another across a network:

- **Delay**—As a packet is sent from one network device to another, its delivery is delayed by some amount of time. This can be caused by the time required to send the packet serially across a wire, the time required for a router or switch to perform table lookups or make decisions, the time required for the data to travel over a geographically long path, and so on. The total delay from start to finish is called the *latency*. This is seen most easily as the time from when a user presses a key until the time the character is echoed and displayed in a terminal session.

- **Jitter**—Some applications involve the delivery of a stream of related data. As these packets are delivered, variations can occur in the amount of delay so that they do not all arrive at predictable times. The variation in delay is called *jitter*. Audio streams are particularly susceptible to jitter; if the audio data is not played back at a constant rate, the resulting speech or music sounds choppy.

- **Loss**—In extreme cases, packets that enter a congested or error-prone part of the network simply are dropped without delivery. Some amount of packet loss is acceptable and recoverable by applications that use a reliable, connection-oriented protocol such as TCP. Other application protocols are not as tolerant, and dropped packets mean data is missing.

To address and alleviate these conditions, a network can employ three basic types of QoS:

- Best-effort delivery

- Integrated Services model

- Differentiated Services model

Keep in mind that QoS works toward making policies or promises to improve packet delivery from a sender to a receiver. The same QoS policies should be used on *every* network device that connects the sender to the receiver. QoS must be implemented end to end before it can be totally effective.

Best-Effort Delivery

A network that simply forwards packets in the order they were received has no real QoS. Switches and routers then make their "best effort" to deliver packets as quickly as possible, with no regard for the type of traffic or the need for priority service.

To get an idea of how QoS operates in a network, consider a fire truck or an ambulance trying to quickly work its way through a crowded city. The lights are flashing and the siren is sounding to signal that this is a "priority" vehicle needing to get through ahead of everyone else. The priority vehicle does not need to obey normal traffic rules.

However, the best effort scenario says that the fire truck must stay within the normal flow of traffic. At an intersection, it must wait in the line or queue of traffic like any other vehicle—even if its lights and siren are on. It might arrive on time or too late to help, depending on the conditions along the road.

Integrated Services Model

One approach to QoS is the *Integrated Services (IntServ)* model. The basic idea is to prearrange a path for priority data along the complete path, from source to destination. Beginning with RFC 1633, the Resource Reservation Protocol (RSVP) was developed as the mechanism for scheduling and reserving adequate path bandwidth for an application.

The source application itself is involved by requesting QoS parameters through RSVP. Each network device along the way must check to see if it can support the request. When a complete path meeting the minimum requirements is made, the source is signaled with a confirmation. Then the source application can begin using the path.

Applying the fire truck example to the IntServ model, a fire truck would radio ahead to the nearest intersection before it left the firehouse. Police stationed at each intersection would contact each other in turn, to announce that the fire truck was coming and to assess the traffic conditions. The police might reserve a special lane so that the fire truck could move at full speed toward the destination, regardless of what other traffic might be present.

Differentiated Services Model

As you might imagine, the IntServ model does not scale very well when many sources are trying to compete with each other to reserve end-to-end bandwidth. Another approach is the *Differentiated Services (DiffServ)* model, which permits each network device to handle packets on an individual basis. Each router or switch can be configured with QoS policies to follow, and forwarding decisions are made accordingly.

DiffServ requires no advance reservations; QoS is handled dynamically, in a distributed fashion. In other words, whereas IntServ applies QoS on a per-flow basis, DiffServ applies it on a per-hop basis to a whole group of similar flows. DiffServ also bases its QoS decisions on information contained in each packet header.

Continuing with the emergency vehicle analogy, here police are stationed at every intersection, as before. However, none of them knows a fire truck is coming until they see the lights or hear the siren. At each intersection, a decision is made as to how to handle the approaching fire truck. Other traffic can be held back, if needed, so that the fire truck can go right through.

Giving premium service to voice traffic focuses almost entirely on the DiffServ model. QoS is a complex and intricate topic in itself. The BCMSN course and exam cover only the theory behind DiffServ QoS, along with the features and commands that address voice QoS specifically.

DiffServ QoS

DiffServ is a per-hop behavior, with each router or switch inspecting each packet's header to decide how to go about forwarding that packet. All the information needed for this decision is carried along with each packet in the header. The packet itself cannot affect how it will be handled. Instead, it merely presents some flags, classifications, or markings that can be used to make a forwarding decision based on QoS policies that are configured into each switch or router along the path.

Layer 2 QoS Classification

Layer 2 frames themselves have no mechanism to indicate the priority or importance of their contents. One frame looks just as important as another. Therefore, a Layer 2 switch can forward frames only according to a best-effort delivery.

When frames are carried from switch to switch, however, an opportunity for classification occurs. Recall that a trunk is used to carry frames from multiple VLANs between switches. The trunk does this by encapsulating the frames and adding a tag indicating the source VLAN number. The encapsulation also includes a field that can mark the *class of service (CoS)* of each frame. This can be used at switch boundaries to make some QoS decisions. After a trunk is unencapsulated at the far-end switch, the CoS information is removed and lost.

The two trunk encapsulations handle CoS differently:

- **IEEE 802.1Q**—Each frame is tagged with a 12-bit VLAN ID and a User field. The User field contains three *802.1p priority bits* that indicate the frame CoS, a unitless value ranging from 0 (lowest-priority delivery) to 7 (highest-priority delivery). Frames from the native VLAN are not tagged (no VLAN ID or User field), so they receive a default CoS that is configured on the *receiving* switch.

- **Inter-Switch Link (ISL)**—Each frame is tagged with a 15-bit VLAN ID. In addition, next to the frame Type field is a 4-bit User field. The lower 3 bits of the User field are used as a CoS value. Although ISL is not standards based, Catalyst switches make CoS seamless by copying the 802.1p CoS bits from an 802.1Q trunk into the User CoS bits of an ISL trunk. This allows CoS information to propagate along trunks of differing encapsulations.

Layer 3 QoS Classification with DSCP

From the beginning, IP packets have always had a *type of service (ToS)* byte that can be used to mark packets. This byte is divided into a 3-bit IP Precedence value and a 4-bit ToS value. This offers a rather limited mechanism for QoS because only the 3 bits of IP Precedence are used to describe the per-hop QoS behavior.

The DiffServ model keeps the existing IP ToS byte but uses it in a more scalable fashion. This byte also is referred to as the *Differentiated Services (DS)* field, with a different format, as shown in Figure 16-3. The 6-bit DS value is known as the *Differentiated Service Code Point (DSCP)* and is the one value that is examined by any DiffServ network device.

Don't be confused by the dual QoS terminology—the ToS and DS bytes are the same, occupying the same location in the IP header. Only the names are different, along with the way the value is interpreted. In fact, the DSCP bits have been arranged to be backward compatible with the IP precedence bits so that a non-DiffServ device still can interpret some QoS information.

Figure 16-3 *ToS and DSCP Byte Formats*

ToS Byte:	P2	P1	P0	T3	T2	T1	T0	Zero
DS Byte:	DS5	DS4	DS3	DS2	DS1	DS0	ECN1	ECN0
	(Class Selector)			(Drop Precedence)				

The DSCP value is divided into a 3-bit class selector and a 3-bit Drop Precedence value. Refer to Table 16-4 to see how the IP Precedence, DSCP per-hop behavior, and DSCP codepoint names and numbers relate.

Table 16-4 *Mapping of IP Precedence and DSCP Fields*

IP Precedence (3 Bits)			DSCP (6 Bits)				
Name	Value	Bits	Per-Hop Behavior	Class Selector	Drop Precedence	Codepoint Name	DSCP Bits (Decimal)
Routine	0	000	Default			Default	000 000 (0)
Priority	1	001	AF	1	1: Low	AF11	001 010 (10)
					2: Medium	AF12	001 100 (12)
					3: High	AF13	001 110 (14)
Immediate	2	010	AF	2	1: Low	AF21	010 010 (18)
					2: Medium	AF22	010 100 (20)
					3: High	AF23	010 110 (22)
Flash	3	011	AF	3	1: Low	AF31	011 010 (26)
					2: Medium	AF32	011 100 (28)
					3: High	AF33	011 110 (30)
Flash Override	4	100	AF	4	1: Low	AF41	100 010 (34)
					2: Medium	AF42	100 100 (36)
					3: High	AF43	100 110 (38)
Critical	5	101	EF			EF	101 110 (46)[*]
Internetwork Control	6	110					(48–55)
Network Control	7	111					(56–63)

[*]IP Precedence value 5 (DSCP EF) corresponds to the range of DSCP bits 101000 through 101111, or 40–47. However, only the value 101110 or 46 is commonly used and is given the EF designation.

The three class selector bits (DS5 through DS3) coarsely classify packets into one of seven classes:

■ Class 0, the default class, offers only best-effort forwarding.

■ Classes 1 through 4 are called *Assured Forwarding (AF)* service levels. Higher AF class numbers indicate the presence of higher-priority traffic.

Packets in the AF classes can be dropped, if necessary, with the lower-class numbers the most likely to be dropped. For example, packets with AF Class 4 will be delivered in preference to packets with AF Class 3.

- Class 5 is known as *Expedited Forwarding (EF)*, with those packets given premium service. EF is the least likely to be dropped, so it always is reserved for time-critical data such as voice traffic.

- Classes 6 and 7 are called *Internetwork Control* and *Network Control*, respectively, and are set aside for network control traffic. Usually, routers and switches use these classes for things such as the Spanning Tree Protocol and routing protocols. This ensures timely delivery of the packets that keep the network stable and operational.

Each class represented in the DSCP also has three levels of *drop precedence*, contained in bits DS2 through DS0 (DS0 is always zero):

- Low (1)

- Medium (2)

- High (3)

Within a class, packets marked with a higher drop precedence have the potential for being dropped before those with a lower value. In other words, a lower drop precedence value gives better service. This gives finer granularity to the decision of what packets to drop when necessary.

TIP   The DSCP value can be given as a codepoint name, with the class selector providing the two letters and a number followed by the drop precedence number. For example, class AF Level 2 with drop precedence 1 (low) is written as *AF21*. The DSCP commonly is given as a decimal value. For AF21, the decimal value is 18. The relationship is confusing, and Table 16-2 should be a handy aid.

You should try to remember a few codepoint names and numbers. Some common values are EF (46) and most of the classes with low drop precedences: AF41 (34), AF31 (26), AF21 (18), and AF11 (10). Naturally, the default DSCP has no name (0).

Implementing QoS for Voice

To manipulate packets according to QoS policies, a switch somehow must identify which level of service each packet should receive. This process is known as *classification*. Each packet is classified according to the type of traffic (UDP or TCP port number, for example), according to parameters matched by an access list or something more complex, such as by stateful inspection of a traffic flow.

Recall that IP packets carry a ToS or DSCP value within their headers as they travel around a network. Frames on a trunk also can have CoS values associated with them. A switch then can decide whether to trust the ToS, DSCP, or CoS values already assigned to inbound packets. If it trusts any of these values, the values are carried over and used to make QoS decisions inside the switch.

If the QoS values are not trusted, they can be reassigned or overruled. This way, a switch can set the values to something known and trusted, and something that falls within the QoS policies that must be met. This prevents nonpriority users in the network from falsely setting the ToS or DSCP values of their packets to inflated levels so that they receive priority service.

Every switch must decide whether to trust incoming QoS values. Generally, an organization should be able to trust QoS parameters anywhere inside its own network. At the boundary with another organization or service provider, QoS typically should not be trusted. It is also prudent to trust only QoS values that have been assigned by the network devices themselves. Therefore, the QoS values produced by the end users should not be trusted until the network can verify or override them.

The perimeter formed by switches that do not trust incoming QoS is called the *trust boundary*. Usually, the trust boundary exists at the farthest reaches of the enterprise network (access-layer switches and WAN or ISP demarcation points). When the trust boundary has been identified and the switches there are configured with untrusted ports, everything else inside the perimeter can be configured to blindly trust incoming QoS values.

TIP   Every switch and router within a network must be configured with the appropriate QoS features and policies. The BCMSN course and exam limit QoS coverage to the switches at the access layer where the trust boundary is configured. Other more involved QoS topics are dealt with in the "Implementing Cisco Quality of Service (QoS)" course.

Figure 16-4 shows a simple network in which the trust boundary is defined at the edges where end users and public networks join. On Catalyst A, port GigabitEthernet2/1 is configured to consider inbound data as untrusted. Catalyst B's port FastEthernet0/2 connects to a PC that also is untrusted. The Cisco IP Phone on Catalyst B port FastEthernet0/1 is a special case because it supports its own voice traffic and an end user's PC. Therefore, the trust boundary can't be defined clearly on that switch port.

Figure 16-4 *A QoS Trust Boundary Example*

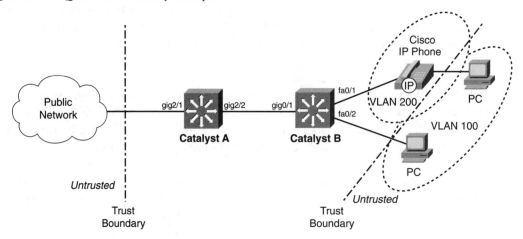

Configuring a Trust Boundary

When a Cisco IP Phone is connected to a switch port, think of the phone as another switch (which it is). If you install the phone as a part of your network, you probably can trust the QoS information relayed by the phone.

However, remember that the phone also has two sources of data:

■ **The VoIP packets native to the phone**—The phone can control precisely what QoS information is included in the voice packets because it produces those packets.

■ **The user PC data switch port**—Packets from the PC data port are generated elsewhere, so the QoS information cannot necessarily be trusted to be correct or fair.

A switch instructs an attached IP Phone through CDP messages on how it should extend QoS trust to its own user data switch port. To configure the trust extension, use the following configuration steps:

Step 1   Enable QoS on the switch:

```
Switch(config)# mls qos
```

By default, QoS is disabled globally on a switch and all QoS information is allowed to pass from one switch port to another. When you enable QoS, all switch ports are configured as untrusted, by default.

Step 2   Define the QoS parameter that will be trusted:

```
Switch(config)# interface type mod/num
Switch(config-if)# mls qos trust {cos | ip-precedence | dscp}
```

You can choose to trust the CoS, IP precedence, or DSCP values of incoming packets on the switch port. Only one of these parameters can be selected. Generally, for Cisco IP Phones, you should use the **cos** keyword because the phone can control the CoS values on its two-VLAN trunk with the switch.

Step 3   Make the trust conditional:

```
Switch(config-if)# mls qos trust device cisco-phone
```

You also can make the QoS trust conditional if a Cisco IP Phone is present. If this command is used, the QoS parameter defined in step 2 is trusted only if a Cisco phone is detected through CDP. If a phone is not detected, the QoS parameter is not trusted.

Step 4   Instruct the IP Phone on how to extend the trust boundary:

```
Switch(config-if)# switchport priority extend {cos value | trust}
```

Normally, the QoS information from a PC connected to an IP Phone should not be trusted. This is because the PC's applications might try to spoof CoS or Differentiated Services Code Point (DSCP) settings to gain premium network service. In this case, use the **cos** keyword so that the CoS bits are overwritten to *value* by the IP Phone as packets are forwarded to the switch. If CoS values from the PC cannot be trusted, they should be overwritten to a value of 0.

In some cases, the PC might be running trusted applications that are allowed to request specific QoS or levels of service. Here, the IP Phone can extend complete QoS trust to the PC, allowing the CoS bits to be forwarded through the phone unmodified. This is done with the **trust** keyword.

By default, a switch instructs an attached IP Phone to consider the PC port as untrusted. The phone will overwrite the CoS values to 0.

What about switch ports that don't connect to end-user or phone devices? Switch uplinks always should be considered as trusted ports. QoS parameters are trusted or overwritten at the network edge, as packets enter the trusted domain. After that, every switch inside the trusted boundary implicitly can trust and use the QoS parameters in any packet passing through.

You can configure a switch uplink port to be trusted with the following commands:

```
Switch(config)# interface type mod/num
Switch(config-if)# mls qos trust cos
```

Here, the trust is not conditional. The switch will trust only the CoS values that are found in the incoming packets.

> **TIP**   A Cisco switch also has a CoS-to-DSCP map that is used to convert inbound CoS values to DSCP values. The CoS information is useful only on trunk interfaces because it can be carried within the trunk encapsulation. CoS must be converted to DSCP or IP Precedence, which can be carried along in the IP packet headers on any type of connection.
>
> Switches use a default CoS-to-DSCP mapping, which can be configured or changed. However, this is beyond the scope of the BCMSN course and exam.

Verifying Voice QoS

A switch port can be configured with a QoS trust state with the connected device. If that device is an IP Phone, the switch can instruct the phone on whether to extend QoS trust to an attached PC.

To verify how QoS trust has been extended to the IP Phone itself, use the following EXEC command:

```
Switch# show mls qos interface type mod/num
```

If the port is trusted, all traffic forwarded by the IP Phone is accepted with the QoS information left intact. If the port is not trusted, even the voice packets can have their QoS information overwritten by the switch. Example 16-5 demonstrates some sample output from the **show mls qos interface** command, where the switch port is trusting CoS information from the attached IP Phone.

Example 16-5   *Verifying QoS Trust to the IP Phone*

```
Switch# show mls qos interface fastethernet 1/0/1
FastEthernet1/0/1
trust state: trust cos
trust mode: trust cos
trust enabled flag: ena
COS override: dis
default COS: 0
DSCP Mutation Map: Default DSCP Mutation Map
Trust device: none
```

Next, you can verify how the IP Phone has been instructed to treat incoming QoS information from its attached PC or other device. This is shown in the **trust device:** line in Example 16-5, where the device is the IP Phone's device. You also can use the following EXEC command:

```
Switch# show interface type mod/num switchport
```

Here, the device trust is called *appliance trust*, as shown in Example 16-6.

Example 16-6 *An Alternate Method for Verifying QoS Trust to an IP Phone*

```
Switch# show interface fast 0/1 switchport
Name: Fa0/1
Switchport: Enabled
[output deleted...]
Voice VLAN: 2 (VLAN0002)
Appliance trust: none
```

Again, the IP Phone's device is not being trusted. If the switch port was configured with the **switchport priority extend trust** command, the appliance trust would show *trusted*.

Example 16-7 shows the configuration commands that have been added to a switch interface where a Cisco IP Phone is connected.

Example 16-7 *Switch Port Configuration Commands to Support a Cisco IP Phone*

```
Switch# show running-config interface fastethernet 1/0/47
Building configuration...
Current configuration : 219 bytes
!
interface FastEthernet1/0/1
 switchport access vlan 10
 switchport trunk encapsulation dot1q
 switchport mode access
 switchport voice vlan 100
 mls qos trust device cisco-phone
 mls qos trust cos
 no mdix auto
end
Switch#
```

If the IP Phone is not connected to the switch port, it is not detected and the trust parameter is not enabled, as Example 16-8 demonstrates.

Example 16-8 *Displaying IP Phone Connection and Trust Status*

```
Switch# show mls qos interface fastethernet 1/0/1
FastEthernet1/0/1
trust state: not trusted
trust mode: trust cos
trust enabled flag: dis
COS override: dis
default COS: 0
DSCP Mutation Map: Default DSCP Mutation Map
Trust device: cisco-phone
Switch#
```

When a Cisco IP Phone is connected, power is applied and the phone is detected. Then the conditional QoS trust (CoS, in this case) is enabled, as demonstrated in Example 16-9.

Example 16-9 *Conditional Trust (CoS) Enabled on a Cisco IP Phone*

```
6d18h: %ILPOWER-7-DETECT: Interface Fa1/0/1: Power Device detected: Cisco PD
6d18h: %ILPOWER-5-POWER_GRANTED: Interface Fa1/0/1: Power granted
6d18h: %LINK-3-UPDOWN: Interface FastEthernet1/0/1, changed state to up
6d18h: %LINEPROTO-5-UPDOWN: Line protocol on Interface FastEthernet1/0/1, chang
ed state to up
6d18h: %SWITCH_QOS_TB-5-TRUST_DEVICE_DETECTED: cisco-phone detected on port Fa1/
0/1, port trust enabled.
Switch# show mls qos interface fastethernet 1/0/1
FastEthernet1/0/1
trust state: trust cos
trust mode: trust cos
trust enabled flag: ena
COS override: dis
default COS: 0
DSCP Mutation Map: Default DSCP Mutation Map
Trust device: cisco-phone
Switch#
```

Foundation Summary

The Foundation Summary is a collection of information that provides a convenient review of many key concepts in this chapter. If you are already comfortable with the topics in this chapter, this summary could help you recall a few details. If you just read this chapter, this review should help solidify some key facts. If you are doing your final preparation before the exam, this summarized information is a convenient way to review the day before the exam.

Table 16-5 *Commands for Configuring IP Telephony on a Catalyst Switch*

Task	Command Syntax
Set power over Ethernet behavior	**power inline {auto	never}**
Enable QoS globally	**mls qos**
Define QoS parameter that will be trusted on an interface	**mls qos trust {cos	ip-precedence	dscp}**
Conditionally trust a Cisco IP Phone	**mls qos trust device cisco-phone**
Define the trunking on a port to a Cisco IP Phone	**switchport voice vlan {***vlan-id* **| dot1p	untagged	none}**
Define the trust relationship of the IP Phone	**switchport priority extend {cos** *value* **| trust}**

You can use the commands in Table 16-6 to verify or troubleshoot IP Telephony on a Catalyst switch.

Table 16-6 *Commands for Troubleshooting IP Telephony on a Catalyst Switch*

Task	Command Syntax
Display Power over Ethernet status	**show power inline [***type mod/num***]**
Verify the voice VLAN	**show interface** *type mod/num* **switchport**
Display how QoS trust is extended to the phone	**show mls qos interface** *type mod/num*

Q&A

The questions and scenarios in this book are more difficult than what you should experience on the actual exam. The questions do not attempt to cover more breadth or depth than the exam; however, they are designed to make sure that you know the answers. Rather than allowing you to derive the answers from clues hidden inside the questions themselves, the questions challenge your understanding and recall of the subject. Hopefully, these questions will help limit the number of exam questions on which you narrow your choices to two options and then guess.

The answers to these questions can be found in Appendix A.

1. How does a Catalyst switch detect that a connected device is capable of using Power over Ethernet?

2. What type of trunk can be used between a Catalyst switch port and a Cisco IP Phone?

3. When a trunk is used on an IP Phone, on which VLAN is the data from an attached PC carried?

4. What is the difference between the VVID and the PVID?

5. Can the CoS information from the voice traffic be passed when the **switchport voice vlan untagged** command is used? If so, how?

6. What is the advantage of using the **switchport voice vlan dot1p** command?

7. By default, does a Cisco IP Phone trust QoS information from an attached PC?

8. The command **switchport priority extend cos 5** is entered for a switch port. Is this a good decision? Why or why not?

9. The **show power inline** command is used to check the power status on each switch port. If the output is as shown here, what can you assume about interface fastethernet 0/1?

    ```
    Interface  Admin   Oper        Power      Device
                                   (Watts)
    ---------- -----   ----------  -------  ------------------
    Fa0/1      auto    off            0     n/a
    Fa0/2      auto    on           6.3     Cisco IP Phone 7960
    ```

10. What command can verify the QoS trust relationship between an IP Phone and its attached PC?

This chapter covers the following topics that you need to master for the CCNP BCMSN exam:

■ **Switch Authentication, Authorization, and Accounting (AAA)**—This section discusses methods that you can use to control switch management access to users.

■ **Port Security Using MAC Addresses**—This section explains how to configure switch ports to allow network access to only hosts with specific or learned MAC addresses.

■ **Port-Based Security Using IEEE 802.1x**—This section discusses a method you can use to require user authentication before network access is offered to a client host.

■ **Mitigating Spoofing Attacks**—This section covers two types of attacks in which a malicious user generates spoofed information to become a man-in-the-middle. When an attacker is wedged between other hosts and a router or gateway, for example, he can examine and exploit all traffic. DHCP snooping and dynamic ARP inspection are two features that can be used to prevent these attacks.

■ **Best Practices for Securing Switches**—This section provides several guidelines for tightening control over Catalyst switches and the protocols they use for switch communication and maintenance.

CHAPTER 17

Securing Switch Access

Traditionally, users have been able to connect a PC to a switched network and gain immediate access to enterprise resources. As networks grow and as more confidential data or restricted resources become available, it is important to limit the access that users receive.

Catalyst switches have a variety of methods that can secure or control user access. Users can be authenticated as they connect to or through a switch, and can be authorized to perform certain actions on a switch. User access can be recorded as switch accounting information. The physical switch port access also can be controlled based on the user's MAC address or authentication.

In addition, Catalyst switches can detect and prevent certain types of attacks. Several features can be used to validate information passing through a switch so that spoofed addresses can't be used to compromise hosts.

"Do I Know This Already?" Quiz

The purpose of the "Do I Know This Already?" quiz is to help you decide what parts of this chapter to use. If you already intend to read the entire chapter, you do not necessarily need to answer these questions now.

The quiz, derived from the major sections in the "Foundation Topics" portion of the chapter, helps you determine how to spend your limited study time.

Table 17-1 outlines the major topics discussed in this chapter and the "Do I Know This Already?" quiz questions that correspond to those topics.

Table 17-1   *"Do I Know This Already?" Foundation Topics Section-to-Question Mapping*

Foundation Topics Section	Questions Covered in This Section	Score
Switch AAA	1–3	
Port Security	4–7	
Port-Based Authentication	8–12	
Mitigating Spoofing Attacks	13–14	
Total Score		

> **CAUTION**   The goal of self-assessment is to gauge your mastery of the topics in this chapter. If you do not know the answer to a question or are only partially sure of the answer, you should mark this question wrong. Giving yourself credit for an answer you correctly guess skews your self-assessment results and might provide you with a false sense of security.

1. If the **username** command is used in a switch configuration, what method of authentication is implied?

   a. Remote

   b. Local

   c. RADIUS

   d. TACACS+

2. Which one of the following commands should be used to configure a vty line to use the myservers authentication method list?

   a. **line authentication myservers**

   b. **authentication myservers**

   c. **authentication method myservers**

   d. **login authentication myservers**

3. If a user needs to be in privileged EXEC or enable mode, which part of AAA must succeed?

   a. Authentication

   b. Authorization

   c. Accounting

   d. Administration

4. Which switch feature can grant access through a port only if the host with MAC address 0005.0004.0003 is connected?

   a. SPAN

   b. MAC address ACL

   c. Port security

   d. Port-based authentication

5. Port security is being used to control access to a switch port. Which one of these commands will put the port into the errdisable state if an unauthorized station connects?

   a. **switchport port-security violation protect**

   b. **switchport port-security violation restrict**

   c. **switchport port-security violation errdisable**

   d. **switchport port-security violation shutdown**

6. If port security is left to its default configuration, how many different MAC addresses can be learned at one time on a switch port?

   a. 0

   b. 1

   c. 16

   d. 256

7. The following commands are configured on a Catalyst switch port. What happens when the host with MAC address 0001.0002.0003 tries to connect?

```
switchport port-security
switchport port-security maximum 3
switchport port-security mac-address 0002.0002.0002
switchport port-security violation shutdown
```

   a. The port shuts down.

   b. The host is allowed to connect.

   c. The host is denied a connection.

   d. The host can connect only when 0002.0002.0002 is not connected.

8. What protocol is used for port-based authentication?

   a. 802.1D

   b. 802.1Q

   c. 802.1x

   d. 802.1w

9. When 802.1x is used for a switch port, where must it be configured?

   a. Switch port and client PC

   b. Switch port only

   c. Client PC only

   d. Switch port and a RADIUS server

10. When port-based authentication is enabled globally, what is the default behavior for all switch ports?

   a. Authenticate users before enabling the port.

   b. Allow all connections without authentication.

   c. Do not allow any connections.

   d. There is no default behavior.

11. When port-based authentication is enabled, what method is available for a user to authenticate?

   a. Web browser

   b. Telnet session

   c. 802.1x client

   d. DHCP

12. The users in a department are using a variety of host platforms, some old and some new. All of them have been approved with a user ID in a RADIUS server database. Which one of these features should be used to restrict access to the switch ports in the building?

   a. AAA authentication

   b. AAA authorization

   c. Port security

   d. Port-based authentication

13. With DHCP snooping, an untrusted port filters out which one of the following?

   a. DHCP replies from legitimate DHCP servers

   b. DHCP replies from rogue DHCP servers

   c. DHCP requests from legitimate clients

   d. DHCP requests from rogue clients

14. Which one of the following should be configured as a trusted port for dynamic ARP inspection?

   a. The port where the ARP server is located

   b. The port where an end-user host is located

   c. The port where another switch is located

   d. None; all ports are untrusted

The answers to the "Do I Know This Already?" quiz are found in Appendix A, "Answers to Chapter 'Do I Know This Already?' Quizzes and Q&A Sections." The suggested choices for your next step are as follows:

- **11 or less overall score**—Read the entire chapter. This includes the "Foundation Topics," "Foundation Summary," and "Q&A" sections.

- **12 or more overall score**—If you want more review on these topics, skip to the "Foundation Summary" section and then go to the "Q&A" section at the end of the chapter. Otherwise, move to Chapter 18, "Securing with VLANs."

Foundation Topics

Switch AAA

You can manage user activity to and through a switch with authentication, authorization, and accounting (AAA) features. AAA uses standardized methods to challenge users for their credentials before access is allowed or authorized. Accounting protocols also can record user activity on a switch.

Authentication

Switch or network access can be granted only after a user's identity has been validated. User authentication commonly is used on switches and routers to limit Telnet access to the network-administration staff. In this case, when someone uses Telnet to log on to a switch, that individual first is challenged with a username and password. The individual's credentials then are submitted to a device that can grant the user access.

User authentication can be handled by several methods:

- Usernames and passwords configured locally on the switch

- One or more external Remote Authentication Dial-In User Service (RADIUS) servers

- One or more external Terminal Access Controller Access Control System+ (TACACS+) servers

Any combination of these methods can be used. In fact, authentication must be defined by grouping the desired methods into a method list. The list contains the types or protocols that will be used, in the sequential order that they will be tried.

To use authentication on a Catalyst switch, you must configure several things in the following order:

Step 1   Enable AAA on the switch.

By default, AAA is disabled. Therefore, all user authentication is handled locally by configuring usernames and passwords. To enable AAA, use the following global configuration command:

```
Switch(config)# aaa new-model
```

The **new-model** refers to the use of method lists, by which authentication methods and sources can be grouped or organized. The new model is much more scalable than the "old model," in which the authentication source was explicitly configured.

Step 2   Define the source of authentication.

You can compare user credentials against locally configured usernames and passwords, or against a database managed by external RADIUS or TACACS+ servers.

Use locally configured usernames and passwords as a last resort, when no other authentication servers are reachable or in use on the network. To define a username, use the following global configuration command:

```
Switch(config)# username username password password
```

RADIUS or TACACS+ servers are defined in groups. First, define each server along with its secret shared password. This string is known only to the switch and the server, and provides a key for encrypting the authentication session. Use one of the following global configuration commands:

```
Switch(config)# radius-server host {hostname | ip-address} [key string]
Switch(config)# tacacs-server host {hostname | ip-address} [key string]
```

Then define a group name that will contain a list of servers, using the following global configuration command:

```
Switch(config)# aaa group server {radius | tacacs+} group-name
```

Define each server of the group type with the following server-group configuration command:

```
Switch(config)# server ip-address
```

You can define multiple RADIUS or TACACS+ servers by repeating these commands.

Step 3   Define a list of authentication methods to try.

You can list switch login authentication methods by giving the method a descriptive name or using the unnamed "default" method. List each method or protocol type in the order that it should be tried. If none of the servers for the first method responds, the switch tries the servers in the next method listed.

Use the following global configuration command to define a method list:

```
Switch(config)# aaa authentication login {default | list-name} method1
  [method2 ...]
```

Here the methods refer to these values:

- **tacacs+**—Each of the TACACS+ servers configured on the switch is tried, in the order that it was configured.

- **radius**—Each of the RADIUS servers configured on the switch is tried, in the order that it was configured.

- **local**—The user's credentials are compared against all the username commands configured on the local switch.

- **line**—The line passwords authenticate any connected user. No usernames can be used.

> **TIP**   Be sure to add either the **local** or **line** methods at the end of the list, as a last resort. This way, if all the RADIUS or TACACS+ servers are unavailable or the switch is completely isolated from the rest of the network, a locally configured authentication method eventually will be used. Otherwise, you will never be able to get into the switch.

Step 4   Apply a method list to a switch line.

First, select a line (console or vty for Telnet access) using the **line** *line* command. Then trigger the user authentication on that line to use an AAA method list. Use the following line-configuration command:

```
Switch(line)# login authentication {default | list-name}
```

You can use the default method list if only one list is sufficient for all circumstances on the switch. Otherwise, if you have configured named method lists, you can reference one of them here.

Step 5   After authentication is configured on a switch, it is a good idea to stay logged in on one session so that the authentication can be tested. If you exit the configuration session, you will not be able to log in again if the authentication is misconfigured. While you stay logged in on the original session, bring up a new Telnet session to the switch. If you can authenticate successfully, everything is configured properly.

Authorization

After a user is authenticated, the switch allows access to certain services or switch commands based on the user's privilege level. Authenticating puts the user at the EXEC level, by default.

Certain commands, such as **show interface**, are available at the EXEC level. Other commands, such as **configure terminal**, are accessible only if the user is able to move into the privileged EXEC or enable mode.

Authorization provides a means of granting specific users the ability to perform certain tasks. As with authentication, authorization is performed by querying external RADIUS or TACACS+ servers. If the authorization server has an entry for a user and a service or command, the switch allows the user to perform that task.

You configure authorization by first defining any RADIUS or TACACS+ servers that will be used. These normally are defined as part of the authentication configuration and do not need to be redefined for authorization.

Next, define a method list of authorization methods that will be tried in sequence using the following global configuration command:

```
Switch(config)# aaa authorization {commands | config-commands | configuration | exec |
network | reverse-access} {default | list-name} method1 [method2 ...]
```

Here you specify the function or service needing authorization with one of the following values:

- **commands**—The server must return permission to use any switch command at any privilege level.

- **config-commands**—The server must return permission to use any switch-configuration command.

- **configuration**—The server must return permission to enter the switch-configuration mode.

- **exec**—The server must return permission for the user to run a switch EXEC session. The server also can return the privilege level for the user so that the user immediately can be put into privileged EXEC (enable) mode without having to type in the **enable** command.

- **network**—The server must return permission to use network-related services.

- **reverse-access**—The server must return permission for the user to access a reverse Telnet session on the switch.

You can identify the method with a descriptive name (*list-name*) if you are configuring more than one list. Otherwise, a single unnamed list is called the *default* list. Each authorization method then is listed in the order it will be tried. The methods can be any of the following values:

- **group** *group-name*—Requests are sent to the servers in a specific group.

- **group** {**radius** | **tacacs+**}—Requests are sent to all servers of this type.

- **if-authenticated**—Requests are granted if the user already is authenticated.

- **none**—No external authorization is used; every user is authorized successfully.

> **TIP** Only TACACS+ servers can authorize users with permission to use specific commands. RADIUS servers offer more of an all-or-nothing approach.

Next, you can apply an authorization method list to a specific line on the switch. Users accessing the switch through that line will be subject to authorization. Use the following line-configuration command:

```
Switch(config-line)# authorization {commands level | exec | reverse-access} {default |
list-name}
```

If you do not use this command, the default group is used for all lines.

Accounting

Catalyst switches also support the capability to use AAA for producing accounting information of user activity. RADIUS and TACACS+ servers also can collect this accounting information from switches, if wanted. Again, the RADIUS and TACACS+ servers already must be configured and grouped as part of the authentication configuration.

As usual, you must define a method list giving a sequence of accounting methods by using the following global configuration command:

```
Switch(config)# aaa accounting {system | exec | commands level} {default | list-name}
{start-stop | stop-only | wait-start | none} method1 [method2 ...]
```

The function triggering the accounting can be one of the following:

- **system**—Major switch events such as a reload are recorded.

- **exec**—User authentication into an EXEC session is recorded, along with information about the user's address and the time and duration of the session.

- **commands** *level*—Information about any command running at a specific privilege level is recorded, along with the user who issued the command.

You can specify that certain types of accounting records be sent to the accounting server using the following keywords:

- **start-stop**—Events are recorded when they start and stop.

- **stop-only**—Events are recorded only when they stop.

■ **none**—No events are recorded.

Next, you can apply an accounting method list to a specific line on the switch. Users accessing the switch through that line will have their activity recorded. Use the following line-configuration command to accomplish this:

```
Switch(config-line)# accounting {commands level | connection | exec} {default | list-name}
```

If you do not use this command, the default group will be used for all lines.

Port Security

In some environments, a network must be secured by controlling what stations can gain access to the network itself. Where user workstations are stationary, their MAC addresses always can be expected to connect to the same access-layer switch ports. If stations are mobile, their MAC addresses can be learned dynamically or added to a list of addresses to expect on a switch port.

Catalyst switches offer the port security feature to control port access based on MAC addresses. To configure port security on an access-layer switch port, begin by enabling it with the following interface-configuration command:

```
Switch(config-if)# switchport port-security
```

Next, you must identify a set of allowed MAC addresses so that the port can grant them access. You can explicitly configure addresses or they can be learned dynamically from port traffic. On each interface that uses port security, specify the maximum number of MAC addresses that will be allowed access using the following interface-configuration command:

```
Switch(config-if)# switchport port-security maximum max-addr
```

By default, only one MAC address will be allowed access on each switch port. You can set the maximum number of addresses in the range of 1 to 1024.

Each interface using port security dynamically learns MAC addresses by default and expects those addresses to appear on that interface in the future. These are called *sticky MAC addresses*. MAC addresses are learned as hosts transmit frames on an interface. The interface learns up to the maximum number of addresses allowed. Learned addresses also can be aged out of the table if those hosts are silent for a period of time. By default, no aging occurs.

For example, to set the maximum number of MAC addresses that can be active on a switch port at any time to two, you could use the following command:

```
Switch(config-if)# switchport port-security maximum 2
```

You also can statically define one or more MAC addresses on an interface. Any of these addresses are allowed to access the network through the port. Use the following interface-configuration command to define a static address:

```
Switch(config-if)# switchport port-security mac-address mac-addr
```

The MAC address is given in dotted-triplet format. If the number of static addresses configured is less than the maximum number of addresses secured on a port, the remaining addresses are learned dynamically. Be sure to set the maximum number appropriately.

You can use the following command to configure a static address entry on an interface:

```
Switch(config-if)# switchport port-security mac-address 0006.5b02.a841
```

Finally, you must define how each interface using port security should react if a MAC address is in violation by using the following interface-configuration command:

```
Switch(config-if)# switchport port-security violation {shutdown | restrict | protect}
```

A violation occurs if more than the maximum number of MAC addresses are learned or if an unknown (not statically defined) MAC address attempts to transmit on the port. The switch port takes one of the following configured actions when a violation is detected:

- **shutdown**—The port immediately is put into the errdisable state, which effectively shuts it down. It must be re-enabled manually or through errdisable recovery to be used again.

- **restrict**—The port is allowed to stay up, but all packets from violating MAC addresses are dropped. The switch keeps a running count of the number of violating packets and can send an SNMP trap and a syslog message as an alert of the violation.

- **protect**—The port is allowed to stay up, as in the **restrict** mode. Although packets from violating addresses are dropped, no record of the violation is kept.

As an example of the **restrict** mode, a switch interface has received the following configuration commands:

```
interface GigabitEthernet0/11
 switchport access vlan 991
 switchport mode access
 switchport port-security
 switchport port-security violation restrict
 spanning-tree portfast
```

When the default maximum of one MAC address is exceeded on this interface, the condition is logged but the interface stays up. This is shown by the following syslog message:

```
Jun  3 17:18:41.888 EDT: %PORT_SECURITY-2-PSECURE_VIOLATION: Security violation
occurred, caused by MAC address 0000.5e00.0101 on port GigabitEthernet0/11.
```

> **TIP** If an interface is undergoing the **restrict** or **protect** condition, you might need to clear the learned MAC addresses so that a specific host can use the switch port. You can clear a MAC address or the complete port cache with the following command:
>
> ```
> Switch# clear port-security dynamic [address mac-addr | interface type mod/num]
> ```

In the **shutdown** mode, the port security action is much more drastic. When the maximum number of MAC addresses is exceeded, the following syslog messages indicate that the port has been shut down in the errdisable state:

```
Jun  3 17:14:19.018 EDT: %PM-4-ERR_DISABLE: psecure-violation error detected on
Gi0/11, putting Gi0/11 in err-disable state
Jun  3 17:14:19.022 EDT: %PORT_SECURITY-2-PSECURE_VIOLATION: Security violation
occurred, caused by MAC address 0003.a089.efc5 on port GigabitEthernet0/11.
Jun  3 17:14:20.022 EDT: %LINEPROTO-5-UPDOWN: Line protocol on Interface Gigabit
Ethernet0/11, changed state to down
Jun  3 17:14:21.023 EDT: %LINK-3-UPDOWN: Interface GigabitEthernet0/11, changed
state to down
```

You also can show the port status with the **show port-security interface** command, as demonstrated in Example 17-1.

Example 17-1 *Displaying Port Security Port Status*

```
Switch# show port-security interface gigabitethernet 0/11
Port Security              : Enabled
Port Status                : Secure-shutdown
Violation Mode             : Shutdown
Aging Time                 : 0 mins
Aging Type                 : Absolute
SecureStatic Address Aging : Disabled
Maximum MAC Addresses      : 1
Total MAC Addresses        : 0
Configured MAC Addresses   : 0
Sticky MAC Addresses       : 0
Last Source Address        : 0003.a089.efc5
Security Violation Count   : 1
Switch#
```

To see a quick summary of only ports in the errdisable state, along with the reason for errdisable, you can use the **show interfaces status err-disabled** command, as demonstrated in Example 17-2.

Example 17-2 *Displaying Summary Information for Ports in the Errdisable State*

```
Switch# show interfaces status err-disabled

Port      Name             Status         Reason
Gi0/11    Test port        err-disabled   psecure-violation
Switch#
```

> **TIP**   When a port is moved to the errdisable state, you must either manually cycle it or configure the switch to automatically re-enable ports after a prescribed delay. To manually cycle a port and return it to service, use the following commands:
>
> ```
> Switch(config)# interface type mod/num
> Switch(config-if)# shutdown
> Switch(config-if)# no shutdown
> ```

Finally, you can display a summary of the port-security status with the **show port-security** command, as demonstrated in Example 17-3.

Example 17-3 *Displaying Port Security Status Summary Information*

```
Switch# show port-security
Secure Port  MaxSecureAddr  CurrentAddr  SecurityViolation  Security Action
             (Count)        (Count)      (Count)

---------------------------------------------------------------------------
    Gi0/11          5             1               0            Restrict
    Gi0/12          1             0               0            Shutdown
---------------------------------------------------------------------------
Total Addresses in System (excluding one mac per port)    : 0
Max Addresses limit in System (excluding one mac per port) : 6176
Switch#
```

Port-Based Authentication

Catalyst switches can support port-based authentication, a combination of AAA authentication and port security. This feature is based on the IEEE 802.1x standard.

Basically, a switch port will not pass any traffic until a user has authenticated with the switch. If the authentication is successful, the user can use the port normally.

For port-based authentication, both the switch and the end user's PC must support the 802.1x standard, using the Extensible Authentication Protocol over LANs (EAPOL). The 802.1x standard is a cooperative effort between the client and the switch offering network service. If the client PC is configured to use 802.1x but the switch does not support it, the PC abandons the protocol and communicates normally. However, if the switch is configured for 802.1x but the PC does not support it, the switch port remains in the unauthorized state so that it will not forward any traffic to the client PC.

> **NOTE**   802.1x EAPOL is a Layer 2 protocol. At the point that a switch detects the presence of a device on a port, the port remains in the unauthorized state. Therefore, the client PC cannot communicate with anything other than the switch by using EAPOL. If the PC does not already have an IP address, it cannot request one. The PC also has no knowledge of the switch or its IP address, so any means other than a Layer 2 protocol is not possible. This is why the PC also must have an 802.1x-capable application or client software.

An 802.1x switch port begins in the unauthorized state so that no data other than the 802.1x protocol itself is allowed through the port. Either the client or the switch can initiate an 802.1x session. The authorized state of the port ends when the user logs out, causing the 802.1x client to inform the switch to revert back to the unauthorized state. The switch also can time out the user's authorized session. In this event, the client must reauthenticate to continue using the switch port.

802.1x Configuration

Port-based authentication uses a variety of methods to authenticate potential clients. A method list is configured, defining the methods to be tried in sequence. Begin by configuring an 802.1x method list with the following global configuration command:

```
Switch(config)# aaa authentication dot1x {default | list-name} method1 [method2 ...]
```

Be sure that the **aaa new-model** command already has been configured. Here, a method is defined by one of the following keywords:

- **group** {*group-name* | **radius** | **tacacs+**}—Authentication servers are used to authenticate the user. These are configured as the group *group-name*. Otherwise, all the available RADIUS or TACACS+ servers are tried. These servers are configured exactly the same as with the AAA feature.

- **enable**—The enable password authenticates the user.

- **line**—The line password authenticates the user. This applies only when 802.1x is being used on a switch line (console or vty).

- **local**—The locally defined usernames and passwords are used to authenticate the user.

- **none**—No authentication is performed.

If RADIUS or TACACS+ servers are used as a method, including one of the local methods at the end of the line is wise. This gives a predictable last-resort method if all the authentication servers are unavailable. Otherwise, users or support staff could be locked out of the switch.

Next, enable the use of 802.1x on the switch with the following global configuration command:

```
Switch(config)# dot1x system-auth-control
```

You must configure each switch port that will use 802.1x. Use the following interface-configuration command to set the authentication state:

```
Switch(config-if)# dot1x port-control {force-authorized | force-unauthorized | auto}
```

Here, the 802.1x state is one of the following:

- **force-authorized**—The port is forced to always authorize any connected client. No authentication is necessary. This is the default state for all switch ports when 802.1x is enabled.

- **force-unauthorized**—The port is forced to never authorize any connected client. As a result, the port cannot move to the authorized state to pass traffic to a connected client.

- **auto**—The port uses an 802.1x exchange to move from the unauthorized to the authorized state, if successful. This requires an 802.1x-capable application on the client PC.

It might be obvious that port-based authentication is tailored to controlling access to a single host PC that is connected to a switch port. However, it also supports cases in which multiple hosts are attached to a single switch port through an Ethernet hub or another access-layer switch.

If the switch should expect to find multiple hosts present on the switch port, use the following interface-configuration command:

```
Switch(config-if)# dot1x multi-hosts
```

Mitigating Spoofing Attacks

Malicious users sometimes can send spoofed information to trick switches or other hosts into using a rogue machine as a gateway. The attacker's goal is to become the "man-in-the-middle," with a naïve user sending packets to the attacker as if it were a router. The attacker can glean information from the packets sent to it before it forwards them normally. This section describes two Cisco Catalyst features—DHCP snooping and dynamic ARP inspection—that prevent certain types of spoofing attack.

DHCP Snooping

A DHCP server normally provides all the basic information a client PC needs to operate on a network. For example, the client might receive an IP address, a subnet mask, a default gateway address, DNS addresses, and so on.

Suppose that an attacker could bring up a rogue DHCP server on a machine in the same subnet as that same client PC. Now when the client broadcast its DHCP request, the rogue server could send a carefully crafted DHCP reply with its own IP address substituted as the default gateway.

When the client receives the reply, it begins using the spoofed gateway address. Packets destined for addresses outside the local subnet then go to the attacker's machine first. The attacker can forward the packets to the correct destination, but in the meantime, it can examine every packet that it intercepts. In effect, this becomes a type of man-in-the-middle attack; the attacker is wedged into the path and the client doesn't realize it.

Cisco Catalyst switches can use the DHCP snooping feature to help mitigate this type of attack. When DHCP snooping is enabled, switch ports are categorized as trusted or untrusted. Legitimate DHCP servers can be found on trusted ports, while all other hosts sit behind untrusted ports.

A switch intercepts all DHCP requests coming from untrusted ports before flooding them throughout the VLAN. Any DHCP replies coming from an untrusted port are discarded because they must have come from a rogue DHCP server. In addition, the offending switch port automatically is shut down in the errdisable state.

DHCP snooping also keeps track of the completed DHCP bindings as clients receive legitimate replies. This database contains the client MAC address, IP address offered, lease time, and so on.

You can configure DHCP snooping first by enabling it globally on a switch with the following configuration command:

```
Switch(config)# ip dhcp snooping
```

Next identify the VLANs where DHCP snooping should be implemented with the following command:

```
Switch(config)# ip dhcp snooping vlan vlan-id [vlan-id]
```

You can give a single VLAN number as *vlan-id* or a range of VLAN numbers by giving the start and end VLAN IDs of the range.

By default, all switch ports are assumed to be untrusted so that DHCP replies are not expected or permitted. Only trusted ports are allowed to send DHCP replies. Therefore, you should identify only the ports where known, trusted DHCP servers are located. You can do this with the following interface-configuration command:

```
Switch(config)# interface type mod/num
Switch(config-if)# ip dhcp snooping trust
```

For untrusted ports, an unlimited rate of DHCP requests is accepted. If you want to rate-limit DHCP traffic on an untrusted port, use the following interface-configuration command:

```
Switch(config)# interface type mod/num
Switch(config-if)# ip dhcp snooping limit rate rate
```

The *rate* can be 1 to 2048 DHCP packets per second.

You also can configure the switch to use DHCP option-82, the *DHCP Relay Agent Information* option, which is described in RFC 3046. When a DHCP request is intercepted on an untrusted port, the switch adds its own MAC address and the switch port identifier into the option-82 field of the request. The request then is forwarded normally so that it can reach a trusted DHCP server.

Adding option-82 provides more information about the actual client that generated the DHCP request. In addition, the DHCP reply (if any) echoes back the option-82 information. The switch intercepts the reply and compares the option-82 data to confirm that the request came from a valid port on itself. This feature is enabled by default. You can enable or disable option-82 globally with the following configuration command:

```
Switch(config)# [no] ip dhcp snooping information option
```

When DHCP snooping is configured, you can display its status with the following command:

```
Switch# show ip dhcp snooping [binding]
```

Using the **binding** keyword results in a display of all the known DHCP bindings that have been overheard. The switch maintains these in its own database. Otherwise, only the switch ports that are trusted or that have rate limiting applied are listed. All other ports are considered to be untrusted with an unlimited DHCP request rate.

As an example, interfaces FastEthernet 0/35 and 0/36 use access VLAN 104, are considered untrusted, and have DHCP rate limiting applied at three per second. A known DHCP server is located on the GigabitEthernet 0/1 uplink. Example 17-4 shows the configuration for this scenario.

Example 17-4 *DHCP Snooping Configuration*

```
Switch(config)# ip dhcp snooping
Switch(config)# ip dhcp snooping vlan 104
Switch(config)# interface range fastethernet 0/35 - 36
Switch(config-if)# ip dhcp snooping limit rate 3
Switch(config-if)# interface gigabitethernet 0/1
Switch(config-if)# ip dhcp snooping trust
```

Example 17-5 shows the resulting DHCP snooping status.

Example 17-5 *DHCP Snooping Status Display*

```
Switch# show ip dhcp snooping
Switch DHCP snooping is enabled
DHCP snooping is configured on following VLANs:
104
Insertion of option 82 is enabled
Interface                    Trusted      Rate limit (pps)
----------------------       -------      ----------------
FastEthernet0/35             no           3
FastEthernet0/36             no           3
GigabitEthernet0/1           yes          unlimited
Switch#
```

Dynamic ARP Inspection

Hosts normally use the Address Resolution Protocol (ARP) to resolve an unknown MAC address when the IP address is known. If a MAC address is needed so that a packet can be forwarded at Layer 2, a host broadcasts an ARP request that contains the IP address of the target in question. If any other host is using that IP address, it responds with an ARP reply containing its MAC address.

The ARP process works well among trusted and well-behaved users. However, suppose that an attacker could send its own crafted ARP reply when it overhears an ARP request being broadcast. The reply could contain its own MAC address, causing the original requester to think that it is bound to the IP address in question. The requester would add the bogus ARP entry into its own ARP cache, only to begin forwarding packets to the spoofed MAC address.

In effect, this scheme places the attacker's machine right in the middle of an otherwise legitimate path. Packets will be sent to the attacker instead of another host or the default gateway. The attacker will be able to intercept packets and (perhaps) will forward them on only after examining the packets' contents.

This attack is known as *ARP poisoning* or *ARP spoofing*, and it is considered to be a type of man-in-the-middle attack. The attacker wedges into the normal forwarding path, transparent to the end users. Cisco Catalyst switches can use the dynamic ARP inspection (DAI) feature to help mitigate this type of attack.

DAI works much like DHCP snooping. All switch ports are classified as trusted or untrusted. The switch intercepts and inspects all ARP packets that arrive on an untrusted port; no inspection is done on trusted ports.

When an ARP reply is received on an untrusted port, the switch checks the MAC and IP addresses reported in the reply packet against known and trusted values. A switch can gather trusted ARP information from statically configured entries or from dynamic entries in the DHCP snooping database. In the latter case, DHCP snooping must be enabled in addition to DAI.

If an ARP reply contains invalid information or values that conflict with entries in the trusted database, it is dropped and a log message is generated. This action prevents invalid or spoofed ARP entries from being sent and added to other machines' ARP caches.

You can configure DAI by first enabling it on one or more client VLANs with the following configuration command:

```
Switch(config)# ip arp inspection vlan vlan-range
```

The VLAN range can be a single VLAN ID, a range of VLAN IDs separated by a hyphen, or a list of VLAN IDs separated by commas.

By default, all switch ports associated with the VLAN range are considered to be untrusted. You should identify trusted ports as those that connect to other switches. In other words, the local switch will not inspect ARP packets arriving on trusted ports; it will assume that the neighboring switch also is performing DAI on all of its ports in that VLAN. Configure a trusted port with the following interface-configuration command:

```
Switch(config)# interface type mod/num
Switch(config-if)# ip arp inspection trust
```

If you have hosts with statically configured IP address information, there will be no DHCP message exchange that can be inspected. Instead, you can configure an ARP access list that defines static MAC-IP address bindings that are permitted. Use the following configuration commands to define the ARP access list and one or more static entries:

```
Switch(config)# arp access-list acl-name
Switch(config-acl)# permit ip host sender-ip mac host sender-mac [log]
[Repeat the previous command as needed]
Switch(config-acl)# exit
```

Now the ARP access list must be applied to DAI with the following configuration command:

```
Switch(config)# ip arp inspection filter arp-acl-name vlan vlan-range [static]
```

When ARP replies are intercepted, their contents are matched against the access list entries first. If no match is found, the DHCP snooping bindings database is checked next. You can give the **static** keyword to prevent the DHCP bindings database from being checked at all. In effect, this creates an implicit deny statement at the end of the ARP access list; if no match is found in the access list, the ARP reply is considered to be invalid.

Finally, you can specify further validations on the contents of ARP reply packets. By default, only the MAC and IP addresses contained within the ARP reply are validated. This doesn't take the actual MAC addresses contained in the Ethernet header of the ARP reply.

To validate that an ARP reply packet is really coming from the address listed inside it, you can enable DAI validation with the following configuration command:

```
Switch(config)# ip arp inspection validate {[src-mac] [dst-mac] [ip]}
```

Be sure to specify at least one of the options:

- **src-mac**—Check the source MAC address in the Ethernet header against the sender MAC address in the ARP reply.

- **dst-mac**—Check the destination MAC address in the Ethernet header against the target MAC address in the ARP reply.

- **ip**—Check the sender's IP address in all ARP requests; check the sender's IP address against the target IP address in all ARP replies.

Example 17-6 demonstrates where DAI is enabled for all switch ports associated with VLAN 104 on an access-layer switch. The uplink to a distribution switch is considered to be trusted.

Example 17-6 *Configuring DAI to Validate ARP Replies*

```
Switch(config)# ip arp inspection vlan 104
Switch(config)# arp access-list StaticARP
Switch(config-acl)# permit ip host 192.168.1.10 mac host 0006.5b02.a841
Switch(config-acl)# exit
Switch(config)# ip arp inspection filter StaticARP vlan 104
Switch(config)# interface gigabitethernet 0/1
Switch(config-if)# ip arp inspection trust
```

You can display DAI status information with the **show ip arp inspection** command.

Best Practices for Securing Switches

You can configure and use many different features on Cisco Catalyst switches. You should be aware of some common weaknesses that can be exploited. In other words, don't become complacent and assume that everyone connected to your network will be good citizens and play by the rules. Think ahead and try to prevent as many things as possible that might be leveraged to assist an attacker.

This section presents a brief overview of many best-practice suggestions that will help secure your switched network.

- **Configure secure passwords**—Whenever possible, you should use the **enable secret** command to set the privileged-level password on a switch. This command uses a stronger encryption than the normal **enable password** command and stores the password in a secure location in NVRAM.

    You also should use external AAA servers to authenticate administrative users whenever possible. The usernames and passwords are maintained externally, so they are not stored or managed directly on the switch. In addition, having a centralized user management is much more scalable than configuring and changing user credentials on many individual switches and routers.

    Finally, you always should use the **service password-encryption** configuration command to automatically encrypt password strings that are stored in the switch configuration. Although the encryption is not strong, it can prevent casual observers from seeing passwords in the clear.

- **Use system banners**—When users successfully access a switch, they should be aware of any specific access or acceptable use policies that are pertinent to your organization. You should configure system banners so that this type of information is displayed right when users log in to a switch. The idea is to warn unauthorized users (if they gain access) that their activities could be grounds for prosecution—or that they are unwelcome, at the very least.

    You should use the **banner motd** command to define the text that is displayed to authenticated users. Try to avoid using other banner types that display information about your organization or the switch before users actually log in. Never divulge any extra information about your network that malicious users could use.

- **Disable unnecessary or insecure services**—Cisco devices sometimes have unused or unnecessary services enabled by default. To tighten security, you should allow only the services, features, and protocols that are needed for your infrastructure. Anything more than that can become a potential weakness that could be exploited.

For example, you should strongly consider disabling the HTTP server on a Catalyst switch. This often is used for a web-based switch-management tool but is usually unneeded in a production environment. You can disable it with the **no ip http server** configuration command.

Although Cisco IOS Software releases have begun to disable other uncommon services as the default, you should make sure that none of the following commands is present in your switch configuration:

```
service tcp-small-servers
service udp-small-servers
service finger
service config
```

If any of these commands are present, disable them by preceding them with the **no** keyword.

- **Secure the switch console**—In many environments, switches are locked away in wiring closets where physical security is used to keep people from connecting to the switch console. Even so, you always should configure authentication on any switch console. It is usually appropriate to use the same authentication configuration on the console as the virtual terminal (vty) lines.

- **Secure virtual terminal access**—You always should configure user authentication on *all* of the vty lines on a switch. In addition, you should use access lists to limit the source IP addresses of potential administrative users who try to use Telnet or Secure Shell (SSH) to access a switch.

  You can use a simple IP access list to permit inbound connections only from known source addresses, as in the following example:

```
Switch(config)# access-list 10 permit 192.168.199.10
Switch(config)# access-list 10 permit 192.168.201.100
Switch(config)# line vty 0 15
Switch(config-line)# access-class 10 in
```

  Be sure you apply the access list to all the **line vty** entries in the switch configuration. Many times, the vty lines are separated into groups in the configuration. You can use the **show user all** command to see every possible line that can be used to access a switch.

- **Use SSH whenever possible**—Although Telnet access is easy to configure and use, Telnet is not secure. Every character you type in a Telnet session is sent to and echoed from a switch in the clear, with no encryption. Therefore, it is very easy to eavesdrop on Telnet sessions to overhear usernames and passwords.

  Instead, you should use SSH whenever possible. SSH uses strong encryption to secure session data. Therefore, you need a strong-encryption IOS image running on a switch before SSH can be configured and used. You should use the highest SSH version that is available on a switch. The early SSHv1 and SSHv1.5 have some weaknesses. SSHv2 is better yet but is available only in recent IOS releases, such as 12.2(25)SEB1 on the Catalyst 3750.

- **Secure SNMP access**—To prevent unauthorized users from making changes to a switch configuration, you should disable any read-write SNMP access. These are commands of the form **snmp-server community** *string* **RW**.

  Instead, you should have only read-only commands in the configuration. In addition, you should use access lists to limit the source addresses that have read-only access. Don't depend on the SNMP community strings for security because these are passed in the clear in SNMP packets.

- **Secure unused switch ports**—Every unused switch port should be disabled so that unexpected users can't connect and use them without your knowledge. You can do this with the **shutdown** interface-configuration command.

  In addition, you should configure every user port as an access port with the **switchport mode access** interface-configuration command. Otherwise, a malicious user might connect and attempt to negotiate trunking mode on a port. You also should consider associating every unused access port with a bogus or isolated VLAN. If an unexpected user does gain access to a port, he will have access only to a VLAN that is isolated from every other resource on your network.

> **TIP** You might consider using the **switchport host** interface-configuration command as a quick way to force a port to support only a single PC. This command is actually a macro, as seen in the following example:
>
> ```
> Switch(config)# interface fastethernet 1/0/1
> Switch(config-if)# switchport host
> switchport mode will be set to access
> spanning-tree portfast will be enabled
> channel group will be disabled
> Switch(config-if)#
> ```

- **Secure STP operation**—A malicious user can inject STP bridge protocol data units (BPDUs) into switch ports or VLANs, and can disrupt a stable, loop-free topology. You always should enable the BPDU guard feature so that access switch ports automatically are disabled if unexpected BPDUs are received.

- **Secure the Use of CDP**—By default, CDP advertisements are sent on *every* switch port at 60-second intervals. Although CDP is a very handy tool for discovering neighboring Cisco devices, you shouldn't allow CDP to advertise unnecessary information about your switch to listening attackers.

For example, the following information is sent in a CDP advertisement in the clear. An attacker might be able to use the device ID to physically locate the switch, its IP address to target Telnet or SNMP attacks, or the native VLAN and switch port ID to attempt a VLAN hopping attack.

```
CDP - Cisco Discovery Protocol
   Version:              2
   Time to live:         180   seconds
   Checksum:             0xD0AE
   Device ID:            BldgA-Rm110
   Version:              Cisco Internetwork Operating System Software .IOS
(tm) C3750 Software (C3750-I9-M), Version 12.2(20)SE4, RELEASE SOFTWARE
(fc1).Copyright  1986-2005 by cisco Systems, Inc..Compiled Sun 09-Jan-05
00:09 by antonino
   Platform:             cisco WS-C3750-48P
   IP Address:           192.168.100.85
   Port ID:              FastEthernet1/0/48
   Capabilities:         0x00000028  Switch   IGMP
   VTP Domain:           MyCompany
   Native VLAN:          101
   Duplex:               0x01  Full
```

CDP should be enabled only on switch ports that connect to other trusted Cisco devices. Don't forget that CDP must be enabled on access switch ports where Cisco IP Phones are connected. When the CDP messages reach the IP Phone, they won't be relayed on to a PC connected to the phone's data port. You can disable CDP on a port-by-port basis with the **no cdp enable** interface-configuration command.

Foundation Summary

The Foundation Summary is a collection of tables that provides a convenient review of many key concepts in this chapter. If you are already comfortable with the topics in this chapter, this summary can help you recall a few details. If you just read this chapter, this review should help solidify some key facts. If you are doing your final preparation before the exam, these tables and figures are a convenient way to review the day before the exam.

Table 17-2 *AAA Configuration Commands*

Task	Command Syntax
Enable AAA on a switch	**aaa new-model**
Use local authentication	**username** *username* **password** *password*
Define individual authentication servers	**radius-server host** {*hostname* ı *ip-address*} [**key** *string*] **tacacs-server host** {*hostname* ı *ip-address*} [**key** *string*]
Define a group of authentication servers	**aaa group server** {**radius** ı **tacacs+**} *group-name* **server** *ip-address*
Define a list of authentication methods to try	**aaa authentication login** {**default** ı *list-name*} *method1* [*method2* ...]
Apply an authentication method list to a line	**login authentication** {**default** ı *list-name*}
Define a list of authorization methods to try	**aaa authorization** {**commands** ı **config-commands** ı **configuration** ı **exec** ı **network** ı **reverse-access**} {**default** ı *list-name*} *method1* [*method2* ...]
Apply an authorization method list to a line	**authorization** {**commands** *level* ı **exec** ı **reverse-access**} {**default** ı *list- name*}
Define a list of accounting methods to try	**aaa accounting** {**system** ı **exec** ı **commands** *level*} {**default** ı *list-name*} {**start-stop** ı **stop-only** ı **wait-start** ı **none**} *method1* [*method2* ...]
Apply an accounting method list to a line	**accounting** {**commands** *level* ı **connection** ı **exec**} {**default** ı *list-name*}

Table 17-3 *Port Security Configuration Commands*

Task	Command Syntax
Enable port security on an interface	**switchport port-security**

Table 17-3 *Port Security Configuration Commands*

Set the maximum number of learned addresses	**switchport port-security maximum** *max-addr*
Define a static MAC address	**switchport port-security mac-address** *mac-addr*
Define an action to take	**switchport port-security violation {shutdown ı restrict ı protect}**

Table 17-4 *Port-Based Authentication Configuration Commands*

Task	Command Syntax
Define a method list for 802.1x	**aaa authentication dot1x {default ı** *list-name*} *method1* [*method2* ...]
Globally enable 802.1x	**dot1x system-auth-control**
Define the 802.1x behavior on a port	**dot1x port-control {force-authorized ı force-unauthorized ı auto}**
Support more than one host on a port	**dot1x multi-hosts**

Table 17-5 *DHCP Snooping Configuration Commands*

Task	Command Syntax
Globally enable DHCP snooping	**ip dhcp snooping**
Define a trusted interface	**ip dhcp snooping trust**
Limit the interface DHCP packet rate	**ip dhcp snooping limit rate** *rate*

Table 17-6 *Dynamic ARP Inspection Configuration Commands*

Task	Command Syntax
Enable DAI on a VLAN	**ip arp inspection vlan** *vlan-range*
Define a trusted interface	**ip arp inspection trust**
Define a static ARP inspection binding	**arp access-list** *acl-name* **permit ip host** *sender-ip* **mac host** *sender-mac* [**log**]
Apply static ARP inspection bindings	**ip arp inspection filter** *arp-acl-name* **vlan** *vlan-range* [**static**]
Validate addresses within ARP replies	**ip arp inspection validate {[src-mac] [dst-mac] [ip]}**

Q&A

The questions and scenarios in this book are more difficult than what you should experience on the actual exam. The questions do not attempt to cover more breadth or depth than the exam; however, they are designed to make sure that you know the answers. Rather than allowing you to derive the answers from clues hidden inside the questions themselves, the questions challenge your understanding and recall of the subject. Hopefully, these questions will help limit the number of exam questions on which you narrow your choices to two options and then guess.

The answers to these questions can be found in Appendix A.

1. What does the acronym AAA stand for?

2. What external methods of authentication does a Catalyst switch support?

3. A RADIUS server is located at IP address 192.168.199.10. What command configures a Catalyst switch to find the server?

4. A Catalyst switch should be configured to authenticate users against RADIUS servers first, followed by TACACS+ servers. What command can define the authentication methods? Make sure users still can authenticate if none of the servers is available.

5. What is the purpose of authorization? What happens if authorization is not used?

6. Is it possible to use different methods to authorize users to run switch commands instead of making configuration changes?

7. When might the command **switchport port-security maximum 2** be used?

8. After port-based authentication is configured and enabled, can any host connect as long as the user can authenticate?

9. When the 802.1x **force-authorized** keyword is used, how does the switch react to users attempting to connect?

10. Can more than one host be authenticated on a single switch port with port-based authentication?

11. In DHCP spoofing and ARP poisoning attacks, what is the goal of the attacker? What Catalyst features can be used to mitigate the risk of these attacks?

12. Which switch ports should be configured as trusted for DHCP snooping?

13. What is the function of a trusted port in DAI?

14. To inspect ARP information from a host that has received its IP address from a DHCP server, what must be enabled in addition to DAI?

This chapter covers the following topics that you need to master for the CCNP BCMSN exam:

- **VLAN Access Lists**—This section discusses how traffic can be controlled within a VLAN. You can use VLAN access control lists (ACL) to filter packets even as they are bridged or switched.

- **Private VLANs**—This section explains the mechanisms that you can use to provide isolation within a single VLAN. Private VLANs have a unidirectional nature; several of them can be isolated yet share a common subnet and gateway.

- **Securing VLAN Trunks**—This section covers two types of attacks that can be leveraged against a VLAN trunk link. If a trunk link is extended to or accessible from an attacker, any VLAN carried over the trunk can be compromised in turn.

- **Switch Port Monitoring**—This section presents the Catalyst features that allow traffic on switch ports or VLANs to be monitored on a different switch port.

CHAPTER 18

Securing with VLANs

Traditionally, traffic has been filtered only at router boundaries, where packets naturally are inspected before forwarding. This is true within Catalyst switches because access lists can be applied as a part of multilayer switching. Catalysts also can filter packets even if they stay within the same VLAN; VLAN access control lists, or VACLs, provide this capability.

Catalyst switches also have the capability to logically divide a single VLAN into multiple partitions. Each partition can be isolated from others, with all of them sharing a common IP subnet and a common gateway address. Private VLANs make it possible to offer up a single VLAN to many disparate customers or organizations without any interaction between them.

VLAN trunks commonly are used on links between switches to carry data from multiple VLANs. If the switches are all under the same administrative control, it is easy to become complacent about the security of the trunks. A few known attacks can be used to gain access to the VLANs that are carried over trunk links. Therefore, network administrators should be aware of the steps that can be taken to prevent any attacks.

Finally, switch ports must be monitored at times for troubleshooting purposes. Catalyst switches can mirror switch ports or VLANs onto other ports so that a network-analysis device can capture or "listen in" on interesting traffic within the switch. The Switch Port Analysis (SPAN) feature can mirror ports on the same switch or across a switched network to a remote switch.

"Do I Know This Already?" Quiz

The purpose of the "Do I Know This Already?" quiz is to help you decide what parts of this chapter to use. If you already intend to read the entire chapter, you do not necessarily need to answer these questions now.

The quiz, derived from the major sections in the "Foundation Topics" portion of the chapter, helps you determine how to spend your limited study time.

Table 18-1 outlines the major topics discussed in this chapter and the "Do I Know This Already?" quiz questions that correspond to those topics.

Table 18-1 *"Do I Know This Already?" Foundation Topics Section-to-Question Mapping*

Foundation Topics Section	Questions Covered in This Section	Score
VLAN ACLs	1–4	
Private VLANs	5–8	
Securing VLAN Trunks	9–10	
Monitoring Switch Ports	11–14	
Total Score		

CAUTION The goal of self-assessment is to gauge your mastery of the topics in this chapter. If you do not know the answer to a question or are only partially sure of the answer, you should mark this question wrong. Giving yourself credit for an answer you correctly guess skews your self-assessment results and might give you a false sense of security.

1. Which one of the following can filter packets even if they are not routed to another Layer 3 interface?

   a. IP extended access lists

   b. MAC address access lists

   c. VLAN access lists

   d. Port-based access lists

2. In what part of a Catalyst switch are VLAN ACLs implemented?

   a. NVRAM

   b. CAM

   c. RAM

   d. TCAM

3. Which one of the following commands can implement a VLAN ACL called *test*?

   a. **access-list vlan test**

   b. **vacl test**

   c. **switchport vacl test**

   d. **vlan access-map test**

4. After a VACL is configured, where is it applied?

   a. Globally on a VLAN

   b. On the VLAN interface

   c. In the VLAN configuration

   d. On all ports or interfaces mapped to a VLAN

5. Which of the following private VLANs is the most restrictive?

   a. Community VLAN

   b. Isolated VLAN

   c. Restricted VLAN

   d. Promiscuous VLAN

6. The **vlan 100** command has just been entered. What is the next command needed to configure VLAN 100 as a secondary isolated VLAN?

   a. **private-vlan isolated**

   b. **private-vlan isolated 100**

   c. **pvlan secondary isolated**

   d. No further configuration is necessary.

7. What type of port configuration should you use for private VLAN interfaces that connect to a router?

   a. Host

   b. Gateway

   c. Promiscuous

   d. Transparent

8. Promiscuous ports must be _____ to primary and secondary VLANs, and host ports must be _____.

   a. mapped, associated

   b. mapped, mapped

   c. associated, mapped

   d. associated, associated

9. In a switch spoofing attack, an attacker makes use of which one of the following?

   a. The switch-management IP address

   b. CDP message exchanges

   c. Spanning Tree Protocol

   d. DTP to negotiate a trunk

10. Which one of the following represents the spoofed information an attacker sends in a VLAN hopping attack?

   a. 802.1Q tags

   b. DTP information

   c. VTP information

   d. 802.1x information

11. Which of the following allows a port to be mirrored to another port on the same switch?

   a. VSPAN

   b. RSPAN

   c. SPAN

   d. CSPAN

12. What must be used to connect switches used for RSPAN?

   a. An 802.1Q trunk

   b. Access-mode switch ports (single VLAN)

   c. A private VLAN over a trunk

   d. An RSPAN VLAN over a trunk

13. What is the most important difference between an RSPAN VLAN and a regular VLAN?

   a. The RSPAN VLAN disables MAC address learning.

   b. The RSPAN VLAN uses static MAC address definitions.

   c. The RSPAN VLAN has the RSPAN source and destination MAC addresses defined in the CAM table.

   d. The RSPAN VLAN cannot be carried over a trunk link.

14. To configure an RSPAN session's source switch, what is used for the session destination?

   a. The switch port leading to the destination switch

   b. The RSPAN VLAN

   c. The final destination switch port

   d. The next-hop router

The answers to the "Do I Know This Already?" quiz are found in Appendix A, "Answers to Chapter 'Do I Know This Already?' Quizzes and Q&A Sections." The suggested choices for your next step are as follows:

■ **11 or less overall score**—Read the entire chapter. This includes the "Foundation Topics," "Foundation Summary," and "Q&A" sections.

■ **12 or more overall score**—If you want more review on these topics, skip to the "Foundation Summary" section and then go to the "Q&A" section at the end of the chapter. Otherwise, move to Chapter 19, "Scenarios for Final Preparation."

Foundation Topics

VLAN Access Lists

Access lists can manage or control traffic as it passes through a switch. When normal access lists are configured on a Catalyst switch, they filter traffic through the use of the Ternary Content Addressable Memory (TCAM). Recall from Chapter 3, "Switch Operation," that access lists (also known as router access lists, or RACLs) are merged or compiled into the TCAM. Each ACL is applied to an interface according to the direction of traffic—inbound or outbound. Packets then can be filtered in hardware with no switching performance penalty. However, only packets that pass *between* VLANs can be filtered this way.

Packets that stay in the same VLAN do not cross a VLAN or interface boundary and do not necessarily have a direction in relation to an interface. These packets also might be non-IP, non-IPX, or completely bridged; therefore, they never pass through the multilayer switching mechanism. VLAN access lists (VACLs) are filters that directly can affect how packets are handled *within* a VLAN.

VACLs are somewhat different from RACLs or traditional access control lists. Although they, too, are merged into the TCAM, they can permit, deny, or redirect packets as they are matched. VACLs also are configured in a route map fashion, with a series of matching conditions and actions to take.

VACL Configuration

VACLs are configured as a VLAN access map, in much the same format as a route map. A VLAN access map consists of one or more statements, each having a common map name. First, you define the VACL with the following global configuration command:

```
Switch(config)# vlan access-map map-name [sequence-number]
```

Access map statements are evaluated in sequence, according to the *sequence-number*. Each statement can contain one or more matching conditions, followed by an action.

Next, define the matching conditions that identify the traffic to be filtered. Matching is performed by access lists (IP, IPX, or MAC address ACLs), which you must configure independently. Configure a matching condition with one of the following access map configuration commands:

```
Switch(config-access-map)# match ip address {acl-number | acl-name}
Switch(config-access-map)# match ipx address {acl-number | acl-name}
Switch(config-access-map)# match mac address acl-name
```

You can repeat these commands to define several matching conditions; the first match encountered triggers an action to take. Define the action with the following access map configuration command:

```
Switch(config-access-map)# action {drop | forward [capture] | redirect type mod/num}
```

A VACL can either **drop** a matching packet, **forward** it, or **redirect** it to another interface. The TCAM performs the entire VACL match and action, as packets are switched or bridged within a VLAN, or routed into or out of a VLAN.

Finally, you must apply the VACL to a VLAN using the following global configuration command:

```
Switch(config)# vlan filter map-name vlan-list vlan-list
```

Notice that the VACL is applied globally to one or more VLANs listed and not to a VLAN interface (SVI). Recall that VLANs can be present in a switch as explicit interfaces or as inherent Layer 2 entities. The VLAN interface is the point where packets enter or leave a VLAN, so it does not make sense to apply a VACL there. Instead, the VACL needs to function *within* the VLAN itself, where there is no inbound or outbound direction.

For example, suppose you need to filter traffic within VLAN 99 so that host 192.168.99.17 is not allowed to contact any other host on its local subnet. Access list **local-17** is created to identify traffic between this host and anything else on its local subnet. Then a VLAN access map is defined: If the **local-17** access list permits the IP address, the packet is dropped; otherwise, the packet is forwarded. Example 18-1 shows the commands necessary for this example.

Example 18-1 *Filtering Traffic Within the Local Subnet*

```
Switch(config)# ip access-list extended local-17
Switch(config-acl)# permit ip host 192.168.99.17 192.168.99.0 0.0.0.255
Switch(config-acl)# exit
Switch(config)# vlan access-map block-17 10
Switch(config-access-map)# match ip address local-17
Switch(config-access-map)# action drop
Switch(config-access-map)# vlan access-map block-17 20
Switch(config-access-map)# action forward
Switch(config-access-map)# exit
Switch(config)# vlan filter block-17 vlan-list 99
```

Private VLANs

Normally, traffic is allowed to move unrestricted within a VLAN. Packets sent from one host to another normally are heard only by the destination host because of the nature of Layer 2 switching.

However, if one host broadcasts a packet, all hosts on the VLAN must listen. You can use a VACL to filter packets between a source and destination in a VLAN if both connect to the local switch.

Sometimes it would be nice to have the capability to segment traffic within a single VLAN, without having to use multiple VLANs and a router. For example, in a single-VLAN server farm, all servers should be capable of communicating with the router or gateway, but the servers should not have to listen to each other's broadcast traffic. Taking this a step further, suppose each server belongs to a separate organization. Now each server should be isolated from the others but still be capable of reaching the gateway to find clients not on the local network.

Another application is a service provider network. Here, the provider might want to use a single VLAN to connect to several customer networks. Each customer needs to be able to contact the provider's gateway on the VLAN. Clearly, the customer sites do not need to interact with each other.

Private VLANs (PVLANs) solve this problem on Catalyst switches. In a nutshell, a normal, or *primary,* VLAN can be logically associated with special unidirectional, or *secondary,* VLANs. Hosts associated with a secondary VLAN can communicate with ports on the primary VLAN (a router, for example), but not with another secondary VLAN. A secondary VLAN is configured as one of the following types:

- **Isolated**—Any switch ports associated with an isolated VLAN can reach the primary VLAN but not any other secondary VLAN. In addition, hosts associated with the same isolated VLAN cannot reach each other. They are, in effect, isolated from everything except the primary VLAN.

- **Community**—Any switch ports associated with a common community VLAN can communicate with each other and with the primary VLAN but not with any other secondary VLAN. This provides the basis for server farms and workgroups within an organization, while giving isolation between organizations.

All secondary VLANs must be associated with one primary VLAN to set up the unidirectional relationship. Private VLANs are configured using special cases of regular VLANs. However, the VLAN Trunking Protocol (VTP) does not pass any information about the private VLAN configuration. Therefore, private VLANs are only locally significant to a switch. Each of the private VLANs must be configured locally on each switch that interconnects them.

You must configure each physical switch port that uses a private VLAN with a VLAN association. You also must define the port with one of the following modes:

- **Promiscuous**—The switch port connects to a router, firewall, or other common gateway device. This port can communicate with anything else connected to the primary or any secondary VLAN. In other words, the port is in promiscuous mode, in which the rules of private VLANs are ignored.

- **Host**—The switch port connects to a regular host that resides on an isolated or community VLAN. The port communicates only with a promiscuous port or ports on the same community VLAN.

Figure 18-1 shows the basic private VLAN operation. Some host PCs connect to a secondary community VLAN. The two community VLANs associate with a primary VLAN, where the router connects. The router connects to a promiscuous port on the primary VLAN. A single host PC connects to a secondary isolated VLAN, so it can communicate only with the router's promiscuous port.

Figure 18-1 *Private VLAN Functionality Within a Switch*

Private VLAN Configuration

Defining a private VLAN involves several configuration steps. These steps are described in the sections that follow so you can use them.

Configure the Private VLANs

To configure a private VLAN, begin by defining any secondary VLANs that are needed for isolation using the following configuration commands:

```
Switch(config)# vlan vlan-id
Switch(config-vlan)# private-vlan {isolated | community}
```

The secondary VLAN can be an isolated VLAN (no connectivity between isolated ports) or a community VLAN (connectivity between member ports).

Now define the primary VLAN that will provide the underlying private VLAN connectivity using the following configuration commands:

```
Switch(config)# vlan vlan-id
Switch(config-vlan)# private-vlan primary
Switch(config-vlan)# private-vlan association {secondary-vlan-list | add secondary-
vlan-list | remove secondary-vlan-list}
```

Be sure to associate the primary VLAN with all its component secondary VLANs using the **association** keyword. If the primary VLAN already has been configured, you can add (**add**) or remove (**remove**) secondary VLAN associations individually.

These VLAN configuration commands set up only the mechanisms for unidirectional connectivity from the secondary VLANs to the primary VLAN. You also must associate the individual switch ports with their respective private VLANs.

Associate Ports with Private VLANs

First, define the function of the port that will participate on a private VLAN using the following configuration command:

```
Switch(config-if)# switchport mode private-vlan {host | promiscuous}
```

If the host connected to this port is a router, firewall, or common gateway for the VLAN, use the **promiscuous** keyword. This allows the host to reach all other promiscuous, isolated, or community ports associated with the primary VLAN. Otherwise, any isolated or community port must receive the **host** keyword.

For a nonpromiscuous port (using the **switchport mode private-vlan host** command), you must associate the switch port with the appropriate primary and secondary VLANs. Remember, only the private VLANs themselves have been configured until now. The switch port must know how to interact with the various VLANs using the following interface-configuration command:

```
Switch(config-if)# switchport private-vlan host-association primary-vlan-id
secondary-vlan-id
```

NOTE   When a switch port is associated with private VLANs, you don't have to configure a static access VLAN. Instead, the port takes on membership in the primary and secondary VLANs simultaneously. This does not mean that the port has a fully functional assignment to multiple VLANs. Instead, it takes on only the unidirectional behavior between the secondary and primary VLANs.

For a promiscuous port (using the **switchport mode private-vlan promiscuous** command), you must map the port to primary and secondary VLANs. Notice that promiscuous-mode ports, or ports that can communicate with any other private VLAN device, are mapped, while other secondary VLAN ports are associated. One (promiscuous-mode port) exhibits bidirectional behavior, while the other (secondary VLAN ports) exhibits unidirectional or logical behavior.

Use the following interface-configuration command to map promiscuous-mode ports to primary and secondary VLANs:

```
Switch(config-if)# switchport private-vlan mapping {primary-vlan-id} {secondary-vlan-
list} | {add secondary-vlan-list} | {remove secondary-vlan-list}
```

As an example, assume that the switch in Figure 18-1 is configured as in Example 18-2. Host PCs on ports FastEthernet 1/1 and 1/2 are in community VLAN 10, hosts on ports FastEthernet 1/4 and 1/5 are in community VLAN 20, and the host on port FastEthernet 1/3 is in isolated VLAN 30. The router on port FastEthernet 2/1 is in promiscuous mode on primary VLAN 100. Each VLAN is assigned a role, and the primary VLAN is associated with its secondary VLANs. Then each interface is associated with a primary and secondary VLAN (if a host is attached) or mapped to the primary and secondary VLANs (if a promiscuous host is attached).

Example 18-2 *Configuring Ports with Private VLANs*

```
Switch(config)# vlan 10
Switch(config-vlan)# private-vlan community
Switch(config)# vlan 20
Switch(config-vlan)# private-vlan community
Switch(config)# vlan 30
Switch(config-vlan)# private-vlan isolated
Switch(config)# vlan 100
Switch(config-vlan)# private-vlan primary
Switch(config-vlan)# private-vlan association 10,20,30
Switch(config-vlan)# exit
Switch(config)# interface range fastethernet 1/1  1/2
Switchconfig# switchport private-vlan host
Switch(config-if)# switchport private-vlan host-association 100 10
Switch(config)# interface range fastethernet 1/4  1/5
Switchconfig# switchport private-vlan host
Switch(config-if)# switchport private-vlan host-association 100 20
Switch(config)# interface fastethernet 1/3
Switchconfig# switchport private-vlan host
Switch(config-if)# switchport private-vlan host-association 100 30

Switch(config)# interface fastethernet 2/1
Switch(config-if)# switchport mode private-vlan promiscuous
Switch(config-if)# switchport private-vlan mapping 100 10,20,30
```

Associate Secondary VLANs to a Primary VLAN SVI

On switched virtual interfaces (SVIs), or VLAN interfaces configured with Layer 3 addresses, you must configure some additional private VLAN mapping. Consider the SVI for the primary VLAN, VLAN 100, that has an IP address and participates in routing traffic. Secondary VLANs 40 (an isolated VLAN) and 50 (a community VLAN) are associated at Layer 2 with primary VLAN 100 using the configuration in Example 18-3.

Example 18-3 *Associating Secondary VLANs to a Primary VLAN*

```
vlan 40
     private-vlan isolated
vlan 50
     private-vlan community
vlan 200
     private-vlan primary
     private-vlan association 40,50
interface vlan 200
     ip address 192.168.199.1 255.255.255.0
```

Primary VLAN 200 can forward traffic at Layer 3, but the secondary VLAN associations with it are good at only Layer 2. To allow Layer 3 traffic switching coming from the secondary VLANs as well, you must add a private VLAN mapping to the primary VLAN (SVI) interface, using the following interface-configuration command:

```
Switch(config-if)# private-vlan mapping {secondary-vlan-list | add secondary-vlan-list
| remove secondary-vlan-list}
```

The primary VLAN SVI function is extended to the secondary VLANs instead of requiring SVIs for each of them. If some mapping already has been configured for the primary VLAN SVI, you can add (**add**) or remove (**remove**) secondary VLAN mappings individually.

For the example, you would map the private VLAN with the following command:

```
interface vlan 200
     private-vlan mapping 40,50
```

Securing VLAN Trunks

Because trunk links usually are bounded between two switches, you might think that they are more or less secure. Each end of the trunk is connected to a device that is under your control, VLANs carried over the trunk remain isolated, and so on.

Some attacks or exploits can be leveraged to gain access to a trunk or to the VLANs carried over a trunk. Therefore, you should become familiar with how the attacks work and what steps you can take to prevent them in the first place.

Switch Spoofing

Recall from Chapter 6, "VLANs and Trunks," that two switches can be connected by a common trunk link that can carry traffic from multiple VLANs. The trunk doesn't have to exist all the time. The switches dynamically can negotiate its use and its encapsulation mode by exchanging Dynamic Trunking Protocol (DTP) messages.

Although DTP can make switch administration easier, it also can expose switch ports to be compromised. Suppose that a switch port is left to its default configuration, in which the trunking mode is **auto**. Normally, the switch port would wait to be asked by another switch in the **auto** or **on** mode to become a trunk.

Now suppose that an end user's PC is connected to that port. A well-behaved end user would not use DTP at all, so the port would come up in access mode with a single-access VLAN. A malicious user, however, might exploit the use of DTP and attempt to negotiate a trunk with the switch port. This makes the PC appear to be another switch; in effect, the PC is spoofing a switch.

After the trunk is negotiated, the attacker has access to any VLAN that is permitted to pass over the trunk. If the switch port has been left to its default configuration, *all* VLANs configured on the switch are allowed onto the trunk. This scenario is shown in Figure 18-2. The attacker can receive any traffic being sent over the trunk on any VLAN. In addition, he can send traffic into any VLAN of his choice.

Figure 18-2 *An Example of Switch Spoofing to Gain Access to a Trunk*

To demonstrate this further, consider the output in Example 18-4, which shows the default access switch port configuration. Notice that trunking is possible because the port is set to dynamic auto mode, awaiting DTP negotiation from a connected device. If a trunk is negotiated, all VLANs are permitted to be carried over it.

Example 18-4 *Displaying the Default Switch Port Configuration*

```
Switch# show interfaces fastethernet 1/0/46 switchport
Name: Fa1/0/46
Switchport: Enabled
Administrative Mode: dynamic auto
Operational Mode: trunk
Administrative Trunking Encapsulation: negotiate
Negotiation of Trunking: On
Access Mode VLAN: 1 (default)
Trunking Native Mode VLAN: 1 (default)
Administrative Native VLAN tagging: enabled
Voice VLAN: none
Administrative private-vlan host-association: none
Administrative private-vlan mapping: none
Administrative private-vlan trunk native VLAN: none
Administrative private-vlan trunk Native VLAN tagging: enabled
Administrative private-vlan trunk encapsulation: dot1q
Administrative private-vlan trunk normal VLANs: none
Administrative private-vlan trunk private VLANs: none
Operational private-vlan: none
Trunking VLANs Enabled: ALL
Pruning VLANs Enabled: 2-1001
Capture Mode Disabled
Capture VLANs Allowed: ALL
Protected: false
Unknown unicast blocked: disabled
Unknown multicast blocked: disabled
Appliance trust: none
Switch#
```

The solution to this situation is to configure *every* switch port to have an expected and controlled behavior. For example, instead of leaving an end-user switch port set to use DTP in auto mode, configure it to static access mode with the following commands:

```
Switch(config)# interface type mod/num
Switch(config-if)# switchport access vlan vlan-id
Switch(config-if)# switchport mode access
```

This way, an end user never will be able to send any type of spoofed traffic that will make the switch port begin trunking.

In addition, you might be wise to disable any unused switch ports to prevent someone from discovering a live port that might be exploited.

VLAN Hopping

When securing VLAN trunks, also consider the potential for an exploit called *VLAN hopping*. Here, an attacker positioned on one access VLAN can craft and send frames with spoofed 802.1Q tags so that the packet payloads ultimately appear on a totally different VLAN, all without the use of a router.

For this exploit to work, the following conditions must exist in the network configuration:

■   The attacker is connected to an access switch port.

■   The same switch must have an 802.1Q trunk.

■   The trunk must have the attacker's access VLAN as its native VLAN.

Figure 18-3 shows how VLAN hopping works. The attacker, situated on VLAN 10, sends frames that are doubly tagged as if an 802.1Q trunk is being used. Naturally, the attacker is not connected to a trunk; he is spoofing the trunk encapsulation to trick the switch into making the frames hop over to another VLAN.

Figure 18-3   *VLAN Hopping Attack Process*

The regular frame—or malicious payload, in this case—first is given an 802.1Q tag with the VLAN ID of the target VLAN. Then a second bogus 802.1Q tag is added with the attacker's access VLAN ID.

When the local switch Catalyst A receives a doubly tagged frame, it decides to forward it out the trunk interface. Because the first (outermost) tag has the same VLAN ID as the trunk's native VLAN, that tag is removed as the frame is sent on the trunk. The switch believes that the native VLAN should be untagged, as it should. Now the second (innermost) tag is exposed on the trunk.

When Catalyst B receives the frame, it examines any 802.1Q tag it finds. The spoofed tag for VLAN 20 is found, so the tag is removed and the frame is forwarded onto VLAN 20. Now the attacker successfully has sent a frame on VLAN 10 and gotten the frame injected onto VLAN 20—all through Layer 2 switching.

Clearly, the key to this type of attack revolves around the use of untagged native VLANs. Therefore, to thwart VLAN hopping, you always should carefully configure trunk links with the following steps:

Step 1   Set the native VLAN of a trunk to a bogus or unused VLAN ID.

Step 2   Prune the native VLAN off both ends of the trunk.

For example, suppose that an 802.1Q trunk should carry only VLANs 10 and 20. You should set the native VLAN to an unused value, such as 800. Then you should remove VLAN 800 from the trunk so that it is confined to the trunk link itself. Example 18-5 demonstrates how to accomplish this.

Example 18-5   *Configuring the 802.1Q Trunk to Carry Only VLANs 10 and 20*

```
Switch(config)# vlan 800
Switch(config-vlan)# name bogus_native
Switch(config-vlan)# exit
Switch(config)# interface gigabitethernet 1/1
Switch(config-if)# switchport trunk encapsulation dot1q
Switch(config-if)# switchport trunk native vlan 800
Switch(config-if)# switchport trunk allowed vlan remove 800
Switch(config-if)# switchport mode trunk
```

> **TIP**   Although maintenance protocols such as CDP, PAgP, and DTP normally are carried over the native VLAN of a trunk, they will not be affected if the native VLAN is pruned from the trunk. They still will be sent and received on the native VLAN as a special case even if the native VLAN ID is not in the list of allowed VLANs.

One alternative is to force all 802.1Q trunks to add tags to frames for the native VLAN, too. The double-tagged VLAN hopping attack won't work because the switch won't remove the first tag with the native VLAN ID (VLAN 10 in the example). Instead, that tag will remain on the spoofed frame as it enters the trunk. At the far end of the trunk, the same tag will be examined, and the frame will stay on the original access VLAN (VLAN 10).

To force a switch to tag the native VLAN on all its 802.1Q trunks, you can use the following command:

```
Switch(config)# vlan dot1q tag native
```

Switch Port Monitoring

Suppose that a problem exists on your switched network and you want to use a network analyzer to gather data. Of interest is a conversation between two hosts connected to the switch, one on interface FastEthernet 1/1 and the other on FastEthernet 4/7. Both ports are assigned to VLAN 100. If you connect your analyzer to another port on VLAN 100, what will your packet capture show?

Recall that, by definition, switches learn where MAC addresses are located and forward packets directly to those ports. The only time a packet is flooded to ports other than the specific destination is when the destination MAC address has not already been located or when the packet is destined for a broadcast or multicast address. Therefore, your packet capture shows only the broadcast and multicast packets that were flooded to the analyzer's port. None of the interesting conversation will be overheard.

Catalyst switches can use the *Switched Port Analyzer (SPAN)* feature to mirror traffic from one source switch port or VLAN to a destination port. This allows a monitoring device, such as a network analyzer or an intrusion-detection system (IDS) sensor, to be attached to the destination port for capturing traffic.

When packets arrive on the source port or VLAN, they are specially marked so that they can be copied to the SPAN destination port along with the true destination port. In this way, the packet capture receives an exact copy of the packets that are being forwarded from the source.

SPAN is available in several different forms:

■ **Local SPAN**—Both the SPAN source and destination are located on the local switch. The source is one or more switch ports.

■ **VLAN-based SPAN (VSPAN)**—A variation of local SPAN in which the source is a VLAN instead of a physical port.

■ **Remote SPAN (RSPAN)**—The SPAN source and destination are located on different switches. Mirrored traffic is copied over a special-purpose VLAN across trunks between switches from the source to the destination.

The sections that follow describe each of these SPAN forms in more detail.

Local SPAN and VSPAN

The SPAN source can be identified as one or more physical switch ports, a trunk, or a VLAN. Packets that are being forwarded from the destination also are copied into the destination port's queue. Because the packets are merely copied, neither the original data nor its being forwarded is affected. Figure 18-4 demonstrates two cases in which a network analyzer on the SPAN destination port is receiving frames that SPAN has copied from the source port. Here, SPAN session A monitors all communication on VLAN 100. SPAN session B uses a normal access-mode source port to monitor communication between a server and its client PCs.

Figure 18-4 *Basic Local SPAN and VSPAN Operation*

What happens if a speed mismatch occurs between the SPAN source and destination ports? This easily could happen if the source is a VLAN with many hosts, or if the source is a GigabitEthernet port and the destination is a FastEthernet port.

Packets are copied only into the destination port's egress queue. If the destination port becomes congested, the SPAN packets are dropped from the queue and are not seen at the destination port. Therefore, if the bandwidth of source traffic exceeds the destination port speed, some packets might not be seen at the destination port. Then traffic from the SPAN source is not affected by any congestion at the SPAN destination.

Local SPAN and VSPAN Configuration

You can configure one or more simultaneous SPAN sessions on a Catalyst switch. These sessions are completely independent because no interaction occurs between the packet mirroring of each.

To configure a SPAN session, start by defining the source of the SPAN session data, using the following global configuration command:

```
Switch(config)# monitor session session source {interface type mod/num | vlan vlan-id}
[rx | tx | both]
```

SPAN sessions must be numbered uniquely using the *session* parameter. The maximum number of supported sessions varies among Catalyst platforms. For example, a Catalyst 3750 can support two sessions, whereas a Catalyst 6500 can support up to 64. If multiple sources are needed, you can repeat this command. The SPAN source can be a physical switch interface or a Layer 2 VLAN (not a logical VLAN interface or SVI).

Traffic can be selected for mirroring based on the direction it is traveling through the SPAN source. For example, you can select only traffic received on the source (**rx**), only traffic transmitted from the source (**tx**), or traffic in both directions (**both**). By default, **both** directions are used.

Next, identify the SPAN destination. You must assign the SPAN source and destination ports to the same VLAN within the switch; otherwise, the switch cannot copy frames from one VLAN to another. Use the following global configuration command to identify the SPAN destination:

```
Switch(config)# monitor session session destination {interface type mod/num | vlan
vlan-id}
```

The session number here must match the one configured for the SPAN source. You can define only one destination port for each SPAN session. In addition, SPAN sessions cannot share a destination port. The destination can be a physical interface (**interface**) or a Layer 2 VLAN (**vlan**, not a VLAN SVI interface).

> **TIP** If the source interface is a trunk, the destination interface also should be configured as an unconditional trunk.

You can narrow the data copied over from the source, if necessary. If the source is a trunk port, you can mirror only traffic from specific VLANs on the trunk with the following global configuration command:

```
Switch(config)# monitor session session filter vlan vlan-range
```

Also, if using a VACL, you can identify and mark interesting traffic for SPAN capture. In this case, use the **capture** keyword in the VACL action statement.

You can delete a SPAN session after the packet analysis is complete. SPAN sessions are numbered, so you can delete them by referencing the number. Use the following global configuration command to delete one or more sessions:

```
Switch(config)# no monitor session {{range session-range} | local | all | session}
```

Session numbers can be given as an individual *session*, a range of sessions, all **local** SPAN sessions, or **all** sessions (local or remote). To see the list of currently active SPAN sessions, use the **show monitor** EXEC command, as shown in Example 18-6. Here, two SPAN sessions are in use on a Catalyst 3750.

Example 18-6 *Displaying the Currently Active SPAN Sessions*

```
Switch# show monitor
Session 1
---------
 Type          : Local Session
Source Ports:
    RX Only:        None
    TX Only:        None
    Both:           Fa1/0/7
Source VLANs:
    RX Only:        None
    TX Only:        None
    Both:           None
Source RSPAN VLAN: None
Destination Ports: Fa1/0/47
    Encapsulation: Native
          Ingress: Disabled
Reflector Port:    None
Filter VLANs:      None
Dest RSPAN VLAN:   None


Session 2
---------
 Type          : Local Session
Source Ports:
    RX Only:        None
    TX Only:        None
    Both:           Gi1/0/1
Source VLANs:
    RX Only:        None
    TX Only:        None
    Both:           None
Source RSPAN VLAN: None
Destination Ports: Gi1/0/2
    Encapsulation: Native
          Ingress: Disabled
Reflector Port:    None
Filter VLANs:      None
Dest RSPAN VLAN:   None
```

CAUTION   When you finish using a SPAN session, you always should disable or delete it. Otherwise, someone later might try to connect to the port that is configured as the SPAN destination. You could spend a good bit of time troubleshooting that user's connectivity problem only to find that you left a SPAN session active.

NOTE   When local SPAN or VSPAN is enabled, the Spanning Tree Protocol (STP) is disabled on the destination port. This allows STP BPDUs to be captured and monitored but also allows the possibility for a bridging loop to form. Never connect a SPAN session's destination port back into an active network. If the monitored packets need to be sent toward another switch, use RSPAN instead.

Remote SPAN

In a large switched network or one that is geographically separated, it might not always be convenient to take a network analysis to the switch where a SPAN source is located. To make SPAN more extensible, Cisco developed the Remote SPAN (RSPAN) feature. With RSPAN, the source and destination can be located on different switches in different locations.

The RSPAN source is identified on one switch, just as with local SPAN. The RSPAN destination is identified on its local switch. Then RSPAN can carry only the mirrored data over a special-purpose VLAN across trunk links and intermediate switches. As long as every switch along the way is RSPAN capable, the source can be located at the far-end switch, while the network analyzer conveniently is located at the switch nearest you.

Figure 18-5 shows an example network using RSPAN where the packets from the file server (source port) on one switch are copied and transported over the RSPAN VLAN on trunk links. At the destination switch, packets are pulled off the RSPAN VLAN and copied to the network analyzer (destination port). The file server and network analyzer are stationed in geographically separate locations.

The RSPAN VLAN has some important differences from a regular VLAN. First, MAC address learning is disabled on the RSPAN VLAN. This is to prevent intermediate switches that transport the RSPAN VLAN from trying to forward the mirrored packets to their real destination MAC addresses. After all, the purpose of SPAN or RSPAN is to simply mirror or copy interesting frames, not forward them normally.

An RSPAN-capable switch also floods the RSPAN packets out all its ports belonging to the RSPAN VLAN, in an effort to send them toward the RSPAN destination. Intermediate switches have no knowledge of the RSPAN source or destination; they know only of the RSPAN VLAN itself.

Figure 18-5 *Example of Remote SPAN Operation*

Remote SPAN Configuration

RSPAN configuration begins with the definition of the special-purpose RSPAN VLAN. If you configure the RSPAN VLAN on a VTP server, VTP correctly propagates it to other intermediate switches. If not using VTP, be sure to configure this VLAN for RSPAN explicitly on each intermediate switch. Otherwise, the RSPAN packets will not be delivered correctly.

In addition, if VTP pruning is in use, the RSPAN VLAN will be pruned from unnecessary trunks, limiting the traffic impact in unrelated areas of the network.

Create and maintain one or more RSPAN VLANs for the special monitoring purpose only. Set aside one RSPAN VLAN for each RSPAN session that will be used. Don't allow any normal hosts to join an RSPAN VLAN. Define an RSPAN VLAN on each switch between the source and destination with the following configuration commands:

```
Switch(config)# vlan vlan-id
Switch(config-vlan)# remote-span
```

Next, you must identify the RSPAN source *and* destination on the two switches where the source and destination are connected. At the source switch, identify the source and destination with the following global configuration commands:

```
Switch(config)# monitor session session source {interface type mod/num | vlan vlan-id}
[rx | tx | both]
Switch(config)# monitor session session destination remote vlan rspan-vlan-id
```

Here, the source is either a physical switch interface or a Layer 2 VLAN (not a VLAN SVI interface). Notice that the command syntax is identical to the local SPAN **source** command. The RSPAN destination is simply the RSPAN VLAN. This allows the mirrored packets to be copied into the special VLAN and sent on their way toward the final RSPAN destination.

At the destination switch, you again must identify the RSPAN source and destination by using the following global configuration commands:

```
Switch(config)# monitor session session source remote vlan rspan-vlan-id
Switch(config)# monitor session session destination {interface type mod/num | vlan
vlan-id}
```

Here the roles are reversed. RSPAN packets are pulled from the RSPAN VLAN and placed onto the destination, which is either a physical switch interface or a Layer 2 VLAN.

NOTE   Be aware that RSPAN traffic can increase the traffic load on a trunk, even though RSPAN is restricted to one special VLAN within the trunk. If the additional load is significant, the normal production and the monitored traffic contend with each other for available bandwidth. As a result, both types of traffic could suffer.

Also, RSPAN must allow the STP to run on the RSPAN VLAN to prevent bridging loops from forming. As a result, STP BPDUs normally are sent and received on the VLAN. You cannot monitor BPDUs with RSPAN.

In Example 18-7, RSPAN is configured on all three switches shown in Figure 18-5. The source is connected to Catalyst A port FastEthernet 1/1. The destination is a network analyzer connected to port FastEthernet 4/48 on Catalyst C. Catalyst B simply passes the RSPAN session traffic over VLAN 999, transported by trunk links.

Example 18-7   *Configuring RSPAN on the Catalyst Switches in Figure 18-5*

```
Catalyst A
vlan 999
     remote-span
monitor session 1 source interface fastethernet 1/1 both
monitor session 1 destination remote vlan 999
Catalyst B
vlan 999
     remote-span
Catalyst C
vlan 999
     remote-span
monitor session 1 source remote vlan 999
monitor session 1 destination interface fastethernet 4/48
```

Foundation Summary

The Foundation Summary is a collection of information that provides a convenient review of many key concepts in this chapter. If you are already comfortable with the topics in this chapter, this summary can help you recall a few details. If you just read this chapter, this review should help solidify some key facts. If you are doing your final preparation before the exam, this information will hopefully be a convenient way to review the day before the exam.

- VLAN Access Lists (VACLs) can control packets that are bridged, switched, or routed. VACLs are effective on packets that stay *within* a single VLAN.

Table 18-2   *VLAN ACL Configuration Commands*

Task	Command Syntax
Define a VACL	**vlan access-map** *map-name* [*sequence-number*]
Define a matching condition	**match** {**ip address** {*acl-number* ∣ *acl-name*}} ∣ {**ipx address** {*acl- number* ∣ *acl-name*} ∣ {**mac address** *acl-name*}}
Define an action	**action** {**drop** ∣ **forward** [**capture**] ∣ **redirect** *interface type mod/num*}
Apply the VACL to VLANs	**vlan filter** *map-name* **vlan-list** *vlan-list*

- Private VLANs provide special unidirectional relationships between entities on a single VLAN.

- Private VLANs are implemented as primary and secondary VLANs.

- Primary VLANs allow hosts to communicate with any other type of private (secondary) VLAN.

- Secondary VLANs allow hosts to communicate with ports on a primary VLAN but not with other secondary VLANs.

- Secondary VLANs are categorized as follows:

  — **Isolated VLAN**—Hosts can communicate only with the primary VLAN, not any other isolated port or secondary VLAN.

  — **Community VLAN**—Hosts can communicate with the primary VLAN and other hosts in the community VLAN but not with any other isolated or community VLAN.

- Secondary VLANs must be associated with one primary VLAN.

You can configure switch ports using private VLANs, as follows:

— **Promiscuous**—Usually connects to a router, firewall, or gateway device; this type of port can communicate with any other type of private VLAN.

— **Host**—Usually connects to regular hosts; this type of port can communicate with a promiscuous port or ports on the same community VLAN.

Table 18-3   *Private VLAN Configuration Commands*

Task	Command Syntax
Define a secondary VLAN	**vlan** *vlan-id* **private-vlan** {**isolated** ⏐ **community**}
Define a primary VLAN; associate it with secondary VLANs	**vlan** *vlan-id* **private-vlan primary** **private-vlan association** {*secondary-vlan-list*⏐ **add** *secondary-vlan-list* ⏐ **remove** *secondary-vlan-list*}
Associate ports with private VLANs	**switchport mode private-vlan** {**host** ⏐ **promiscuous**}
Associate nonpromiscuous ports with private VLANs	**switchport private-vlan host-association** *primary-vlan-id secondary-vlan-id*
Associate promiscuous ports with private VLANs	**switchport private-vlan mapping** {*primary-vlan-id*} {*secondary-vlan-list*} ⏐ {**add** *secondary-vlan-list*} ⏐ {**remove** *secondary-vlan-list*}
Associate secondary VLANs with a primary VLAN Layer 3 SVI	**private-vlan mapping** {*secondary-vlan-list* ⏐ **add** *secondary-vlan-list* ⏐ **remove** *secondary-vlan-list*}

- Switch port monitoring can monitor or capture interesting traffic on a Catalyst switch.

- Local SPAN copies frames from a source to a destination port on the local switch.

- VLAN SPAN (VSPAN) copies frames from a source VLAN to a destination port on the local switch.

- Remote SPAN (RSPAN) copies frames from a source on one switch to a destination on another switch. Frames are carried over a special RSPAN VLAN across intermediate switches and trunks.

Table 18-4 *Local or VLAN SPAN Commands*

Task	Command Syntax
Identify a SPAN session source	**monitor session** *session* **source** {**interface** *type* | **vlan** *vlan-id*} [**rx** | **tx** | **both**]
Identify a SPAN session destination	**monitor session** *session* **destination** {{**interface** *type mod/num*} | {**vlan** *vlan-id*} | {**analysis-module** *slot-number*} | {**data-port** *port-number*}}
Filter VLANs from a SPAN source trunk	**monitor session** *session-number* **filter vlan** *vlan-range*
Remove a SPAN session	**no monitor session** {{**range** *session-range*} | **local** | **all** | *session*}

Table 18-5 *RSPAN Commands*

Task	Command Syntax
Define an RSPAN VLAN for transport (all switches from source to destination)	**vlan** *vlan-id* **remote-span**
Source switch: Identify the RSPAN source and destination	**monitor session** *session* **source** {**interface** *type mod/num* | **vlan** *vlan-id*} [**rx** | **tx** | **both**] **monitor session** *session* **destination remote vlan** *rspan-vlan-id*
Destination switch: Identify the RSPAN source and destination	**monitor session** *session* **source remote vlan** *rspan-vlan-id* **monitor session** *session* **destination** {**interface** *type mod/num* | **vlan** *vlan-id*}

Q&A

The questions and scenarios in this book are more difficult than what you should experience on the actual exam. The questions do not attempt to cover more breadth or depth than the exam; however, they are designed to make sure that you know the answers. Rather than allowing you to derive the answers from clues hidden inside the questions themselves, the questions challenge your understanding and recall of the subject. Hopefully, these questions will help limit the number of exam questions on which you narrow your choices to two options and then guess.

You can find the answers to these questions in Appendix A.

1. When a VACL is implemented on a switch, how is the switching speed affected?

2. What actions can be taken on packets matching a VACL?

3. After a VACL is applied using the **vlan filter** command, how is the traffic direction (inbound or outbound) specified?

4. A secondary community VLAN is associated with a primary VLAN on a switch. Can hosts assigned to the community VLAN communicate with each other?

5. A secondary isolated VLAN is associated with a primary VLAN on a switch. Can hosts assigned to the isolated VLAN communicate with each other?

6. What command is needed to configure a promiscuous VLAN?

7. A router is identified as the central gateway for a private VLAN. What command is needed to configure the switch port where a router is connected?

8. How many actual VLANs must be configured to implement a common router with two community VLANs?

9. In a switch spoofing attack, what is the attacker's goal?

10. What should be configured to prevent a switch spoofing attack?

11. Describe some methods that can be used to prevent a VLAN hopping attack.

12. How is switching performance affected when several SPAN sessions are enabled?

13. What command can specify the source of a SPAN session as VLAN 100?

14. When a SPAN session is enabled, what direction of traffic flow (relative to the source port) is mirrored for analysis?

15. What two things can identify more granular traffic to be mirrored to a SPAN destination?

16.   Three switches are connected in series with trunk links. The RSPAN source is on the first switch and the destination is on the third. How does the intermediate (second) switch learn about the RSPAN's source and destination locations?

17.   What must be configured on all switches connecting an RSPAN source and destination? What commands can be used?

18.   One of the advantages of RSPAN is that mirrored traffic can be isolated in the RSPAN VLAN on a trunk. If a GigabitEthernet port is to be monitored on one switch, which is better to use as a transport for the RSPAN VLAN: a GigabitEthernet trunk already carrying user traffic in other VLANs, or an isolated GigabitEthernet trunk link set aside for RSPAN?

PART V

Scenarios for Final Preparation

CHAPTER 19

Scenarios for Final Preparation

This chapter presents scenarios that you can use to review most of the concepts contained in this book. The scenarios are designed to assist you in final preparation for the BCMSN exam. Case studies are presented with network diagrams and questions covering many switching topics.

This chapter emphasizes an overall understanding of switching concepts, configuration commands, and network operation. Although the Cisco BCMSN exam might not contain scenarios of this type, you can become better prepared by thinking about the "bigger picture" of a network and how you can apply each switching topic.

Scenario 1: Trunking and DTP

This scenario is built around a network of switches connected by trunking links. You need to think about how DTP operates and how trunks are negotiated (or not) between switches. Consider the network shown in Figure 19-1 and answer the questions that follow. Assume that all switches shown support DTP.

Figure 19-1 *Diagram for Scenario 1*

1. What is the mode of the link between Catalyst A and Catalyst B?

2. Suppose that the network administrator types these commands for interface GigabitEthernet 0/1 on Catalyst B:

```
Switch(config)# interface gigabitethernet 0/1
Switch(config-if)# switchport mode trunk
Switch(config-if)# switchport nonegotiate
```

    What will the link mode be now?

3. Catalyst B has been given the command **no switchport nonegotiate** for interface GigabitEthernet 0/1. What is the link mode now?

4. What is the mode of the link between Catalyst A and Catalyst C?

5. Assume that all links between Catalyst switches are in trunking mode, transporting VLANs 1 through 1005. Can PC-2 ping PC-4?

6. Suppose that PC-1 begins to generate a broadcast storm. Where would the effects of this storm be experienced in this network? Consider both devices and links. Will PC-4 receive the broadcasts?

Scenario 2: VLANs, Trunking, and VTP

This scenario is designed to stir your thinking about VLAN and trunking connectivity. You also need to examine switch configurations and apply them to a network diagram. See the diagram shown in Figure 19-2 and answer the questions that follow. Portions of the configurations of the three Catalyst switches are shown above them.

Figure 19-2 *Diagram for Scenario 2*

1. PC-1 and PC-2 both are configured with IP addresses on the same subnet. Notice that each PC connects to a different VLAN number. Given the switch configurations shown, can PC-1 ping PC-2?

2. PC-2 and PC-3 are assigned to the same IP subnet (using subnet mask 255.0.0.0) and the same VLAN. Can PC-2 and PC-3 ping each other?

3. Will the trunk link between Catalyst B and Catalyst C come up successfully?

4. Suppose that the trunk between Catalyst B and Catalyst C is configured properly. Where will VLAN1 be pruned? Why?

5. Suppose that Catalyst A is a VTP server, Catalyst C is a VTP client, and Catalyst B is configured for VTP transparent mode. All switches are in the Bermuda management domain. If VLAN14 is created on Catalyst A, which switches also will create VLAN 14 using VTP?

6. If VLAN 15 is created on Catalyst B, what other switches also will create VLAN 15 through VTP?

7. If VLAN 16 is created on Catalyst C, what will happen?

Scenario 3: EtherChannels

This scenario focuses on EtherChannel links between switches. See the diagram shown in Figure 19-3 and answer the questions that follow.

Figure 19-3 *Diagram for Scenario 3*

1. Four GigabitEthernet interfaces on Catalyst A are to be bundled into a Gigabit EtherChannel with Catalyst B. If each of these interfaces also is configured as a trunk, what must be similar about them on both switches?

2. Catalyst A should actively initiate an EtherChannel with Catalyst B. PAgP negotiation should be used. What commands should be used on each of Catalyst A's ports to configure negotiation of EtherChannel 1?

3. What is the default load-distribution algorithm, assuming that the switches are Catalyst 6500s?

4. Suppose that the EtherChannel is a Layer 3 interface on both switches so that each switch uses one MAC and one IP address. Should you choose the **src-dst-mac** or **src-dst-ip** algorithm to maximize the load distribution across all the links?

Scenario 4: Traditional STP

This scenario exercises your ability to think through the Spanning Tree Protocol operation. You are presented with a simple network of two switches. This keeps the STP complexity to a minimum while forcing you to think through the STP convergence process on a live network. Given the network diagram shown in Figure 19-4, complete the following exercises.

Figure 19-4 *Network Diagram for Scenario 4*

32768.00-d0-58-a3-83-c9

fa1/1	fa1/2	g2/1
10 Mbps	100 Mbps	1000 Mbps
fa1/1	fa1/2	g2/1

32768.00-d0-58-a3-83-ca

1. Manually compute the spanning-tree topology. Note which switch is the root bridge, which ports are root ports and designated ports, and which ports are in the Blocking state.

2. If the 100-Mbps link (port FastEthernet 1/2) is disconnected, what happens with the STP?

3. If the 1000-Mbps link (port GigabitEthernet 2/1) is disconnected, how much time will elapse before the two switches can communicate again? (Assume that both switches use the default STP timer values and no additional features for faster convergence.)

4. Assume that the physical 1000-Mbps link (port GigabitEthernet 2/1) stays up and active, but BPDUs are not allowed to pass (that is, an access list filter is blocking BPDUs). What happens and when?

Scenario 5: Advanced STP

A small network consists of two core switches, Catalyst C1 and C2, and an access switch, A1, as shown in Figure 19-5. Advanced Spanning Tree Protocol features will improve the convergence times and reduce the number of STP instances. Answer these questions.

Figure 19-5   *Network Diagram for Scenario 5*

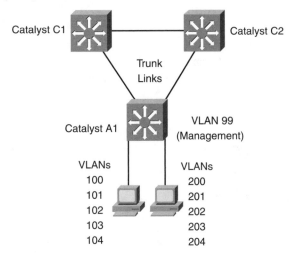

1. To prevent the possibility of a unidirectional link occurring on switch A1's uplinks, what switch feature can be used? What commands are necessary to enable this feature? Assume that the links should be disabled if a unidirectional condition is found. Which switches need to be configured this way?

2. On Catalyst A1, what feature and command should be used to prevent unexpected STP BPDUs from being received on the ports connected to end users?

3. For the links between switch A1 and the user PCs, what command is needed to configure these as RSTP edge ports?

4. By default, the traditional PVST+ mode is enabled on a switch. What command can be used to enable RSTP to be used with PVST+?

5. Suppose that MST is to be configured to reduce the number of STP instances because 12 unique VLANs are being used across the network. How many MST instances are needed for the three switches shown in Figure 21-4, assuming that traffic should be load-balanced across the two uplinks of switch A1?

6. What commands are needed to configure switch C1 for MST?

7. Now make sure that C1 is configured as the root bridge for one MST instance. What commands are needed?

Scenario 6: Router Redundancy with HSRP and GLBP

This scenario covers two methods by which you can configure multilayer switches to provide redundant router or gateway functionality: HSRP and GLBP.

A network consists of two VLANs: 101 and 102. Suppose that the PCs in VLAN 101 (192.168.101.0/24) use address 192.168.101.1 as their default gateway. The PCs in VLAN 102 (192.168.102.0/24) use 192.168.102.1.

1. What commands are necessary to configure HSRP on a Catalyst switch so that it becomes the active router for VLAN 101 and the standby router for VLAN 102? If a failed router interface is restored, control should be passed back to it from the HSRP standby router. (You can use IP addresses 192.168.101.2 and 192.168.102.2, if needed.)

2. What commands can you use to configure VRRP for the network described in question 1?

3. GLBP is to be used in the network shown in Figure 19-6. Answer the following questions about this network.

Figure 19-6 *Network Diagram for Scenario 6*

a. What command should you use to make Catalyst B become the active virtual gateway (AVG) for GLBP group 10?

b. The virtual gateway address is 192.168.10.1. Which switches should be configured for this, and with what command?

    c. Give the command needed on the AVG to implement round-robin load balancing, evenly distributing the virtual gateway MAC addresses across the set of AVFs.

    d. Each of the AVF switches must be configured to become members of GLBP group 10. How can this be accomplished?

Scenario 7: Multicast

This scenario tests your knowledge of various multicast switching features. Think about how multicast traffic traverses a network and how switches can be configured to participate in building multicast topologies. Then consider how you can configure the switches to limit the forwarding of unnecessary multicast traffic.

1. Under what conditions is IGMP snooping more suitable than CGMP for handling multicast traffic?

2. Figure 19-7 shows a network diagram. Assume that all switches use the default multicast configurations. Where in the network will multicast traffic originating from PC-1 on Catalyst A (VLAN 101) be seen?

Figure 19-7 *Network Diagram for Scenario 7*

3. What configuration is needed on Catalysts C and D to limit multicast traffic to only those ports that explicitly join multicast groups, using CGMP with PIM dense mode? Assume that this is needed on both VLANs 101 and 102. What configuration is needed on Catalysts A and B, which are not capable of IGMP snooping?

Scenario 8: IP Telephony in a Switched Network

This scenario uses a simple two-switch network to reinforce the concepts needed to properly implement IP telephony. Think about supplying power to the Cisco IP Phone, as well as how to implement QoS trust within this network. Use Figure 19-8 as a reference for the following questions.

Figure 19-8 *Network Diagram for Scenario 8*

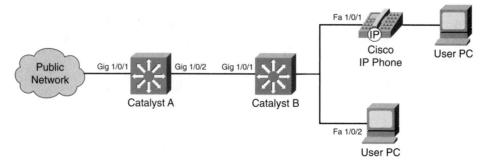

1. Assume that Catalyst B supports Power over Ethernet. If interface Fa1/0/1 has its default configuration, will power be supplied to the IP Phone? Now suppose that someone has entered the **power inline never** command for that interface. What command could you use to begin supplying power to the phone dynamically?

2. Where should a QoS trust boundary be implemented? In other words, which switches should trust incoming QoS information and which ones should not?

3. On Catalyst B, configure interface FastEthernet 3/1 to inform the IP Phone to use VLAN 17 for voice traffic. Also add a configuration command to ensure that no QoS trust is extended to the IP Phone's PC data port.

4. What configuration commands would be necessary to enable QoS trust on Catalyst B's Gig 1/0/1 uplink and to disable trust on port Fa1/0/2 where the user PC is connected?

Scenario 9: Securing Access and Managing Traffic in a Switched Network

This scenario is designed to stir your thinking about how to control access to switched networks, how to control traffic within a VLAN, and how to monitor traffic.

1. Network administrators want to have tight control over hosts moving around within their network. A Catalyst 3750 needs to have port-level security enabled on all 48 of its FastEthernet access-layer ports. Only one host should be connected per port, so the default behavior of shutting down the port is acceptable. What commands are necessary to do this?

2. Port-level security is desired on a Catalyst 3750 interface FastEthernet 1/0/18, where 24 users are connected through an Ethernet hub. Rather than have the switch port shut down upon a security violation, network administrators want only the hosts in violation to be rejected. What command can accomplish this?

3. Configure a VLAN access control list that can perform packet filtering within a VLAN. Users in the 192.168.191.0 255.255.255.0 network should be allowed to use only HTTP (www) traffic to the web server 192.168.191.199/24, on VLAN 180. How can you configure the VACL to accomplish this?

4. An access-layer switch has ports FastEthernet 1/0/1 through 1/0/48 connected to end-user PCs. Is it possible for a user to make one of these ports come up in trunking mode? If so, what commands should you enter to prevent unexpected trunk negotiation?

5. Suppose that a switch has a trunk link GigabitEthernet 1/0/1 configured with the following commands:

```
Switch(config)# interface gigabitethernet 1/0/1
Switch(config-if)# switchport
Switch(config-if)# switchport trunk encapsulation dot1q
Switch(config-if)# switchport trunk native vlan 100
Switch(config-if)# switchport trunk allowed vlan 100-300
Switch(config-if)# switchport mode trunk
```

VLANs 100, 200, and 300 all are used for user traffic. What, if anything, should be done to the trunk configuration to prevent a VLAN hopping attack from occurring?

6. A Catalyst switch has users connected to ports FastEthernet 1/0/1 through 1/0/30. These users are associated with VLAN 50. Two production DHCP servers are connected to ports FastEthernet 1/0/40 and 1/0/41. What commands should be entered to enable DHCP snooping so that DHCP spoofing attacks can be detected and prevented?

7. Assume that a server is connected to interface GigabitEthernet 3/3 on a Catalyst 6500. What command can be used to monitor traffic transmitted and received on the server port with a network analyzer connected to interface GigabitEthernet 5/8 on the same switch?

8. Suppose that the only network analyzer available has a 10/100 Ethernet NIC. It is connected to Catalyst 6500 interface FastEthernet 2/1, to monitor the server on GigabitEthernet 3/3. Explain any problems you might encounter with this setup.

Scenario Answers

Scenario 1 Answers

1. The link is still an access link, with no trunking established, because both switches are set to auto mode. The switches are passively waiting for the other to initiate trunking.

2. Trunking is still not established. Catalyst A is waiting to be asked to trunk, and Catalyst B is set to nonegotiate. Catalyst B will never try to negotiate trunking because its DTP packets have been silenced.

3. Trunking finally has been established. Both switches A and B will use DTP, and B will effectively ask A to bring up a trunk link.

4. Trunking. Catalyst A expects trunking on the link, while Catalyst C actively tries to negotiate trunking.

5. No. The two PC devices are connected to different VLANs. Without a router or Layer 3 device connecting the VLANs, no traffic will cross between them.

6. All hosts on VLAN 1 (PC-1, PC-2, and PC-3) will experience the broadcast storm. All trunk links between switches will transport the broadcast frames. In addition, all switch supervisor CPUs will receive and process the broadcasts because each switch has an IP address for management assigned to VLAN 1. (For this reason, it is recommended to reserve VLAN 1 for control protocol traffic only. User-generated broadcasts can overload the switch supervisor to the extent that it no longer can keep track of its control or "overhead" protocols, such as VTP, CDP, and so forth. Instead, all user traffic should be kept off VLAN 1.)

Scenario 2 Answers

1. Yes. PC-1 and PC-2 are connected to access VLAN switch ports, VLAN 2 and VLAN 10, respectively. Normally, if these were assigned to different VLANs, they could not ping each other unless a Layer 3 device were present to route between the Layer 2 VLANs. In this case, however, the link between Catalyst A and B is the key. On one switch, the link is an access VLAN port on VLAN 2; on the other end, it is an access VLAN port on VLAN 10. These are physically connected, and each switch has no knowledge of what VLAN the other has assigned to the link. Therefore, data can pass across the link freely, connecting the two VLANs.

2. No. Again, the key is the link between Catalyst B and C. Catalyst B has the link configured as an ISL trunk, whereas Catalyst C has it configured as an 802.1Q trunk. Because the trunk encapsulations are different, no data will pass between them.

3. Yes, the trunk link on each switch will come up successfully, even though the trunk will not work end to end because of the encapsulation mismatch. This is because DTP packets will be exchanged, but both ends of the link are configured to trunk unconditionally.

    As a side note, DTP and CDP packets will be exchanged between the switches. Both of these protocols are sent over VLAN 1 in ISL encapsulation and over the native VLAN (VLAN 1, by default) in dot1Q encapsulation. Because the trunk encapsulation is different on each end of the link, each switch will tag VLAN 1 differently. Therefore, VLAN 1 will not be contiguous across the link, and these protocols will not pass successfully.

4. VLAN 1 will not be pruned. Although VLAN 1 is present on all switches, it is not pruned because VLAN 1 is ineligible for pruning by definition.

5. Only Catalyst C creates VLAN 14 in response to VTP advertisements. Catalyst B in transparent mode relays only the VTP information, without interpreting the information.

6. Only Catalyst B creates VLAN 15. Because it is in transparent mode, no VLAN activity will be advertised to other neighboring switches. However, Catalyst B is allowed to create, delete, and rename VLANs freely. These VLANs are significant only to the local switch.

7. Catalyst C will not allow any VLANs to be created unless they are learned from a VTP server in the bermuda domain. Because it is in VTP client mode, no VLAN changes can be performed from the console.

Scenario 3 Answers

1. All bundled ports must have the same set of allowed VLANs, the same native VLAN, the same trunk encapsulation, and the same trunk mode. (In addition, the switch ports all must have identical speed and duplex settings.)

2. You can use the following configuration commands:

    ```
    CatalystA(config)# interface range gigabitethernet 3/1 - 4
    CatalystA(config-if)# channel-protocol pagp
    CatalystA(config-if)# channel-group 1 mode desirable
    ```

3. The Catalyst 6500 default algorithm is the XOR of the source and destination IP addresses, using the **port-channel load-balance src-dst-ip** command.

4. Most of the traffic crossing the EtherChannel will have the same two MAC addresses as source or destination—that of the two Layer 3 interfaces. Therefore, the **src-dst-mac** algorithm always will use only one of the four links within the EtherChannel. The source and destination IP addresses, however, probably will be varied and will yield the best distribution.

Scenario 4 Answers

1. The spanning-tree topology should look like the diagram in Figure 19-9. Catalyst A is the root bridge, and only the 1000-Mbps link is forwarding. The root ports (RP) and designated ports (DP) are labeled on the diagram.

Figure 19-9   *Resulting Spanning-Tree Topology for Scenario 4*

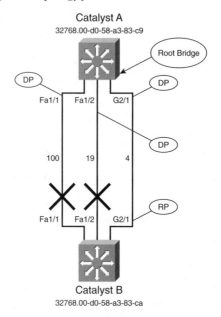

2. Because the 100-Mbps link is in the Blocking state on Catalyst B, no major change in the topology occurs. Effectively, this link already was "disconnected." However, after the physical link status goes down, both Catalyst A and Catalyst B sense the change and begin sending TCN BPDUs to notify each other of the topology change. Because Catalyst A is the root bridge, it acknowledges the TCN to Catalyst B. Both switches age out their MAC address tables in Forward Delay seconds.

3. Disconnecting the 1000-Mbps link causes Catalyst B to immediately find another root port. Ports 1/1 and 1/2 go into the Listening state, waiting to receive BPDUs. Port 1/2, with a cost of 19, becomes the next root port as soon as Catalyst B computes the root path cost (0+19) for it. Port 1/2 stays in the Listening state for Forward Delay (15 seconds), and then in the Learning state for Forward Delay (15 seconds). Port 1/2 moves into the Forwarding state, restoring connectivity in 30 seconds. (If PAgP is operating on the port, an additional delay of 20 seconds occurs.)

4. Because the 1000-Mbps link's status stays up, neither Catalyst detects a link failure. Therefore, no immediate attempt to find another root port occurs. Instead, Catalyst B will not receive BPDUs from Catalyst A over link GigabitEthernet 2/1 because they are being filtered out. After the MaxAge Timer expires (20 seconds), Catalyst B ages out the stored BPDU for Catalyst A on port GigabitEthernet 2/1. Catalyst B moves ports FastEthernet 1/1 and 1/2 into the Listening state to determine a new root port. As in step 3, port FastEthernet 1/2 becomes the root port with a lower root path cost than port FastEthernet 1/1. The port moves through the Listening (15 seconds) and Learning (15 seconds) states and into the Forwarding state. The total time that has elapsed before connectivity restores is 20 + 15 + 15 = 50 seconds. (Again, if PAgP is active on the port, an additional 20 seconds can be added to the delay.)

Scenario 5 Answers

1. The Unidirectional Link Detection (UDLD) feature can be used. You can use the **udld aggressive** global-configuration command to enable UDLD on all fiber-optic ports. UDLD must be enabled on *both ends* of a link, so it should be enabled on switches A1 and also C1 and C2.

2. The BPDU Guard feature can be used to detect and stop unexpected BPDUs from being received on access layer ports. You can use the following interface-configuration command to enable this feature:

   ```
   Switch(config-if)# spanning-tree bpduguard enable
   ```

3. The **spanning-tree portfast** interface-configuration command defines an edge port.

4. You can use the following global configuration command to enable rapid PVST+:

   ```
   Switch(config)# spanning-tree mode rapid-pvst
   ```

5. A minimum of two MST instances are needed so that traffic can be load-balanced. One instance can support VLANs 100 through 104; the other can support VLANs 200 through 204. To load-balance, traffic from one instance must be carried over one uplink while the other instance is carried over the second uplink.

6. You can use these configuration commands:

   ```
   Switch(config)# spanning-tree mode mst
   Switch(config)# spanning-tree mst configuration
   Switch(config-mst)# name NorthWestDivision
   Switch(config-mst)# revision 1
   Switch(config-mst)# instance 1 vlan 100,101,102,103,104,99
   Switch(config-mst)# instance 2 vlan 200,201,202,203,204
   Switch(config-mst)# exit
   ```

Notice that VLAN 99, used for switch-management traffic, also is mapped to an MST instance. It is sometimes easy to forget about nonuser or nonaccess VLANs.

7. This command makes C1 become the MST root bridge for instance 1:

```
Switch(config)# spanning-tree mst 1 root primary
```

This causes the uplink from C1 to A1 to be used for instance 1 by keeping it in the Forwarding state. Switch C2 also should be configured as the root for MST instance 2 so that the other uplink can be used for those VLANs.

Scenario 6 Answers

1. You can configure HSRP load balancing with the following Catalyst configuration commands:

```
Switch(config)# interface vlan 101
Switch(config-if)# ip address 192.168.101.2 255.255.255.0
Switch(config-if)# standby 101 priority 110
Switch(config-if)# standby 101 preempt
Switch(config-if)# standby 101 ip 192.168.101.1
Switch(config-if)# interface vlan 102
Switch(config-if)# ip address 192.168.102.2 255.255.255.0
Switch(config-if)# standby 102 priority 100
Switch(config-if)# standby 102 preempt
Switch(config-if)# standby 102 ip 192.168.102.1
```

The default gateway address that is shared between the switches is configured as 192.168.101.1 for VLAN 101 and 192.168.102.1 for VLAN 102. In VLAN 101, the virtual interface has an IP address of 192.168.101.2. Two HSRP groups are defined, one for each VLAN. Interface VLAN 101 will be the active router for VLAN 101 because of its higher priority of 110 (over a default of 100 on the other Catalyst). If control is passed to the standby router, this router can assume control again through the use of the **preempt** command. For VLAN 102, the roles are reversed. This router becomes the standby router in Group 102, with its lower priority of 100. (The other switch will be configured with priority 110 for VLAN 102 to take the active router role.)

2. Functionally, VRRP is very similar to HSRP. The following commands can be used to configure VRRP. No commands are necessary to enable the router to pre-empt for VRRP; pre-emption is the default.

```
Switch(config)# interface vlan 101
Switch(config-if)# ip address 192.168.101.2 255.255.255.0
Switch(config-if)# vrrp 101 priority 110
Switch(config-if)# vrrp 101 ip 192.168.101.1
Switch(config-if)# interface vlan 102
Switch(config-if)# ip address 192.168.102.2 255.255.255.0
Switch(config-if)# vrrp 102 priority 100
Switch(config-if)# vrrp 102 ip 192.168.102.1
```

3. The four-part answers to question 2 are as follows:

   a. By default, all switches have a GLBP priority of 100. Catalyst B's priority can be raised with the **glbp 10 priority 200** command.

   b. Only the AVG switch, Catalyst B, needs to be configured with the gateway address. It will inform all other members of the group. You should use the **glbp 10 ip 192.168.10.1** command.

   c. **glbp 10 load-balancing round-robin**

   d. Each AVF switch should receive the **glbp 10 ip** interface-configuration command. No IP address is needed here because the virtual gateway address is learned from the group's AVG.

Scenario 7 Answers

1. With IGMP snooping, a switch can listen to IGMP activity for itself. Although this burdens the switch supervisor with examining IGMP reports from multicast group members, the learning process does not require a router or multilayer switch. However, if a switch does not have hardware capable of IGMP snooping natively, CGMP and help from an external router are required.

2. By default, a switch must forward broadcast and multicast frames out all available ports on a VLAN. The multicast traffic will be seen on all VLAN 101 ports on Catalyst A. In addition, Catalyst C and Catalyst D bridge the multicast traffic over the trunk links between them. Finally, all VLAN 101 ports on Catalyst B also forward the multicasts.

3. In this network, CGMP configuration is needed on both types of switches, whether or not IGMP snooping can be used. You can use the following commands on one of the multilayer switches:

   ```
   Switch(config)# ip multicast-routing
   Switch(config)# interface vlan 101
   Switch(config-if)# ip pim dense-mode
   Switch(config-if)# ip cgmp
   Switch(config-if)# interface vlan 102
   Switch(config-if)# ip pim dense-mode
   Switch(config-if)# ip cgmp
   ```

   On Catalyst A and B, only the following global-configuration command **cgmp** is needed.

Scenario 8 Answers

1. In the default configuration, PoE will automatically be supplied if a powered device is detected. If someone has disabled PoE on that interface, you can re-enable it by using the **power inline auto** interface-configuration command.

2. The QoS domain should consist of the two Catalyst switches, A and B. QoS trust should be extended to the IP Phone connected to Catalyst B. QoS information should be trusted on the ports connecting switches A and B.

   QoS information should not be trusted on Catalyst A port Gig1/0/1 (the public network), Catalyst B port Fa1/0/2 (PC), or the IP Phone's PC data port. At these locations, incoming QoS information should be overwritten to known and trusted values, such as COS 0 or DSCP 0.

3. The following commands define VLAN 17 as the voice VLAN (VVID) and the IP Phone's data port as untrusted:

   ```
   Switch(config)# interface fastethernet 3/1
   Switch(config-if)# switchport voice vlan 17
   Switch(config-if)# switchport priority extend cos 0
   ```

4. To enable trust on the uplink, you can use the following commands:

   ```
   CatalystB(config)# interface gigabitethernet 1/0/1
   CatalystB(config-if)# mls qos trust cos
   ```

   Then to disable trust on Fa 1/0/2, you can use these commands:

   ```
   CatalystB(config)# interface fastethernet 1/0/2
   CatalystB(config-if)# no mls qos trust
   ```

Scenario 9 Answers

1. On a Catalyst 3750, you can use the following commands:

   ```
   Switch(config)# interface range fastethernet 1/0/1 - 48
   Switch(config-if)# switchport port-security
   ```

2. On a Catalyst 3750, you can use the following commands:

   ```
   Switch(config)# interface fastethernet 1/0/18
   Switch(config-if)# switchport port-security
   Switch(config-if)# switchport port-security maximum 24
   Switch(config-if)# switchport port-security violation restrict
   ```

   The first command line enables port-level security on the switch port. The second line configures port security to learn up to 24 MAC addresses dynamically on that port. The last line configures the switch to restrict any MAC addresses found to be in violation (any additional addresses learned beyond the 24). The port stays up, allowing the other users to communicate.

3. You can use the following commands:

   ```
   Switch(config)# access-list 101 permit tcp 192.168.191.0 0.0.0.255 host
   192.168.191.199 eq www
   Switch(config)# vlan access-map myfilter
   Switch(config-access-map)# match ip address 101
   Switch(config-access-map)# action forward
   ```

```
Switch(config-access-map)# match
Switch(config-access-map)# action drop
Switch(config-access-map)# exit
Switch(config)# vlan filter myfilter vlan-list 180
```

The first line configures an access list that will be used only to match against traffic being forwarded on a VLAN. The **permit** keyword causes matching traffic only to be eligible for an action by the VACL; it does not cause the matching traffic to be forwarded or not. The VACL is configured to first match traffic with access list 101; this traffic is forwarded as normal. Then a simple **match** statement is given so that all other traffic is matched; this remaining traffic is dropped so that it does not reach its destination. The VACL then is applied to VLAN 180.

4.   In the default configuration, a switch port uses the **switchport mode dynamic auto** command. Therefore, it passively waits for a switch on the far end to initiate DTP negotiation to enter trunking mode. A malicious user could spoof the DTP exchange, causing the switch to bring the port into trunking mode.

You can use the following commands to prevent unexpected trunk negotiation:

```
Switch(config)# interface range fastethernet 1/0/1 - 48
Switch(config-if)# switchport mode access
```

In addition, you should disable any unused access ports and set the access VLAN to an unused or isolated VLAN ID.

5.   The trunk configuration does have a weakness that could allow attackers to inject packets that essentially "hop" from one VLAN to another. The trunk has VLAN 100 as its native VLAN — a VLAN that also is used for user traffic elsewhere in the network.

The solution is to configure the trunk to have an unused VLAN ID for its native VLAN. Then the native VLAN should be manually pruned or disallowed from entering the trunk. By adding the shaded command to the following interface configuration, the native VLAN becomes VLAN 9, which is not allowed on the trunk:

```
Switch(config)# interface gigabitethernet 1/0/1
Switch(config-if)# switchport
Switch(config-if)# switchport trunk encapsulation dot1q
Switch(config-if)# switchport trunk native vlan 9
Switch(config-if)# switchport trunk allowed vlan 100-300
Switch(config-if)# switchport mode trunk
```

6.   You can use the following commands to enable DHCP snooping on the switch:

```
Switch(config)# ip dhcp snooping
Switch(config)# ip dhcp snooping vlan 50
Switch(config)# interface range fastethernet 1/0/40 - 41
Switch(config-if)# ip dhcp snooping trust
```

Only the two ports where legitimate DHCP servers are connected are configured as trusted ports. All other ports are considered to be untrusted, by default. If the switch has an uplink to other switches, you also should use the **ip dhcp snooping trust** command to configure the uplink as trusted. This assumes that the upstream switches have DHCP snooping configured also; it's wise to extend trust to an uplink only if the trusted domain also extends to the neighboring switches.

7. The following commands can configure a local SPAN session on the Catalyst 6500:

```
Switch(config)# monitor session 1 source interface gigabitethernet 3/3 both
Switch(config)# monitor session 1 destination interface gigabitethernet 5/8
```

8. The only potential problem is with the mismatch in connection speeds. The server has a Gigabit Ethernet connection, while the analyzer is limited by its Fast Ethernet connection. If the server has a low utilization on its connection, the network analysis might turn out fine. Otherwise, if the server's connection is using most of the available 1000 Mbps of bandwidth, the analyzer misses a large portion of the mirrored packets.

The server and its connection will not suffer from the speed mismatch. The Catalyst switch continues to forward packets to and from the server as if no port mirroring was occurring. Only when the packets are being copied to the monitor port queue can they potentially be dropped.

Appendix

Answers to Chapter "Do I Know This Already?" Quizzes and Q&A Sections

Chapter 1

"Do I Know This Already?"

1. c

2. e

3. d

4. d

5. a

6. c

7. b

8. c

9. c

10. c

11. d

12. c

Q&A

1. For each layer of the OSI model, match the forwarding criteria used by a switch:

___ Layer 1	A. IP address
___ Layer 2	B. UDP/TCP port
___ Layer 3	C. None
___ Layer 4	D. MAC address

Answer:

C Layer 1	A. IP address
D Layer 2	B. UDP/TCP port
A Layer 3	C. None
B Layer 4	D. MAC address

2. What is multilayer switching (MLS)?

    Answer: MLS forwards traffic using information from Layer 2, Layer 3, and Layer 4—all in hardware at wire speed.

3. Fill in the blanks in the following statement:

    In the 20/80 rule of networking, 20 percent of the traffic on a segment usually stays _____, while 80 percent travels _____.

    Answer: local, travels across the network

4. What is a collision domain, and where does it exist in a switched LAN?

    Answer: A collision domain is a network segment where shared media access is supported. Devices on the shared media must compete for access when transmitting data. In a switched network, the collision domain is restricted to a single switch port and does not extend across the switch.

5. What is a broadcast domain, and where does it exist in a switched LAN?

    Answer: A broadcast domain is the extent of a network where broadcast frames propagate. Basically, a broadcast domain covers an area where Layer 2 devices are located and terminates at the boundary of a Layer 3 device. In a switched network, the broadcast domain extends to all switch ports assigned to a common VLAN. This is because a switch forwards broadcasts out all available ports in a VLAN.

6. What is a VLAN, and why is it used?

    Answer: A virtual LAN (VLAN) is a group of switch ports that communicate as if they were attached to a single shared-media LAN segment. VLANs can extend across buildings or backbones, as long as the VLAN is connected end to end through trunking or physical connections. A VLAN is a broadcast domain. VLANs segment networks for ease of management and better performance.

7. At what OSI layer(s) do devices in the distribution layer usually operate?

    Answer: Layers 2, 3, and 4

8. What is network segmentation? When is it necessary, and how is it done in a campus network design?

    Answer: Segmentation is the process of dividing a LAN into smaller, discrete collision domains. If a large percentage of collisions is observed on a LAN, segmentation is appropriate. In a campus network design, segmentation occurs at each switch port. A similar form of segmentation involves reducing the size of broadcast domains. Placing Layer 3 devices in the distribution and core layers terminates the broadcast domains at those layer boundaries.

9. Is it possible to use Layer 2 switches in the distribution layer rather than Layer 3 switches? If so, what are the limitations?

    Answer: It is generally best practice to use Layer 3 or multilayer switches in the distribution layer, as outlined in this chapter. However, in some environments, this might not be possible because of cost or implementation logistics. Layer 2 switches will work fine in the distribution layer but will not provide a VLAN or broadcast domain boundary in that layer. As a result, broadcasts will propagate into the core layer, using unnecessary bandwidth.

Chapter 2

"Do I Know This Already?"

1. c
2. c, d, e
3. a, b
4. a, c
5. c
6. d
7. a, c
8. c, d, e
9. b
10. b, c

11. c, d

12. a, b, c

13. b

14. c

Q&A

1. Where is the most appropriate place to connect a block of enterprise (internal) servers? Why?

Answer: You should connect a block of enterprise servers into the core, just as you would switch blocks. The server farm building block should have a layer of access and distribution switches, just as in any switch block. This maximizes connectivity from the servers to all other devices in the network. In effect, all users will see the same number of switch "hops" to access a server. Connecting into the core also provides maximum scalability because you can add more server blocks in the future.

2. How can you provide redundancy at the switch and core block layers? (Consider physical means, as well as functional methods using protocols, algorithms, and so on.)

Answer: In a switch block, you can provide redundancy through two distribution switches. Each access switch can be linked to both distribution switches for fault tolerance. The Layer 3 distribution layer allows both uplinks to be used at the same time, with little or no failover time required. In the core layer, a dual core can be used with two core switches. Each distribution switch has dual uplinks, with one link to each core switch. Here, the redundant links can stay active for load sharing and redundancy, thanks to the Layer 3 routing protocols running in the distribution and core layers.

3. What factors should you consider when sizing a switch block?

Answer: Consider traffic types, flows, and patterns, as well as the size and number of common workgroups. Additionally, the Layer 3 switching capacity in the distribution layer should be sized according to the amount of traffic crossing from one VLAN to another.

4. What are the signs of an oversized switch block?

Answer: The distribution switches begin to become bottlenecks in handling the interVLAN traffic volume. Access list processing in the distribution layer also can become a rate-limiting factor. Broadcast and multicast traffic forwarding can slow the Layer 2 and Layer 3 switches in the block.

5. What are the attributes and issues of having a collapsed core block?

Answer:
Attributes: Cost savings (no separate high-end core switches) and design simplicity.
Issues: Scalability becomes limited.

6. How many switches are sufficient in a core block design?

Answer: Two switches are usually sufficient in a core block, offering load sharing and redundancy. However, you can add core switches as the size of the network and core traffic flow dictates.

7. What building blocks are used to build a scalable campus network?

Answer: The switch block is the template used to group access-layer switches and their respective distribution-layer switches. Switch blocks then are connected into the core block to build a scalable network. Depending on the other resources that are present in a campus network, other building blocks can include a server farm block, a network management block, and an enterprise edge block. The service provider edge block exists outside the campus network, although it does interface with the enterprise edge block.

8. What are two types of core, or backbone, designs?

Answer: Collapsed core and dual core.

9. Why should links and services provided to remote sites be grouped in a distinct building block?

Answer: Remote sites and roaming VPN users should be considered corporate users, as if they were connected directly inside the enterprise network. These users should enjoy the same efficient access to any enterprise resource that internal users have. Additionally, VPN tunnels should terminate in a secure area of the enterprise network.
Connections into the Internet (through service providers) are just the inverse—users from all parts of the enterprise need equal and efficient access to resources located out on the Internet. Therefore, a separate building block connected into the core is justified.

10. Why should network-management applications and servers be placed in a distinct building block?

Answer: Network-management applications must be capable of polling, querying, or accessing devices anywhere in the campus network. Moving these resources into a distinct building block provides redundant and efficient access into the network core so that all devices can be managed with equal access.

Chapter 3

"Do I Know This Already?"

1. b
2. b
3. b
4. c
5. d
6. b
7. d
8. d
9. b
10. c
11. d
12. b

Q&A

1. By default, how long are CAM table entries kept before they are aged out?

   Answer: 300 seconds

2. A TCAM lookup involves which values?

   Answer: Mask, Value, Result

3. How many table lookups are required to find a MAC address in the CAM table?

   Answer: 1

4. How many table lookups are required to match a packet against an access list that has been compiled into 10 TCAM entries?

   Answer: 1

5. How many value patterns can a TCAM store for each mask?

   Answer: 8

6. Can all packets be switched in hardware by a multilayer switch?

Answer: No; some must be flagged for process switching by the switch CPU.

7. Multilayer switches must rewrite which portions of an Ethernet frame?

Answer:
Source and destination MAC addresses
IP Time-To-Live
Checksums

8. If a station receives only Ethernet frames and doesn't transmit anything, how will a switch learn of its location?

Answer: You must configure a static CAM entry with the station's MAC address and the switch port where it is located. Otherwise, the switch must flood every frame destined for that host out every switch port in an effort to find it.

9. What is a TCAM's main purpose?

Answer: To process access lists as a single table lookup

10. Why do the TCAM mask and pattern fields consist of so many bits?

Answer: So that a combination of several address fields in a frame can be inspected at once

11. In a multilayer switch with a TCAM, a longer access list (more ACEs or statements) takes longer to process for each frame. True or false?

Answer: False

12. A multilayer switch receives a packet with a certain destination IP address. Suppose that the switch has that IP address in its Layer 3 forwarding table but has no corresponding Layer 2 address. What happens to the packet next?

Answer: The switch CPU sends an ARP request.

13. Suppose that a multilayer switch can't support a protocol with CEF, and it relies on *fallback bridging*. Can the switch still route that traffic?

Answer: No. That traffic is transparently bridged. An external multilayer switch or router is required to route the bridged packets.

14. To configure a static CAM table entry, the **mac address-table static** *mac-address* command is used. Which two other parameters also must be given?

    Answer:
    vlan *vlan-id*
    interface *type mod/num*

15. As a network administrator, what aspects of a switch TCAM should you be concerned with?

    Answer: The size of the TCAM resources

16. What portion of the TCAM is used to evaluate port number comparisons in an access list?

    Answer: LOU

17. Someone has asked you where the host with MAC address 00-10-20-30-40-50 is located. Assuming that you already know the switch it is connected to, what command can you use to find it?

    Answer: show mac address-table dynamic address 0010.2030.4050

18. Complete this command to display the size of the CAM table: **show mac** _____.

    Answer: address-table count

19. What protocol is used to advertise CAM table entries among neighboring switches?

    Answer: None; the entries are not advertised.

20. Suppose that a host uses one MAC address to send frames and another to receive them. In other words, one address will always be the source address sent in frames, and the other is used only as a destination address in incoming frames. Is it possible for that host to communicate with others through a Layer 2 switch? If so, how?

    Answer: Yes, but not very efficiently. The Layer 2 switch will learn one of the host's MAC addresses as the host sends frames. That address will be seen as the source address on frames arriving at the switch. However, because the second MAC address never is used to send frames, the switch will never be capable of learning of its existence. When frames are sent to the host using that second MAC address, the switch is forced to flood the frames out all relevant switch ports. The host receives those frames only because it is connected to a port where the frames were flooded. All other hosts on the same VLAN also receive the flooded frames, even though they have no interest in that traffic.

Chapter 4

"Do I Know This Already?"

1. b

2. b

3. b

4. c

5. d

6. c

7. b

8. c

9. d

10. a

11. d

12. d

Q&A

1. When Cisco IOS Software is used on a Catalyst switch, the switch must perform routing. True or false?

   Answer: False

2. What is the major difference between the Cisco IOS Software and CatOS command sets?

   Answer: Cisco IOS Software uses the familiar router configuration commands and a hierarchy of configuration modes. CatOS uses **set** commands with no explicit configuration mode. Also, IOS configuration commands are not saved automatically across a power failure, whereas CatOS commands are. IOS also offers the capability to switch packets at Layer 3, whereas CatOS never was extended beyond Layer 2.

3. What switch command will enter privileged EXEC or "enable" mode on a Catalyst 4500?

   Answer: enable

4. Match these default command-line prompts with their respective modes:

   a. Switch#   ____Normal user EXEC mode

   b. Switch(config)   ____Privileged EXEC or enable

   c. Switch(config-if)#   ____Global configuration

   d. Switch>   ____Interface configuration

Answer:

__d__	Normal user EXEC mode
__a__	Privileged EXEC or enable
__b__	Global configuration
__c__	Interface configuration

5. With the command-line prompt **testlab#**, what command has been used to customize the prompt?

Answer: hostname testlab

6. The following commands have just been entered, assuming that interface VLAN 10 did not previously exist:

```
interface vlan 10
ip address 192.168.199.10 255.255.255.0
no shutdown
```

Suddenly, the power cord is pulled out of the switch. What will happen when the power is restored?

Answer: Not only will interface VLAN 10 have no IP address, but there will not even be an interface VLAN 10. Those commands were entered into the running-config configuration file, so they were not applied permanently. When the power is restored, the contents of the startup-config will be read and executed. Because the running-config was not saved, the VLAN 10 commands no longer will exist.

7. Can you configure an enable secret password (**enable secret** *password*) for the switch console and a different enable secret password for Telnet access?

Answer: No, only one global enable secret password is allowed, and it applies to all lines on the switch.

8. When you configure an IP address and subnet mask on a Layer 2 switch for management purposes, which VLAN are you required to use?

    a. VLAN 1

    b. VLAN 0

    c. VLAN 1001

    d. Any VLAN that is appropriate

    e. You cannot assign an IP address to a VLAN.

    Answer: d

9. What commands will allow Telnet and ping access to a switch-management interface at 192.168.200.10, subnet mask 255.255.255.0, on VLAN 5? A router is available at address 192.168.200.1.

    Answer:
    ```
    interface vlan 5
    ip address 192.168.200.10 255.255.255.0
    ip default-gateway 192.168.200.1
    no shutdown

    interface vlan 5
    ip address 192.168.200.10 255.255.255.0
    ip default-gateway 192.168.200.1
    ```

10. CDP advertisements occur every _____ seconds.

    Answer: 60

11. When a Cisco Catalyst switch receives a CDP multicast frame, it relays it to neighboring switches. True or false?

    Answer: False

12. Eight access-layer switches connect to a central distribution-layer switch using Gigabit Ethernet connections. Each connection is assigned to VLAN 1 so that no link is in trunking mode. On one of the access switches, how many neighboring switches will be shown by the **show cdp neighbor gigabit 0/1**?

    Answer: Only one neighboring switch will be shown—the single distribution-layer switch that is connected directly. CDP messages are not forwarded; they are received and processed only by the neighboring switch. Because all eight access switches are connected by another switch, CDP messages don't pass between them.

13. Which Cisco IOS Software image file is more recent:

c3550-i5q3l2-mz.121-12c.EA1.bin

or

c3550-i9q3l2-mz.121-11c.EA1.bin?

Answer: c3550-i5q3l2-mz.121-12c.EA1.bin

14. A new switch has just been configured with 100 command lines from the console. You realize the need to save the new configuration and type **copy start run**. Where will your configuration be stored?

Answer: Unfortunately, the configuration you made might be lost or drastically changed. The startup-config file will be copied into, or overlaid onto, the running-config. Any commands that are different in the startup-config will overwrite the commands you entered in the running-config. Because this is a new switch containing only the default commands, you could end up effectively overwriting your changes with the default values that the switch had when it powered up for the first time. The correct command should have been **copy run start.**

15. What command can you use to see what Cisco IOS software version currently is running on a switch?

Answer: show version

16. Complete this command so that the output is displayed starting with the configuration for interface VLAN 100:

show run _____

Answer: | begin Vlan100

17. The **debug spanning-tree all** command has been given from the EXEC mode command line. What commands can you use to stop or disable the debugging output?

Answer:
```
no debug all
no debug spanning-tree all
undebug all
```

18. What command can you use to verify CDP configuration on switch port GigabitEthernet 3/1?

Answer: show cdp interface gigabit 3/1

Chapter 5

"Do I Know This Already?"

1. c

2. b

3. a

4. b

5. b

6. b

7. c

8. c

9. c

10. d

11. e

Q&A

1. Put the following Ethernet standards in order of increasing bandwidth:

    a. 802.3z

    b. 802.3ae

    c. 802.3

    d. 802.3u

    Answer: c, d, a, b

2. What benefits does switched Ethernet have over shared Ethernet?

    Answer: Switched Ethernet ports receive dedicated bandwidth, have a reduced collision domain, and show increased performance because of segmentation or fewer users per port.

3. When a 10/100 Ethernet link is autonegotiating, which will be chosen if both stations can support the same capabilities—10BASE-T full duplex, 100BASE-TX half duplex, or 100BASE-TX full duplex?

    Answer: 100BASE-TX full duplex will be chosen because it has the highest autonegotiation priority and is common to both end stations.

4.   How many pairs of copper wires does a 1000BASE-T connection need?

   Answer: Four pairs

5.   A switch port is being configured as shown here. What command is needed next to set the port to full-duplex mode?

```
Switch(config)# interface fastethernet 0/13
Switch(config-if)#
```

   Answer: Enter the command **duplex full** at the prompt.

6.   If a full-duplex Gigabit Ethernet connection offers 2 Gbps throughput, can a single host send data at 2 Gbps?

   Answer: No, a full-duplex Gigabit Ethernet connection allows only 1 Gbps simultaneously in each direction across the link.

7.   Which GBIC would you use for a connection over multimode fiber (MMF)?

   Answer: You could use either a 1000BASE-SX or a 1000BASE-LX/LH.

8.   A Category 5 cable having only pins 1,2 and 3,6 has been installed and used for a Fast Ethernet link. Can this same cable be used for a migration to Gigabit Ethernet using 1000BASE-T GBICs, assuming that the length is less than 100 m?

   Answer: No. 1000BASE-T requires all four pairs of wires to be present.

9.   A Catalyst 3550 switch port has been configured for 100 Mbps full-duplex mode, but a link cannot be established. What are some commands that you could use to investigate and correct the problem?

   Answer: To see the current state of one or more ports, you could use the **show interface** command. This would show the ports' speed and duplex modes, and whether a link has been established. One reason the link is not established could be that the port is shut down or disabled. To enable the port, use the **no shutdown** interface-configuration command. Because the port has been set to 100 Mbps full-duplex mode, it is possible that the end station can support only 10 Mbps at half duplex. Therefore, set the port for autonegotiate mode with the **speed auto** and **duplex auto** commands. Otherwise, you could set the port to a fixed speed and mode that would match that of the end station.

10.   The 10-Gigabit Ethernet is backward-compatible with other forms of Ethernet at Layer _____ but not at Layer _____.

   Answer: 10-Gigabit Ethernet is backward compatible with other forms of Ethernet at Layer **2** but not at Layer **1**.

11. What one switch command will select Fast Ethernet interfaces 4/1 through 48 for a common configuration?

Answer: interface range fastethernet 4/1 − 48
(Don't forget spaces around the dash.)

12. What is the purpose of a GBIC?

Answer: A GBIC is used as a modular medium-independent connection for Gigabit Ethernet. A switch with a GBIC port will accept GBIC modules that support various network media types. Changing network media cabling requires only a low-cost GBIC module change.

13. Suppose you need to apply several different common configurations to Fast Ethernet interfaces 3/1 through 12, 3/34, 3/48, and 5/14 through 48. What commands are needed to create an interface macro to accomplish this, and what command would apply the macro?

Answer:

```
define interface-range mymacro fastethernet 3/1 - 12, fastethernet 3/34 -
48 , fastethernet 5/14 - 48
interface range macro mymacro
```

14. If a switch port is configured with the **speed 100** and **duplex full** commands, what will happen if the PC connected to it is set for autonegotiated speed and duplex? Now, reverse the roles. (The switch will autonegotiate, but the PC won't.) What will happen?

Answer: When the PC attempts to autonegotiate the link settings, it will detect the switch port's speed of 100 Mbps. However, the duplex cannot be detected without a two-way information exchange, so the PC probably will fall back to half duplex. The results are similar when the roles are reversed because the switch will decide on 100 Mbps half duplex. In either case, a duplex mismatch will occur.

15. By default, what will a switch do if one of its ports has a serious error condition, and how can you tell when this has happened?

Answer: By default, every possible error condition is detected on every port. If any one of these conditions occurs, the port automatically will be shut down in the errdisable state. The **show interface status err-disabled** command shows a brief summary of all ports in the errdisable state.

16. What port speeds can you assign to a UTP Gigabit Ethernet switch port? Consider both 1000BASE-T GBIC and native RJ-45 copper switch module ports.

Answer: A 1000BASE-T GBIC is fixed at 1 Gbps, whereas switch modules with UTP Gigabit Ethernet ports can be 10 Mbps, 100 Mbps, or 1000 Mbps.

17. What command can you use to make sure that no switch ports automatically are shut down in an errdisable state for any reason?

Answer: Use the **no errdisable detect cause all** interface-configuration command. Remember that all causes are enabled by default, so you must disable all causes first.

18. Suppose you commonly find that switch ports are being shut down in errdisable because users are making their connections go up and down too often. Thinking that this might be the result of odd PC behavior, you would like to visit each user to troubleshoot the problem; however, this is a minor error and you don't want to inconvenience the end users too much. What commands can you use to have the switch automatically re-enable the ports after 10 minutes? Make sure a flapping link will be recovered automatically in this time frame.

Answer:
```
errdisable recovery interval 600
errdisable recovery cause link-flap
```

19. Look at the following **show interfaces** output. Does the high number of collisions indicate a problem? Why or why not?

```
FastEthernet0/6 is up, line protocol is up
  Hardware is Fast Ethernet, address is 000a.f4d2.5506 (bia 000a.f4d2.5506)
  Description: Front Office PC
  MTU 1500 bytes, BW 10000 Kbit, DLY 1000 usec,
     reliability 255/255, txload 1/255, rxload 1/255
  Encapsulation ARPA, loopback not set
  Keepalive set (10 sec)
  Half-duplex, 10Mb/s
  input flow-control is off, output flow-control is off
  ARP type: ARPA, ARP Timeout 04:00:00
  Last input never, output 00:00:00, output hang never
  Last clearing of "show interface" counters never
  Input queue: 0/75/0/0 (size/max/drops/flushes); Total output drops: 0
  Queueing strategy: fifo
  Output queue :0/40 (size/max)
  5 minute input rate 0 bits/sec, 0 packets/sec
  5 minute output rate 0 bits/sec, 0 packets/sec
     1321140 packets input, 227738894 bytes, 0 no buffer
     Received 13786 broadcasts, 0 runts, 0 giants, 0 throttles
     1 input errors, 1 CRC, 0 frame, 0 overrun, 0 ignored
     0 watchdog, 42 multicast, 0 pause input
     0 input packets with dribble condition detected
     87798820 packets output, 2662785561 bytes, 1316 underruns
     6 output errors, 406870 collisions, 3 interface resets
     0 babbles, 0 late collision, 19458 deferred
     0 lost carrier, 0 no carrier, 0 PAUSE output
     1316 output buffer failures, 0 output buffers swapped out
```

Answer: Yes, this probably would be normal, considering that the interface is set for 10 Mbps half duplex. Collisions are to be expected on a link with shared bandwidth; in this case, the link is part of a collision domain. If the link were showing full duplex at any speed, collisions never should be detected.

Chapter 6

"Do I Know This Already?"

1. c

2. b

3. b

4. b

5. b

6. c

7. d

8. c

9. b

10. a

11. c

12. a

Q&A

1. What is a VLAN? When is it used?

    Answer: A VLAN is a group of devices on the same broadcast domain, such as a logical subnet or segment. VLANs can span switch ports, switches within a switch block, or closets and buildings. VLANs group users and devices into common workgroups across geographical areas. VLANs help provide segmentation, security, and problem isolation.

2. When a VLAN is configured on a Catalyst switch port, in how much of the campus network will the VLAN number be unique and significant?

    Answer: The VLAN number will be significant in the local switch. If trunking is enabled, the VLAN number will be significant across the entire trunking domain. In other words, the VLAN will be transported to every switch that has a trunk link supporting that VLAN.

3. Name two types of VLANs in terms of spanning areas of the campus network.

    Answer:
    Local VLAN
    End-to-end VLAN

4. What switch commands configure Fast Ethernet port 4/11 for VLAN 2?

Answer:
```
interface fastethernet 4/11
switchport mode access
switchport access vlan 2
```

5. Generally, what must be configured (both switch and end-user device) for a port-based VLAN?

Answer: The switch port

6. What is the default VLAN on all ports of a Catalyst switch?

Answer: VLAN 1

7. What is a trunk link?

Answer: A trunk link is a connection between two switches that transports traffic from multiple VLANs. Each frame is identified with its source VLAN during its trip across the trunk link.

8. What methods of Ethernet VLAN frame identification can be used on a Catalyst switch trunk?

Answer:
802.1Q
ISL

9. What is the difference between the two trunking methods? How many bytes are added to trunked frames for VLAN identification in each method?

Answer: ISL uses encapsulation and adds a 26-byte header and a 4-byte trailer. 802.1Q adds a 4-byte tag field within existing frames, without encapsulation.

10. What is the purpose of the Dynamic Trunking Protocol (DTP)?

Answer: DTP allows negotiation of a common trunking method between endpoints of a trunk link.

11. What commands are needed to configure a Catalyst switch trunk port Gigabit 3/1 to transport only VLANs 100, 200 through 205, and 300 using IEEE 802.1Q? (Assume that trunking is enabled and active on the port already. Also assume that the **interface gigabit 3/1** command already has been entered.)

Answer:
```
switchport trunk allowed vlan 100, 200-205, 300
```

12. Two neighboring switch trunk ports are set to the *auto* mode with *ISL* trunking encapsulation mode. What will the resulting trunk mode become?

Answer: Trunking will not be established. Both switches are in the passive auto state and are waiting to be asked to start the trunking mode. The link will remain an access link on both switches.

13. Complete the following command to configure the switch port to use DTP to actively ask the other end to become a trunk:

```
switchport mode _____
```

Answer:
```
switchport mode dynamic desirable
```

14. Which command can set the native VLAN of a trunk port to VLAN 100 after the interface has been selected?

Answer:
```
switchport trunk native vlan 100
```

15. What command can configure a trunk port to stop sending and receiving DTP packets completely?

Answer:
```
switchport nonegotiate
```

16. What command can be used on a Catalyst switch to verify exactly what VLANs will be transported over trunk link gigabitethernet 4/4?

Answer:
```
show interface gigabitethernet 4/4 switchport
```

or
```
show interface gigabitethernet 4/4 trunk
```

17. Suppose that a switch port is configured with the following commands. A PC with a nontrunking NIC card then is connected to that port. What, if any, traffic will the PC successfully send and receive?

```
interface fastethernet 0/12
switchport trunk encapsulation dot1q
switchport trunk native vlan 10
switchport trunk allowed vlan 1-1005
switchport mode trunk
```

Answer: The PC expects only a single network connection, using a single VLAN. In other words, the PC can't participate in any form of trunking. Only untagged or unencapsulated frames will be understood. Recall that an 802.1Q trunk's native VLAN is the only VLAN that has untagged frames. Therefore, the PC will be capable of exchanging frames only on VLAN 10, the native VLAN.

Chapter 7

"Do I Know This Already?"

1. c
2. a
3. c
4. b
5. b
6. b and c
7. a
8. c
9. c
10. b
11. d
12. b

Q&A

1. True or false: You can use VTP domains to separate broadcast domains.

   Answer: False. Broadcast domains can be separated only with VLANs because a VLAN defines a broadcast domain's boundaries. A VTP domain is a different concept; it defines the management domain where a set of switches can exchange information about VLAN configuration.

2. What VTP modes can a Catalyst switch be configured for? Can VLANs be created in each of the modes?

   Answer: Server, client, and transparent modes. VLANs can be created in server mode. VLANs cannot be created in client mode. In transparent mode, VLANs can be created, but only on the local switch; they are not advertised to other switches.

3. How many VTP management domains can a Catalyst switch participate in? How many VTP servers can a management domain have?

   Answer: A switch can be a member of only one VTP management domain. A domain must have at least one server for VLAN changes to be propagated throughout the domain. There can be more than one server, for redundancy.

4. What conditions must exist for two Catalyst switches to be in the same VTP management domain?

    Answer: Both switches must have the same VTP domain name defined and enabled, both switches must be adjacent on a trunk link, and trunking must be enabled and active between them.

    Two switches also can operate in the same VTP domain if one of them is new and has the default NULL domain name. That switch will listen and pick up the first VTP domain name it hears in VTP advertisements.

5. On a VTP server switch, identify what you can do to reset the VTP configuration revision number to 0.

    Answer:
    Set the VTP domain name to a bogus value and change it back.

    Configure the switch for VTP transparent mode and then configure the switch back to server mode.

6. How can you clear the configuration revision number on a VTP client?

    Answer: You can't. The VTP client bases all VLAN and VTP information on advertisements from a VTP server. Therefore, the configuration revision number on the client comes directly from the same number on the server.

7. Complete this command to make all VLANs other than 30 and 100 eligible for pruning on the trunk interface:

    ```
    switchport trunk pruning vlan_____
    ```
    Answer:
    ```
    switchport trunk pruning vlan except 30,100
    ```

8. Which VLAN numbers are never eligible for VTP pruning? Why?

    Answer: VLAN numbers 1 and 1001 to 1005. VLAN 1 is reserved as a VLAN for control protocol traffic, and VLANs 1002 to 1005 are reserved as the default FDDI and Token Ring function VLANs.

9. What does the acronym VTP stand for?

    Answer: VLAN Trunking Protocol

10. What VTP domain name is defined on a new switch with no configuration?

    Answer: A NULL or empty string. The switch defaults to server mode and learns a VTP domain name from the first VTP server heard on a trunk link. Otherwise, you manually must configure the domain name.

11. In a network of switches, VTP domain Engineering has been configured with VLANs 1, 10 through 30, and 100. The VTP configuration revision number is currently at 23. Suppose a new switch is connected to the network, and it has the following configuration: VTP domain Engineering, VTP server mode, only VLANs 1 and 2 defined, and configuration revision number of 30.

What happens when the switch is connected to the network?

Answer: Because the new switch has a higher configuration revision number, the other switches in the VTP domain Engineering will learn all its VLAN and VTP configuration information. The new switch has two VLANs configured on itself: VLAN 1 and 2. The other switches will assume that they should delete all VLANs except for VLAN 1, and VLAN 2 will be created. Obviously, this will cause a major outage on the network because active VLANs 10 through 30 and 100 will be deleted and will go inactive. A network administrator will have to manually restore the configurations of those VLANs.

12. A VTP client switch has VLANs 1, 2, 3, 10, and 30 configured as part of a VTP domain; however, the switch has users connected only to access switch ports defined on VLANs 3 and 30. If VTP pruning is enabled and all VLANs are eligible, which VLANs will be pruned on the upstream switch?

Answer: 2, 10

13. The VTP domain Area3 consists of one server and several clients. The server's VTP configuration revision number is at 11. A new switch is added to the network. It has VTP domain name Area5 and a configuration revision number of 10. What happens when the new switch is added to the network? What happens when the VTP domain name is changed to Area3 on the new switch?

Answer: Domain Area5 will experience no change when the switch is added. The two domains, Area3 and Area5, will coexist on the same network with different sets of clients. The configuration revision numbers on both servers will stay unchanged.

When the domain is changed to Area3, that domain then will have two VTP servers. The switch that has the newly configured domain name has a lower configuration revision number, so it will learn all VTP information from the existing server. The new switch's revision number will become 11, and its list of defined VLANs will change to match the existing server.

14. What command shows information about the VTP configuration on a Catalyst 3550?

Answer:
```
show vtp status
```

Chapter 8

"Do I Know This Already?"

1. e

2. c

3. c

4. d

5. c

6. c

7. a

8. d

9. b

10. c

11. c

12. c

13. c

Q&A

1. What are some benefits of an EtherChannel?

   Answer:
   Increased bandwidth
   Link redundancy

2. How many links can be aggregated into an EtherChannel?

   Answer: 2 to 8

3. Traffic between two hosts will be distributed across all links in an EtherChannel. True or false?

   Answer: False. Packets are distributed onto the EtherChannel links based on the load-distribution method or algorithm that is configured. It is entirely possible that traffic passing between two hosts will end up on just one link within the bundle if a method involving source or destination addresses is used.

4. Which methods can you use to distribute traffic in an EtherChannel?

Answer:
MAC address
IP address
Layer 4 port

5. How does an EtherChannel distribute broadcasts and multicasts?

Answer: Broadcasts and multicasts are distributed across the links within an EtherChannel, just like any other traffic. The broadcast or multicast addresses are used in the hash or load-balancing algorithm to determine the link index.

6. When load balancing, what hashing functions choose a link for a frame?

Answer: If the hashing function is based on a single address (MAC, IP, or port), the low-order bits of that address are used as a link index. If two addresses or port numbers are used, the exclusive-OR (XOR) of those two values is used to derive the low-order bits that form a link index.

7. What protocols can negotiate an EtherChannel between two switches?

Answer:
PAgP and LACP

8. Suppose a switch at one end of an EtherChannel is configured to use source MAC addresses for load balancing. The switch on the other end is configured to use both source and destination IP addresses. What happens?

Answer: The EtherChannel successfully will transport traffic between the two switches. However, the traffic load will not be distributed evenly or symmetrically across the links in the channel.

9. Two switches have a four-port EtherChannel between them. Both switches are load balancing using source and destination IP addresses. If a packet has the source address 192.168.15.10 and destination address 192.168.100.31, what is the EtherChannel link index?

Answer: The link index is computed by an XOR of the source and destination IP addresses. Because this is a four-port link, only the 2 low-order bits are needed. 10 XOR 31 can be computed by using binary values: 00001010 XOR 00011111 = 00010101. The lowest 2 bits (01) give a link index of 1.

10. What does the acronym PAgP stand for?

    Answer: Port Aggregation Protocol

11. Two switches should be configured to negotiate an EtherChannel. If one switch is using PAgP auto mode, what should the other switch use?

    Answer: PAgP desirable mode

12. What is the LACP system priority value used for?

    Answer: The switch with the lowest system ID (system priority + MAC address) is allowed to make decisions regarding which ports actively will participate in an EtherChannel and which ones will be held in a standby state.

13. Complete the following command to put an interface into EtherChannel group 3 and to use PAgP to ask the far-end switch to participate in the EtherChannel. This switch port also should require PAgP packets back from the far-end switch.

    ```
    Switch(config-if)# channel-group _____
    ```

    Answer:
    ```
    Switch(config-if)# channel-group 3 mode desirable non-silent
    ```

14. What interface configuration command is needed to select LACP as the EtherChannel negotiation protocol?

    Answer:
    ```
    channel-protocol lacp
    ```

15. What command could you use to see the status of every port in an EtherChannel?

    Answer:
    ```
    show etherchannel summary
    ```

16. What command could you use to verify the hashing algorithm used for EtherChannel load balancing?

    Answer:
    ```
    show etherchannel load-balance
    ```

17. Suppose that a switch is used in a small data center where one server offers an IP-based application to many clients throughout the campus. An EtherChannel connects the data-center switch to a Layer 3 core switch, which routes traffic to all clients. What EtherChannel load-balancing method might be most appropriate at the data-center switch?

    a. Source MAC address

    b. Source IP address

    c. Destination MAC address

    d. Destination IP address

    e. Source and destination MAC address

    f. Source and destination IP address

Answer:
d. Remember that the EtherChannel will load-balance only outbound traffic, or that from the server toward the clients. Here are brief explanations of each of the choices, to help clarify the answer.

a. **Source MAC address**—Not very useful. The source MAC address (the server) always is the same. One link in the channel always would be selected.

b. **Source IP address**—Not very useful. Again, the source IP address (the server) is constant.

c. **Destination MAC address**—Not very useful. Because a Layer 3 switch is positioned in the core layer, it always appears as the destination MAC address for all client destinations.

d. **Destination IP address**—This is the best choice because the destination IP addresses of the clients are diverse and are not modified along the path.

e. **Source and destination MAC address**—Not very useful. Because the destination MAC address always is the Layer 3 switch, only one link will be used.

f. **Source and destination IP address**—This would make a good choice, although the combination of addresses doesn't add anything. The source IP address (the server) always is constant. Therefore, source XOR destination always yields something similar to the destination address itself.

18. Suppose that a mainframe is connected to a switch that has an EtherChannel uplink to a campus network. The EtherChannel has been configured with the **port-channel load-balance src-dst-ip** command. Most of the mainframe traffic is SNA (non-IP). What will happen to the SNA frames when they are switched? Would it be better to reconfigure the channel with **port-channel load-balance src-dst-mac**?

    Answer: The SNA frames are non-IP, so only MAC addresses are relevant. The switch has been configured to load-balance according to the XOR of the source and destination IP addresses. Obviously, the SNA frames will have neither of these values present. The switch will realize this and fall back to the "lower" method of src-dst-mac (XOR of the source and destination MAC addresses) for each SNA frame. No configuration changes are necessary for this to occur.

    There really isn't a good reason to reconfigure for src-dst-mac because the switch can forward the SNA frames already. However, if it were reconfigured, any IP packets would be encapsulated in Ethernet frames, providing MAC addresses within the frames.

19. What attributes of a set of switch ports must match to form an EtherChannel?

Answer:
Port speed
Port duplex
Trunking mode
Trunking encapsulation
Access or native VLAN

20. What happens if one port of an EtherChannel is unplugged or goes dead? What happens when that port is reconnected?

Answer: Traffic on the disconnected port is moved to the next available link in the EtherChannel bundle. When the port is reconnected, traffic does not automatically move back to the bundle's original port. Instead, new traffic is learned and applied to the restored link.

Chapter 9

"Do I Know This Already?"

1. c
2. c
3. b
4. b
5. c
6. c
7. a
8. b
9. d
10. b
11. b
12. c

Q&A

1. What is a bridging loop? Why is it bad?

Answer: A bridging loop is a path through a bridged or switched network that provides connectivity in an endless loop. Unknown unicast, broadcast, or multicast frames introduced into the loop are propagated by each switch, causing the frames to circulate around and around the loop. Network bandwidth and CPU resources can be absorbed completely by the increasing amount of broadcast traffic. Breaking the loop connectivity can end bridging loops.

2. Put the following STP port states in chronological order:

  a. Learning

  b. Forwarding

  c. Listening

  d. Blocking

Answer: d, c, a, b

3. Choose two types of STP messages used to communicate between bridges:

  a. Advertisement BPDU

  b. Configuration BPDU

  c. ACK BPDU

  d. TCN BPDU

Answer: b, d

4. What criteria are used to select the following?

  a. Root Bridge

  b. Root Port

  c. Designated Port

  d. Redundant (or secondary) Root Bridges

Answer:
a. Lowest Bridge ID (Bridge priority, MAC address)
b. Lowest Root Path Cost
c. Lowest Root Path Cost on a shared segment
d. Next-to-lowest Bridge ID

If a tie occurs, these parameters are used to decide:
1. Lowest Bridge ID
2. Lowest Root Path Cost
3. Lowest Sender Bridge ID
4. Lowest Sender Port ID

5. Which of the following switches becomes the Root Bridge, given the information in the following table? Which switch becomes the secondary Root Bridge if the Root Bridge fails?

Switch Name	Bridge Priority	MAC Address	Port Costs
Catalyst A	32,768	00-d0-10-34-26-a0	All are 19
Catalyst B	32,768	00-d0-10-34-24-a0	All are 4
Catalyst C	32,767	00-d0-10-34-27-a0	All are 19
Catalyst D	32,769	00-d0-10-34-24-a1	All are 19

Answer: Catalyst C will become the primary Root because of its lower Bridge Priority value. (Bridge Priority has a greater weight on the election than a lower MAC address.) The secondary Root will be Catalyst B; both A and B have the next-lowest Bridge Priorities, but B also has a lower MAC address.

6. What conditions cause an STP topology change? What effect does this have on STP and the network?

Answer: A topology change occurs when a port moves to the Forwarding state, or from Forwarding or Learning to the Blocking state. During a topology change, addresses are aged out in Forward Delay seconds, whereas active stations are not aged out of the bridging table. The STP is not recomputed; TCN BPDUs are sent throughout the network, notifying other switches of the topology change. Only the port where the topology change is occurring is affected, by moving through the STP states.

7. A Root Bridge has been elected in a switched network. Suppose that a new switch is installed with a lower Bridge ID than the existing Root Bridge. What will happen?

Answer: The new switch will begin life by advertising itself as the Root Bridge, thinking it is the only bridge on the network. Because it has a lower Bridge ID than the current Root, it will win the election after the BPDUs converge and when all switches have a knowledge of the new, better choice.

8. Suppose that a switch receives Configuration BPDUs on two of its ports. Both ports are assigned to the same VLAN. Each of the BPDUs announces Catalyst A as the Root Bridge. Can the switch use both of these ports as Root Ports? Why?

Answer: The STP doesn't allow more than one Root Port per switch (bridge). Because of this, both ports cannot become Root Ports. Only the port with the lowest Root Path Cost (or one of the successive STP tie-breaker decisions) will become the Root Port.

9. How is the Root Path Cost calculated for a switch port?

   Answer: The Root Path cost is a cumulative value that is incremented as Configuration BPDUs are passed from switch to switch. A switch adds the Port Cost of the local port to the current Root Path Cost value as a BPDU is received.

10. What conditions can cause ports on a network's Root Bridge to move into the Blocking state? (Assume that all switch connections are to other switches. No crossover cables are used to connect two ports on the same switch.)

    Answer: By definition, all ports on the Root Bridge are Designated Ports because they are in the closest possible location to the Root Bridge. Therefore, those ports never can be put into the Blocking state. The only exception to this is if two of the Root Bridge switch's ports are connected, a situation that could but shouldn't occur.

11. What parameters can be tuned to influence the selection of a port as a Root or Designated Port?

    Answer: Port Cost

12. After a bridging loop forms, how can you stop the endless flow of traffic?

    Answer: Turn off the switch or unplug a cable on a port that is part of the loop. Turning off the switch is obviously a drastic measure, but it does help to clear the loop. Any method might be used, as long as the loop manually is broken or disconnected. In some cases, the traffic volume caused by the loop can overwhelm the switch CPU. If that happens, you won't be able to connect to the switch CLI to shut down an interface or reload the switch.

13. In a BPDU, when can the Root Bridge ID have the same value as the Sender Bridge ID?

    Answer: When the switch that is sending the BPDU is also the Root Bridge

14. Which of these is true about the Root Path Cost?

    a. It is a value sent by the Root Bridge that cannot be changed along the way.

    b. It is incremented as a switch receives a BPDU.

    c. It is incremented as a switch sends a BPDU.

    d. It is incremented by the Path Cost of a port.

    Answer: b, d

15. Suppose that two switches are connected by a common link. Each must decide which one will have the Designated Port on the link. Which switch takes on this role if these STP advertisements occur?

    a. The link is on switch A's port number 12 and on switch B's port number 5.

    b. Switch A has a Bridge ID of 32,768:0000.1111.2222, and switch B has 8192:0000.5555.6666.

    c. Switch A advertises a Root Path Cost of 8, while B advertises 12.

    Answer:
    Switch A will have the Designated Port. The STP tie-breaking sequence must be used for the decision. The first relevant decision is that of the lowest Root Path Cost, advertised by switch A. If both switches advertised an identical Root Path Cost, the lowest Sender Bridge ID (that of switch B) would be used.

16. Using the default STP timers, how long does it take for a port to move from the Blocking state to the Forwarding state?

    Answer: 30 seconds

17. If the Root Bridge sets the Topology Change flag in the BPDU, what must the other switches in the network do?

    Answer: Shorten their bridge table aging times

18. Over what VLAN(s) does the CST form of STP run?

    a. VLAN 1

    b. All active VLANs

    c. All VLANs (active or inactive)

    d. The native VLAN

    Answer: d

19. What is the major difference between PVST and PVST+?

    Answer: PVST+ interoperates with CST and PVST.

20. Two switches are connected by a common active link. When might neither switch have a Designated Port on the link?

    a. When neither has a better Root Path Cost.

    b. When the switches are actually the primary and secondary Root Bridges.

   c. When one switch has its port in the Blocking state.

   d. Never; this can't happen.

Answer: d

Chapter 10

"Do I Know This Already?"

   1. c

   2. c

   3. d

   4. c

   5. c

   6. c

   7. b

   8. d

   9. c

   10. a

   11. a

   12. d

Q&A

   1. What commands can configure a Catalyst 4500 switch as the root bridge on VLAN 10, assuming that the other switches are using the default STP values?

   Answer:
```
spanning-tree vlan 10 root primary
```

   2. Using your root bridge answer from question 1, what commands can configure a Catalyst 3550 switch as a secondary or backup root bridge on VLAN 10?

   Answer:
```
spanning-tree vlan 10 root secondary
```

3. Which of the following switches will become the root bridge, given the information in the following table? Which switch will become the secondary root bridge if the root bridge fails?

Switch Name	Bridge Priority	MAC Address	Port Costs
Catalyst A	32,768	00-d0-10-34-26-a0	All are 19
Catalyst B	32,768	00-d0-10-34-24-a0	All are 4
Catalyst C	32,767	00-d0-10-34-27-a0	All are 19
Catalyst D	32,769	00-d0-10-34-24-a1	All are 19

Answer: The root bridge will be Catalyst C because its bridge priority has the lowest value. The bridge priority is more significant because it is stored in the upper bits of the Bridge ID field. If Catalyst C fails in its duty as root bridge, Catalyst B will take over as the secondary root bridge. Because Catalyst B has the default bridge priority (32,768), along with another switch, the lowest MAC address will be the deciding factor.

Questions 4 through 7 are based on a network that contains two switches, Catalyst A and B. Their bridge priorities and MAC addresses are 32,768:0000.aaaa.aaaa and 32,768:0000.bbbb.bbbb, respectively.

4. Which switch will become the root bridge?

    Answer: Catalyst A. The bridge priorities are equal, so the lowest MAC address is the deciding factor.

5. If switch B's bridge priority is changed to 10,000, which one will be root?

    Answer: Catalyst B will become the new root bridge because its new priority is the lowest.

6. If switch B's bridge priority is changed to 32,769, which one will be root?

    Answer: Catalyst A will become the root again because B's priority is slightly higher.

7. If switch C is introduced with 40000:0000.0000.cccc, which will be the secondary root?

    Answer: Catalyst B was previously the secondary root, with the second-highest bridge priority. It will remain the secondary root because Catalyst C has a higher bridge priority.

8.   Suppose that a switch is configured with the **spanning-tree vlan 10 root primary** command. Then another switch is connected to the network. The new switch has a bridge priority of 8192. Which one of the following happens?

  a.   When the new switch advertises itself, the original root bridge detects it and lower its bridge priority to 4096 less than the new switch.

  b.   The new switch becomes and stays the root bridge (bridge priority 8192).

  c.   No change; both switches keep their current bridge priorities.

  d.   The new switch detects that a root bridge already exists and raises its own bridge priority to 32,768.

Answer: b

9.   Three switches in a network have the following bridge priorities: 32,768, 16,384, and 8192. If a fourth switch is configured with **spanning-tree vlan 1 root secondary**, what is the bridge priority of the switches that become the primary and secondary root bridges?

Answer: Primary root: 8192; secondary root: 16,384. (The switch configured with the **root secondary** keywords can't detect any other potential secondary roots, so it can set its priority only to 28,672.)

10.   What STP timer values automatically can be modified by setting the network diameter?

Answer: Hello timer
Forward Delay timer
Max Age timer

11.   Which STP timer determines how long a port stays in the Listening state? What is its default value?

Answer: The Forward Delay timer; default 15 seconds

12.   What is the purpose of the Max Age timer?

Answer: It sets the length of time received BPDUs are held if a neighboring switch is not heard from on a nondesignated port. After the Max Age timer expires, the BPDU for the neighbor is flushed and that port enters the Listening state, eventually becoming the new designated port on the segment.

13.   Three switches are connected to each other, forming a triangle shape. STP prevents a loop from forming. What is the most accurate value that could be used for the network diameter?

Answer: 3

14. Which of the following will not benefit from STP UplinkFast?

   a. An access-layer switch with one uplink port

   b. An access-layer switch with two uplink ports

   c. An access-layer switch with three uplink ports

   d. An access-layer switch with four uplink ports

   Answer: a

15. What command can enable the STP PortFast feature on a switch? What configuration mode must you enter first?

   Answer: spanning-tree portfast, in interface-configuration mode

16. What happens if the STP Hello Time is decreased to 1 second in an effort to speed up STP convergence? What happens if the Hello Time is increased to 10 seconds?

   Answer: Setting the Hello timer to 1 second doubles the number of configuration BPDUs that a switch sends, as compared to the default 2-second timer. Although this does share BPDU information more often, it doesn't help the long convergence delay when a port comes up. The significant delays come from the Forward Delay timer, which is used to move a port through the Listening and Learning states. By default, this process takes 30 seconds and is unaffected by the Hello timer.

17. What switch command safely can adjust the STP timers on the root bridge in VLAN 7? Assume that the network consists of Catalysts A, B, and C, all connected to each other in a triangle fashion.

   Answer: Because the three switches form a triangle loop, one link eventually will be placed in the Blocking state. Therefore, the maximum distance across the network is 3 switch hops. This value can be used to define the network diameter to safely adjust the STP timers for faster convergence:

   ```
   spanning-tree vlan 7 root primary diameter 3
   ```

   For questions 18 and 19, refer to the following output:

   ```
   Switch# show spanning-tree vlan 50
   VLAN50
     Spanning tree enabled protocol ieee
     Root ID    Priority    8000
                Address     00d0.0457.3831
                Cost        12
                Port        49 (GigabitEthernet0/1)
                Hello Time   2 sec  Max Age 20 sec  Forward Delay 15 sec

     Bridge ID  Priority    32818  (priority 32768 sys-id-ext 50)
                Address     0009.b7ee.9800
                Hello Time   2 sec  Max Age 20 sec  Forward Delay 15 sec
   ```

```
            Aging Time 300

Interface                                    Designated
Name             Port ID Prio  Cost Sts  Cost Bridge ID              Port ID
---------------- ------- ---- ------ ---  ---- -------------------- -------
FastEthernet0/1   128.1   128     19 FWD    12 32818 0009.b7ee.9800 128.1
FastEthernet0/2   128.2   128     19 FWD    12 32818 0009.b7ee.9800 128.2
FastEthernet0/4   128.4   128    100 FWD    12 32818 0009.b7ee.9800 128.4
FastEthernet0/7   128.7   128     19 FWD    12 32818 0009.b7ee.9800 128.7
FastEthernet0/8   128.8   128     19 FWD    12 32818 0009.b7ee.9800 128.8
FastEthernet0/9   128.9   128     19 FWD    12 32818 0009.b7ee.9800 128.9
FastEthernet0/10  128.10  128     19 FWD    12 32818 0009.b7ee.9800 128.10
FastEthernet0/11  128.11  128     19 FWD    12 32818 0009.b7ee.9800 128.11
FastEthernet0/12  128.12  128     19 FWD    12 32818 0009.b7ee.9800 128.12
FastEthernet0/17  128.13  128     19 FWD    12 32818 0009.b7ee.9800 128.13
FastEthernet0/20  128.16  128     19 FWD    12 32818 0009.b7ee.9800 128.16
FastEthernet0/21  128.17  128     19 FWD    12 32818 0009.b7ee.9800 128.17
FastEthernet0/23  128.19  128     19 FWD    12 32818 0009.b7ee.9800 128.19
FastEthernet0/24  128.20  128     19 FWD    12 32818 0009.b7ee.9800 128.20
```

18. What is the Bridge ID for the current root bridge? Is the switch that produced this output the actual root bridge?

    Answer: The root Bridge ID is 8000:00d0.0457.3831. The local switch is not the root bridge because its Bridge ID (32818:0009.b7ee.9800) is different from the root.

19. What is the path cost of interface FastEthernet 0/4, and why is it different from the others?

    Answer: The path cost is 100. This is because that interface currently is operating at 10Mbps (STP cost 100), whereas the others are operating at 100Mbps (STP cost 19).

20. Why does the column marked "Designated Bridge ID" have the same value for every switch port?

    Answer: Each of the switch ports shown has won the election to become the designated port for its local segment. Each designated port must identify its own Bridge ID, which is 32818:0009.b7ee.9800. Naturally, the Bridge ID is the same for all ports on VLAN 50.

21. Suppose that you need to troubleshoot your spanning-tree topology and operation. What commands and information can you use on a switch to find information about the current STP topology in VLAN 39?

    Answer: The **show spanning-tree vlan 39 root** command displays the current root bridge and the root port for VLAN 39. The **show spanning-tree vlan 39 brief** command shows a listing of every switch port on VLAN 39, along with its path cost and STP state. The designated Bridge ID is also shown on every switch port segment. For a quick summary of the total number of ports participating in each active VLAN, use the **show spanning-tree summary** command.

Chapter 11

"Do I Know This Already?"

1. b
2. c
3. c
4. b
5. b
6. a
7. b
8. b
9. c
10. c
11. c
12. b

Q&A

1. Why would a unidirectional link be bad?

   Answer: Switches must exchange BPDUs in both directions across a link. If one side of the link is disrupted and the switches think the link is still operational, one of the switches will not receive BPDUs. If that switch had its end of the link in the Blocking state to prevent a bridging loop, the absence of BPDUs will cause it to promote the link toward the Forwarding state. At that point, the loop will form.

2. What condition must be met to keep a switch port in the Blocking state?

   Answer: A constant flow of BPDUs. Without them, the switch thinks there is no need to block the port any longer.

3. If a switch port is shown to be in the root-inconsistent state, what has happened on it?

   Answer: Root guard has detected someone advertising a BPDU that is superior to the current Root Bridge.

4. When root guard has been triggered on a switch port, what must be done to enable the port for use again?

Answer: Root guard automatically allows the port to be moved through the STP states as soon as the superior BPDUs no longer are received.

5. When BPDU guard is enabled on a switch port, what state will the port be put in if a BPDU is received on it?

Answer: errdisable

6. When BPDU guard has been triggered on a switch port, what must be done to enable the port for use again?

Answer: If the errdisable timeout feature has been enabled, the switch automatically puts the switch port back into service after a set amount of time. Otherwise, the port remains disabled until you manually enable it again.

7. When loop guard is enabled on a switch port, what state will the port be put in if BPDUs are noted to be missing?

Answer: loop-inconsistent

8. Can STP loop guard be enabled on all switch ports?

Answer: Yes. Only the nondesignated ports are affected by loop guard.

9. When UDLD is enabled on a switch port, what else must be done to detect a unidirectional link on the port?

Answer: Enable UDLD on the far-end switch on the same link

10. What is the difference between the UDLD normal and aggressive modes?

Answer: Normal mode detects and reports a unidirectional link condition. Aggressive mode detects the condition, reports it, and moves the port to the errdisable state so that it can't be used.

11. What command enables UDLD aggressive mode on a switch interface?

Answer: udld aggressive

12. If two switches enable UDLD on the ports that have a common link, do their UDLD message times have to agree?

Answer: No. The UDLD messages are just echoed back, so the message times are only locally significant.

13. UDLD should be used on switch ports with what type of media?

Answer: Fiber-optic media

14. Can UDLD be used on all switch ports without causing problems?

Answer: Yes, although it is needed only on all fiber-based ports. The device on the far end of the port connection also must support UDLD so that UDLD messages can be echoed back to the switch.

15. Is it possible to disable STP on a single switch port without disabling the whole STP instance? If so, how can you do that?

Answer: Yes, you can use BPDU filtering to effectively disable STP on a switch port. BPDUs are neither processed when they arrive nor sent on the switch port. You can use the **spanning-tree bpdufilter enable** interface-configuration command to enable BPDU filtering. Otherwise, the whole STP instance for a VLAN must be disabled.

16. Complete the following command to display all ports that are disabled because of STP protection features:

```
show spanning-tree _____
```

Answer:
```
show spanning-tree inconsistent ports
```

Chapter 12

"Do I Know This Already?"

1. b

2. c

3. a

4. c

5. a

6. b

7. c

8. d

9. c

10. d

11. b

12. c

Q&A

1. What is synchronization in RSTP?

Answer: Because RSTP works to converge a switched network, each switch effectively isolates itself from the next layer of neighbors until an agreement can be reached about who will have the designated port on each segment.

2. What is an alternate port?

Answer: A port with an alternate path to the root. The path is less desirable than the one through the root port but is flagged for immediate use if the root port path fails.

3. What is the difference between an alternate port and a backup port?

Answer: An alternate port connects to a different segment than the root port to provide an alternate path to the root. A backup port connects to the same segment as another port on the local switch to provide another path out of the switch, but not necessarily another path back to the root.

4. Can a switch port be a designated port and be in the Discarding state?

Answer: Yes. RSTP removes the link between a port's role and its state. In 802.1D, a designated port must be forwarding, but RSTP doesn't have the same requirement.

5. Which port type *cannot* participate in RSTP synchronization?

Answer: Edge port

6. What two messages must be exchanged during RSTP synchronization?

Answer: Proposal and agreement

7. After an agreement message is received from a neighboring switch, how much time elapses before the port can begin forwarding? (Consider any timers that must expire or other conditions that must be met.)

Answer: The port is moved to the Forwarding state immediately after the agreement message is received. With RSTP, no other conditions are necessary because two switches have completed a quick handshake by exchanging proposal and agreement messages.

8. After a switch receives news of a topology change, how long does it wait to flush entries from its CAM table?

Answer: The switch flushes entries immediately instead of employing the timer reduction that 802.1D uses.

9. What command configures a port as an RSTP edge port?

Answer:
```
spanning-tree portfast
```

10. Suppose interface FastEthernet 0/1 is in half-duplex mode, but you want it to be considered a point-to-point link for RSTP. What command can accomplish this?

Answer:
```
spanning-tree link-type point-to-point
```

11. Put the following in order of the number of supported STP instances, from lowest to highest:

  a. MST

  b. PVST+

  c. CST

  d. 802.1D

Answer: d, c, a, b (d and c both have a single instance.)

12. What three parameters must be configured to uniquely define an MST region?

Answer: The region name, configuration revision number, and instance-to-VLAN mappings

13. What parameter does a switch examine to see if its neighbors have the same VLAN-to-MST instance mappings? How is that information passed among switches?

Answer: The VLAN-to-instance mapping is kept in a table of 4096 entries. This information is passed along in the MST BPDUs. Instead of passing the entire table, switches include only a digest of their current table contents.

14. Which MST instance in a region corresponds to the CST of 802.1Q?

Answer: The Internal Spanning Tree (IST) instance

15. Which MST instance is the IST?

Answer: IST is instance 0. Instances 1 through 15 are available for other use.

16. When an MST region meets a PVST+ domain, how is each MST instance propagated into PVST+?

Answer: The BPDUs from each instance are replicated and sent into all the appropriate VLANs in the PVST+ switch.

17. Is it wise to assign VLANs to MST instance 0? Why or why not?

Answer: No. By default, all VLANs are mapped to instance 0, the IST. You should select the number of instances needed and map all active VLANs to them. Otherwise, you can't have full control over the topologies independent of IST and CST.

18. The commands have just been entered to define an MST region on a switch. You are still at the MST configuration prompt. What command must you enter to commit the MST changes on the switch?

Answer: exit (When the MST configuration mode is exited, the changes are committed immediately.)

19. How can MST configuration information be propagated to other Cisco switches?

Answer: The MST information must be configured manually in each switch within the MST region. Currently, no method or protocol automatically can propagate the MST configuration.

20. A switch can interact with both 802.1D and RSTP. Can it run both PVST+ and MST simultaneously?

Answer: No. A switch can run either PVST+ or MST. If a switch is running MST, it can interact and interoperate with PVST+, 802.1D, and RSTP.

Chapter 13

"Do I Know This Already?"

1. d

2. a

3. a

4. b

5. c

6. c

7. c

8. d

9. c

10. c

11. d

12. c

Q&A

1. What might you need to implement interVLAN routing?

   Answer:
   One or more Layer 3 interfaces
   One or more SVIs
   Static routes
   A dynamic routing protocol

2. Can interVLAN routing be performed over a single trunk link?

   Answer: Yes. Packets can be forwarded between the VLANs carried over the trunk.

3. To configure an SVI, what commands are needed?

   Answer: First, make sure the VLAN is defined on the switch.
   ```
   interface vlan vlan-id
   ip address ip-address mask
   no shutdown
   ```

4. What command can verify the VLAN assignments on a Layer 2 port?

Answer:

```
show interface type mod/num switchport
```

or

```
show interface status
```

5. A switch has the following interface configurations in its running configuration:

```
interface fastethernet 0/1
 switchport access vlan 5
!
interface vlan 5
 ip address 192.168.10.1 255.255.255.0
 no shutdown
```

What is necessary for packets to get from the FastEthernet interface to the VLAN 5 SVI?

Answer: Nothing. Both are assigned to VLAN 5, so normal Layer 2 transparent bridging will take care of all forwarding between the two.

6. What is the source of FIB information?

Answer: The routing table, as computed by the Layer 3 engine portion of a switch.

7. How often is the FIB updated?

Answer: As needed. It is downloaded or updated dynamically by the Layer 3 engine whenever the routing topology changes or an ARP entry changes.

8. What is meant by the term "CEF punt"?

Answer: A packet can't be forwarded or switched by CEF directly because it needs further processing. The packet is "punted" to the Layer 3 engine, effectively bypassing CEF for a more involved resolution.

9. What happens to the FIB when distributed CEF (dCEF) is used?

Answer: It is simply replicated to each of the independent CEF engines. The FIB itself remains intact so that each engine receives a duplicate copy.

10. What happens during a "CEF glean" process?

Answer: The MAC address (ARP reply) for a next-hop FIB entry is not yet known. The Layer 3 engine must generate an ARP request and wait for a reply before CEF forwarding can continue to that destination.

11. What does a multilayer switch do to the IP TTL value just before a packet is forwarded?

    Answer: The TTL is decremented by one, as if a router had forwarded the packet.

12. What is fallback bridging?

    Answer: On switch platforms that cannot multilayer-switch (route) all routable protocols, those protocols can be bridged transparently between VLANs instead.

13. Is it possible for an SVI to go down? If so, for what reasons?

    Answer: Yes. The SVI can be shut down administratively with the **shutdown** command, as with any other interface. Also, if the VLAN associated with the SVI is not defined or active, the SVI will appear to be down.

Chapter 14

"Do I Know This Already?"

1. d
2. d
3. c
4. b
5. b
6. b
7. c
8. c
9. c
10. b
11. b
12. c

Q&A

1. A multilayer switch has been configured with the command **standby 5 priority 120**. What router-redundancy protocol is being used?

    Answer: HSRP

2.   What feature can you use to prevent other routers from accidentally participating in an HSRP group?

Answer: HSRP authentication

3.   What command can configure an HSRP group to use a virtual router address of 192.168.222.100?

Answer: standby 1 ip 192.168.222.100

4.   The **show standby vlan 271** command produces the following output:

```
Vlan271 - Group 1
  Local state is Active, priority 210, may preempt
  Hellotime 3 holdtime 40 configured hellotime 3 sec holdtime 40 sec
  Next hello sent in 00:00:00.594
  Virtual IP address is 192.168.111.1 configured
    Secondary virtual IP address 10.1.111.1
    Secondary virtual IP address 172.21.111.1
  Active router is local
  Standby router is unknown expires in 00:00:37
  Standby virtual mac address is 0000.0c07.ac01
  2 state changes, last state change 5d17h
```

If the local router fails, which router takes over the active role for the virtual router address 192.168.111.1?

Answer: None. There is no known standby router, so it also has failed.

5.   What is meant by pre-empting in HSRP?

Answer: Normally, if the active router (highest priority) fails, another router takes over its active role. The original active router is not allowed to resume the active role when it is restored until the new active router fails. Pre-empting allows a higher-priority router to take over the active role immediately or after a configurable delay.

6.   What protocols discussed in this chapter support interface tracking?

Answer: HSRP, GLBP

7.   The **show standby brief** command has been used to check the status of all HSRP groups on the local router. The output from this command is as follows:

```
Switch# show standby brief
                     P indicates configured to preempt.
                     |
   Interface  Grp Prio P State    Active addr  Standby addr   Group addr
   Vl100       1   210 P Active   local        192.168.75.2   192.168.75.1
   Vl101       1   210 P Active   local        192.168.107.2  192.168.107.1
   Vl102       1   210 P Active   local        192.168.71.2   192.168.71.1
```

Each interface is shown to have Group 1. Is this a problem?

Answer: No, as long as there is no bridging between VLANs. The HSRP group number can be repeated because each group is isolated on its own VLAN.

8. How many HSRP groups are needed to load-balance traffic over two routers?

   Answer: Two

9. What load-balancing methods can GLBP use?

   Answer: Round robin, weighted, host dependent

10. What command can you use to see the status of the active and standby routers on the VLAN 171 interface?

    Answer: show standby vlan 171

11. How many GLBP groups are needed to load-balance traffic over four routers?

    Answer: One

12. To use NSF on a multilayer switch with redundant supervisor modules, what must be configured in addition to the redundancy mode? What else must be present in the network?

    Answer: First, the SSO redundancy mode must be enabled with the **redundancy** and **mode sso** configuration commands. NSF can be enabled only when it is configured within the respective routing protocol configurations. When NSF is configured on a switch, there must be other neighboring switches or routers that are NSF-aware. The local switch depends on these devices to provide it with routing information during a failover.

13. How is SSO different from SRM with SSO redundancy mode?

    Answer: There is no difference. SRM refers to Single Router Mode, in which only one of the two route processors can be active at any time. Only one route processor can be active for the Stateful Switchover (SSO) mode, so SRM is used inherently with SSO.

14. If two Catalyst 6500 power supplies are configured with the **power redundancy-mode combined**, what will happen if one of them fails?

    Answer: In combined mode, both power supplies actively share the total power load of the chassis. As long as the total power budget is less than the maximum capacity of one power supply, the one working power supply can continue to power the switch. Otherwise, the supervisor will begin removing power from switch modules until the power load becomes less than the power supply capacity.

Chapter 15

"Do I Know This Already?"

1. a

2. c

3. b

4. d

5. c

6. c

7. b

8. a

9. b

10. c

11. c

12. c

Q&A

1. By default, what does a router or Layer 3 switch do with multicast packets?

   Answer: It drops them because multicast routing is not enabled by default.

2. By default, what does a Layer 2 switch do with a multicast packet?

   Answer: It floods the packet out all ports on the source VLAN, as if it were a broadcast packet.

3. What high-order bit combination signals that an IP address is used for multicast?

   Answer: 1110

4. If the IP-to-MAC multicast address mapping is somewhat ambiguous, how can a frame be forwarded to the correct destination group?

   Answer: The IP header must be examined in addition to the multicast MAC destination address.

5.   What IP multicast address range is set aside for use only on the local network segment?

Answer: 224.0.0.0 to 224.0.0.255

6.   For the RPF check, the source IP address is looked up in the unicast routing table. To forward the packet, what should the result of the test be?

Answer: The unicast route to the source must be out the interface where the packet arrived.

7.   What important difference exists between IGMPv1 and IGMPv2?

Answer: Hosts can request to leave a multicast group immediately with IGMPv2. IGMPv1 doesn't have any mechanism for leaving a group other than an aging-out process.

8.   To join a multicast group, what type of message is sent? Where is this message sent?

Answer: An IGMP membership report is sent. The IGMP message is with a destination address of the multicast group itself so that the nearest multicast router will receive it.

9.   What is the purpose of the IGMP querier?

Answer: It is a router that periodically asks all hosts if any of them want to join the multicast group. Interested hosts must respond with a membership report.

10. For PIM dense mode, how is the multicast tree built?

Answer: The source is the root of the tree, and all dense-mode routers are included by default. After all of these have joined the group, a pruning phase occurs so that routers with no member hosts are pruned off the tree.

11. Where is the root of the PIM sparse-mode tree located?

Answer: At a rendezvous point (RP) router

12. With PIM sparse-dense mode, is the PIM mode determined per interface or per group?

Answer: Per group. If the group has an RP, sparse mode is used; otherwise, dense mode is used.

13. What routing table is used for PIM?

Answer: The unicast routing table is used. PIM does not build or maintain its own multicast routing table.

14. What command is used to configure an interface for the hybrid PIM mode?

    Answer: ip pim sparse-dense-mode

15. When a switch performs IGMP snooping, what is it snooping for?

    Answer: It listens to all IGMP membership reports so that it can learn the location of hosts joining and leaving multicast groups.

16. What else does a Layer 2 switch need when it is configured for CGMP?

    Answer: A multicast router. The router relays group join and leave requests as CGMP packets that the switch can use.

17. When should IGMP snooping and CGMP be used together on a switch?

    Answer: Never; they are mutually exclusive features.

18. At a trade show, several PCs and servers are connected to a single Layer 2 switch. The switch has CGMP enabled. When a server begins to send video data to a multicast address, what happens to that traffic?

    Answer: Even though CGMP is enabled, no multicast router is available to assist the switch with its multicast forwarding decisions. Therefore, the video packets will be flooded out all switch ports on the server's VLAN.

Chapter 16

"Do I Know This Already?"

1. b

2. d

3. c

4. b

5. a

6. d

7. a

8. d

9. c

10. b

11. b

12. d

Q&A

1. How does a Catalyst switch detect that a connected device is capable of using Power over Ethernet?

Answer: The device first must loop the Ethernet connection's transmit and receive pairs. The switch then can hear its own test tone, confirming that the device does need inline power. When the power is enabled on the port, the switch and the device can exchange CDP messages so that the amount of power can be adjusted.

2. What type of trunk can be used between a Catalyst switch port and a Cisco IP Phone?

Answer: A special-case 802.1Q trunk with only two VLANs

3. When a trunk is used on an IP Phone, on which VLAN is the data from an attached PC carried?

Answer: PC data always is carried over the native (untagged) VLAN in the trunk. Voice packets can be carried over the native VLAN, too, or over a unique voice VLAN.

4. What is the difference between the VVID and the PVID?

Answer: VVID refers to the voice VLAN ID, whereas PVID refers to the port VLAN ID.

5. Can the CoS information from the voice traffic be passed when the **switchport voice vlan untagged** command is used? If so, how?

Answer: Yes, CoS information is passed within the 802.1p portion of the 802.1Q trunk encapsulation.

6. What is the advantage of using the **switchport voice vlan dot1p** command?

Answer: Voice traffic is carried over VLAN 0 on the IP Phone trunk, so a unique voice VLAN is not necessary. This can be an advantage when a new VLAN can't be added to a network or switch. CoS information still is carried over the trunk in the 802.1p field.

7. By default, does a Cisco IP Phone trust QoS information from an attached PC?

Answer: No. The phone will overwrite all QoS information (both CoS and DSCP) to 0, considering the PC an untrusted source.

8. The command **switchport priority extend cos 5** is entered for a switch port. Is this a good decision? Why or why not?

    Answer: Probably not. After that is done, all packets from an attached PC will be marked with CoS 5, the same value the phone gives to its voice-bearer packets. Any upstream switches will be incapable of distinguishing the two types of traffic just by examining the CoS value.

9. The **show power inline** command is used to check the power status on each switch port. If the output is as shown here, what can you assume about interface fastethernet 0/1?

    ```
    Interface  Admin  Oper      Power      Device
                                (Watts)

    ----------  -----  ----------  -------  --------------------
    Fa0/1      auto   off              0   n/a
    Fa0/2      auto   on             6.3   Cisco IP Phone 7960
    ```

    Answer: Interface fastethernet 0/1 shows an operational inline power state of "off," with 0W of power. This could mean that nothing is plugged into that switch port. It also could mean that an IP Phone is connected to the port but that the port has inline power set to the "off" state.

10. What command can verify the QoS trust relationship between an IP Phone and its attached PC?

    Answer:
    show mls qos interface
    or
    show interface switchport

Chapter 17

"Do I Know This Already?"

1. b

2. d

3. b

4. c

5. d

6. b

7. b

The trick is in the "maximum 3" keywords. This sets the maximum number of addresses that can be learned on a port. If only one static address is configured, two more addresses can be learned dynamically.

8. c

9. a

10. b

11. c

12. c

Because of the variety of user host platforms, port-based authentication (802.1x) cannot be used. The problem also states that the goal is to restrict access to physical switch ports, so AAA is of no benefit. Port security can do the job by restricting access according to the end users' MAC addresses.

13. b

14. c

Q&A

1. What does the acronym AAA stand for?

Answer: Authentication, authorization, and accounting

2. What external methods of authentication does a Catalyst switch support?

Answer: RADIUS and TACACS+

3. A RADIUS server is located at IP address 192.168.199.10. What command configures a Catalyst switch to find the server?

Answer: radius-server host 192.168.199.10

4. A Catalyst switch should be configured to authenticate users against RADIUS servers first, followed by TACACS+ servers. What command can define the authentication methods? Make sure users still can authenticate if none of the servers is available.

Answer: aaa authentication login default radius tacacs+ local

5. What is the purpose of authorization? What happens if authorization is not used?

   Answer: Authorization allows an external server to decide whether the authenticated user can gain access to specific resources or switch commands. If authorization is not used, the default behavior is that all users must authenticate as they move to the appropriate privilege level to run switch commands.

6. Is it possible to use different methods to authorize users to run switch commands instead of making configuration changes?

   Answer: Yes; The **aaa authorization** command separates these functions so that each can have its own method list.

7. When might the command **switchport port-security maximum 2** be used?

   Answer: The **switchport port-security maximum 2** command might be used if it is too much trouble to manually configure MAC addresses into the port security feature. Up to two MAC addresses then would be learned dynamically. The network administrator also might want to control what is connected to that switch port. If another switch or a hub were connected, the total number of active stations easily could rise above two.

8. After port-based authentication is configured and enabled, can any host connect as long as the user can authenticate?

   Answer: No, only hosts that have 802.1x-capable applications can communicate with the switch port to properly authenticate.

9. When the 802.1x **force-authorized** keyword is used, how does the switch react to users attempting to connect?

   Answer: The switch always authorizes any connecting user, without any authentication.

10. Can more than one host be authenticated on a single switch port with port-based authentication?

    Answer: Yes, if the **dot1x multi-hosts** command is configured on the switch port interface.

11. In DHCP spoofing and ARP poisoning attacks, what is the goal of the attacker? What Catalyst features can be used to mitigate the risk of these attacks?

    Answer: In both types of attacks, the attacker is attempting to be positioned as a man-in-the-middle, to be used as the default gateway address by unsuspecting clients. Sitting between a client and other resources, the attacker then can intercept and inspect packets coming from the client. The DHCP snooping and dynamic ARP inspection (DAI) Catalyst switch features can be used to detect and prevent these attacks when they are attempted.

12. Which switch ports should be configured as trusted for DHCP snooping?

    Answer: You should configure a port as trusted only if it connects to a known, trusted DHCP server. In addition, you can make a port trusted if it connects to another switch that also is performing DHCP snooping.

13. What is the function of a trusted port in DAI?

    Answer: No ARP inspection is performed on a trusted port; the inspection process is reserved for ARP replies on untrusted ports only. You can configure a port as trusted if it connects a neighboring switch that also has DAI enabled or if it connects to a trusted host.

14. To inspect ARP information from a host that has received its IP address from a DHCP server, what must be enabled in addition to DAI?

    Answer: DHCP snooping must be enabled, too. The DHCP snooping feature maintains a database of dynamic MAC–to–IP address mappings. This information is used by DAI to validate the ARP responses it inspects.

Chapter 18

"Do I Know This Already?"

1. c

2. d

3. d

4. a

5. b

6. a

7. c

8. a

9. d

10. a

11. c

12. d

13. a

14. b

Q&A

1. When a VACL is implemented on a switch, how is the switching speed affected?

   Answer: It isn't; VACLs are implemented in hardware, so packets can be inspected as they are being switched, with no performance penalty.

2. What actions can be taken on packets matching a VACL?

   Answer: Packets can be forwarded, dropped, marked for capture, or redirected to a different Layer 2 switch port.

3. After a VACL is applied using the **vlan filter** command, how is the traffic direction (inbound or outbound) specified?

   Answer: It isn't; VACLs operate on packets as they are being forwarded within a VLAN. Therefore, there is no concept of direction within the VLAN. A direction can't be specified.

4. A secondary community VLAN is associated with a primary VLAN on a switch. Can hosts assigned to the community VLAN communicate with each other?

   Answer: Yes, they can. However, they can't communicate with any other community or isolated VLAN.

5. A secondary isolated VLAN is associated with a primary VLAN on a switch. Can hosts assigned to the isolated VLAN communicate with each other?

   Answer: No, hosts on an isolated VLAN can't communicate even among themselves. They can reach only the promiscuous host on the primary VLAN.

6. What command is needed to configure a promiscuous VLAN?

   Answer: This isn't possible. The primary VLAN can communicate with all the secondary VLANs that are associated with it. The only promiscuous objects that can be configured are promiscuous hosts, located on the primary VLAN.

7. A router is identified as the central gateway for a private VLAN. What command is needed to configure the switch port where a router is connected?

   Answer: switchport mode private-vlan promiscuous

8. How many actual VLANs must be configured to implement a common router with two community VLANs?

Answer: Three VLANs must be used: one for the primary VLAN where the router is connected and two more for the secondary community VLANs. The primary VLAN will be logically associated with the two community VLANs, but all three must be configured.

9. In a switch spoofing attack, what is the attacker's goal?

Answer: An attacker spoofs DTP messages on a normal access-layer switch port, hoping that the switch responds and will negotiate trunking mode. If that happens, the attacker can spoof VLAN ID tags to inject traffic onto any VLAN that is carried over the trunk.

10. What should be configured to prevent a switch spoofing attack?

Answer: You always should configure every access-layer switch port to a fixed mode so that DTP is disabled, preventing the possibility of trunk negotiation with an attacker. Switch ports default to the **switchport mode dynamic auto** mode, allowing a connected device to actively negotiate the port into the trunking mode. You can use the **switchport mode access** command to force static access mode, thereby disabling DTP negotiation completely.

11. Describe some methods that can be used to prevent a VLAN hopping attack.

Answer: You always should configure a trunk's native VLAN to an unused VLAN number and prune the native VLAN from each end of the trunk. This isolates the native VLAN completely so that no traffic can be injected onto it.

In addition, you can configure Catalyst switches to require a tag on *all* VLANs carried over a trunk, including the native VLAN.

12. How is switching performance affected when several SPAN sessions are enabled?

Answer: Switching performance is not affected. Packets simply are marked and copied into another switch port's queue during a SPAN session. The original traffic still is forwarded without being modified or affected.

13. What command can specify the source of a SPAN session as VLAN 100?

Answer: monitor session 1 source vlan 100

14. When a SPAN session is enabled, what direction of traffic flow (relative to the source port) is mirrored for analysis?

    Answer: By default, traffic in both directions is mirrored.

15. What two things can identify more granular traffic to be mirrored to a SPAN destination?

    Answer: A VLAN ACL (VACL) can match and mark packets for capture. A SPAN VLAN filter also can identify specific VLANs to mirror if the source is a trunk port.

16. Three switches are connected in series with trunk links. The RSPAN source is on the first switch and the destination is on the third. How does the intermediate (second) switch learn about the RSPAN's source and destination locations?

    Answer: It doesn't. The intermediate switch has no knowledge that RSPAN is being used. The only configuration needed is to define the RSPAN VLAN and to allow that VLAN on the trunk links. Beyond that, the intermediate switch can flood only the RSPAN packets to all ports carrying the RSPAN VLAN.

17. What must be configured on all switches connecting an RSPAN source and destination? What commands can be used?

    Answer: The special-purpose RSPAN VLAN must be configured. Define the VLAN number and then use the **remote-span** command.

18. One of the advantages of RSPAN is that mirrored traffic can be isolated in the RSPAN VLAN on a trunk. If a GigabitEthernet port is to be monitored on one switch, which is better to use as a transport for the RSPAN VLAN: a GigabitEthernet trunk already carrying user traffic in other VLANs, or an isolated GigabitEthernet trunk link set aside for RSPAN?

    Answer: The existing trunk will work fine because the RSPAN traffic will be isolated in its own VLAN. However, you must be careful not to place an excessive load on that trunk link. RSPAN traffic easily can add to the bandwidth burden on a link, considering that the source here is also a GigabitEthernet port. In this case, it might be better to transport the RSPAN mirrored traffic over its own trunk link, if one is available and cost-effective.

O-P

Q

R

W

X–Y–Z

SEARCH THOUSANDS OF BOOKS FROM LEADING PUBLISHERS

Safari® Bookshelf is a searchable electronic reference library for IT professionals that features more than 2,000 titles from technical publishers, including Cisco Press.

With Safari Bookshelf you can

- **Search** the full text of thousands of technical books, including more than 70 Cisco Press titles from authors such as Wendell Odom, Jeff Doyle, Bill Parkhurst, Sam Halabi, and Karl Solie.

- **Read** the books on My Bookshelf from cover to cover, or just flip to the information you need.

- **Browse** books by category to research any technical topic.

- **Download** chapters for printing and viewing offline.

With a customized library, you'll have access to your books when and where you need them—and all you need is a user name and password.

Safari®
BOOKS ONLINE
ENABLED

THIS BOOK IS SAFARI ENABLED

INCLUDES FREE 45-DAY ACCESS TO THE ONLINE EDITION

The Safari® Enabled icon on the cover of your favorite technology book means the book is available through Safari Bookshelf. When you buy this book, you get free access to the online edition for 45 days.

Safari Bookshelf is an electronic reference library that lets you easily search thousands of technical books, find code samples, download chapters, and access technical information whenever and wherever you need it.

TO GAIN 45-DAY SAFARI ENABLED ACCESS TO THIS BOOK:

- Go to **http://www.ciscopress.com/safarienabled**

- Enter the ISBN of this book (shown on the back cover, above the bar code)

- Log in or Sign up (site membership is required to register your book)

- Enter the coupon code found in the front of this book before the "Contents at a Glance" page

If you have difficulty registering on Safari Bookshelf or accessing the online edition, please e-mail customer-service@safaribooksonline.com.